100
ALL-TIME FAVORITE
MOVIES
OF THE 20TH CENTURY

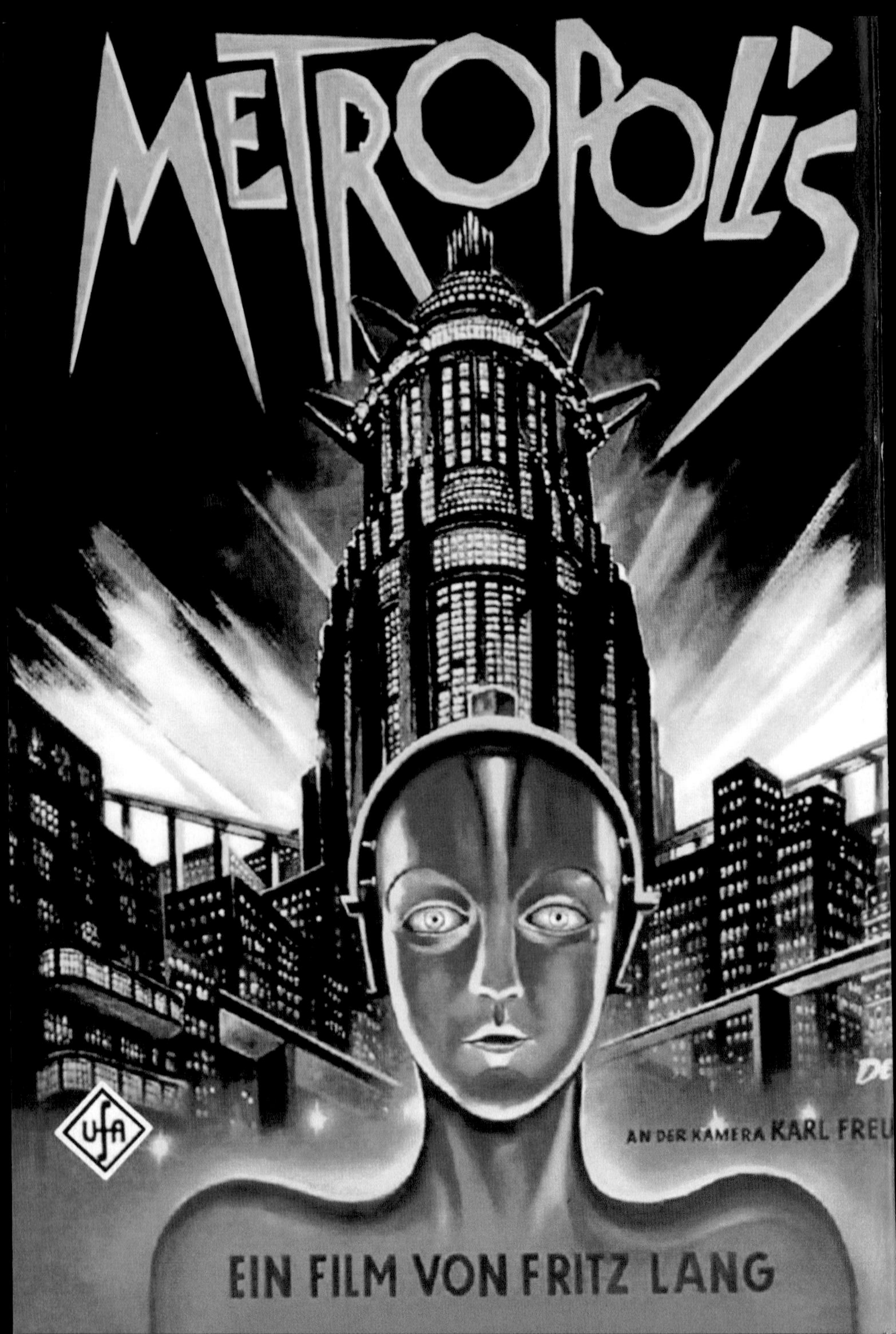
METROPOLIS
AN DER KAMERA KARL FREU
EIN FILM VON FRITZ LANG

Ed. Jürgen Müller

100 ALL-TIME FAVORITE MOVIES

OF THE 20TH CENTURY

In collaboration with
ddp images, Hamburg / Deutsche Kinemathek, Berlin /
British Film Institute, London / Bibliothèque du Film, Paris /
Herbert Klemens Filmbild Fundus Robert Fischer, Munich

TASCHEN

Bibliotheca Universalis

THE '20^s

THE '30^s

THE '40s

THE '50ˢ

THE '60s

THE '70s

THE '80s

THE '90s

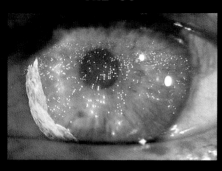

THE BIRTH OF A NATION

1915 - USA - 187 MIN.

DIRECTOR

D. W. GRIFFITH (1875–1948)

SCREENPLAY

D. W. GRIFFITH, FRANK E. WOODS, THOMAS F. DIXON JR.,
based on the novel and stage play *The Clansman: An Historical Romance of the Ku Klux Klan,*
and the novel The Leopard's Spots: A Romance of the White Man's Burden,
1865–1900 by THOMAS F. DIXON JR.

DIRECTOR OF PHOTOGRAPHY

G. W. BITZER

EDITING

JAMES SMITH, D. W. GRIFFITH, JOSEPH HENABERY, ROSE SMITH, RAOUL WALSH

MUSIC

JOSEPH CARL BREIL, D. W. GRIFFITH

PRODUCTION

D. W. GRIFFITH, DAVID SHEPARD for DAVID W. GRIFFITH CORP.

STARRING

LILLIAN GISH (Elsie Stoneman), ELMER CLIFTON (Phil Stoneman),
MAE MARSH (Flora Cameron), HENRY B. WALTHALL (Colonel Ben Cameron),
MIRIAM COOPER (Margaret Cameron), MARY ALDEN (Lydia Brown),
BESSIE LOVE (Piedmont Girl), RAOUL WALSH (John Wilkes Booth),
DONALD CRISP (General Ulysses S. Grant), HOWARD GAYE (General Robert E. Lee)

- The Fiery Cross of the Ku Klux Klan -

D.W. GRIFFITH'S MIGHTY SPECTACLE
THE BIRTH OF A
NATION FOUNDED ON THOMAS DIXON'S 'THE CLANSMAN'

"This sidewalk belongs to us as much as it does to you, Colonel Cameron."

The American Civil War was fought between the industrialized states of the North and the still largely agricultural South. The war lasted from 1861 to 1865 and ended in defeat for the South, whose economic power was almost completely destroyed, not least because around four million slaves were freed. *The Birth of a Nation,* David Wark Griffith's great, controversial American epic, tells the stories of the effects of the war on two families: the Stonemans of Pennsylvania in the North and, in the South, the Camerons of Piedmont, South Carolina. The families are friends; their sons were at school together. Shortly before the outbreak of war, Phil Stoneman (Elmer Clifton) and his younger brother pay a visit to Piedmont and enjoy the hospitality of their Southern friends. Phil immediately falls in love with Flora Cameron (Mae Marsh). Ben (Henry B. Walthall), the Camerons' eldest son, is enchanted when he sees a picture of Elsie Stoneman (Lillian Gish), which he will carry with him right through the war.

Such gatherings of family and friends are portrayed with great freshness and vitality, without any of the pathos characteristic of so many silent movies. The film is also ahead of its time in its depiction of the war. Griffith's crowd and battle scenes are more complex and more extravagant than anything seen before. *The Birth of a Nation* is one of the first truly "modern" feature films, exploiting to the full the technical possibilities of the medium, and using exclusively cinematic techniques to tell the story without a trace of theatricality. Griffith's editing is masterly. He constantly switches back and forth between crowd scenes and small "human" interactions, and at the end very effectively crosscuts between three plot lines to bring about a last-minute rescue.

The Birth of a Nation is now recognized as the first blockbuster and the first big box-office success in the history of the motion pictures. Until then, all the industry had to offer were films between 3 and 18 minutes long – known as one- or two-acters. Griffith himself had made more than 400 of these mini-features. As a rule they cost no more than a thousand dollars to make, but *The Birth of a Nation* soaked up an amazing 100,000 dollars. By 1932

DAVID WARK GRIFFITH Film historian George Sadoul described David Wark Griffith (1875–1948) as not the inventor so much as the creator of a new cinematic language founded on editing. Griffith grew up on a farm in Kentucky and was raised as a typical "Southern gentleman." After touring as an actor with a traveling theater troupe, he worked for the Biograph Company, first as an actor then as a screenwriter and director. Biograph produced short features for the small movie theaters that by then were springing up everywhere. Griffith made more than 400 shorts for Biograph, working in many of them with the actress Lillian Gish and the cameraman G. W. Bitzer. In them, he experimented with the narrative structure and content he would later use in his full-length features. One of his short films was *The Rose of Kentucky* (1911), which, interestingly, was much more clearly critical of the Ku Klux Klan than *The Birth of a Nation* (1915). This and *Intolerance* (1916) are two outstanding examples of Griffith's art. The two epics established him as a great visionary and immortalized him as the father of modern cinematography. Afterwards, he made two famous melodramas starring Lillian Gish, *Broken Blossoms* (1919) and *Way Down East* (1920). But his successful career was soon over. His films were less and less well received and Griffith turned to drink for comfort. In 1936 he received a special Academy Award for lifetime achievement, but in 1948 he died in a Hollywood hotel, lonely and virtually forgotten.

1 Elsie Stoneman (Lillian Gish) fears for her brother, who has helped the Cameron family to flee from black leader Silas and his militia.

2 Never suspecting that they have had their day, slave-owning Southerners march proudly to war.

3 She does her duty – but with a few regrets: Flora Cameron (Mae Marsh) donates her beautiful gowns to swell the war chest of the Northern States.

4 A terrible accident: because she believes a black man is about to rape her, Flora Cameron jumps over a precipice and dies in the arms of her elder brother Ben (Henry B. Walthall).

it had grossed 90 times its production costs and remained the most successful movie of all time before being superseded in 1939 by *Gone with the Wind* – another film about the American Civil War.

Griffith's masterwork has further claims to fame. It was the first film to be screened for a U.S. president – Woodrow Wilson – at the White House and one of the first-ever cinema epics. The scope of the film extends beyond the end of the Civil War. Griffith not only tells of the war itself but also covers the postwar period, especially the situation created by the emancipation of slaves. The first part of the film ends with the careful reenactment of the

"With its sweeping battle scenes, tender moments of human drama, and the skillful (if highly inflammatory) ride of the Ku Klux Klan for a rousing climax, the film was a sensation, and Griffith was hailed as the 'Shakespeare of the screen.'" *Leonard Maltin*

assassination of President Abraham Lincoln, on April 1, 1865. In the second part, entitled *Reconstruction*, the action is confined exclusively to the South and – it has to be said – is blatantly racist, its black characters no more than stereotypes.

"Reconstruction" – the term was introduced to describe the reintegration of the Southern States into the Union after the war – tells of the supposedly intolerable conditions that would result from the emancipation of the slaves. African Americans (often played by "blacked-up" white actors) are shown humiliating white men and lusting after their women, making a spectacle of themselves in

the legislature and generally undermining the social order. The white people are rescued and what Griffith sees as the natural order is restored by the intervention of the Ku Klux Klan, that murderous gang with their pointed hoods and burning crosses. The moral of the story leaves a bad taste today and did so even then. When it was released in 1915, the film unleashed a storm of controversy and was banned in some U.S. states. Director Griffith felt misunderstood, insisting on his right to freedom of speech and immediately starting work on a new film. *Intolerance* (1916) – a title loaded with meaning – was, he claimed, an ode to the essential goodness of the human race.   HJK

NOSFERATU

NOSFERATU – EINE SYMPHONIE DES GRAUENS

1922 - GERMANY - 84 MIN.

DIRECTOR

F. W. MURNAU (1888–1931)

SCREENPLAY

HENRIK GALEEN, based on
the novel *Dracula* by BRAM STOKER

DIRECTOR OF PHOTOGRAPHY

FRITZ ARNO WAGNER

MUSIC

HANS ERDMANN

PRODUCTION

ALBIN GRAU, ENRICO DIECKMANN
for PRANA-FILM GMBH

STARRING

MAX SCHRECK (Count Orlok, Nosferatu), GUSTAV VON WANGENHEIM (Hutter),
GRETA SCHRÖDER (Ellen, his Wife), ALEXANDER GRANACH (Knock, a Real Estate Agent),
GEORG HEINRICH SCHNELL (Harding, a Shipowner), RUTH LANDSHOFF (Ruth, his Sister),
JOHN GOTTOWT (Professor Bulwer), GUSTAV BOTZ (Professor Sievers, a Doctor),
MAX NEMETZ (Captain), GUIDO HERZFELD (Innkeeper)

"Your wife has a lovely neck."

Knock (Alexander Granach), a shady real-estate agent in the town of Wisborg, dispatches his young assistant Hutter (Gustav von Wangenheim) to faraway Transylvania. There he is to meet with Count Orlok who wishes to buy a house in the North German seaport. The eager young man bids farewell to his wife Ellen (Greta Schröder) who stays at home, full of apprehension. Her feelings of terrible foreboding are confirmed when, after an arduous journey, Hutter arrives at Orlok's castle in the Carpathians. The mysterious Count (Max Schreck) proves to be a vampire who attacks his visitor during the night. When the blood-sucking fiend discovers a picture of Ellen among Hutter's things, his interest immediately switches to her. Without warning, he sets off by sea to Wisborg. Realizing the danger, Hutter pursues him overland, but to no avail. Nothing can prevent Orlok from reaching his new home. Soon after his arrival, plague breaks out and Ellen saves the city by sacrificing herself to the vampire.

Nosferatu was the first popular success for the still relatively inexperienced director, Friedrich Wilhelm Murnau. It was also the first-ever screen adaptation of Bram Stoker's 1897 novel *Dracula*, marking the debut appearance of what would become a remarkably popular film fantasy character – the vampire. Although screenplay writer

FRIEDRICH WILHELM MURNAU Born in 1888 into a wealthy middle-class family, Friedrich Wilhelm Murnau studied literature and art history at university. However, his academic career ended when the famous Berlin theater director Max Reinhardt saw him in a student production and invited him to join his company of actors. World War I, in which he served as a fighter pilot, interrupted Murnau's acting career. When he returned to Berlin in 1919, like so many artists of his generation he was bitten by the movie bug. In partnership with the actor Ernst Hoffmann he set up a production company and made his first film *The Blue Boy / The Emerald of Death (Der Knabe in Blau / Der Todessmaragd)* in the same year. Like most of his early work, the film has not survived. In the space of only two years, Murnau made eight more movies and from surviving material there emerge the characteristics that would mark his later masterpieces. As well as a fascination with the unconscious and a tendency towards the melancholy and the romantic, Murnau's early movies have certain painterly qualities and a predilection for combining studio-based shots with location filming. *Nosferatu* (1922) established Murnau once and for all in the front rank of German directors. He became internationally known when he caused a sensation with the use of an "unchained" camera in the 1924 UFA production of *The Last Laugh (Der letzte Mann)*. Even more lavish was *Faust* (1925/26), whose rich visual imagery, including what the renowned German film critic Lotte Eisner described as some of "the most remarkable examples of German chiaroscuro," still fascinates modern audiences. Soon afterwards, studio mogul William Fox lured the young director to Hollywood with a sensational contract that allowed him to make his next movie with complete artistic freedom. Although, from an aesthetic point of view, *Sunrise – A Song of Two Humans* (1927) fulfilled all expectations, box-office takings came nowhere near to covering the cost of making the movie. In his next assignments for Fox, *Four Devils* (1928) and *City Girl*, a.k.a. *Our Daily Bread* (1929/30), Murnau was forced to make so many compromises that he finally terminated his contract and took off for Tahiti to shoot his next movie (1930/31). Murnau never lived to see this wonderful film set in the South Seas. He was killed in 1933 in an automobile accident a few days before the premiere.

"This is film: ghostly carriages flit through wooded gorges, nightmarish monsters hunt people down, pestilence breaks out, ships sail unmanned into harbors, coffins full of earth and mice are spirited out of cellars onto wagons, into ships and into moldering, dilapidated houses. This is film: a being creeps and clambers, half man, half ghost, over the screen – and meanwhile, as a concession to typical audiences, there is a love story with a tragic ending."

Vossische Zeitung

1 The classic horror movie: Nosferatu (Max Schreck), however, has little in common with the gentleman bloodsuckers of later vampire films. Murnau portrays him as a monstrous, spider-like creature.

2 The start of a fatal passion: Count Orlok gazes at the photograph of Hutter's (Gustav von Wangenheim) wife Ellen.

3 Architecture made to measure: the ubiquitous pointed Gothic arches suggest Nosferatu's otherworldliness and at the same time create a visual link between the castle in the Carpathians and the port of Wisborg in the north of Germany.

Henrik Galeen changed names and places, removed some leading characters and rewrote the ending, the film recognizably follows the plot of the legendary Gothic novel. Even so, the bald, skeletal monster in the film has as little in common with his counterpart in the novel as he does with the debonair bloodsuckers of later vampire films. With his hooked nose, black-ringed eyes, rodent teeth and long claws, Orlok is both grotesque and frightening, a nightmare figure with the power to bring to life our most terrifying fantasies.

The vampire's bizarre appearance is certainly one of the main reasons for *Nosferatu's* enduring popularity. But most of all the film owes its classic status to its outstanding visual quality, due to Murnau's masterly handling of Expressionistic light and shade. It is clear, too, that the director was inspired by Scandinavian cinema and the 19th-century Romantic movement in painting. Unusually for the period, *Nosferatu* was largely filmed away from the studio, on location in northern Germany and Romania. And between them, Murnau and his director of photography Fritz Arno Wagner impressively succeeded in transforming real locations into fearful, eerie places. The film shows – a touch ironically – naïve young Hutter's adventures as a journey into darkness. Having left summery, carefree Wisborg, the villages and landscapes through which he passes become increasingly inhospitable until he is finally imprisoned in Orlok's shadowy realm. Similarly, as the vampire sets sail for Wisborg, this once tranquil town is slowly overwhelmed by shadows. Murnau vividly portrays encroaching horror as Orlok's black ship of death is steered by a ghostly hand into the harbor. Soon afterwards, a procession of black-clad men is seen moving through the street – pallbearers carrying the coffins of plague victims to a mass grave.

In the face of such spine-chilling imagery, it comes as no surprise that *Nosferatu* was often seen as a commentary on the contemporary political situation. Many interpreted the deaths of so many citizens of Wisborg as an allegory for the horror of World War I. Others saw the scene where Knock, presumed to be a treacherous troublemaker, is hounded by a lynch mob, as a reminder of the hysterical social climate under the Weimar Republic. Admittedly, it makes more sense to see *Nosferatu* as an erotic fantasy, an evocative tale about the darkest depths of human desire. Since Murnau was gay, Orlok's nightly visits could be read as an "in joke." More disturbing is Ellen's relationship with the vampire. A mysterious telepathy links the melancholy young woman with the sinister Count Orlok, with whom she shares a fondness for nocturnal wanderings. Bizarrely, as she stands on the beach awaiting her beloved, she looks out to sea – in other words, in the direction from which not her husband but the vampire is approaching. It seems that, in her act of self-sacrifice, she is abandoning herself to masochistic sexual excitement, surrendering to a terrifying lover who makes her worthy spouse look like a passionless bourgeois, and the seemingly idyllic Wisborg like a dismal one-horse town of narrow-minded conformists.   JH

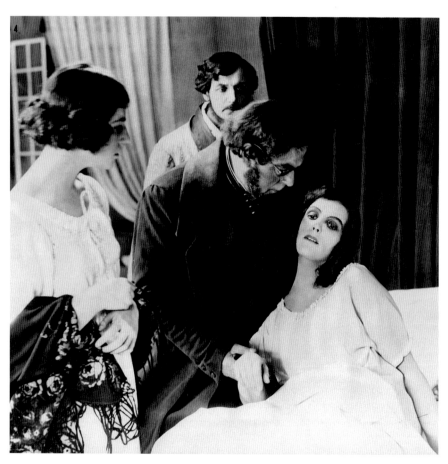

4 Strange fascination: there seems to be a mysterious attraction between Ellen (Greta Schröder) and the vampire, which neither her family nor the doctor suspect.

5 Threat to the small-town idyll: from the very beginning Ellen introduces a note of sinister melancholy to seemingly peaceful Wisborg. Her innocent husband notices nothing.

"Every gesture, every costume (from around 1840), every step and every movement must have been carefully calculated according to the laws of psychological effect on the viewer. In this, Grau and Murnau achieve a remarkably detailed work, without neglecting a wider, more majestic span." *Der Film*

THE TEN COMMANDMENTS

1923 - USA - 136 MIN.

DIRECTOR

CECIL B. DEMILLE (1881–1959)

SCREENPLAY

JEANIE MACPHERSON

DIRECTOR OF PHOTOGRAPHY

BERT GLENNON, J. PEVERELL MARLEY, ARCHIE STOUT,
FRED WESTERBERG, RAY RENNAHAN

EDITING

ANNE BAUCHENS

MUSIC

HUGO RIESENFELD, MILAN RODER

PRODUCTION

CECIL B. DEMILLE for FAMOUS PLAYERS-LASKY CORPORATION

STARRING

THEODORE ROBERTS (Moses), CHARLES DE ROCHEFORT (Rameses),
ESTELLE TAYLOR (Miriam, Sister of Moses), JAMES NEILL (Aaron, Brother of Moses),
EDYTHE CHAPMAN (Mrs. Martha McTavish), RICHARD DIX (John McTavish),
ROD LA ROCQUE (Dan McTavish), LEATRICE JOY (Mary Leigh),
NITA NALDI (Sally Lung)

The Ten Commandments

PRODUCED BY

Cecil B. DeMille

WITH

THEODORE ROBERTS	LEATRICE JOY
RICHARD DIX	NITA NALDI
ROD LA ROCQUE	ESTELLE TAYLOR
CHARLES de ROCHE	EDYTHE CHAPMAN
ROBERT EDESON	JULIA FAYE

STORY BY

Jeanie Macpherson

Thou shalt not

a Paramount Production

Presented by ADOLPH ZUKOR *and* JESSE L. LASKY

"You cannot break the Ten Commandments – they will break you!"

In 1922 the *Los Angeles Times*, together with the Famous Players-Lasky Corporation, organized a competition. A prize of $1000 was to be awarded to the member of the public who could come up with the most convincing idea for a movie. There were a striking number of biblical themes among the host of suggestions. In the office of director Cecil B. DeMille they were amazed. Could the Bible be the source of a mass-appeal movie?

One entry stuck in DeMille's mind. It came from F. C. Nelson, a blue-collar worker from Michigan, who said he would like to see a film about the Ten Commandments. Mr. Nelson even proposed an advertising slogan: "You cannot break the Ten Commandments – they will break you!" He and seven other competitors suggesting the same subject each received the $1000 prize – a modest sum considering the expenditure on *The Ten Commandments* and the money it would bring in. The production cost around $1.5 million and box-office receipts totaled a then record $4.2 million. DeMille envisaged a movie in two parts, taking Old Testament themes and applying them to a story of modern-day life. The film began with a biblical prologue and moved on to a contemporary tale of two brothers, quite unlike each other, but both pursuing the same woman. The historical part was based on the Book of Exodus, recounting the escape of the Israelites from Egypt, the parting of the Red Sea, Moses receiving the Ten Commandments on Mount Sinai, and the debauched celebrations around the Golden Calf. DeMille commissioned a young screenwriter and actress called Jeanie Macpherson to create the script for the modern story.

THE GUADALUPE SET The citizens of the little coastal town of Guadalupe, not far from Santa Maria, were surprised when, in the spring of 1923, a small army of workmen began building a vast structure of iron, concrete, and wood amid the white sand dunes along the Pacific shore. Two months later, when the whole thing was finished, the locals stared in disbelief. Before them loomed a great gate in the wall of an Ancient Egyptian city, over 750 feet long and 110 feet high, flanked on either side by massive statues of pharaohs, above which hung two huge bas-reliefs. An avenue with 21 faux-marble sphinxes led straight up to the immense gate. A short distance away a pyramid rose into the sky. Barely 100 miles northwest of Los Angeles, Cecil B. DeMille had resurrected the capital of the biblical pharaoh, Ramses II.

To recreate the exodus of the Israelites and the destruction of Pharaoh's army on an equally massive scale, DeMille hired 2500 extras, who were housed, along with 3000 animals, in a huge purpose-built camp. It was just like a military base with its own infrastructure supplying water, electricity, and telephone lines. There were regular jazz and orchestral concerts and a school for the children. The camp had its own police to enforce Prohibition. DeMille even thought to provide kosher meals for the 250 Orthodox Jews recruited to walk at the head of the procession led by Moses. He was convinced that they would play their part with real commitment and was particularly touched when, as the sequence was shot, they began singing their traditional songs. DeMille spent so much of the backers' money buying two thoroughbred horses to draw Pharaoh's chariot that it nearly cost him the movie.

But finally the whole movie was in the can and only slightly over the million-dollar budget. There was no cash left over to pay for storage of the biggest sets in cinema history, so they were simply dismantled and buried in the sand. In his autobiography, DeMille joked that some day in the distant future archeologists would uncover an interesting find in the dunes of Guadalupe. But he was only partly right. In 1983, three movie enthusiasts, Peter Brosnan, Bruce Cardozo, and Richard Eberhardt, began excavations at the site; due to lack of funds these are still incomplete today.

"The best photoplay ever made. The greatest theatrical spectacle in history. The greatest sermon on the tablets which form the basis of all law ever preached." *Photoplay Magazine*

The director knew exactly how the Bible scenes should look. He took his inspiration from a King James version with illustrations by Gustave Doré. At the beginning of 1923 DeMille finally gave Paul Iribe the contract to build the gigantic set for the city of Ramses II in the sand dunes near the town of Guadalupe, northwest of Los Angeles. The set surpassed everything ever before constructed for a movie. The biblical epic, the genre that was to prove Hollywood's biggest money-spinner, was built on a few sand dunes.

It was not only the colossal sets and the spectacular but beautifully controlled crowd scenes that caused a sensation. The biblical prologue also showcased an innovative piece of film technology. A relatively new company by the name of Technicolor offered DeMille an additional camera

that operated with the new two-color system. If he wanted the results it produced, he could buy them; if not, Technicolor would destroy them. DeMille already had some experience of coloring with the Handschiegel process, which he also used on a special nitrate copy of the prologue that he made for himself. But he liked the Technicolor pictures. The selective application of color not only intensified the content of the images, but it was also ideally suited to the screen representation of stories from the Bible. Furthermore, black-and-white pictures were associated with the unvarnished on-screen portrayal of reality, while color suggested the unreal, the dreamlike, and the atmospheric.

A lot has been written about how the parting of the Red Sea was accomplished by the trick of splitting a huge lump of gelatin up the middle. But there are also two

4

1 Moses receives the Ten Commandments from God: Theodore Roberts as the biblical father of the Israelites, a tribe persecuted and driven into exile.

2 Preparing to cross the Red Sea: the movie's biblical episodes were filmed using the very latest two-color system.

3 This was the most expensive movie of its time, not least because of the cost of the gigantic sets built amid the sand dunes near the town of Guadalupe and the huge camp provided for the extras.

4 Estelle Taylor as Moses's sister Miriam. DeMille's movie comprised an epic biblical prologue and a dramatic story set in the present day.

scenes from the modern section of the film that are no less impressive today. One is a female protagonist's dizzying ascent to the roof of a church – a sequence clearly influenced by the "new vision" photography rooted in the technological culture of the 20th century, very much in vogue in the 1920s. The other is the often-quoted murder scene where the victim – a mistress, not a wife – falls against a heavy velvet curtain, tearing it section by section from its rod.

Critics raved most of all about the biblical prologue. The tale of the two dissimilar sons of a bigoted mother (Edythe Chapman), the smart, go-getting Dan (Rod La Rocque), and upright John McTavish (Richard Dix) who

lives by the scriptures, was somewhat lost beneath the spectacular wizardry of the prologue. At the end, it is the honest, decent John who wins the heart of the beautiful young woman while sinful Dan is dashed to pieces on the rocky shore. However, the interplay between good and evil, between instinctive understanding and out-of-hand rejection, delighted audiences. And moviegoers were not too upset to see Mother McTavish killed by the collapse of a church wall, shaped just like the tablets bearing the Ten Commandments given to Moses in the prologue. But then they had not read the letter from a certain Mr. Nelson in Michigan.

SR

THE GOLD RUSH

1925 - USA - 82 MIN.

DIRECTOR
CHARLES CHAPLIN (1889–1977)

SCREENPLAY
CHARLES CHAPLIN

DIRECTOR OF PHOTOGRAPHY
ROLAND H. TOTHEROH

MUSIC
CHARLES CHAPLIN, RICHARD WAGNER,
PYOTR ILYICH TCHAIKOVSKY, NIKOLAY RIMSKY-KORSAKOV

PRODUCTION
CHARLES CHAPLIN for CHARLES CHAPLIN PRODUCTIONS

STARRING
CHARLES CHAPLIN (The Lone Prospector), MACK SWAIN (Big Jim McKay),
TOM MURRAY (Black Larson), GEORGIA HALE (Georgia),
BETTY MORRISSEY (Georgia's Friend), KAY DESLYS (Georgia's Friend),
JOAN LOWELL (Georgia's Friend), MALCOLM WAITE (Jack Cameron),
HENRY BERGMAN (Hank Curtis)

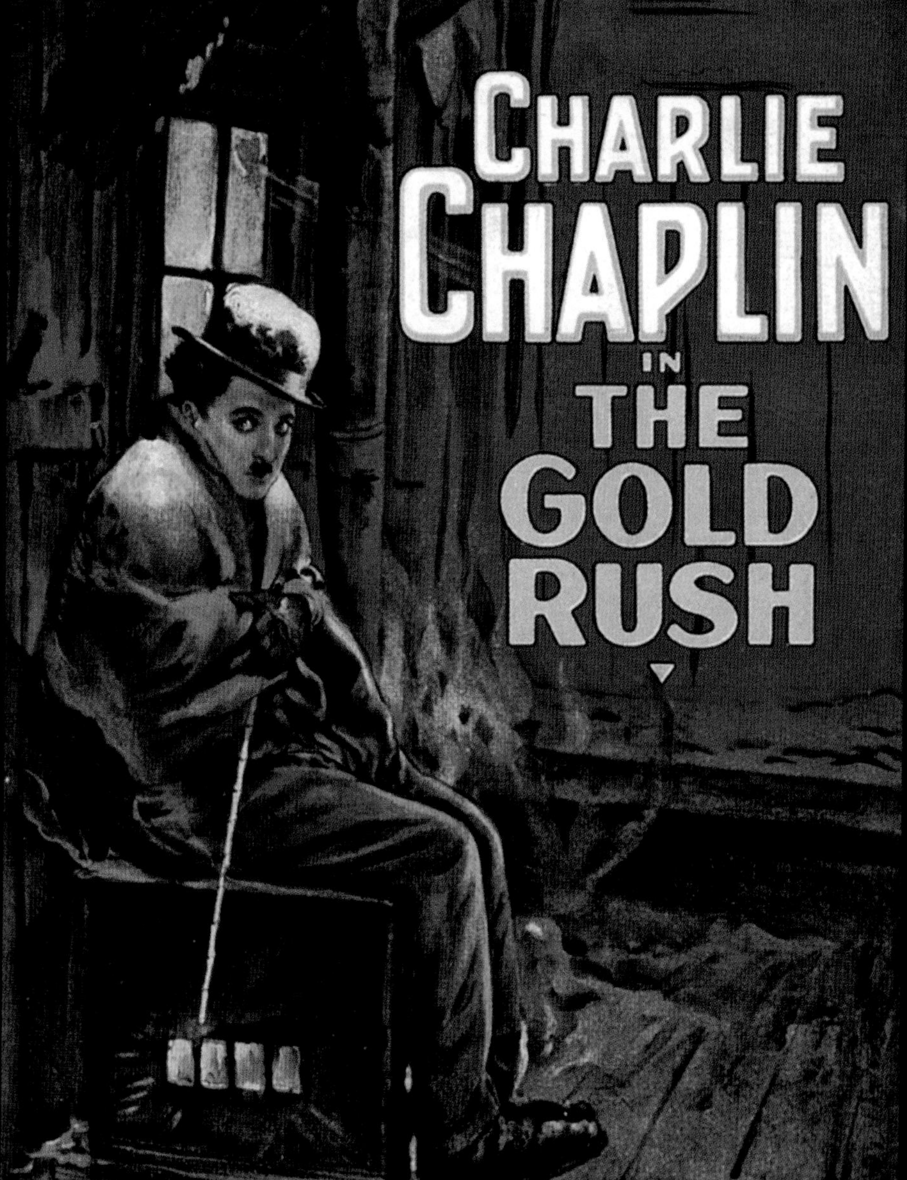
CHARLIE
CHAPLIN
IN
THE
GOLD
RUSH

"With a hunch of his shoulders and a gesture of his left hand Chaplin tells more than many a player can do with his eyes and mouth."

A snowstorm keeps Charlie, the Little Tramp (Charles Chaplin), and morose gold prospector Big Jim (Mack Swain) holed up for days in a log cabin miles from anywhere. There is nothing to eat, so Charlie cooks one of his boots and serves it up as ceremoniously as a turkey at Thanksgiving. This does not prevent his companion, suffering in adversity and delirious with hunger, from mistaking him for a chicken and trying to eat him. In a second table scene, our hero, who has found his way to a shoddy town knocked together by prospectors, invites Georgia (Georgia Hale), with whom he has fallen madly in love, and her girlfriends to a New Year's Eve dinner. The lovingly prepared meal is a great success, but now Charlie must find a way to entertain his guests. He grabs two forks and with them spears two bread rolls, creating a comical pair of legs that execute a hilarious dance on the table, to everyone's delight. But then the Little Tramp wakes up. He is all alone. The candles have burnt down. Georgia has stood him up. The wonderful evening was only a dream.

Rarely have the near-delirium of starvation and the pains of love been more vividly, movingly, and comically portrayed on screen than in these famous scenes from *The Gold Rush*, the movie which Chaplin himself considered his masterpiece. And none of the great comic's other films came so close to the ideal of a universally accessible comedy drama. The Alaska gold rush of 1898, a great adventure for some, a traumatic and tragic experience for others, provided Chaplin's inspiration.

GEORGIA HALE Georgia Hale (1905–1985) owed her most important movie role to a Hollywood scandal. Originally, the virtually unknown Lita Grey was lined up to play the pretty bar girl who is the female lead in *The Gold Rush* (1925), but when filming was under way, the 16-year-old told Chaplin she was expecting his child. He was obliged not only to marry her but also to recast her role. Chaplin chose Hale, whom he had spotted in her screen debut in Josef von Sternberg's first film as director, *The Salvation Hunters* (1924/25). It proved to be an excellent decision. Hale, with her attractive blend of vulnerability and self-assured femininity, was perfect as the woman of the Little Tramp's dreams. Her work with the famous comic earned the former Miss Chicago a contract with Paramount. In the second half of the 1920s she was among the studio's most promising young stars, until she fell victim to the introduction of the soundtrack in 1928. Studio bosses thought her voice unsuitable for speaking parts. Chaplin considered hiring her for *City Lights* (1931), but things never got past the screen-test stage. Hale ended her career playing opposite a quite different male star of the period. In 1931, she took the female lead in *The Lightning Warrior* – the last screen appearance of Rin Tin Tin, the legendary German Shepherd dog.

1 The Little Tramp surrounded by ice and snow: Charles Chaplin's Gold Rush is one of the all-time great movies.

2 Never has hunger been so vividly and grotesquely depicted onscreen as in this scene where Charlie makes a meal for himself and his buddy out of an old boot.

3 Chaplin's camera work was generally regarded as unadventurous. But who could capture loneliness better than the comic genius and his loyal cameraman Rollie Totheroh?

4 Delirious with hunger, Big Jim (Mack Swain) mistakes the puny Little Tramp for a nice plump chicken. Charlie constantly has to stand up to physically much stronger men.

As he sends his weedy little wanderer stumbling, innocent as a baby, across the icy wastes of the American North and into one hair-raising situation after another, he presents us with the whole gamut of human affliction, weakness, and longing, most of all the need for love and comradeship.

For present-day tastes, Chaplin's films often come across as rather too sentimental. The Gold Rush, however, strikes a perfect balance between adventure, comedy, and melodrama, giving the movie enormous and enduring emotional power, with the minimum of mawkishness. There can be no doubt that Chaplin's skill as a

mime is at the very heart of the film. His inspired playing not only succeeds in stirring our emotions, but also lends total credibility to even the most bizarre situations. In the scene when Charlie's image dissolves into a man-sized chicken, we know it is the product of his starving companion's crazy imaginings. But it is only through precise camera technique that the transformation seems astonishingly plausible. Crucially, too, the Little Tramp has already started imperceptibly to move like a chicken, bending forward as if pecking for grains, frantically flapping his arms, and shuffling his feet. Chaplin's subtle

"The Gold Rush is a distinct triumph for Charlie Chaplin from both the artistic and commercial standpoints, and is a picture certain to create a genuine riot at theater box offices. It is the greatest and most elaborate comedy ever filmed, and will stand for years as the biggest hit in its field." *Variety*

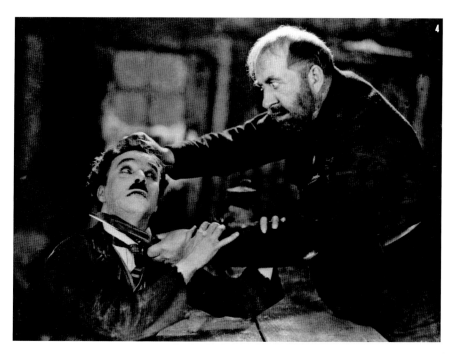

5 No other Chaplin movie managed to be simultaneously as touching, funny, and dramatic as *The Gold Rush*. Here Charlie tries to prise a bone away from the dog of bandit Black Larson (Tom Murray).

6 With the huge success of *The Gold Rush*, Chaplin, "The Most Famous Man in the World," reached the peak of his career. From then on his problems with the more conservative elements in the U.S. became more and more serious.

body language creates associations, inviting us to dream with eyes wide open.

While Chaplin's films are brilliantly acted, from a technical point of view they are often regarded as old-fashioned, mainly because of their static, mostly frontal, camera positions. *The Gold Rush* is all the more surprising for the trick photography that is still convincing today, as in the astonishing scene in which an avalanche sweeps the brutal killer Black Larson (Tom Murray) to his death.

Equally unforgettable is the sequence in which Charlie and his fat friend wake to find their log cabin teetering over the edge of a precipice, carried away in an overnight storm. There follows a breathtaking ballet as the floor pitches and tosses like a ship at sea. Life, Chaplin seems to be saying, is like an absurd, neverending dance performed on unstable ground. Only by working together can we find the right balance.

JH

BATTLESHIP POTEMKIN
BRONENOSETS POTYOMKIN
1925 - USSR - 75 MIN.

DIRECTOR

SERGEI M. EISENSTEIN (1898–1948)

SCREENPLAY

NINA AGADZHANOVA-SHUTKO, SERGEI M. EISENSTEIN

DIRECTOR OF PHOTOGRAPHY

EDOUARD TISSÉ

EDITING

SERGEI M. EISENSTEIN

PRODUCTION

GOSKINO

STARRING

ALEKSANDR ANTONOV (Vakulinchuk, Bolshevik Sailor),
VLADIMIR BARSKY (Commander Golikov), GRIGORI ALEKSANDROV
(Chief Officer Giliarovsky), ALEKSANDR LEVSHIN (Petty Officer),
MIKHAIL GOMOROV (Matiushenko, Militant Sailor)

ХУДОЖЕСТВЕННЫЙ ФИЛЬМ   ПОСТАНОВКА   СЕРГЕЯ ЭЙЗЕНШТЕЙНА
АВТОР СЦЕНАРИЯ Н.А.ГАДЖАНОВА   ОПЕРАТОР Э.ТИССЭ   КОМПОЗИТОР Н. КРЮКОВ
ПРОИЗВОДСТВО ГОСКИНО (1-я Ф-КА) 1925 г.   ПОВТОРНО ОЗВУЧЕН В 1950 с. „МОСФИЛЬ"

БРОНЕНОСЕЦ «ПОТЁМКИН»

"Comrades, the time has come to act!"

There are some films that have to succeed abroad before they receive the attention they deserve in their homeland. Such was the case with *The Cabinet of Dr. Caligari (Das Cabinet des Dr. Caligari*, 1919/20), directed by Robert Wiene, which was a major hit in Paris before it went on to be acknowledged in Berlin as a groundbreaking movie. Later, the same thing happened to Rainer Werner Fassbinder's films, which won acclaim in Paris, London and New York before finding recognition in the director's native Germany. A prime example of a film taking a similarly roundabout route to success is *Battleship Potemkin*. Sergei M. Eisenstein's masterpiece created a sensation in Berlin in the 1920s before making its triumphant way across Europe and securing its place in cinema history. Even now, it numbers among the most revered classic movies, regularly cropping up on lists of the best films of all time and inspiring generations of film students.

However, no one could have guessed as much when the leadership of the newly created Soviet Union commissioned the 27-year-old Sergei Eisenstein to make a film with the working title *The Task of Remembering the Pre-Revolutionary Revolts in 1905*. After being forced to abandon his engineering studies and working in the theater with the great innovator Karl Theodor Meyerhold, Eisenstein came to the attention of Soviet cultural officials with *Strike (Statchka*, 1924), his first full-length feature. Originally, the story of the rebellion aboard the warship *Potemkin* was intended as only one of several episodes, but as Eisenstein explored the subject in ever-greater depth the other episodes were finally abandoned.

EISENSTEIN'S MONTAGE OF ATTRACTIONS Sergei M. Eisenstein is not only regarded as one of the most important directors in the history of cinema, but he also left a no less significant mark on the theory of film. For this revolutionary moviemaker, the art of directing and the theory of cinematic effect were far from irrelevant to one another. On the contrary, he saw them as inseparable, dialectic halves of the same phenomenon. Central to Eisenstein's theory and practice of cinema was the concept of montage. Not by chance did he use a term borrowed from the construction industry, in other words from the world of work in the Marxist sense.

What Eisenstein called "montage of attractions," which he initially developed while working in the theater in the early 1920s, was the juxtaposition of seemingly arbitrary images to create the greatest possible impact on the viewer and produce a different level of meaning. He borrowed the principles of shock and surprise from forms of popular entertainment such as the circus and traveling fairs. The showcase for this type of montage was Eisenstein's first full-length feature *Strike (Statchka*, 1924), which, like *Battleship Potemkin (Bronenosets Potyomkin*, 1925), told the story of a revolutionary rebellion. Shots of the bloody suppression of the strike were crosscut with images of a bull being slaughtered. Later, Eisenstein developed the concept even further to create intellectual montage, through which new ideas emerge from a sequence of shots.

"It is a travesty of sentimentality and prejudice and is full of bloodthirsty scenes on board the cruiser and shooting and panic in Odessa. Though its naval technique is full of palpable absurdities, it has an extraordinary effect on the public, which takes sides in the theatre, as the film shows infuriated sailors murdering their officers." *The Times*

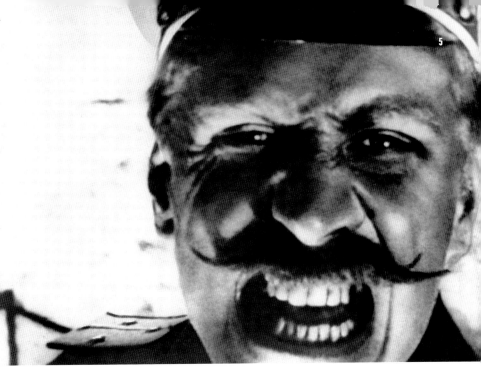

1 The battleship's revolutionary crew celebrate their victorious rebellion against their officers.

2 Eisenstein's dynamic and dramatic imagery and exciting montage turned the movie's premiere into a major political event.

3 Eisenstein used what he called the principle of "typage" to choose his actors: instead of experienced professionals he hired amateurs who looked right for the roles of officers, workers, or representatives of the bourgeoisie.

4 Eisenstein uses space and carefully calculated geometric configurations to underpin the drama unfolding on the quarterdeck.

5 Expressive faces communicate emotions to the audience: here an officer is filled with hate.

The film is clearly divided into five acts: the deplorable conditions on the ship, the sailors' revolt against the officers, the alliance of the townspeople with the revolutionary crew, the Cossacks' massacre of the innocent on the Odessa steps, and finally rescue by the ships of the Black Sea fleet. But, then as now, what really moves the viewer is not so much the story itself but the way in which it is told. Eisenstein was the first to make radical changes in editing techniques and to develop his own theory of montage and a style of editing characterized by the rapid, rhythmic juxtaposition of short shots and jump cuts building up to a climactic moment in the narrative. Accustomed as we are to music videos and TV commercials, nowadays there seems to be nothing particularly innovative about *Battleship Potemkin*. But in the mid-1920s it represented

a revolution in world cinema. More conservative critics and audiences viewed the movie with deep concern, fearing it could mark the beginning of radical political change. In many German states it was banned. For example, moviegoers in Bavaria and Württemberg were unable to see *Battleship Potemkin* until after World War II.

Writing in defense of the film in 1927, the distinguished German literary critic Walter Benjamin described it as "ideologically solid as concrete, as meticulously calculated in every detail as the arch of a bridge" – in other words a masterly achievement of engineering by Eisenstein, the former student engineer. And the structure still holds good today as the film continues to work its magic. Few scenes are so often quoted or adapted as the massacre on the harbor steps in Odessa with the runaway

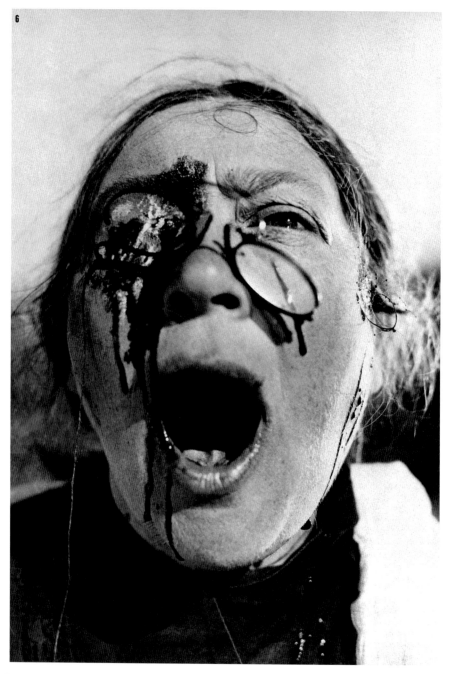

baby carriage, whether in *The Untouchables*, Brian De Palma's 1986 movie set in Chicago in the Prohibition era, or Anno Saul's tale of life in Hamburg's cosmopolitan Schanze district, *Kebab Connection* (2004).

So *Battleship Potemkin* owes its longevity not only to numerous revivals but also to the endless allusions that have appeared in popular culture over the years. In 2004 the film, complete with a brand new soundtrack recorded by the Pet Shop Boys, made a spectacular comeback at an open-air screening in London's Trafalgar Square, while in 2005 a restored version was presented at several film festivals. Maybe all these references and quotations are simply more roundabout ways leading right back to Eisenstein's original masterwork.   MH

"*Potemkin* is a huge film of rare success ... However, the film is ideologically solid, minutely calculated in every detail like the arch of a bridge. The harder the blows rain down on it, the better it roars. Only those who shake it with gloved hands hear and move nothing." *Walter Benjamin*

6 The pain in the face of this Odessa woman has become an iconic image of a cataclysmic event.

7 A milestone in movie history: Eisenstein's montage of the Cossacks' massacre of civilians on the Odessa Steps.

THE GENERAL

1926/27 - USA - 75 MIN.

DIRECTOR

BUSTER KEATON (1895–1966), CLYDE BRUCKMAN (1894–1955)

SCREENPLAY

AL BOASBERG, CHARLES HENRY SMITH, CLYDE BRUCKMAN,
BUSTER KEATON, based on the book *The Great Locomotive Chase:
A History of the Andrews Railroad Raid into Georgia in 1862* by WILLIAM PITTENGER

DIRECTOR OF PHOTOGRAPHY

DEVEREAUX JENNINGS, BERT HAINES

EDITING

SHERMAN KELL, BUSTER KEATON

PRODUCTION

JOSEPH M. SCHENCK, BUSTER KEATON FOR BUSTER KEATON PRODUCTIONS INC.

STARRING

BUSTER KEATON (Johnnie Gray), MARION MACK (Annabelle Lee),
CHARLES HENRY SMITH (Annabelle's Father), FRANK BARNES (= Richard Allen)
(Annabelle's Brother), GLEN CAVENDER (Captain Anderson), JIM FARLEY (General Thatcher),
FREDERICK VROOM (Confederate General), JOE KEATON (Union General),
MIKE DONLIN (Union General), TOM NAWN (Union General)

"There were two loves in his life."

Marietta, Georgia, 1861. Johnnie (Buster Keaton) has two great loves: a steam locomotive proudly named *The General* and his sweetheart Annabelle (Marion Mack). All spruced up in his Sunday suit, he goes to woo the young lady at her parents' house, just as news arrives that the Southern States have declared war on the North. Annabelle's father (Charles Henry Smith) and brother (Frank Barnes) immediately enlist. It does not take Johnnie long to volunteer as well, for he knows only too well that unless he is wearing a Confederate uniform, he will not be able to face his beloved. So much the worse for him when he is rejected because he is considered worth more to the war effort as an engineer. Annabelle fails to understand; she thinks he is a coward and not worthy of her. But Johnnie gets the chance to prove himself when Yankee spies steal *The General* as part of a plot to sabotage the supply

JOSEPH M. SCHENCK The extraordinary story of Joseph M. Schenck's life reads like something straight out of a movie. Born in 1878 in Russia, he came to New York with his younger brother Nicholas in 1893. Within the space of a few years they rose from being practically penniless to owning a chain of drugstores. The brothers' astonishing business acumen soon led them into the entertainment industry. They bought two amusement parks and their success brought them into contact with Marcus Loew, who made them partners in his vaudeville and movie theater chain, which later became Hollywood's legendary MGM studios.

From then on, the Schencks became part of movie business aristocracy. In 1916 Joe married the up-and-coming screen star Norma Talmadge. While Nicholas, soon to be appointed president of Loew's Inc., remained in New York, the couple went to Hollywood where Joe launched his movie career as an independent producer. He produced films not only for his wife and her sisters, Natalie and Constance, but also for Roscoe "Fatty" Arbuckle and Buster Keaton. Most importantly, he joined the management of United Artists and became president in 1927.

But he did not stop there. In 1933, Schenck cofounded 20th Century Pictures with Darryl F. Zanuck. And when the studio merged with the Fox Film Corporation in 1935, as chairman of this new major studio he finally became one of Hollywood's most powerful moguls. However, his position of power led him into some shady dealings. In 1941 he was jailed for a few months for tax evasion and corruption, but received a presidential pardon from President Truman and did not have to serve the full term. Back in business, Schenck witnessed the creeping decline of the studio system but the Hollywood veteran also struck up a friendship with Marilyn Monroe, one of the last great stars whose career he helped to launch. In 1953 Joseph M. Schenck received a special Academy Award for long and distinguished service to the motion picture industry. He died in 1961 in Los Angeles.

1 The man who never laughs: Buster Keaton always achieved maximum effect with minimum use of mime.

2 Johnnie (Buster Keaton) and his beloved locomotive: as in many of this brilliant comedian's movies, the plot revolves around man and machine.

3 A dramatic chase: Keaton spared no expense or effort on action sequences.

"They're kidding about everything now; any day you may expect to see U.S. Grant and Robert E. Lee break into a Charleston. Not that they do it in *The General*, but Buster Keaton does spoof the Civil War most uncivilly in his new comedy." *Photoplay*

4 It is not only the almost documentary camera style that illustrates Keaton's insistence on authenticity – the extras were real soldiers!

5 Comic turned acrobat: Buster Keaton always performed his own stunts, even the most dangerous.

route to the South. Grimly determined, he sets off in pursuit of the train, first on foot, then on a handcart, a penny-farthing bicycle, and finally aboard another locomotive, *The Texas.*

The General is by far the best loved of Buster Keaton's films and it was the famous silent movie comedian's own particular favorite. He regarded it as a work that was entirely his own, in which he managed to blend to perfection a dazzling array of weird ideas and an exciting plot. The story is based on real-life incidents from the

American Civil War, which Keaton read about in William Pittenger's personal account, *The Great Locomotive Chase: A History of the Andrews Railroad Raid into Georgia in 1862,* published in 1863. While he and the author freely adapted the story from the book, when it came to historical detail, Keaton laid great store by authenticity. The film was shot many miles away from the Hollywood studios, in Oregon, because the state boasted suitable railroad installations and the landscape offered an attractive and credible backdrop to the pursuit of *The General.*

6 The inner child: the seriousness with which Johnnie approaches his work is just like a child at play.

7 Is there anything in there? With weird scenes like this, it's no wonder the Surrealists were big fans of Keaton's movies.

8 The rejected volunteer: Johnnie does not lose his cool when the recruiting officer turns him down.

9 Like Charles Chaplin and Harold Lloyd, Keaton's brand of comedy was based not least on extraordinary physical control – riding an old-fashioned penny-farthing was one of the easier feats required of the vaudeville artist's son.

"A pleasant piece of celluloid without any rollicking moments." *Motion Picture Classic*

So insistent was Keaton on realism, he went so far as to make a burning bridge collapse under *The Texas* and the locomotive fall into a riverbed. The shot, the spectacular climax of the movie, was the most expensive of the whole silent era.

The careful composition of the Civil War scenes – often reminiscent of the famous photographs by Matthew B. Brady – made a considerable contribution to the movie's success. Most of all, the story provided ideal material for

Keaton's special brand of comedy. As so often in Keaton's films, a machine, in this case the steam locomotive of the title, played second lead. It was the focal point from which the comedian could develop a whole series of visual gags. But, unlike *The Navigator* (1924), in which Keaton plays a millionaire's son who finds himself on board an abandoned ocean liner, the joke in *The General* is not sparked off by the unequal relationship between man and mighty machine. Quite the opposite. It is precisely

Johnnie's familiarity with the steel colossus that makes him seem like an eccentric who lives in his own world. Grown-ups regard him as a good-for-nothing, whereas in fact he has his own crazy professional ethos. Typical is the situation when the lovesick Johnnie perches on one of the loco's connecting rods and completely fails to notice that it has started moving and lifting him up and down. It is a scene full of typical Keaton poetry and an impressive example of the comic's physical control, for, had he moved an inch or two backwards, he would have ended up under the wheels.

As though seemingly oblivious to danger, Johnnie sleepwalks his way through the most hair-raising situations with the instinctive confidence with which Keaton executes all his stunts. He even sticks his head up the barrel of a cannon to see what is blocking it. Johnnie seems not the least surprised when it fires just as he withdraws his head and, by a complete fluke, instead of hitting his own train the cannonball reaches its real target. So the absurd but completely logical behavior of the puny little guy with the sad face makes him a war hero, and wins him back the heart of the girl he loves.   UB

METROPOLIS

1926 - GERMANY - 147 MIN.

DIRECTOR

FRITZ LANG (1890–1976)

SCREENPLAY

THEA VON HARBOU, based on her
novel of the same name

DIRECTOR OF PHOTOGRAPHY

KARL FREUND, GÜNTHER RITTAU

EDITING

FRITZ LANG

MUSIC

GOTTFRIED HUPPERTZ

PRODUCTION

ERICH POMMER for UFA

STARRING

ALFRED ABEL (Johann "Joh" Fredersen), GUSTAV FRÖHLICH
(Freder Fredersen), BRIGITTE HELM (Maria / The Robot), RUDOLF KLEIN-ROGGE
(Rotwang), FRITZ RASP (Slim), THEODOR LOOS (Josaphat / Joseph),
ERWIN BISWANGER (N°. 11 811), HEINRICH GEORGE (Grot),
OLAF STROM (Jan), HANNS LEO REICH (Marinus)

METROPOLIS

DEGEN

"... it was their hands that built this city of ours, Father, but where do the hands belong in your scheme?" "In their proper place!"

Metropolis stands alongside D. W. Griffith's *Intolerance* (1916) and Sergei M. Eisenstein's *Battleship Potemkin (Bronenosets Potyomkin*, 1925) as one of the great masterpieces of early cinema. It is also about a revolution, but what makes the movie so memorable is not its shamelessly trivial plot but its visionary landscapes that are both portents of the industrial age and harbingers of postmodernism. In a movie made at a time of transition between German Expressionism and the Neue Sachlichkeit (New Objectivity) movement, the architecture itself plays a crucial role in the development and telling of the story. Even now, the city still impresses with its trademark skyscrapers, traversed by automobiles and airplanes. Metropolis is a corporate city-state strictly segregated along class lines. The city above belongs to the privi-

leged ruling classes, while the downtrodden workers toil away in the subterranean city below. An immense "New Tower of Babel" dominates the cityscape, and inside it a mad scientist works in perpetual darkness to clone a mechanical being – a robot, the first cyborg. Makers of sci-fi movies, from *Bride of Frankenstein* (1935) to *Blade Runner* (1982) and *The Fifth Element* (1997), have continued to draw on this theme, which has provided the pretext for an inexhaustible series of sensational effects. In the late 1920s, there was only one man who could come up with this kind of science fiction – the mad architect of German cinema, Fritz Lang.

He was inspired by a visit to the U.S. To him, the New York skyline seemed like a magnificent stage set and, like many Germans in the turbulent period between the wars,

OTTO HUNTE Along with Walter Reimann, Walter Röhrig, and Rochus Gliese, Otto Hunte (1881–1960) was one of the leading German art directors of the 1920s and '30s. Many of UFA's major productions were particularly admired for their atmospheric sets proclaiming the primacy of architecture in the art of cinema. In his review of *Metropolis* (1926), Luis Buñuel paid tribute to Hunte's work, observing: "Henceforth and for ever more the scenic designer has been replaced by the architect." A veteran of World War I, Hunte began his career painting stage sets, a job which brought him into contact with some of the best-known German directors of the period. With his assistants Erich Kettelhut and Karl Vollbrecht, he was a member of the successful design team that worked on Joe May's spectacular eight-part *Mistress of the World (Die Herrin der Welt*, 1919). Fritz Lang engaged all three men for most of his German productions, including *Dr. Mabuse, the Gambler (Dr. Mabuse, der Spieler*, 1921/22, Parts 1 & 2); *Die Nibelungen* (1922–24, Parts 1 & 2); *Metropolis; Spies (Spione*, 1927/28); and *Woman in the Moon (Frau im Mond*, 1928/29) – although Kettelhut did not work on the last two. Just as significant as these epoch-making visions of past and future were Hunte's designs for Joseph von Sternberg's drama *The Blue Angel (Der blaue Engel*, 1930), for which he created a striking contrast between dens of iniquity and small-town tranquility. And in the successful 1930 comedy *Three Good Friends (Die Drei von der Tankstelle)*, he showed a keen eye for the minutiae of everyday life in Germany.

However, Hunte's exceptional artistic career followed a typically German pattern. During the Nazi period, his name appeared in the credits of some propaganda films, including Veit Harlan's violently anti-Semitic *Jew Suss (Jud Süß*, 1940). Later, with Wolfgang Staudte's *The Murderers Are Among Us (Die Mörder sind unter uns*, 1946), he lent his support to the postwar anti-Nazi education campaign. From 1948 until his death in 1960 he devoted himself entirely to landscape painting.

1 Awe-inspiring cityscape: the breath-taking skyline of the big city was both a symbol and a portent of things to come in the modern age.

2 A dreamer in the underworld: Freder (Gustav Fröhlich) is shocked.

3 Vorsprung durch Technik: the inventor Rotwang clones a cyborg from the virtuous Maria (Brigitte Helm).

4 Lang's robot became an icon of the modern age. The floating circles of light were the result of a multiple exposure.

> "*Metropolis* does what many great films do, creating a time, place and characters so striking that they become part of our arsenal of images for imagining the world. The ideas of *Metropolis* have been so often absorbed into popular culture that its horrific future city is almost a given. Lang filmed for nearly a year, driven by obsession, often cruel to his colleagues, a perfectionist madman, and the result is one of those seminal films without which the others cannot be fully appreciated." *Chicago Sun-Times*

he was both intoxicated and repelled by its immensity. The result was a futuristic fairy tale of the sinister kind, a crude mixture of American fantasy, modern social criticism and backward-looking occultism. On a visit to the subterranean city Freder (Gustav Fröhlich) gains an insight into the hierarchical power structure created by his tyrannical father Joh Fredersen (Alfred Abel). Moved by a call for peace and understanding by the virtuous and beautiful Maria (Brigitte Helm), he joins the cause of the dissatisfied workers. Meanwhile, the brilliant inventor Rotwang (Rudolf Klein-Rogge), who is also a master of black magic, creates a robot modeled on Maria – the evil Maria (also played by Brigitte Helm). This lascivious *femme fatale* both seduces the bright young men of the city above and uses her

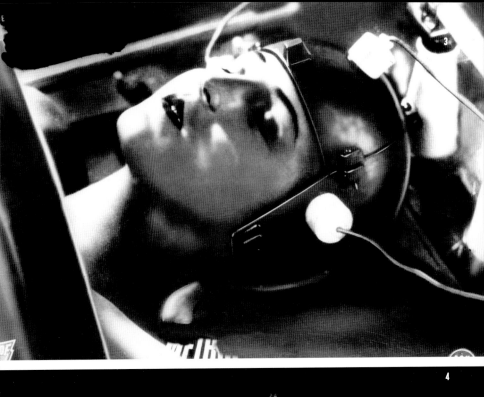

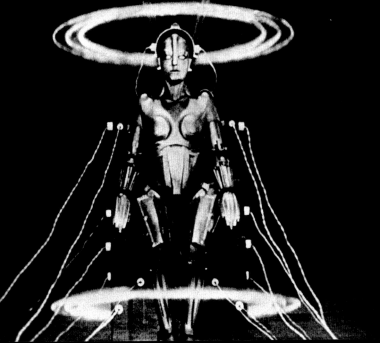

5 Rotwang (Rudolf Klein-Rogge) is a cross between Faust and Dr. Frankenstein.

6 Freder and Maria's love for each other brings reconciliation between all sides. Metaphor, allegory, and parables replace social analysis.

7 Manipulation of the masses: a man-made sex symbol, the bad Maria turns the heads of the bright young men of the city above.

8 Power struggle: Fredersen (Alfred Abel) and Rotwang.

9 One of the movie's main characteristics is pseudo-religious symbolism, drawing on various ideologies.

"Between brain and hands, the intermediary must be the heart." *Intertitle: the film's motto*

vampish charm to persuade the workforce to revolt. What was intended as personal revenge against Fredersen leads to disaster. Workers trying to wreck machinery unwittingly flood their city, but the "good" Maria brings all sides to their senses, a compromise is reached, and social harmony is achieved with a handshake and the words, "The heart must mediate between head and hands."

Hitler and Goebbels, who was to become his Minister for Propaganda, were both impressed by the film's sumptuous sets and equally enthusiastic about the model

it presented of an archaic but modern community founded on revolutionary pathos and pseudo-religious ideology. Critics, meanwhile, hated its naïve solution to serious political problems. H. G. Wells saw it as a "concentration of almost every possible foolishness, cliché and platitude." Luis Buñuel was kinder, overwhelmed by what he called "the most marvelous picture book imaginable." He laid the blame for the movie's naïve and tasteless sociological message squarely at the door of the screenplay writer Thea von Harbou. The accusations leveled at Lang's then

wife, who later became a loyal member of the Nazi Party, persist even now despite Lang's attempts at damage limitation. He stated that she was responsible for the main theme but added that "I was at least 50 percent responsible since I made the movie." He continued: "I was not as politically aware as I am now. One can't make a socially conscious film that says the heart mediates between head and hands – I think that is actually a fairy tale. But I was very interested in machines ..." In making *Metropolis* Fritz Lang created an engineer's dream. The pace of the film is set, not by the script but by the throb of pistons as they move up and down, by the revolution of cogs, and Joh Fredersen's ten-hour clock. In order to bring the director's vision to the screen, the movie had to become an industry in its own right. Filming took 310 days and 60 nights. Most of the six-million-mark production costs were swallowed up by the 25,000 special effects. The famous street scenes took four months to complete and legendary art director Otto Hunte's sets then had to be shot a frame at a time. Every single miniature automobile was driven forward using the laborious stop-motion technique. The Schüfftan Process was used in scenes featuring aircraft

10 The Black Madonna of the electrical age, the bad Maria has the power to destroy.

12 Labor costs: Freder has to learn that clocks and machines in Metropolis move at their own murderous pace.

13 A warning sign: people die like flies, a sacrifice to the machine god Moloch.

11 Architecture and film: the gong in the workers' city was built to a design by Bauhaus architect Walter Gropius.

and long columns of people. This involved scraping away the silver on part of a mirror and placing the mirror at a 45-degree angle to the camera. The action was then filmed through the clear portion of the mirror while the silvered portion reflected the artificial background, combining the two into a single image. The towering Club of the Sons stadium in the upper city was also created via this technique, which was developed by cameraman and special effects expert Eugen Schüfftan. So, too, was Freder's nightmare in which the great generators that run the city become the machine-god Moloch, demanding human sacrifice. Rotwang's transformation of the good Maria into a Madonna-like robot has become one of the icons of science-fiction cinema, a creative act performed amid rings of light and flashes of lightning, a first attempt at morphing, without the aid of computer-generated imagery.

Lang's methods of maintaining control of his idiosyncratic creation were not unlike those of the dictator Fredersen. Before shooting began on the flood sequence, the extras – Lang had recruited an army of 3600 of them – had to stand in the water for hours on end. Brigitte Helm was made to perform perilous leaps and, in the scene in which the robot Maria meets her end at the stake, to contend with real flames.

The film was a commercial disaster. After its glittering premiere, it continued to play in cinemas for a matter of weeks, with audiences staying away in droves. Some six months later, it was re-released in a drastically cut version. The silent film only recovered one-seventh of its production costs, a disaster not only for UFA but also for the whole German movie industry. In 1925, UFA, MGM, and Paramount had agreed to cooperate in the making and distribution of

movies for both the German and U.S. markets. But the so-called Parafumet Agreement, which UFA had hoped would be a way in to the American market, proved to be a disappointment. Frustrated by the very public wrangling over production costs, Lang left the studio, which was then taken over by the publisher and National Socialist sympathizer Alfred Hugenberg. The decline in the quality of its output became all too apparent in subsequent years. *Metropolis* was cut several times for the export market and the leftover footage scattered to the four winds. Although the film now exists in an outstanding restored version, up to a quarter of the footage is regarded as lost. Only much later was it transformed from a forgotten fossil to a much-admired cult movie. In 1984, Giorgio Moroder launched a shortened, color-tinted version with a pop soundtrack onto the market. Although not to everyone's taste, it testified to the continuing fascination with *Metropolis*. With its combination of styles and time frames, of Constructivist industrial design and Art Deco, of Old Testament mysticism and belief in the future, and a muddled erratic plot alternating Bolshevistic machine wrecking and crypto-Fascist ideology, it is precisely this eclecticism, reflecting the period in which the movie was made, that makes it relevant to today's world.

PB

THE BLUE ANGEL
DER BLAUE ENGEL
1930 - GERMANY - 107 MIN.

DIRECTOR

JOSEF VON STERNBERG (1894–1969)

SCREENPLAY

ROBERT LIEBMANN, JOSEF VON STERNBERG, based on a free adaptation
of HEINRICH MANN'S novel *Professor Unrat oder das Ende eines Tyrannen
(Small Town Tyrant or Professor Unrat)* by
CARL ZUCKMAYER and KARL VOLLMOELLER

DIRECTOR OF PHOTOGRAPHY

GÜNTHER RITTAU, HANS SCHNEEBERGER

EDITING

SAM WINSTON

MUSIC

FRIEDRICH HOLLAENDER

PRODUCTION

ERICH POMMER for UFA

STARRING

EMIL JANNINGS (Professor Immanuel Rath), MARLENE DIETRICH (Lola Lola),
KURT GERRON (Kiepert the Magician), ROSA VALETTI (Guste, Kiepert's Wife),
HANS ALBERS (Mazeppa the Strong Man), REINHOLD BERNT (Clown),
EDUARD VON WINTERSTEIN (School Principal), JOHANNES ROTH (Pedell the Janitor),
ROLF MÜLLER (Angst), ROLAND VARNO (Lohmann),
CARL BALHAUS (Ertzum), ROBERT KLEIN-LÖRCK (Goldstaub)

THE BLUE ANGEL

"Falling in love again, never wanted to. What am I to do? I can't help it."

Professor Immanuel Rath (Emil Jannings) runs a tight ship. As a master at a small-town boys' high school he subjects his students to an extremely pedantic and doctrinaire style of teaching. As if that were not enough, the middle-aged, middle-class professor is particularly zealous in dealing with his pupils' moral misdemeanors. When he discovers that every night some of the boys are going to the Blue Angel, a seedy nightclub down by the docks, to see the singer Lola Lola (Marlene Dietrich), he decides to pay the place a visit. But instead of catching his students *in flagrante* and chastising them for immoral behavior, the professor himself falls under the spell of the happy-go-lucky young woman. It is a passion that will ultimately destroy him.

Josef von Sternberg's *The Blue Angel* has come to be seen as the great classic German movie, not least because it saw the birth of Germany's one and only true screen icon: Marlene Dietrich. Who can forget the moment when, wearing top hat and garter belt, she launches into her famous number "Falling in Love Again"? Laid-back and provocative, she perches on a beer barrel, her left leg seductively drawn up, looking languidly over her bare shoulder as she confesses her little weakness. This legendary, self-confidently sexy pose became Dietrich's trademark. And even though, as Lola Lola, she had not yet acquired the aura of the sophisticated, slightly kinky femme fatale of her later movies with von Sternberg, she already radiates the down-to-earth sensuality which saw

KURT GERRON Alongside Rosa Valetti and Hans Albers, Kurt Gerron (1897–1944) is one of the outstanding supporting actors in *The Blue Angel (Der blaue Engel*, 1930), making a vital contribution to the movie's lasting appeal. The role of Kiepert the magician was tailor-made for this talented entertainer. It was not just his portly figure that made him one of the most striking theater and cinema personalities under the Weimar Republic. Gerron began his career in cabaret in the 1920s. Halfway through the decade he made his movie debut, at first tending to play down-to-earth characters but later moving on to quirky portrayals of more upper-crust types. Acting in successful movies such as *Three Good Friends (Die Drei von der Tankstelle*, 1930) and *Bombs Over Monte Carlo (Bomben auf Monte Carlo,* 1931) in the early 1930s, Gerron was not only among the best-known faces of German cinema, but he had also launched a promising career as a director. The son of Jewish parents, he was forced to flee when Hitler came to power. He finally reached Amsterdam after traveling via Austria and France. Gerron's fate is a chilling illustration of the barbarity of the National Socialist regime. After the German invasion of the Netherlands, Gerron found himself in several concentration camps until the Nazis finally coerced him into making a propaganda "documentary" about the camp which presented a totally false version of conditions there. Once filming was completed, Gerron, his wife, and all those who had worked with him on the film were transported to Auschwitz and murdered.

her typecast as a woman of low morals, a prostitute, or a singer in a third-rate nightclub.

In Dietrich's erotic presence even Emil Jannings, the German movie star of the era, paled into insignificance. In fact, it was to be Jannings's task to attract publicity outside Germany for UFA's first major talkie. Just how much The Blue Angel was built around the great actor is clear from the fact that Jannings was able to persuade UFA bosses to hire the American director von Sternberg. The two men had already worked together in Hollywood making *The Last Command* (1927/28), which earned Jannings the

"Not only is Mr. Jannings' and Miss Dietrich's acting excellent, but they are supported by an unusually competent cast. Having quite a good story, Mr. von Sternberg's direction is infinitely superior to that of *Morocco*, and the settings are very effective."
The New York Times

1 "Falling in love again, never wanted to." The role of the seductive Lola Lola shot Marlene Dietrich to stardom and created her screen sex goddess image.

2 Marlene Dietrich sang Friedrich Hollaender's wonderfully ribald songs with inimitable sassy charm.

3 Alongside Marlene Dietrich (left) and Emil Jannings (right), the star-studded cast of *The Blue Angel* also included the young Hans Albers (center), who later became one of Germany's best-loved screen actors …

4 … and Kurt Gerron, one of German cinema's outstanding personalities of the period, now sadly almost forgotten. The wonderful comic actor and director was murdered in Auschwitz in 1944.

Oscar for Best Actor. However, while von Sternberg's direction was acclaimed, especially his convincing use of sound in his atmospheric interpretation of the story, many critics found Jannings's style of acting in *The Blue Angel* outmoded.

Others complained that in turning Heinrich Mann's social satire *Small Town Tyrant or Professor Unrat* (1904/05) into an individual tragedy the moviemakers had completely missed the point of the book. But it is precisely Jannings's mannered performance that works against this idea. Even though the pathos of the great German actor is seldom broken by any suggestion of irony, the solid bourgeois character can be seen as representing a distinctive type. And the sets, whose stylization links them closely to the

Expressionist tradition of silent movies, harmonize perfectly with Jannings's portrayal of the professor. The old town with its rickety, steep-pitched roofs and narrow winding streets is the perfect setting for a man whose petty-mindedness has been warped even further by an exaggerated belief in authority.

All of which makes the nightclub an alluring alternative world. As the professor creeps along the dark alleyways towards the Blue Angel with the sound of foghorns echoing from the harbor, it seems as though the upright citizen is being drawn by a siren song into the realms of the unconscious, where he will have to confront his innermost desires. Indeed, the tyrannical teacher will be unmasked as a repressed masochist, who ends by cutting a

5 Emil Jannings was really intended to be the star of the movie. But newcomer Marlene Dietrich stole the show from the great Oscar-winning actor.

6 Heinrich Mann's famous novel of social mores, *Small Town Tyrant*

(Professor Unrat), portrayed the high-school teacher as a typical petit bourgeois of the days of the Kaiser …

7 … but von Sternberg placed him at the center of a drama of humiliation and self-abasement.

8 "Men cluster to me like moths around a flame." After *The Blue Angel*, Marlene Dietrich went to Hollywood with Josef von Sternberg and became the first – and for a long time the only – international star from Germany.

"You'll try in vain, you can't explain / The charming, alarming, blonde women." *Film quote: Lola Lola (Marlene Dietrich)*

pitiful figure. Robbed of his respectable bourgeois existence and his former position of power, he becomes a pathetic victim. The sadistic jokes and humiliations he once inflicted on his former students are now meted out to him by mediocre entertainers and other denizens of the seedy seamen's quarter.

These desolate scenes of frustration and cruelty clearly suggest that *The Blue Angel* can be interpreted as a commentary on the situation in German society only a few years before the far less inhibited middle classes would help bring the Fascists to power. But, above all, the movie still stands as a dazzling masterpiece of a crucial era in German cinema – a golden age that was soon to be lost forever.

JH

"On top of the drawing power of Jannings comes the discovery of a new magnet, Marlene Dietrich, who should be as much to the American taste as to that of the Continent." *Variety*

UNDER THE ROOFS OF PARIS

SOUS LES TOITS DE PARIS

1929/30 - FRANCE - 92 MIN.

DIRECTOR
RENÉ CLAIR (1898–1981)

SCREENPLAY
RENÉ CLAIR

DIRECTOR OF PHOTOGRAPHY
GEORGES PÉRINAL, GEORGES RAULET

EDITOR
RENÉ LE HÉNAFF, RENÉ CLAIR

MUSIC
ARMAND BERNARD, ANDRÉ GAILHARD,
RAOUL MORETTI & RENÉ NAZELLES (Songs)

PRODUCTION
FRANK CLIFFORD for
SOCIÉTÉ DES FILMS SONORES TOBIS

STARRING
ALBERT PRÉJEAN (Albert), POLA ILLÉRY (Pola),
EDMOND T. GRÉVILLE (Louis), BILL BOCKET (Bill),
GASTON MODOT (Fred), RAYMOND AIMOS (Thief),
THOMY BOURDELLE (François), PAUL OLLIVIER (Customer),
JANE PIERSON (Fat Woman)

"Do you speak French?"

René Clair's first talkie, described in the publicity as "France's first all-talking, all-singing movie," tells a gentle story from the life of Parisian bohemia, finding its poetry in the picture-postcard milieu of little bakeries and smoky pubs, where musicians, artists, streetwalkers, pickpockets, and profiteers seem quite naturally at home. The film opens with a daring diagonal track from the picturesque roofs down to the street to frame the singer Albert (Albert Préjean), who is practicing his song there together with the entire neighborhood. The symbiosis of image and music is complete. This is Paris as it sings and laughs. But then the sound is abruptly interrupted. The romantic storyline about a likeable street musician and a Romanian girl Pola (Pola Illéry) starts off as a silent movie. Shortly afterwards, the music begins again, and behind the win-dows everyone starts singing, each in his own way, the new song that no one can avoid: "Under the Roofs of Paris."

René Clair, like many others, was skeptical about the arrival of the talkies, something that is quickly made apparent by the fact that the lovely *chanson* soon gets on everyone's nerves. His rejection was not absolute and had nothing to do with the technical difficulties that, in the transition period, could barely be surmounted. Like Chaplin or Eisenstein, Clair feared that artistic expression would be paralyzed by dialogue. Music and individual sounds, on the other hand, he considered an enrichment. In a similar way to, for instance, Fritz Lang in *M (M – Eine Stadt sucht einen Mörder*, 1931), produced at the same time, in *Under the Roofs of Paris* Clair was experimenting with sound rather than trying to achieve a fluid synchronization with

GEORGES PÉRINAL Alongside masters such as Gregg Toland, James Wong Howe, Edouard Tissé, and Karl Freund, Georges Périnal (1897–1965) was one of the most respected and innovative cinematographers in the world. In fact, the Frenchman played a decisive part in some of the most important pioneer productions as well as in sound and color films. The former cinema operator made a name for himself through his collaborations with René Clair, including *Under the Roofs of Paris (Sous les toits de Paris*, 1929/30) and *Liberty for Us (À nous la liberté*, 1931). In Jean Cocteau's experimental fantasy *The Blood of a poet (Le Sang d'un poète*, 1930), his work principally consisted of astounding camera tricks. Périnal's real strength, however, lay in the well-balanced, shadow-free illumination of scenes that were able to blur the difference between realism and artificiality. The producer Alexander Korda was particularly impressed by his work. In fact, the Hungarian brought Périnal to his adoptive country, England, where he put some of the milestones of British prewar cinema in the frame. Films such as *The Private Life of Henry VIII* (1933), *Rembrandt* (1936), and *The Four Feathers* (1939) substantiated his outstanding reputation. Périnal's skill developed fully with the arrival of Technicolor. The colorful oriental spectacle *The Thief of Bagdad* (1940) and the ambitious Powell/Pressburger production *The Life and Death of Colonel Blimp* (1943) are still among the best Technicolor films of all time. The Parisian had in the meantime turned down an offer to emigrate to the United States with Korda. Among his final well-known films were Charlie Chaplin's *A King in New York* (1957) and Otto Preminger's *Bonjour Tristesse* (1957). Georges Périnal died in London in 1965.

"From its graceful opening pan across the (studio-recreated) roof tops of the title to the multiple variations on its naggingly memorable theme song, the enchantment of Clair's first talkie has remained intact. Even the slight awkwardness of the semi-synchronised soundtrack, as scratchy as if played on a wind-up phonograph, complements its nostalgic, almost anachronistic visuals. That, plus Lazare Meerson's elegantly spare sets, George van Parys' jingly score, and the naïve if still affecting performances, make for a miniaturist masterpiece." *Time Out Film Guide*

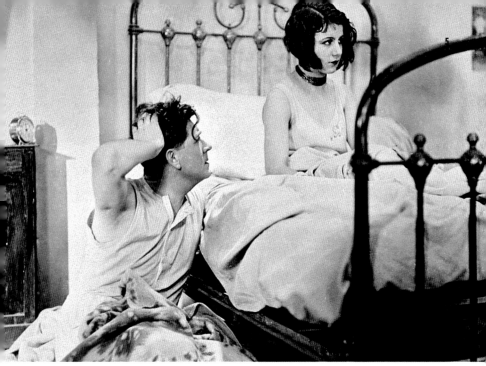

1 Romanian Pola Illéry plays the bohemian Pola, sometimes speaking in her native tongue.

2 In the wonderful opening shot, the camera travels down from the Parisian rooftops to Albert and his little choir.

3 Shy to begin with: Albert (Albert Préjean) sees Pola home.

4 The rascally Fred (Gaston Modot) also fancies his chances.

5 Unfulfilled expectations: kind-hearted Albert spends an uncomfortable night on his own floor.

the images. The songs and omnipresent accordion playing are reminiscent of a musical. Dialogue, on the other hand, is kept extremely short and often serves merely to introduce silent scenes. Furthermore, the really important exchanges are drowned out by the music, or take place behind closed windows. In an inversion of this principle, Clair turns the lights out when Albert and Pola – who only hesitantly returns his love – spend their first night together. Their argument over bed space, accompanied by the rustling of sheets, can only be heard, not seen. All in all, the film was calculated to thoroughly subvert the expectations of French audiences.

In France, people closed their minds to the experiment and felt themselves cheated out of a "proper" talkie.

In Germany, however, and later throughout the entire world, from the United States to Japan, the film received the highest admiration. This was chiefly garnered by the magnificent camerawork that Clair had developed together with Georges Périnal, his longstanding director of photography. It was precisely the relatively new, motorized cameras of the talkies that allowed the maneuverability that gave this film, and all Clair's later work, its lyrical quality.

The plot here has roughly the importance of an operetta libretto and suits the Paris created in the studio by the renowned production designer Lazare Meerson. Albert's happiness with Pola is short-lived. Thanks to some dirty dealings on the part of the villainous crook Fred (Gaston Modot) from whom he took her away, he ends up

6 The artist's life: the poor singer makes a living selling his songs.

7 A real good friend: while Albert is in jail, Louis (Edmond T. Gréville) looks out for Pola.

> **"Instead of simply enjoying synchronous sound techniques he chose to use sound only when needed – not content with tossing in dialogue just for the sake of doing so. Clair expressed the film's meaning 'essentially in images with words used only when helpful and to avoid lengthy visual explanations.'"** *Motion Picture Guide*

in prison. When he is released, she is going out with his best friend Louis (Edmond T. Gréville). In a bittersweet finale, the dice, an altruistic deception, and ultimately life itself take the decision that turns Albert back into a lonely singer again. It is a melancholy love story, full of irony and wit, of the sort that have been associated with Paris throughout history. Love and its songs, wine and baguettes are always there; only the girls never really know where they belong. René Clair was one of those great directors for whom reality and artificiality did not exclude each other, but rather determined each other. And *Under the Roofs of Paris* is the most beautiful expression of that. PB

M

M – EINE STADT SUCHT EINEN MÖRDER

1931 - GERMANY - 117 MIN. / 108 MIN.
(restored version)

DIRECTOR

FRITZ LANG (1890–1976)

SCREENPLAY

THEA VON HARBOU and FRITZ LANG

DIRECTOR OF PHOTOGRAPHY

FRITZ ARNO WAGNER

EDITING

PAUL FALKENBERG

PRODUCTION

SEYMOUR NEBENZAHL and
ERNST WOLFF for NERO FILM AG

STARRING

PETER LORRE (Hans Beckert, the Murderer), ELLEN WIDMANN
(Frau Beckmann), INGE LANDGUT (Elsie Beckmann), OTTO WERNICKE
(Inspector Karl Lohmann), THEODOR LOOS (Inspector Groeber),
GUSTAF GRÜNDGENS ("Schränker," the Safecracker), FRIEDRICH GNASS
(Franz, the Burglar), THEO LINGEN (Bauernfänger, the Con Artist),
RUDOLF BLÜMNER (Beckert's Defender), GEORG JOHN (the Blind Balloon Seller)

EIN
FRITZ LANG
FILM
DER HERO

TONVERFAHREN
TOBIS
KLANGFILM

 VERLEIH: VER. STAR-FILM G·M·B·H

M

"This monster does not have the right to exist. He must be removed, stamped out, exterminated. Without mercy!"

The city's going mad. A harmless old man is being dragged to the police station by a couple of rough workers; just around the corner, an angry mob is jumping on a fare dodger who's being escorted off the bus by a policeman. What's going on? For the last eight months, someone has been murdering children, and the police still have no idea who he is or where he's hiding. The tension is palpable: everyone is a suspect, and the killer has just struck again, after luring little Elsie Beckmann (Inge Landgut) into an open field with a colorful balloon. He even sends an open letter to the press, announcing that he's not finished yet …

Inspector Lohmann (Otto Wernicke) gathers his colleagues for an emergency meeting. One idea is to check every patient who has come out of psychiatric care over the last few years, and investigations soon lead the police officers to Hans Beckert (Peter Lorre). Beckert is an unobtrusive lodger who likes to take walks in the city, on the lookout for little girls who will follow him on the promise of some candy or a toy.

But the police aren't the only ones looking for the killer. An underworld organization known as "The Ring" also has an interest in tracking him down, as the heavy police presence is driving business to the wall. While the

PETER LORRE Born in Hungary, Ladislav Loewenstein (1904–1964) started an apprenticeship as a bank clerk after graduating from high school, but soon dropped out in favor of an acting career. The "Lorre" part of his pseudonym is a wordplay on "Rolle," German for "role." After a difficult start, he was offered his first theater roles in Vienna and Zurich, and his first, albeit modest appearance on film was in *The Woman Who Disappeared (Die verschwundene Frau*, 1928/29).
Lorre's role as the child murderer Hans Beckert in Fritz Lang's *M* (1931) made him an overnight sensation. Sadly, he was denied a sustained career in German film. Lorre emigrated to the United States following periods of exile in Austria, France, and Britain, where he played a number of major parts (such as in Alfred Hitchcock's *The Man Who Knew Too Much* in 1934). In Hollywood, Lorre was predominantly typecast as a psychotic character, a part his diminutive physique, child-like face, and disproportionately large eyes seemed to cut him out for. Mostly playing supporting roles, Lorre brought his unique flair to many movie classics, including *The Maltese Falcon* (1941), *Arsenic and Old Lace* (1942/44), and *Casablanca* (1942). As agent "Mr. Moto" he even had his own series of B-flicks (1937–1939).
Dissatisfied with the course of his career – Lorre's ambitions lay in serious drama – he returned to Germany in 1949, where he wrote and directed *The Lost One (Der Verlorene*, 1950/51), a passionate and critical examination of the Nazi period in which he also played the lead role. The film did not meet with the acclaim Lorre expected, and he returned to the United States, where he starred in numerous film and television productions until his death in 1964.

cops are dithering about how to proceed, "Schränker" (Gustaf Gründgens), the infamous safecracker – "the best man for the job between Berlin and Frisco" – is holding his own crisis session. Soon, all the beggars and drifters in the city are patrolling every corner and alleyway on the lookout for suspicious characters. Beckert eventually betrays himself with a sign of his pathological compulsiveness – he whistles a particular melody whenever his urge to kill surfaces, and a blind balloon seller (Georg John) identifies him thanks to the haunting tune. Branded with a letter M chalked on the back of his coat, the murderer can

"It was just a matter of time before someone recognized that there was an undeniably cinematic story to be told in the much-publicized murder trials of names like Haarmann, Großmann or Kürten. What a boon it is that Fritz Lang was the man who braved the waters of this subject matter; for he possessed both the necessary finesse and skill to tackle something this complex." *Filmwelt*

1 The murderer in the mirror: Beckert (Peter Lorre) is horrified to discover that he is a marked man.

2 Playmates and playthings: no one knows his toys like a pervert.

3 Supreme court: Hans is put on trial by the people in this signature Lang tableau.

4 The hot lights: the roof of this office building seemed like a good hiding place – until somebody tripped the switch.

no longer elude his pursuers. They corner him in the attic of an office building, and drag him back to their headquarters, where these criminals become his judge and jury.

In *Metropolis* (1926), Fritz Lang had already depicted society – specifically urban society – as a system with strict divisions between the upper and lower classes. That film had shown a privileged, wealthy minority pursuing a life of pleasure in the rooftop gardens of gigantic skyscrapers, while an anonymous mass of laborers lan-

guished in bleak, subterranean housing compounds. In *M*, a similar social dichotomy is presented in a more realistic, contemporary setting. The city is no longer a futurist construct, but a modern metropolis with all its familiar trappings – tenement houses, factories and industry, dense urban traffic, splendid shopping boulevards, etc. – but here, too, there is an "underworld". Beneath the visible surface of city life lurk criminal organizations; only this time, they happen to share the authorities' interest in

5 Wall to wall terror: a murderer at the mercy of the masses.

6 Slayed in the shade: despite the round-the-clock criminal investigation, Beckert is always one step

ahead of the law. Inge Landgut as little Elsie Beckmann.

7 Name that tune: a blind balloon vendor (Georg John) identifies the killer.

8 Sign language: baby-faced Peter Lorre adopted some alarming expressions for this star-making role.

> **"This film has got plenty of everything that normally rattles the censors from a mile off. Here, the murderer reaches into his pocket, sharpens his knife and is the epitome of sadism. The government is mocked and organized crime is cheered on."** *Die Weltbühne*

capturing a psychopath on the loose. Lang was so inspired by the notion of criminals hunting a murderer in order to curb unwelcome police activity that he lived in constant fear that someone else would beat him to capturing the idea on film. Like *Metropolis*, *M* presents a situation in which the underworld and the "overworld" are compelled to reach an agreement.

For this disturbing film, Lang chose a visual language that emphasizes the model character of his societal con-

struct. Again and again, the camera shows us fullscreen street maps, ground plans, fingerprints, and even samples of the murderer's handwriting. These "blueprints" provide novel perspectives on the familiar city, and they are examined meticulously for signs of alien life: Where is the killer hiding? What psychotic traits are expressed in his handwriting? Where is the unique twist in his fingerprint? Fritz Lang's choice of the attic as the disturbed murderer's refuge was no accident: even when Beckert's murderous compulsion is repressed, it remains as physical and real as the forgotten junk in the loft. In this sense, there is an analogous relationship between the body of the killer and the architecture of the city.

Beckert's "judges" are the assembled denizens of the underworld, and when they charge him with his crimes, the truth erupts: in a gripping monologue, he tells of the inner voices that compel him to kill. Among the assembled listeners are some who can identify with the confessions of this tortured soul, and Beckert's "advocate" (Rudolf Blümner) urges the massed vigilantes to acknowledge the killer's insanity and hand him over to the authorities. Led by the safecracker, the angry mob shouts down his plea.

Shaken by economic crises and political unrest, the Weimar Republic could appeal to no values that were universally acknowledged. In this moral vacuum, a promise of resolute action and "a firm hand" presented a tempting alternative to the protean unpredictability of modern city life. The risk inherent in the freedom of anonymity is that an alienated man can kill without being noticed. Seen from this perspective, *M* is an apt portrayal of German sensibilities on the eve of the Nazis' rise to power. When Beckert is saved from lynching by a last-minute police bust and made to face a proper court of law, Lang's preference for the legal enforcement of justice is unmistakable.

EP

DUCK SOUP

1933 - USA - 68 MIN.

DIRECTOR
LEO MCCAREY (1898–1969)

SCREENPLAY
BERT KALMAR, HARRY RUBY,
ARTHUR SHEEKMAN, NAT PERRIN

DIRECTOR OF PHOTOGRAPHY
HENRY SHARP

EDITING
LEROY STONE

MUSIC
HARRY RUBY, BERT KALMAR

PRODUCTION
HERMAN J. MANKIEWICZ for PARAMOUNT PICTURES

STARRING
GROUCHO MARX (Rufus T. Firefly), HARPO MARX (Pinky),
CHICO MARX (Chicolini), ZEPPO MARX (Lieutenant Bob Roland),
MARGARET DUMONT (Gloria Teasdale), RAQUEL TORRES (Vera Marcal),
LOUIS CALHERN (Ambassador Trentino of Sylvania),
EDMUND BREESE (Zander), CHARLES MIDDLETON (Prosecutor),
EDGAR KENNEDY (Lemonade Vendor)

"You wanna be a public nuisance?"
"Sure, how much does the job pay?"

This brief exchange between the newly inaugurated President of Freedonia, Rufus T. Firefly (Groucho Marx), and the agent Chicolini (Chico Marx), who is disguised as a peanut vendor, encapsulates the Marx Brothers' mission perfectly: *Duck Soup* is an all-out attack on the pathetic illusion that the world is rationally ordered and that decent, law-abiding citizens can have any influence at all on the way things are run.

The tiny state of Freedonia is just like its inhabitants: free, but broke. The only person with a few million at her disposal is banker's widow Mrs. Teasdale (the indomitable Margaret Dumont, in one of her best roles), but she's only prepared to invest in the bankrupt economy if Firefly agrees to take over the running of the country "toot sweet." For some unfathomable reason, this brawny lady on the verge of a nervous breakdown has fallen for Rufus, a shady cigar addict with a painted-on mustache who misses no opportunity to wisecrack at her and everyone else's expense. But in order to ruin an entire country, even a chaos machine like President Firefly needs some reliable support. The dialogue with Chicolini continues: "Have you got a license?" – "No, but my dog's got a million." – "How about

WAR SATIRES Most films in a military setting give an idealized picture of the army, and they aim, more often than not, to sanctify the business of soldiering. By contrast, movies that satirize war almost inevitably take a very dim view of the military. The Marx Brothers' *Duck Soup* (1933) depicted war as rooted in the vanity and arrogance of politicians. In one of the most famous war satires, *Dr. Strangelove or: How I Learned to Stop Worrying and Love the Bomb* (1963), Stanley Kubrick showed war as the work of an unholy and uncontrollable alliance between mad scientists and unscrupulous military leaders. The grunts on the ground have also been subjected to withering satire, as in Richard Lester's *How I Won the War* (1967), which starred John Lennon. The personal failures of individuals reveal the essential absurdity of war, for inhuman circumstances are hardly likely to bring out the best in human beings – quite the contrary.

As one might expect, war satires tend to proliferate during periods of actual war: generally, though, they deal with safely historical conflicts rather than directly addressing the current slaughter. Good examples of this phenomenon are two satirical movies produced during the Vietnam War years: Robert Altman's *M*A*S*H* (1969), which is set in an army field hospital during the Korean conflict, and Mike Nichols's *Catch-22* (1970), which examines the dubious deployment of Allied troops in Italy during WWII.

1 Working out the menu: dictator of
Freedonia Rufus T. Firefly (Groucho
Marx) considers what sort of
mayhem to serve up next.

2 Life's a breeze: until Chicolini (Chico
Marx) and Pinky (Harpo Marx) show
up and it spirals into a tornado.

3 Soda jerk: Pinky teaches the guy at
the refreshment stand a thing or two
about seltzer.

4 Lose something? When the Marx
Brothers are on the case, things are
likely to turn up in the oddest of
places. Just be sure you're not
bending over when they do.

5 Knock knock jokes: wealthy widow
Gloria Teasdale (Margaret Dumont)
and Rufus T. Firefly fool around after
hours.

"The last man nearly ruined this place, he didn't know what to do with it. If you think this country's bad off now, just wait till I get through with it."

Film quote: National Anthem of Freedonia

a job in the mint?" – "No, I no like a mint. What other flavor you got?" The whole bizarre "job interview" takes less than a minute, and the Marx Brothers sustain this breakneck tempo for the remaining 67.

Champion lunatic in this festival of madness is Chicolini's companion Pinky (Harpo Marx), a man who's remarkably noisy for someone who can't speak. Armed with a car horn and a pair of scissors, he even manages to pack the other Marx Brothers into his endlessly capacious pockets, from which he's also capable of conjuring a blowtorch (lit, of course). Anyone rash enough to approach this jovial one-man army is soon missing several

6 Army fatigue: after making *Duck Soup*, Zeppo (second from the left) backed out of the troop's screen antics. His role as the fourth Marx brother often spotlighted him as the voice of reason and a ladies' man. In real life, however, jokester Zeppo was anything but suave.

7 Surefire comedy: when it comes to knocking 'em dead, these guys never miss their Marx.

items of apparel along with his sanity and equanimity. Instead of shaking hands with you, he's more than likely to offer you his foot. "You're pulling my leg" indeed. The Marx Brothers' anarchy is their response to the pomposity of the powerful, a principled objection to communicating with windbags, a stubborn refusal to take anyone or anything seriously. From their point of view, an actual war is just the continuation of everyday lunacy by other means.

The battle between the Peanut Vendors and the Lemonade Vendors is one of the funniest film sequences ever made, and it demonstrates that there can be no winner in such a conflict – unless it's the person who can rise above the tedium of reality by laughing out loud at it. What's comforting is the knowledge that, ultimately, all parties involved will end up looking equally dumb.

And the dialogue is glorious: "If you're found, you're lost." – "You're crazy. How can I be lost if I'm found?" In 1933, at the peak of the Depression, many people were grateful for an hour's liberation through the forces of surrealism. Nonetheless, the Marx Brothers' last film for Paramount was a financial flop; and a short time later, MGM president Irving Thalberg ordered Groucho & Co. to cut down on the gags and work on their plotlines.

His advice was taken to heart. Many "Marxists" regard the first MGM movie, *A Night at the Opera* (1935), as their very best work. But for those who prefer Groucho, Harpo, Chico, and Zeppo as unbridled Lords of Misrule, *Duck Soup* remains the pinnacle of the Marx Brothers' achievement.

SH

KING KONG

1933 - USA - 100 MIN.

DIRECTORS

MERIAN C. COOPER (1893–1973), ERNEST B. SCHOEDSACK (1893–1979)

SCREENPLAY

MERIAN C. COOPER, EDGAR WALLACE, JAMES ASHMORE CREELMAN, RUTH ROSE

DIRECTORS OF PHOTOGRAPHY

EDWARD LINDEN, J. O. TAYLOR, VERNON L. WALKER, KENNETH PEACH

EDITING

TED CHEESMAN

MUSIC

MAX STEINER

PRODUCTION

MERIAN C. COOPER, ERNEST
B. SCHOEDSACK for RKO

STARRING

FAY WRAY (Ann Darrow), ROBERT ARMSTRONG (Carl Denham),
BRUCE CABOT (John 'Jack' Driscoll), FRANK REICHER (Captain Englehorn),
SAM HARDY (Charles Weston), NOBLE JOHNSON (Native Chief),
STEVE CLEMENTE (Witch King), JAMES FLAVIN (Shipmate Briggs),
VICTOR WONG (Charlie), LYNTON BRENT (Reporter)

"Beauty killed the Beast."

King Kong reflects the artistic techniques established by its documentary filmmaker protagonist, Carl Denham (Robert Armstrong), as elements of scientific expedition meet the sensationalism of cinematic horror. It all starts when Denham embarks on the search for an actress willing to play vulnerable in his upcoming wildlife movie. A victim of the Great Depression, Ann Darrow (Fay Wray) is desperate enough to take on any job if it means getting out of New York. Six weeks later, she and an entire film team drop anchor on an East Indian island, where a skull-shaped mountain is the only thing more imposing than insurmountable cliffs. Those cliffs form a huge wall dividing the terrain, with humans inhabiting the one half and an untamable beast occupying the other. This creature is, of course, none other than the legendary King Kong, a 40-foot gorilla that can only be appeased with human female sacrifices. Needless to say, a love-struck Kong wants Ann from the moment he sees her, and the young woman is powerless to resist his advances.

In the rescue mission that follows, a spectacular prehistoric rainforest unfolds beyond the divisive wall. Dinosaurs claim a good portion of the ship's crew before Ann's love interest Jack Driscoll (Bruce Cabot) finally manages to free his dream girl from captivity. Carl Denham uses gas explosives to knock out King Kong and ship him back to the urban jungle of New York City.

On Broadway, billboards advertise the colossal ape as the wonder of the century. Then, at his stage debut, press photographers flashbulb him into a frenzy and he breaks free of his chains. Kong's next move is to reclaim Ann. This accomplished, he seeks seclusion at the top of the Empire State Building ... only the National Guard has its own interpretation of his actions and sends in an airborne unit to shoot him down.

STOP MOTION PHOTOGRAPHY Used to animate three-dimensional models and machines, stop motion is one of the oldest techniques in cinematic trick photography. As early as 1910, Ladislas Starevich (1882–1965) was employing it in Russia and France to make entire movies. The principle was simple: stationary figures were placed on a set before a painted backdrop, where they were photographed and then minutely repositioned for the following shot. While the Starevich pieces demonstrate a degree of seamless perfection that would rarely be topped let alone matched by any other filmmaker, *King Kong* (1933) is considered to have made the most significant breakthrough in stop motion photography. Credited with this accomplishment is Willis O'Brien and his team of painters, miniaturists, and technicians.

Stop motion would continue to improve in the decades to come. In particular, Ray Harryhausen's special effects for films like *Jason and the Argonauts* (1963) were hailed by industry experts and audiences alike. Even recent movies like *Wallace & Gromit: A Grand Day Out* (1988/89) and *The Nightmare Before Christmas* (1993) were filmed according to the principles of the age-old technique. Movies like *Toy Story* (1995) then brought the stop-motion look into the digital age.

"Imagine a 50-foot beast with a girl in one paw climbing up the outside of the Empire State Building ... clutching at airplanes, the pilots of which are pouring bullets from machine guns into the monster's body." *The New York Times*

1 Hanging by a thread: not to worry, King Kong hasn't let Ann Darrow (Fay Wray) down yet.

2 Battle royal: King Kong knocks down opponent after opponent to save the woman he loves.

3 Scream queen: Robert Armstrong can't calm Fay Wray's nerves for the life of him.

King Kong tickets sold like hot cakes. The movie's many prehistoric animals appealed to an audience that had been won over by a silent era classic entitled *The Lost World* (1924/25, directed by Harry O. Hoyt). Indisputably, evolutionary theory was a popular topic in '30s cinema. One could argue that bottle-blond Fay Wray a.k.a. Ann was the nexus between the "big black beast" from the virgin forest and the superior "civilized world" as presented by the film.

King Kong's main theme is views of other forms of society: Carl Denham comes across as a typically arrogant colonialist when he attempts to film the secret ritual of the island's inhabitants; conversely, the people he spies on look like something out of a spoof on voodoo tribal worship. It follows that heavy makeup, grass skirts, shell necklaces, and coconut bras are all the rage with these peculiarly black natives. India, it seems, looked a whole lot like Africa back in the '30s, with Hollywood's confusion of the two at its most striking in the scenes of King Kong's slave-trade inspired journey from his homeland to America, followed by the caged scenes, which are reminiscent of old New York freak shows and living village exhibits. There are no two

4 Dinner at ape: tonight's entrée is sacrificial lamb.

5 New Yorkers won't allow King Kong to play with dolls.

6 Air show: the U.S. military disposes of Kong and reclaims its title as king of the skies.

ways about it: *King Kong* equates dark skin with savagery and worse. Its representation of the United States, on the other hand, is of a rational society rooted in order and progress. The overgrown baboon's fate is thus already sealed as he climbs to the then newly completed Empire State Building (1931); for the modern machinery of war must reign supreme in this piece of colonial propaganda. There is, however, more to the story than meets the eye. Having worked as ethnographic filmmakers in the '20s, directors Merian C. Cooper and Ernest B. Schoedsack were quick to

show how even a documentary examination of far-off worlds can be prone to the artificiality of media hype. The Denham character proves this by having his actress practice her big scene while still on board the ship. As the scene suggests, real documentary films did in fact rely on paid actors, or ape costumes if necessary, to make other cultures and wild animals behave according to viewer expectations. As with any other cinematic genre, much of what appears so strange on screen is nothing more than a construct of the filmmaker's mind.   PLB

MODERN TIMES

1936 - USA - 87 MIN.

DIRECTOR
CHARLES CHAPLIN (1889–1977)

SCREENPLAY
CHARLES CHAPLIN

DIRECTORS OF PHOTOGRAPHY
ROLAND H. TOTHEROH, IRA H. MORGAN

EDITING
WILLARD NICO

MUSIC
CHARLES CHAPLIN

PRODUCTION
CHARLES CHAPLIN for CHARLES CHAPLIN PRODUCTIONS,
UNITED ARTISTS

STARRING
CHARLES CHAPLIN (A Factory Worker), PAULETTE GODDARD (A Gamine),
HENRY BERGMAN (Café Proprietor), STANLEY SANDFORD (Big Bill),
CHESTER CONKLIN (Mechanic), HANK MANN (Burglar),
LOUIS NATHEAUX (Burglar), STANLEY BLYSTONE (The Gamine's Father),
AL ERNEST GARCIA (President of the Electro Steel Corp.),
SAMMY STEIN (Turbine Operator)

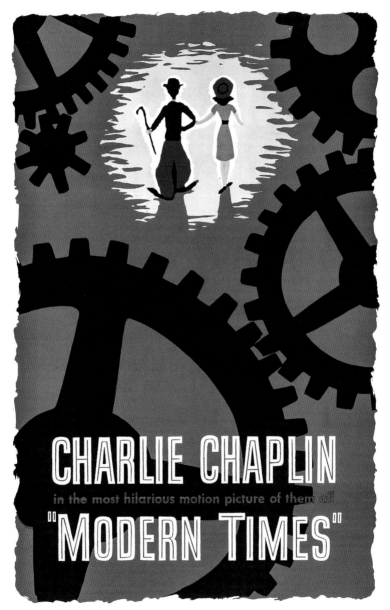

CHARLIE CHAPLIN

in the most hilarious motion picture of them all

"MODERN TIMES"

WRITTEN, DIRECTED AND PRODUCED BY CHARLES CHAPLIN • RELEASED THRU LOPERT FILMS, INC.

"Se bella pui satore, je notre so catore, Je notre qui cavore, je la qu', la qui, la quai!"

The first thing we see is a herd of sheep, then a quick cross-fade takes us to a herd of workers streaming into a factory. One of them is Charlie (Charles Chaplin). Our former Tramp is now standing at a conveyor belt. A slave to the rhythm of the machine, he tightens one bolt after another. As the tempo increases, he can't keep up, and the machine swallows him and spits him back out. Dazed, disoriented, almost entranced, he grasps his monkey wrench and tightens everything in sight: noses, buttons, whatever comes his way ... In a bizarre, balletic sequence, he reduces the entire factory to chaos. They end up carting him off to the mental ward.

When the talkies were born in 1927, Charlie Chaplin was probably their most vehement opponent. Language, he believed, would destroy the universality of the cinema. By 1936, it was clear that the sound medium had triumphed; but with *Modern Times*, Chaplin created something that was neither talkie nor silent film. In the entire hour and a half, the actors speak not a single understandable word, and the sound track consists solely of music, the racket of the factory machines, and commands from the boss, barked from enormous, futuristic screens. It's a sideswipe at the "talking" cinema, which Chaplin thereby equates with the philistinism and brutality of the times.

This unconventional use of sound is undoubtedly one reason why *Modern Times* is now regarded as one of the timeless masterpieces of the cinema. Like no other film character, Chaplin's Tramp gives touchingly comic form to humanity's existential struggle in a dehumanized world. Through no fault of his own, the little fellow is thrown into an industrialized world. Here, far from making the workers' lives easier, technology makes instruments of the workers themselves. The men are the meat part of a giant machine for manufacturing profit.

PAULETTE GODDARD Jean Cocteau once described her as "a little lion with a wild mane and splendid claws." The role of the lively vagabond in Charles Chaplin's *Modern Times* (1936) seemed tailor-made for Paulette Goddard, and they were in fact a couple at the time. Goddard (1911–1990) grew up in poverty in New York City. Ambition and talent meant that she was already a Ziegfeld girl by the time she was 14. Two years later, she married a wealthy playboy, divorced him, and went to Hollywood. There, she played minor roles until she met Chaplin in 1932. *Modern Times* made her famous, but her alleged "unofficial" marriage with Chaplin – it's said that they married for real in 1936 – was apparently not good for her career. Legend has it that David O. Selznick refused to cast her as Scarlett in *Gone with the Wind* (1939) because he feared bad publicity. After *The Great Dictator* (1940), Chaplin and Goddard went their separate ways. In the years that followed, Paulette Goddard became a popular star of musicals and comedies for Paramount. Her performance as a nurse in Mark Sandrich's *So Proudly We Hail!* (1942) brought her an Oscar nomination, though her title role in Jean Renoir's *The Diary of a Chambermaid* (1946) was a far more interesting piece of work. Thereafter, Paulette Goddard devoted more time to the theater. In the mid-'50s, she emigrated to Switzerland and married the German writer Erich Maria Remarque. From then on, she rarely appeared on the screen.

1 *Homo faber*: Charlie Chaplin shows technology who's boss in *Modern Times* and raises eyebrows in industrial America.

2 Here's mud in your eye: Charlie has better luck defending his individuality in the slammer than he does at the factory.

3 Getting the belt: eight hours of mindless work is the worst whipping there is.

4 Interchangeable parts: Chaplin misuses his instruments and starts playing a silly symphony.

5 You want a knuckle sandwich? Charlie's co-workers don't tolerate his mechanized behavior during lunch hour.

Yet it is also very clearly a film of its time: the Depression era. In contrast to Chaplin's earlier works, *Modern Times* presents the misery straight, without picturesque embellishment. At times, the camera work is almost documentary-style in its sober mustering of an impoverished environment. Chaplin is also alive to the political tensions of the period. In one scene, Charlie picks up a red flag that's fallen off the back of a passing truck. When a crowd of demonstrators appear around the corner, the police take Charlie for their leader and haul him off to jail.

Scenes like these reinforced Chaplin's reputation as a left-winger – thereby bolstering the animosity of right-wing Americans who had always had their suspicions about this immigrant Brit. In fact, the film's true position seems less socialist than profoundly humanist; for Charlie is innocent of the meaning of the red flag he picks up, and his wild dance in the factory is not the deliberate act of a

"For those still unfamiliar with the picture, the first thing that needs to be said of *Modern Times* (1936) is that it's very funny and occasionally hilarious."

San Francisco Chronicle

"I go to a lot of movies, and I can't remember the last time I heard paying audience actually applaud at the end of a film. But this one did. And the talk afterward in the aisles, the lobby, and in line at the parking garage was genuinely excited; maybe a lot of these people hadn't seen much Chaplin before, or were simply very happy to find that the passage of time has not diminished the man's special genius." *Chicago Sun-Times*

7

6 Get into gear: in one of the film's most beloved scenes, Chaplin is eaten alive by the machinery he services.

7 Too pooped to pop: at the side of an orphan (Paulette Goddard), a worn-out Charlie falls in love – and sleeps through the good parts.

8 Sneak attack: staying true to his slapstick pantomime while giving a nod to innovation, Charlie Chaplin shot *Modern Times* with a dialogue-free sound track. He did, however, have the Tramp sing a bit towards the end – in gobbledygook.

machine-wrecker – it is his body that rebels, with the unconscious directness of genuine naïveté. Even modern times can't turn the vagabond into a class-conscious proletarian. Kitted out as ever with his baggy pants, too-tight tailcoat, shabby shoes, black 'tache, walking stick, and bowler, he remains true to himself as a dandy in rags. Luxuriating in every tiny free space he can make for himself, the Tramp is his very own man – he is, quite literally, in a class of his own.

Back on the street, Charlie meets a young orphan (Paulette Goddard) who has stolen some bread. They flee the police together, and dream of a brighter future: of a country cottage, where you only have to reach out the window to find a bunch of grapes or fill your glass with milk from a friendly passing cow. To achieve such a heaven on earth, Charlie is even prepared to go to work again – but

everything he tries, from laboring to night-portering, ends in disaster. For the first time, Chaplin provides his protagonist with an almost-equal partner, a kind of Trampess (so to speak). She is played by Paulette Goddard, his companion of many years. It's this that makes the film, ultimately, an expression of optimism. The Tramp's love for the girl is so great that he even breaks his silence by getting up on stage in a dance hall and singing a song. And because he can't remember the words, he resorts to a kind of nonsensical Esperanto that's only comprehensible because his gestures make it so. The song seems to indicate that Chaplin has made his peace with the talkies. The age of the Tramp was over. Yet there's something comforting about the little man's last exit: for the very first time, he's not walking that country road alone, but hand-in-hand with a pretty girl. UB

THE GRAND ILLUSION
LA GRANDE ILLUSION
1937 - FRANCE - 114 MIN.

DIRECTOR

JEAN RENOIR (1894–1979)

SCREENPLAY

CHARLES SPAAK, JEAN RENOIR

DIRECTOR OF PHOTOGRAPHY

CHRISTIAN MATRAS

EDITING

MARGUERITE RENOIR

MUSIC

JOSEPH KOSMA

PRODUCTION

FRANK ROLLMER, ALBERT PINKOVITCH
for R. A. C. – RÉALISATIONS D'ART CINÉMATOGRAPHIQUE

STARRING

JEAN GABIN (Maréchal), PIERRE FRESNAY (Capt. de Boeldieu),
ERICH VON STROHEIM (Capt. von Rauffenstein), DITA PARLO (Elsa),
MARCEL DALIO (Lt. Rosenthal), JULIEN CARETTE (Cartier, the actor),
GASTON MODOT (The Engineer), JEAN DASTÉ (The Teacher),
JACQUES BECKER (An English Officer), GEORGES PÉCLET (A French Soldier)

JEAN GABIN
PIERRE FRESNAY
et
ERIC VON STROHEIM
dans

LA GRANDE ILLUSION

adaptation et dialogues de
JEAN RENOIR et **CHARLES SPAAK**
Musique de **KOSMA**
avec **DALIO**

Un film de
JEAN RENOIR

RAC
DISTRIBUTION

"There's the border, designed by men – but nature doesn't give a damn!"

Captain de Boeldieu (Pierre Fresnay) and Lieutenant Maréchal (Jean Gabin) – the former an aristocrat, the latter a proletarian – are shot down in a plane during World War I. Captured and imprisoned in a German POW camp, the two French soldiers find themselves amongst a mixed bag of compatriots who form a real community despite their differences. Their solidarity is strongest in the shared enterprise of digging a tunnel; but before it can be used as an escape route, the men are transferred to a different camp. Following the failure of further escape attempts, Maréchal and de Boeldieu eventually end up imprisoned in a castle, where the commanding officer, Captain von Rauffenstein (Erich von Stroheim), immediately pays his respects to his fellow aristocrat. But instead of taking the opportunity to enjoy the privileges of rank, de Boeldieu resolves to help Maréchal and his Jewish comrade Rosenthal (Marcel Dalio) in yet another bid for freedom. By creating a distraction, he confuses the guards and forces von Rauffenstein to shoot him. As de Boeldieu dies, Maréchal and Rosenthal make good their escape.

When *La Grande Illusion* premiered in 1937, a new world war was already in the air. Jean Renoir's film didn't just hit a nerve with the French public; it also attracted the attention of politicians all over Europe. The movie's pacifist stance led to its being banned in the Fascist countries, and Germany's Propaganda Minister Goebbels went so far as to call it "Cinematic Enemy No. 1." In the United States, however, Franklin D. Roosevelt vehemently

---

MARCEL DALIO Small, dark, mercurial, and elegant, Marcel Dalio (1900–1983) seemed predestined for roles such as the Jewish banker's son Rosenthal in *The Grand Illusion (La Grande Illusion*, 1937). Yet Dalio, born in Paris to a Romanian Jewish family, was too good an actor to be typecast as he was. In *The Rules of the Game (La Règle du jeu*, 1939), another of Renoir's masterpieces, he gave a brilliant performance as the vain but sensitive aristocrat Robert de la Cheyniest. Marcel Dalio was one of the most instantly recognizable actors in the French cinema of the '30s, appearing in famous films such as Julien Duvivier's *Pépé le Moko* (1936/37) and Robert Siodmak's *Mollenard / Capitaine Corsaire* (1937), yet only *The Rules of the Game* provided him with a truly important leading role. In 1940, he fled France when the Germans invaded, and this undoubtedly saved his life: the Nazis even used his portrait for their anti-Semitic propaganda. Dalio went to Hollywood, where he suffered the fate of many immigrants from the European film industry. As a supporting actor in anti-Nazi films, he was generally cast as a cultivated Frenchman with a charming accent. Thus, he appeared alongside Humphrey Bogart as the croupier in Michael Curtiz's *Casablanca* (1942) and as the proprietor of a bar in Howard Hawks's *To Have and Have Not* (1944). After the war, Dalio worked on both sides of the Atlantic, but he rarely found films that did justice to his talent. Nonetheless, Dalio was capable of wryly parodying his own image, as he did in the Louis de Funès vehicle *The Adventures of Rabbi Jacob (Les Aventures de Rabbi Jacob*, 1973).

defended the movie, saying that every democrat should see it. In fact, *La Grande Illusion* is one of the few antiwar films that truly deserves to be called great, not least because it keeps its distance from the stereotypes and the all-too-easy spectacle of the battlefront. Renoir refused to subject his audience to an orgy of "thrilling" bloodshed; and just as he declined to exploit the spectacle of war, he was also only marginally interested in the story's potential for suspense. The escape scenario intrigued him for another reason: it gave him an opportunity to share his perspective on the world – a world in which nations and

"Jean Renoir tells his story with an almost unbelievable sense of balance. There are no monsters in the ranks of soldiers, not even among the Germans. All of them are – to a certain extent – the victims of their particular circumstances ... Renoir focuses more on the differences between social classes than on differences between nationalities. A man's way of yawning tells us more about him than his uniform, or the fact that he wears white gloves." *die tageszeitung*

1 Am I seeing things? Nazi propaganda minister Joseph Goebbels detested *The Grand Illusion* for allowing a regular working-class guy like Maréchal (Jean Gabin, left) to befriend the son of an affluent Jewish banker (Marcel Dalio). Goebbels confiscated the film's print as soon as Germany occupied France.

2 It takes all kinds: war proves to be the great social equalizer when a commoner, an aristocrat, a black man, and a Jew find themselves on equal footing at a prison camp.

3 You and whose army: rather than assuming the off-screen command of *The Grand Illusion*, actor-director Erich von Stroheim settles for calling

the shots in the role of Capt. von Rauffenstein and graces the cinema with one of his finest performances.

4 No such thing as a free lunch: *Grand Illusion* director Jean Renoir would never have been able to secure his producer had he not sparked French star Jean Gabin's interest in the project first.

the conflicts between them seem merely arbitrary, and in which the real barriers are those between classes.Thus, Renoir arranges the microcosm of the prison camp as a kind of cross-section of society. Alongside Maréchal and de Boeldieu, this enforced community includes an engi-

neer, a somewhat naïve schoolteacher, a Jewish banker's son, and an actor. What's astonishing is that one hardly notices how schematic this arrangement is. On the contrary: the ensemble is refreshingly lively and absolutely credible – even when the film is emphasizing the subtle

5 No tongues: French soldier Maréchal and German Fräulein Elsa (Dita Parlo) communicate through glances and body language.

6 Take the bait: Capt. de Boeldieu (Pierre Fresnay) diverts the guards'

attention so that his friends can escape unscathed.

7 Put a spike in my vein: Jean Renoir depicts the friendship between blue-bloods Rauffenstein and de Boeldieu much like a tragic love story.

8 Wash my feet: in *The Grand Illusion*, actors like Carette, Dalio, Modot, and Gabin demonstrate their grandeur in front of the camera.

signs by which the men's social ranking is made manifest. The characters are never reduced to mere types or given crude psychological motivations. Renoir leaves the actors time and space enough to do their work, and if the performances sometimes seem exaggerated, then this too has its reasons. It's one of the mysteries of Renoir that his obvious sympathy for the art of acting is precisely the means by which life itself enters his films. So, although *La Grande Illusion* is regarded as a classic of cinematic realism, it does have a peculiarly larger-than-life quality, and yet it never descends into cliché. Renoir can indicate the absurdity of war through various grotesque situations without ever disrupting the rhythm of the film. In one scene, for example, a soldier tries on a suit of women's clothes for a stage appearance – and his comrades respond to this feeble imitation of femininity with an embarrassed silence.

There is one surprisingly melodramatic thread in the film: the relationship between Rauffenstein and de Boeldieu. Renoir directs it like a love story with a tragic ending. When the Frenchman dies of his bullet wound, the German places a flower on his lifeless body. It is the only flower in the whole castle. This pathos-laden gesture is not merely Renoir's tribute to the actor Erich von Stroheim, one of the great film directors of the silent era, but also signifies the feeling for social class that links men across national boundaries.

As in *The Rules of the Game (La Règle du jeu*, 1939), Renoir depicts the aristocracy as a species heading for extinction – while other classes remain. And when Maréchal, the metalworker, and Rosenthal, the Jewish *grand bourgeois*, trudge side-by-side through the snow towards Switzerland, it's no accident that we are reminded of the famous finale of Chaplin's *Modern Times* (1936). For this odd couple, it seems, there is no room in cold reality; their friendship is an illusion, but a great and beautiful illusion.

JH

"From the first image to the last, the picture not only sustains but intensifies its grip on the audience. The film is 'orchestrated,' conducted, and we are left with an extraordinary impression of a realism that is powerful and compelling, stripped of any vestige of classicism and orthodoxy." *Cinémonde*

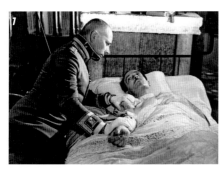

GONE WITH THE WIND ♟♟♟♟♟♟♟

1939 - USA - 222 MIN. (original release) / 238 MIN.
(restored version)

DIRECTOR
VICTOR FLEMING (1883–1949)

SCREENPLAY
SIDNEY HOWARD, based on the novel of the same name by MARGARET MITCHELL

DIRECTOR OF PHOTOGRAPHY
ERNEST HALLER

EDITING
HAL C. KERN, JAMES E. NEWCOM

MUSIC
MAX STEINER

PRODUCTION
DAVID O. SELZNICK for SELZNICK INTERNATIONAL PICTURES

STARRING
CLARK GABLE (Rhett Butler), VIVIEN LEIGH (Scarlett O'Hara),
LESLIE HOWARD (Ashley Wilkes), OLIVIA DE HAVILLAND (Melanie Hamilton),
THOMAS MITCHELL (Gerald O'Hara), BARBARA O'NEIL (Ellen O'Hara),
EVELYN KEYES (Suellen O'Hara), ANN RUTHERFORD (Carreen O'Hara),
HATTIE MCDANIEL (Mammy), OSCAR POLK (Pork),
BUTTERFLY MCQUEEN (Prissy), RAND BROOKS (Charles Hamilton),
CARROLL NYE (Frank Kennedy), LAURA HOPE CREWS (Aunt Pittypat Hamilton)

ACADEMY AWARDS 1939
OSCARS for BEST PICTURE (David O. Selznick), BEST DIRECTOR (Victor Fleming),
BEST ACTRESS (Vivien Leigh), BEST SUPPORTING ACTRESS (Hattie McDaniel),
BEST ADAPTED SCREENPLAY (Sidney Howard), BEST CINEMATOGRAPHY (Ernest Haller,
Ray Rennahan), BEST EDITING (Hal C. Kern, James E. Newcom),
and BEST ART DIRECTION / INTERIOR DECORATION (Lyle R. Wheeler)

"After all ... tomorrow is another day."

In Hollywood, greatness is written on the wind. And grand sweeping statements can hit like a tempest as early as the opening titles. Their message: *Gone with the Wind* was and is the most magnificent of all epics, a triumph in moviemaking, and an ode to the Old South unlike any other. Return to a world upheld by masters and slaves, where chivalry has yet to die. Hear the Civil War cannons roar as they crumble the walls, but not the foundations of a great society. And see it all as only novelist Margaret Mitchell could tell it. Able to spot a hit from a mile off, producer David O. Selznick paid a then incredible 50,000 dollars to secure the rights to adapt the story for the cinema. The year was 1936, and the novel – the only one Mitchell would ever write – had been in print for approximately a month. Immediately, Selznick launched a publicity campaign that transformed the book into a bestseller.

A media-propagated "search for Scarlett" would follow, although the decision had already been made: Vivien Leigh, a virtually unknown British actress, had signed on to play the shameless Southern Belle. A bold heroine, in an era when Hollywood preferred to see women as meek, Scarlett braves an inferno for her Tara home and a shot at true love with the wrong man. Between Secession and Reconstruction, her obstinacy will have worn down as many husbands

as the filming of her story did directors: personal differences with male lead Clark Gable caused George Cukor to jump ship; and Victor Fleming suffered fits of exhaustion that forced him to temporarily pass the baton to Sam Wood. Then again, sleep deprivation and frayed nerves seem a small price to pay in exchange for over three and a half hours of the finest cinema the world had ever seen.

At the center of this Technicolor extravaganza of magnolias and antebellum estates is the larger-than-life Scarlett. Desperately in love with foolish dreamer Ashley Wilkes (Leslie Howard) from the moment they meet, the pampered plantation owner's daughter simply won't take no for an answer. And until shortly before the curtain falls, neither Ashley's happy marriage to his cousin Melanie (Olivia de Havilland) nor the cunning advances of warhorse Rhett Butler (Clark Gable) can steer Scarlett's heart from its path. While Rhett alone sees her for the wolf she is, even he underestimates the extent of her singled-mindedness; for no matter whom she marries, she'll relinquish her sexual autonomy to no one. Melanie respects her for it, whereas Rhett claims not to "give a damn." How telling it is that male and female viewers also tend to differ in their interpretations of the film.

From today's standpoint, *Gone with the Wind's* romance may seem trite and its attitude towards slavery

CLARK GABLE Ohio native Clark Gable (1901–1960) was born the son of a freelance oil driller. Several small stage appearances sparked the future star's lifelong interest in theater and prompted him to seek out professional acting training. His coach, Josephine Dillon, an actress who was 17 years his senior, soon became the first Mrs. Clark Gable.

MGM took the screen hopeful under contract in 1930 and proceeded to make a leading man out of him. In no time flat, the sly dog with Mickey Mouse ears and pomade mustache had become what every woman of the era was looking for. Nonetheless, it wasn't until MGM lent Gable to the smaller Columbia for Frank Capra's hit comedy *It Happened One Night* (1934) that the actor won his first Oscar.

Numerous adventure picture roles followed, with Gable often being paired opposite leading ladies like Jean Harlow or Myrna Loy. His most memorable performance in the genre came as Lieutenant Fletcher Christian in *Mutiny on the Bounty* (1935), rated by many fans as a highlight in his career. Later, when David O. Selznick needed someone to play Rhett Butler in *Gone with the Wind* (1939), Gable was the only man the producer so much as considered.

In 1942, after losing third wife Carole Lombard in a plane crash, the man nicknamed the "King of Hollywood" was overcome by depression and enlisted in the army. Well over 40, Gable carried out missions over Nazi Germany as a U.S. fighter pilot and returned home a war hero. Despite enjoying the respect of the entire industry, it was clear that his Hollywood heyday was behind him. Be that as it may, the never-say-die Gable still insisted on performing his own daredevil stunts for his final film, John Huston's *The Misfits* (1960). In all likelihood, the strain was too much for him. Two days after wrapping up the shoot, he suffered a heart attack that claimed his life two weeks later.

"*Gone with the Wind* presents a sentimental view of the Civil War, in which the 'Old South' takes the place of Camelot and the war was fought not so much to defeat the Confederacy and free the slaves as to give Miss Scarlett O'Hara her comeuppance. But we've known that for years; the tainted nostalgia comes with the territory. Yet as *Gone with the Wind* approaches its 60th anniversary, it is still a towering landmark of film, quite simply because it tells a good story, and tells it wonderfully well." *Chicago Sun-Times*

1   Well, I'll be damned: heartthrob Clark Gable sizzles things up down South as dashing rogue Rhett Butler.

2   As God is my witness, I'll never be hungry again: Scarlett may not have to endure poverty again, but only time will tell whether or not she'll end up love-starved.

3   I don't know nothing about birthing no babies: although Prissy (Butterfly McQueen, left) often doubts herself in emergencies, Scarlett always rises to the occasion.

4   A walk in the park: Melanie (Olivia de Havilland) and Ashley (Leslie Howard) have a picture-perfect romance that

knows not the sound and the fury of Scarlett and Rhett.

5   Tara firma: in just a few years time, the life Scarlett so loved as a child will be but a distant memory.

questionable at best. The picture, however, presents us with two very "real" characters. Scarlett is the first. Beyond good and evil, and riddled with flaws, she seems infinitely more human than the angelic Melanie. Mammy (Hattie McDaniel), the story's second great heroine, gains depth through a resoluteness that commands more respect than all the other characters put together. It was a poignant

performance that made history as Hattie McDaniel became the first black actress to receive an Oscar.

Beyond the characters themselves, uncompromising images of the Civil War continue to breathe life into this epic as the camera chronicles the burning of Atlanta in blood-red. From here, a panoramic crane shot reveals a field hospital where limbless and fallen soldiers reach as

"As God is my witness, as God is my witness they're not going to lick me. I'm going to live through this and when it's all over, I'll never be hungry again. No, nor any of my folk. If I have to lie, steal, cheat or kill. As God is my witness, I'll never be hungry again."

Film quote: Scarlett O'Hara (Vivien Leigh)

far as the eye can see. Such gruesome confrontations with American history, in particular with the Civil War, were categorically regarded as box-office poison prior to *Gone with the Wind.* And nobody, other than Selznick himself, reckoned on a hit.

Star appeal, color symbolism – green for Scarlett, black for Rhett, ash yellow for Ashley, etc. – and the fusion of individual destiny with historical events created a blueprint for what would become the gold standard in filmmaking. Even so, the then astronomical four-million-dollar budget did more to end an era in filmmaking than usher in a new one. The fact that *Gone with the Wind* continues to bowl over contemporary audiences as a total work of art

of Wagnerian complexity is the single-handed accomplishment of old-school producer David O. Selznick. He was the one who effectively pulled all the strings in terms of directing, screenwriting, and editing. Forget the director's cut, Selznick knew exactly what he wanted from start to finish and sat at editor Hal C. Kern's side to get a perfectly mastered negative. Needless to say, *Gone with the Wind* was made at a point in time prior to the creation of unions and workers' rights. Eight Oscars and gross U.S. ticket sales totaling 200 million dollars made it one of the most impressive undertakings in cinematic history and attest to the majesty of a production that could never be replicated today.   PB

6 Standing grand: gunrunner and adventurer Rhett Butler doesn't flinch in the face of adversity.

7 Pride and prejudice: Vivien Leigh embodies the legacy of the antebellum South as the steadfast Scarlett O'Hara.

8 Southern gentleman gone south: knowing that he could never live up to Scarlett's expectations, Ashley (Leslie Howard) rejects her in no uncertain terms.

9 Mass exodus: Atlantans evacuate the town to escape the wrath of the Union Army.

10 Sherman's March to the Sea: in one of the most infamous acts in U.S. history, the Northern troops sweep over Georgia like a ball of fire.

11 Life under glass: having faced war head-on, Scarlett emerges from a purple haze with new-found humanity.

FANTASIA ♟♟

1940 - USA - 120 MIN.

DIRECTORS

SAMUEL ARMSTRONG (1893–1976) [Segment 1, 2],
JAMES ALGAR (1912–98) [Segment 3], BILL ROBERTS, PAUL SATTERFIELD [Segment 4],
HAMILTON LUSKE (1903–1968), JIM HANDLEY, FORD BEEBE (1888–1978) [Segment 5],
T. HEE (1911–1988), NORMAN FERGUSON (1902–1957) [Segment 6],
WILFRED JACKSON (1906–1988) [Segment 7]

SCREENPLAY

LEE BLAIR, ELMER PLUMMER, PHIL DIKE [Segment 1],
SYLVIA MOBERLY-HOLLAND, NORMAN WRIGHT, ALBERT HEATH, BIANCA MAJOLIE,
GRAHAM HEID [Segment 2], PERCE PEARCE, CARL FALLBERG [Segment 3],
WILLIAM MARTIN, LEO THIELE, ROBERT STERNER, JOHN MCLEISH [Segment 4],
OTTO ENGLANDER, WEBB SMITH, ERDMAN PENNER, JOSEPH SABO, BILL PEET, VERNON
STALLINGS [Segment 5], CAMPBELL GRANT, ARTHUR HEINEMANN, PHIL DIKE [Segment 7]

DIRECTORS OF PHOTOGRAPHY

MAXWELL MORGAN, JAMES WONG HOWE

MUSIC

JOHANN SEBASTIAN BACH [Segment 1], PIOTR ILYICH TCHAIKOVSKY [Segment 2],
PAUL DUKAS [Segment 3], IGOR STRAVINSKY [Segment 4],
LUDWIG VAN BEETHOVEN [Segment 5], AMILCARE PONCHIELLI [Segment 6],
MODEST MUSSORGSKY [Segment 7], FRANZ SCHUBERT [Segment 7]

PRODUCTION

WALT DISNEY for WALT DISNEY PICTURES

SPEAKER

LEOPOLD STOKOWSKI (Himself), DEEMS TAYLOR (Narrator),
WALT DISNEY (Voice of Mickey Mouse)

ACADEMY AWARDS 1941

HONORARY AWARD for the outstanding contribution to the advancement of the
use of sound in motion pictures (Walt Disney, William E. Garity, J. N. A. Hawkins),
and HONORARY AWARD for unique achievement in the creation of a new form
of visualized music (Leopold Stokowski and his associates)

Walt Disney's
TECHNICOLOR FEATURE TRIUMPH
FANTASIA
with
Stokowski
Distributed by RKO Radio Pictures, Inc.

"Congratulations to you, Mickey!"

Two hours of classical music and often abstract visuals isn't exactly a recipe for a Hollywood blockbuster. Still, prior to *Fantasia* (1940), no one had ever attempted to make a film along those lines. Walt Disney originally dreamed up the concept for the picture with his studio's music director, Carl W. Stalling, back in 1929 – long before the cartoon mogul's astounding success with the world's first full-length animated feature *Snow White and the Seven Dwarfs* (1937) and its successor *Pinocchio* (1940). Ten years later, Leopold Stokowski, the director of the Philadelphia Orchestra, suggested to Disney that he combine a number of the animated shorts known as "Silly Symphonies" in a single concert-length production. *Fantasia*

began to take shape, and Disney had plans to update it regularly with new pieces that reflected current trends and innovations in animation. Sixty years later, that dream finally became a reality with the Walt Disney Company's release of *Fantasia 2000*.

For the version completed in his lifetime, Disney chose Bach's *Toccata and Fugue in D minor* to initiate the viewer into the action. The orchestra, first seen in colorful silhouette, quickly evolves from an assembly of stylized instruments into an array of ever-shifting graphic images. Waves, clouds, and other natural shapes visually depict musical sounds and vibrations but soon dissolve into utterly abstract representations. Avant-garde filmmaker

SILLY SYMPHONIES *Fantasia* (1940) was by no means the first of Walt Disney's cartoons to be so in tune with its music. Unlike *Fantasia*, however, the point of Walt's Silly Symphonies series (1929–1939) was to build a short cartoon around a musical score. The symphonies were the brainchild of Disney musical director Carl W. Stalling, a former silent movie pianist. Kicking off the series was *The Skeleton Dance* (1929), a piece Ub Iwerks animated to match a Stalling composition inspired by the work of Edvard Grieg. Silly Symphony *Flowers and Trees* (1932) was the first cartoon ever to be shot in three-color Technicolor, and went on to win an Oscar for Best Animated Short. Disney turned the cartoon into an art form of its own by inspiring his animators to use music and a wide range of artistic techniques to breathe life into the inanimate. Indeed, Disney's experiments with music in cinema's early days of sound set motion picture standards for animation and live-action films alike. Over the course of its ten-year run, the Silly Symphony series served as a great creative outlet for animators and helped foster new techniques in the field. A number of beloved Disney characters, such as Donald Duck, also got their start thanks to these shorts. The final cartoon in the series, *Ugly Duckling* (1939), an animated adaptation of the Hans Christian Andersen fairy tale of the same name, was recognized with an Oscar in 1940. That same year, *Fantasia*, which was awarded two honorary Oscars, marked both the zenith and the grand finale of Disney's revolutionary project.

"Yesterday night's long-awaited world premiere of Disney's *Fantasia* at the Broadway Theatre went down in film history. Let us all agree, like almost everyone who was there, that Mickey Mouse, Snow White and the assembled darlings of animated film created something that throws tradition overboard and takes film in quite a new direction. The simple verdict is: *Fantasia* is fantastic." The New York Times Directory of the Film

1 Disney's greatest star: *Fantasia* is a fireworks display of classical music and animation. "The Sorcerer's Apprentice" sequence is one of the film's many highlights.

2 Fetch a pail of water: Mickey learns that working magic can be a chore.

3 From one maestro to another: Philadelphia Orchestra conductor Leopold Stokowski collaborates with pop culture icon Mickey Mouse on a full-length cartoon symphony.

Oskar Fischinger helped created these images, which are at times reminiscent of the work of Expressionist painter Wassily Kandinsky. Unfortunately, the uncompromising Fischinger, who had directed his own abstract animated shorts, left the project disillusioned as later segments began to resemble more traditional cartoons. In fact, during the very next sequence, the audience is presented with a rendition of Tchaikovsky's *Nutcracker Suite* packaged as a fairy ballet that climaxes in a mushroom dance. And from here on, *Fantasia*'s music almost exclusively relies on concrete and often kitsch illustrations.

In the central and undoubtedly most famous segment of the film, Mickey Mouse magically commands a broom to carry buckets of water for him as Paul Dukas's "Sorcerer's Apprentice." Things, however, soon get out of control when the broom inadvertently causes a flood while performing the

chore, leaving the sorcerer to intervene and clean up the mess, a mishap that gives rise to a whole range of water images that bear witness to the impeccable artistry and boundless creativity of the Disney animators.

The fourth segment, occupied by Igor Stravinsky's *Rite of Spring*, documents the history of the earth from the planet's cosmic – and thus necessarily abstract – infancy to the age of dinosaurs. For this piece, the initial images of life's violent beginnings are in fact so awe-inspiring that the ensuing prehistoric fight for survival is almost anti-climactic in comparison.

Following a lighthearted intermezzo in which various musical sounds are illustrated by a moving line, the mood changes again as the film leads into Beethoven's *Pastoral Symphony*. Instead of its original setting of Heiligenstadt, Austria, the piece is relocated to the heights of Mount

4 The devil made me do it: the Lord of Darkness hosts the soirée of the century atop Bald Mountain

5 Mule-tilated: regardless of what the photo may suggest, it was not Disney's intention to make asses of the great masters of classical music.

7 The wind beneath my wings: Beethoven's *Pastoral* reaches new heights through color animation.

6 I'll be hard to handle: Mickey learns that you should never send a broom to do a mouse's work.

Olympus, where it now chronicles the flirtations of centaurs. This altogether "free" interpretation of the musical composition had some music aficionados up in arms, as did the Stravinsky segment which preceded it. Still, Disney took just as much artistic license with his adaptation of Ponchielli's *Dance of the Hours*, which he staged as a parodic animal ballet starring hippos and crocodiles.

The film concludes with a wonderful grand finale, Mussorgsky's *Night on a Bare Mountain* and Schubert's "Ave Maria." The fusion of these two musically contrasting pieces is among *Fantasia*'s most extraordinary technical and artistic achievements. The medley begins with the Prince of Darkness conjuring up an army of demonic creatures for the highly expressionistic Mussorgsky piece,

images which are replaced by an angelic procession of lantern bearers and souls floating up to heaven against a foggy backdrop as "Ave Maria" announces the dawn of a new day.

Perhaps inevitably, *Fantasia* was snubbed by audiences of the day. Advocates of high culture claimed it defiled classical music, whereas the general public found it overwhelming – even after it was later shortened by more than 40 minutes. Disney's vision of reconciling popular and elite culture had failed for the time being. He was, nonetheless, convinced that education entails the "freedom to have faith in one's own choices, and to read, think and express whatever one wishes." *Fantasia* is the artistic expression of Walt Disney's commitment to these liberties. SH

"It is this faith in the discrimination of the average person that led us to make such a radically different type of entertainment as *Fantasia*. We simply figured that if ordinary folk like ourselves find entertainment in these visualizations of so-called classical music, so would the average person." *Walt Disney, in: Robert D. Feild, The Art of Walt Disney*

CITIZEN KANE 🏆

1941 - USA - 119 MIN.

DIRECTOR
ORSON WELLES (1915–1985)

SCREENPLAY
HERMAN J. MANKIEWICZ, ORSON WELLES

DIRECTOR OF PHOTOGRAPHY
GREGG TOLAND

EDITING
ROBERT WISE

MUSIC
BERNARD HERRMANN

PRODUCTION
ORSON WELLES for MERCURY PRODUCTIONS INC., RKO

STARRING
ORSON WELLES (Charles Foster Kane), JOSEPH COTTEN
(Jedediah Leland), DOROTHY COMINGORE (Susan Alexander Kane),
AGNES MOOREHEAD (Mary Kane), RUTH WARRICK (Emily Kane),
RAY COLLINS (James W. Gettys), ERSKINE SANFORD (Herbert Carter),
EVERETT SLOANE (Mr. Bernstein), WILLIAM ALLAND (Jerry Thompson),
PAUL STEWART (Raymond), GEORGE COULOURIS (Walter Parks Thatcher)

ACADEMY AWARDS 1941
OSCAR for BEST SCREENPLAY (Herman J. Mankiewicz, Orson Welles)

EVERYBODY'S TALKING ABOUT IT!

It's Terrific!

ORSON WELLES

CITIZEN KANE

The Mercury Actors

JOSEPH COTTEN
DOROTHY COMINGORE

EVERETT SLOANE
RAY COLLINS
GEORGE COULOURIS
AGNES MOOREHEAD
PAUL STEWART
RUTH WARRICK
ERSKINE SANFORD
WILLIAM ALLAND

RKO RADIO PICTURES

"Rosebud ..."

When newspaper tycoon Charles Foster Kane dies, a film is made about his life. The producer is dissatisfied with the results; it's not enough, he says, to show what Kane had achieved: "The people want to know who and what he was." Maybe "Rosebud" holds the key? This was the mysterious last word spoken by Kane on his deathbed. It's an enigma that demands to be solved, so the reporter Jerry Thompson (William Alland) is given the task of finding and interviewing the people closest to Kane. Who, or what, was Rosebud?

Welles's film presents the memories of five people in a series of flashbacks. Piece by piece, we are shown the major incidents and decisive moments in the great man's life. These images are complemented by verbal commentaries from those who had known him. Kane, we discover, had been born into modest circumstances; but when his mother (Agnes Moorehead) suddenly acquired wealth, she placed the boy in the care of a legal guardian, who ensured that he was educated at the best schools. Having begun as a dynamic young publisher, Charles Foster Kane (Orson

Welles) went on to build a massive press empire – before eventually losing it all. We see how Kane fails in his ambition to become governor, and how he fails, too, in each of his two marriages. He becomes a passionate art collector, but his passion is restricted to mere acquisition. He creates an absurdly gigantic home for himself: the palace of Xanadu, in which he will die alone and embittered, a victim of his own hubris. François Truffaut paid tribute to the film in the following words: "It is a hymn to youth and a meditation on old age; an essay on the vanity of human ambitions and a poem about decay; and, beyond all this, it's a reflection on the loneliness of exceptional men."

For Thompson, the reporter, as for everyone else in the film, the word "Rosebud" remains an enigma: "just a piece in a jigsaw puzzle – a missing piece." As viewers, however, we're privileged beings. After Kane's death, the junk that fills his home is dumped on a bonfire; and the camera takes a closer look as an old wooden sled goes up in flames: "Rosebud" is the maker's name. The sled had

ORSON WELLES Born in 1915, actor and director Orson Welles had already made a name for himself by 1938, when he directed a radio adaptation of H. G. Wells's *The War of the Worlds*. It threw the people of New York into a panic. Suddenly, Welles was famous, or notorious; and when he signed the contract with RKO Studios for his first major film, *Citizen Kane* (1941), he was granted a number of unusual privileges. *The Magnificent Ambersons* followed in 1942; but as the box-office returns from *Kane* had proved disappointing, he was not allowed to edit the latter film as he had wished. And so began a series of projects that were completed by other directors, or remained entirely unfinished or suffered mutilation at the hands of studio bosses, like his late noir movie, *Touch of Evil* (1958). Welles responded with various strategies, including a low-budget movie version of his theater production, *Macbeth* (1948). It was followed by two further Shakespeare adaptations; with *Othello* (1952), he won the Golden Palm at Cannes in the same year. From 1948 onwards, he worked repeatedly in Europe, both as a director and as an actor. Filmmakers who employed him included Claude Chabrol, Fred Zinnemann, and Sergei Bondartschuk. Apart from Kane, his most memorable acting role was probably as Harry Lime in Carol Reed's *The Third Man* (1949). Among his many works for cinema and TV in the years after 1960, *F for Fake* (1975) stands out – an eccentric, episodic documentary about great forgers and his own passion for charlatanism. Orson Welles died in Los Angeles in 1985.

1 Stop press: Charles Foster Kane (Orson Welles) is running for office.

2 All's Welles that ends Welles: even after losing the election, Kane still ain't down for the count.Pictured here with close friend and campaign manager Jedediah Leland (Joseph Cotten).

3 Xanadu bound: Kane's mother places her son in the guardianship of Mr. Thatcher (George Coulouris) and launches him on his path to greatness.

4 The keys to his soul: as the second Mrs. Kane discovers, music can access the hidden chambers of the mogul's heart.

5 Up on a soap box winning isn't everything – it's the only thing.

been the boy's only means of resisting his guardian and coping with his mother's rejection. "Rosebud": the word stood symbolically for his lost childhood. Yet even this knowledge cannot serve as *the* key to Kane's personality. And so the *New York Times* critic wasn't the only one to complain that the film provides no "clear image of the man's character or of what motivated him."

It now seems clear that this alleged weakness was in fact intentional, and it has contributed greatly to the film's legendary status. Seen in the context of contemporary discourse on the "construction" of biographical narrative, the film's strategy of multiple perspectives is among its most revolutionary achievements. *Citizen Kane* allows its protagonist to emerge as a collage of subjective, fragmentary,

"As the cinema celebrates its 100th birthday, prominent directors and producers from around the world have named Orson Welles' *Citizen Kane* the best film ever made." *Frankfurter Allgemeine Zeitung*

6 To hell with fun and games: second Mrs. Kane, Susan Alexander (Dorothy Comingore) goes to pieces in Xanadu.

7 Make me your muse: Emily Norton (Ruth Warrick), the first Mrs. Kane, charms her way to fame and fortune.

8 Smear campaign: Kane and Susan Alexander get their names dragged through the mud by the opposition.

9 A letter to the editor: Kane's former guardian, Walter Parks Thatcher, criticizes his ward's unorthodox means of conducting business.

10 Another victory for yellow journalism: the editors of the *Inquirer* prove once again that the pen is mightier than the sword. Kane pictured with Leland and Bernstein (Everett Sloane, left).

and sometimes conflicting recollections from a variety of sources. If the film never provides any definitive "clarity," we are entitled to regard this as a reflection on the ineluctable subjectivity of memory.

The visual form of the film is equally worthy of attention. A hard lighting design helps to sustain the film's mysterious atmosphere; various scenes feature figures as silhouettes, their faces emerging only gradually, and only partially, from the shadows. *Citizen Kane* is a highly stylized work of art, with its extreme camera angles and its penchant for visual symbols: the film begins and ends with the same image – the barred windows that keep the world away from Xanadu. Above all, Welles's movie was pioneering in its use of depth of field. Many scenes are no longer divided up "classically" into individual shots, with the viewer's eye guided by composition and editing. Instead, Welles shot entire scenes as single, continuous, static shots; it is the movement of the actors in this deep visual field that excites the spectator's attention. In many scenes, foreground and background are equally accentuated; thus, a new technical development enabled a striking stylistic innovation, and Welles exploited its possibilities with something approaching passion. As André Bazin wrote admiringly: "The extended depth of field enabled Welles to restore to reality its quality of perceptible continuity." JS

"It is cynical, ironic, sometimes oppressive and as realistic as a slap. But it has more vitality than fifteen other films we could name." *The New York Times*

TO BE OR NOT TO BE

1942 - USA - 99 MIN.

DIRECTOR

ERNST LUBITSCH (1892–1947)

SCREENPLAY

EDWIN JUSTUS MAYER, MELCHIOR LENGYEL

DIRECTOR OF PHOTOGRAPHY

RUDOLPH MATÉ

EDITING

DOROTHY SPENCER

MUSIC

WERNER R. HEYMANN

PRODUCTION

ERNST LUBITSCH for
ROMAINE FILM CORPORATION

STARRING

CAROLE LOMBARD (Maria Tura), JACK BENNY (Joseph Tura),
ROBERT STACK (Lieutenant Stanislav Sobinski), STANLEY RIDGES
(Professor Alexander Siletsky), SIG RUMAN (Colonel Ehrhardt), FELIX BRESSART
(Greenberg), TOM DUGAN (Bronski), CHARLES HALTON (Dobosh),
HENRY VICTOR (Schultz), LIONEL ATWILL (Rawitch)

Alexander
KORDA
presents

Carole
LOMBARD

Jack
BENNY

Ernst
LUBITSCH'S
COMEDY

TO BE or NOT to BE

Produced and Directed by **ERNST LUBITSCH**
RELEASED THRU UNITED ARTISTS

with
ROBERT STACK
FELIX BRESSART
LIONEL ATWILL
STANLEY RIDGES
SIG RUMAN
original story by
Ernst Lubitsch and
Melchior Lengyel
screenplay by
Edwin Justus Mayer

"Shall we drink to a blitzkrieg?"
"I prefer a slow encirclement."

How far is satire permitted to go? As far as it wants, so long as it doesn't insult the Führer. This, at least, is the view of the theater managers in Warsaw when they cancel Theater Polski's latest production, a Hitler parody entitled *Gestapo*, shortly before its premiere. In August 1939, they feel, it might be advisable to show a little more respect. One month later, their scruples haven't helped them a bit, for Hitler has invaded Poland. Now it's the Nazis who are running the show, and the whole country is their stage.

And it's here that the ensemble will finally have the opportunity to perform the roles they've rehearsed. This time, however, they'll be playing for their lives. The actors don the uniforms of their enemies in order to deal with a spy – and because the female star Maria Tura (Carole Lombard) just happened to get involved with the Resistance fighter Sobinski (Robert Stack). Maria's husband, vain *Hamlet*-actor Joseph Tura (Jack Benny), becomes SS Gruppenführer Ehrhardt in order to lure the spy Siletsky (Stanley Ridges) into a trap. After successfully disposing of the traitor, Tura disguises himself as Siletsky, and enters the SS headquarters where he meets the real Ehrhardt (Sig Ruman). The extra Bronski (Tom Dugan) gets the role of his

life, as Adolf Hitler. In this pandemonium of trickery and deceptions, the situation remains deadly serious, and a false beard can mean the difference between life and death. To be, or not to be? In the end, Tura saves himself and everyone else in a truly hair-raising scene involving the shaving of a corpse.

Are there limits to satire? Today, almost all critics are in agreement that *To Be or Not to Be* shows the great director Ernst Lubitsch at the height of his ability. When the film first came out, reactions were very different. Lubitsch's tightrope act ended with a fall, the biggest catastrophe of his career. The German filmmaker was accused of making fun of the Polish people's suffering. Between the start of filming and the first preview, the world had changed radically, and the extent of Hitler's aggression was becoming all too apparent. The Americans had joined the war. In 1940, Chaplin's *The Great Dictator* had been greeted with benevolent indifference; by '42, jackbooted Nazis screaming "Heil Hitler!" no longer seemed like the stuff of comedy.

Lubitsch reacted to the wave of disapproval by writing letters to his critics. The sole targets of his film, he

CAROLE LOMBARD The premiere of *To Be or Not to Be* (1942) was overshadowed not only by the gathering storm that was World War II; shortly beforehand, Carole Lombard, the film's 33-year-old leading actress, was killed in a plane crash. She had been on tour, encouraging people to purchase war bonds, and with her death, Hollywood lost one of its biggest and best-paid stars. Born in 1908 as Jane Alice Peters, she was discovered at the age of 13, playing basketball on the street. In the '20s, she was popular in mediocre silent melodramas and Westerns, and only with difficulty did she manage the transition to the talkies. In 1926, an automobile accident left her with a scar on her face, but a combination of plastic surgery and makeup made it practically invisible.

Blessed with elegance and esprit in equal measure, Carole Lombard eventually made her breakthrough. In Howard Hawks's *Twentieth Century* (1934), she became "the queen of screwball comedy." In *My Man Godfrey* (1936), she appeared alongside her ex-husband William Powell (their marriage having ended in 1933). This movie brought her her only Oscar nomination. The highpoints of her short career were Hitchcock's marriage drama *Mr. & Mrs. Smith* (1941), and Lubitsch's anti-Nazi satire *To Be or Not to Be*. She married Clark Gable in 1939.

1. The sound and the führer: married actors Maria (Carole Lombard) and Joseph Tura (Jack Benny) undermine the Nazis with a bit of thespian savvy.

2. The jig is up: Professor Siletsky (Stanley Ridges) is quick to recognize that the Nazis aren't the only ones sporting battle fatigues.

3. Live the part: the Turas could lose their heads if they don't follow Mr. Dobosh's (Charles Halton) direction to the letter.

4. Dying on stage: Tura breaks character when the audience bolts during his delivery of "to be or not to be."

5. Caught in the act: Hitler's impostor (Tom Dugan) walks in on General Ehrhardt (Sig Ruman) and Maria's game of hanky panky.

6. Curtain call: the actors are unmasked as news of the real Hitler's march on Poland reaches the theater.

said, were the Nazis and their ridiculous ideology – and the actors who remain just actors, no matter how perilous their situation. This barb was directed against the intellectuals of the time: people like Tura, whose professional vanity and egotism endanger all those around them. The fake Siletsky asks the real Ehrhardt whether he knows "the great actor Tura." Oh yes, says the beefy officer: "What he did to Shakespeare, we are doing to Poland." With gags like these, Lubitsch captures perfectly the cynical tone of the Nazis. The thespians are no less perfect at imitating that tone; actors, one and all. The tragedy is that someone like Ehrhardt could terminate a life with a stroke of his pen, when he might have made a perfectly good theater critic …

Ernst Lubitsch was a German Jew. In every second of this film, we can feel how appalled he was by the fact that a bunch of third-rate actors were able to enslave half of Europe. Here, humor is a weapon used in self-defense – the only weapon at his disposal. In scenes often arranged so that they mirror each other, Lubitsch depicts a game for very high stakes. The killers and the killed, the stage and the world, appearance and reality, real beards and false ones, laughter and tears; here, in fact, only a decent measure of egoism and vanity will ensure the protagonists' survival. Lubitsch clearly sympathizes with Greenberg, the Jewish bit-part actor who would so love to play Shylock: "It would get a laugh." And as any actor will tell you, a good laugh is not to be sniffed at.   PB

"With his comedy *To Be or Not to Be*, Ernst Lubitsch embarrassed the Nazis by showing them as they really were: brutal, sneaky, gutless and dumb — buffoons, each and every one of them. Lubitsch must have thought, 'If we can't literally laugh them off the world stage, let's at least raise our own spirits by having some fun at their expense.'" *die tageszeitung*

CASABLANCA ⚔⚔⚔

1942 - USA - 102 MIN.

DIRECTOR
MICHAEL CURTIZ (1888–1962)

SCREENPLAY
JULIUS J. EPSTEIN, PHILIP G. EPSTEIN, HOWARD KOCH, based on
the play *Everybody Comes to Rick's* by MURRAY BURNETT and JOAN ALISON

DIRECTOR OF PHOTOGRAPHY
ARTHUR EDESON

EDITING
OWEN MARKS

MUSIC
MAX STEINER

PRODUCTION
HAL B. WALLIS for LOEW'S INC., WARNER BROS.

STARRING
HUMPHREY BOGART (Rick Blaine), INGRID BERGMAN (Ilsa Lund Laszlo),
PAUL HENREID (Victor Laszlo), CLAUDE RAINS (Chief of Police Louis Renault),
CONRAD VEIDT (Major Strasser), SYDNEY GREENSTREET (Signor Ferrari),
PETER LORRE (Guillermo Ugarte), DOOLEY WILSON (Sam), S. Z. SAKALL (Carl),
MADELEINE LEBEAU (Yvonne), JOY PAGE (Annina Brandel),
CURT BOIS (Pickpocket)

ACADEMY AWARDS 1943
OSCARS for BEST PICTURE (Hal B. Wallis), BEST DIRECTOR (Michael Curtiz),
and BEST SCREENPLAY (Julius J. Epstein, Philip G. Epstein, Howard Koch)

Humphrey **BOGART** · Ingrid **BERGMAN** · Paul **HENREID**

A
HAL B. WALLIS
PRODUCTION

"Casablanca"

CLAUDE **RAINS** · CONRAD **VEIDT** · SYDNEY **GREENSTREET** · PETER **LORRE**

Directed by **MICHAEL CURTIZ**

"Louis, I think this is the beginning of a beautiful friendship."

A Moroccan desert city serves as the last outpost in what's left of unoccupied French territory, and refugees, pickpockets, racketeers, gamblers, and boozers of every race, creed, and color flock to this spot like bees to honey. The time is World War II; the place, Casablanca.

At Rick's Café Américain, the best address for scarce U.S. visas, personal dramas have supplanted stage shows. The owner, Rick Blaine (Humphrey Bogart), watches it all from the sidelines, but knows better than to get involved: "I stick my neck out for nobody," or so he says.

Then one night it happens. Of all the gin joints in all the towns in all the world, she had to walk into his: Ilsa Lund (Ingrid Bergman), the woman who disappeared with Rick's heart the day the Germans marched on Paris, re-enters his life. Only, rather than coming alone, the newly wed Ilsa brings husband and high-profile Resistance fighter Victor Laszlo (Paul Henreid) along with her. As if things weren't complicated enough, Rick is soon faced with a moral dilemma when transit papers fall into his hands: will he be the patriot he claims to be and supply the couple with a chance at freedom, or will undying love undermine his doing "the right thing"?

Contrary to popular belief, the beloved words "Play it again, Sam" are never spoken in *Casablanca*. Yet sometimes, it takes an apocryphal line such as this to capture the spirit of a film. *Casablanca* is an extraordinary cinematic romance that calls us back time and again. And once there, we succumb to the power of its last goodbye as if we were living it ourselves. But what marked an eternal parting of ways for Bogart and Bergman's characters was just the beginning of a beautiful friendship for film enthusiasts worldwide. Even those unfamiliar with the picture have felt its power in the countless phrases from *Casablanca's* dialogue that turn up in everyday conversation, such as "Here's looking at you kid," "Round up the usual suspects," or "We'll always have Paris," to name but a few examples.

One need but look to the star-studded selection of international actors to understand why *Casablanca* struck such a personal chord with audiences worldwide. As only three of the 14 roles listed in the opening credits are meant to be played by Americans, the remaining majority of the cast is free to fly its foreign colors at will – be it as emigrants in exile or government officials. And with the likes of Claude Rains as the corrupt yet magnetizing police

MICHAEL CURTIZ Critics of his work consider *Casablanca* (1942) a pure fluke. To them, Michael Curtiz will always be the director who diligently cranked out pictures for Warner Bros. And yet many of the 100-odd pictures he shot were the studio's best and most profitable. In nearly 30 years of service at Warner, Curtiz captained classics like *Captain Blood* (1935), *The Adventures of Robin Hood* (1938), *Yankee Doodle Dandy* (1942), and *Mildred Pierce* (1945).

Like so many of the actors he worked with in *Casablanca*, Michael Curtiz was born a million miles from Hollywood. The man who entered the world in 1886 as Mihály Kertész in Budapest, Austria-Hungary, directed numerous pictures before relocating to Vienna in 1919. His success in Europe prompted Harry Warner to put him under contract in 1926. Still, the Hungarian wasn't one to cater to Hollywood aesthetics if he could help it, and *Casablanca* is the product of a European eye: the expert interplay of shadow and light coupled with his distinct visual style. These were the talents that compensated for his poor command of foreign languages: his English was as bad as his German had been before.

As is documented in countless biting anecdotes that have come to be known collectively as "Curtizisms," a great many of his actors detested his autocratic ways. This, however, didn't prevent them from sharing in the credit for his cinematic successes. In 1954, Warner terminated Curtiz's contract and his reputation within the industry reached an all-time low. Be that as it may the filmmaker continued to win with audiences, directing pictures like *White Christmas* (1954) and *We're No Angels* (1955). His Elvis picture, *King Creole* (1958), was among the King's more successful movies. In 1962, Curtiz died in Hollywood after losing a battle with cancer.

"Seeing the film over and over again, year after year, I find it never grows over-familiar. It plays like a favorite album; the more I know it, the more I like it. The black-and-white cinematography has not aged as color would, and the dialogue is so spare and cynical it has not grown old-fashioned."

Chicago Sun-Times

5

1 You must remember this: bar owner Rick Blaine (Humphrey Bogart) welcomes us at the door to the last outpost of the free world – Casablanca.

2 Not for all the tea in China: Signor Ferrari (Sydney Greenstreet) can bargain all he likes – Rick's Café Américain simply isn't for sale.

3 The foreign legion: Renault (Claude Rains, right) and Major Strasser (Conrad Veidt) debate the military future of Vichy France while getting bombed at Rick's.

4 A game of do or die: Rick isn't about to become a pawn in Ugarte's (Peter Lorre) black market operation.

5 Play it again, Sam: a pianist who drowns out the sorrows of the world with a smile and a song. Dooley Wilson as Sam.

chief Louis Renault, Peter Lorre as the smarmy fence Ugarte, and Conrad Veidt as despicable Nazi Major Strasser, no member of the cast is expendable. In addition to turning Humphrey Bogart into a global icon, *Casablanca* was arguably the first cult classic of all time.

What makes cult cinema unique is the fact that it improves with subsequent viewings. There is so much we miss when we enter Rick's café for the first time, details that initially get lost in the commotion. It takes time before Rick and Ilsa's past liaison in Paris comes to light. Similarly, the love triangle gathers shape little by little via stolen glances and innuendoes. The legendary "battle of the anthems" at Rick's café indicates the extent of structural complexity: fed up with the crude Nazi rendition of the "Wacht am Rhein"

"Even when spoken by supporting actors, the dialogue is filled with innuendoes, ambiguities and ironies. In fact, many of the men and women playing waiters, refugees or nameless customers were Europeans who had emigrated to Hollywood to escape Nazism. Nervously hopeful, coldly indifferent or patient and resigned, the presence of these minor characters intensifies the oppressive atmosphere of the film."

Reclams Filmklassiker

6

6 Here's lookin' at you kid: Rick and Ilsa (Ingrid Bergman) reminisce about days gone by before putting the past behind them once and for all.

7 A is for alibi: Ugarte pleads with Rick to verify his story, but the bar owner refuses to risk his neck for the pint-sized fence.

8 Toasting misfortune: pain and suffering keep the liquor flowing at Rick's café.

9 The merry men: rather than arresting freedom fighter Victor Laszlo (Paul Henreid), Renault prefers to see, hear, and speak no evil.

("The Watch on the Rhine"), Laszlo asks the bar's bandleader to play the "Marseillaise," a selection that would reverse the nature of the audience's divide; Rick gestures his approval with a subtle nod and the crowd goes into a patriotic display that drowns out the Nazi tune. The scene also attests to Michael Curtiz's brilliance in terms of dramatic economy: Laszlo gets an idea; Rick gives the go-ahead, and Ilsa, the great divider, is granted a moment of peace.

Casablanca's script, co-developed by the Epstein Brothers and Howard Koch, is the stuff of Hollywood legend.

10 Round up the usual suspects: Louis and Rick begin a beautiful friendship as Ilsa and Victor escape to freedom in one of Hollywood's most fantastic finales.

11 Forget Paris: as far as the audience is concerned Rick and Ilsa's legendary affair unfolds during their time in Casablanca.

"It's a great ensemble, but it's the heat between Rick and Ilsa that makes *Casablanca* work so very well. Rick has been terribly wounded, and has built a life to avoid repeated injury. Ilsa has buried their shared past and resigned herself to loyal support of her husband. We all know that their love is submerged, but still very much alive. And as the pressure builds for Ilsa's husband to get out of Casablanca and continue his work in America, she and Rick face terrible decisions." *Apollo Movie Guide*

Julius J. and Philip G. Epstein came up with the tight caper plot and much of the dialogue. However, as the picture was not considered a top studio priority, the team was reassigned to Frank Capra's propagandistic war spectacular *Why We Fight* (1942–45) once shooting began. Koch picked up where they left off, feverishly filling the gaps with emotion and idealism. Chaos was an everyday occurrence with scenes being penned at the last minute and Ingrid Bergman allegedly only finding out whom she'd end up with when the time came to shoot the final scene. Indeed, the film betrays an underlying uncertainty as indicative of shooting conditions as it is of the times. The battle against evil, however, ultimately inspires the world to stand tall for its beliefs. As Rick sees to it that Ilsa and Laszlo board the airplane, political idealism wins out over personal interest and Hollywood propaganda takes to the sky. PB

THE BIG SLEEP

1946 - USA - 114 MIN.

DIRECTOR

HOWARD HAWKS (1896–1977)

SCREENPLAY

WILLIAM FAULKNER, JULES FURTHMAN, LEIGH BRACKETT, based on the
novel of the same name by RAYMOND CHANDLER

DIRECTOR OF PHOTOGRAPHY

SID HICKOX

EDITING

CHRISTIAN NYBY

MUSIC

MAX STEINER

PRODUCTION

HOWARD HAWKS for
FIRST NATIONAL PICTURES INC., WARNER BROS.

STARRING

HUMPHREY BOGART (Philip Marlowe), LAUREN BACALL (Vivian Rutledge),
MARTHA VICKERS (Carmen Sternwood), JOHN RIDGELY (Eddie Mars), CHARLES WALDRON
(General Sternwood), SONIA DARRIN (Agnes), REGIS TOOMEY (Bernie Ohls),
ELISHA COOK JR. (Jones), BOB STEELE (Canino),
LOUIS JEAN HEYDT (Joe Brody), CHARLES D. BROWN (Norris),
DOROTHY MALONE (Acme Bookstore Proprietress), JOY BARLOW
(Taxi Driver), PEGGY KNUDSEN (Mona Mars)

A WARNER HIT!!!

HUMPHREY

BOGART

The picture they were born for!

AND

LAUREN

BACALL

"THE BIG SLEEP"

MARTHA VICKERS · DOROTHY MALONE

HOWARD HAWKS PRODUCTION

MUSIC BY MAX STEINER · SCREEN PLAY BY WILLIAM FAULKNER, LEIGH BRACKETT & JULES FURTHMAN · FROM THE NOVEL BY RAYMOND CHANDLER · A WARNER BROS.–FIRST NATIONAL PICTURE

"Such a lot of guns around town and so few brains!"

Old, wealthy, and sick, General Sternwood (Charles Waldron) has a problem on his plate: his loose-living daughter Carmen (Martha Vickers) is being subjected to blackmail. The General hires private eye Philip Marlowe (Humphrey Bogart) to help him out, and before long Marlowe is on the trail of a murderous conspiracy that in some way involves Vivian (Lauren Bacall), Sternwood's second daughter. When Marlowe falls in love with her, he soon finds himself dodging bullets from rival gangsters.

This short synopsis shouldn't deceive anyone into thinking that the plot of *The Big Sleep* is anywhere near intelligible. One famous anecdote tells of Hawks and Bogart arguing on set about how a certain character had actually died: murder, or suicide? Hawks tried to settle the dispute by asking Raymond Chandler, who'd written the novel on which the film was based. But not even the author could help. An earlier version of *The Big Sleep* had included a scene that cast some light on the obscurity of the plot. This scene was cut, however, because test audiences simply hadn't liked it. As a result, the movie acquired an exceptionally fast narrative tempo, even by Hawks's standards, and the plot is even more labyrinthine than it would

DOROTHY MALONE Her appearance in *The Big Sleep* (1946) lasts barely three minutes, but they're worth waiting for. Dorothy Malone, born in Chicago in 1925, plays the seductive proprietress of the Acme Bookstore. Marlowe only enters the shop to inquire after some information, but when she takes off her glasses, lets down her hair, and locks the door, he makes an abrupt change of plans and spends the afternoon there with her, drinking whisky. Despite this famous scene with Bogart and her obvious potential, Dorothy Malone spent a further ten years appearing in minor Westerns before briefly entering the major league of Hollywood stars. Sadly, her success never matched her considerable talents. The highpoint of her career was marked by roles in two of Douglas Sirk's finest films: *The Tarnished Angels* (1957); and, above all, the wonderful melodrama *Written on the Wind* (1956). In the latter, she played the nymphomaniac daughter of a Texas oil baron. The role brought her an Oscar as Best Supporting Actress, but it also influenced her subsequent career: from then on, she was typecast as a "loose woman," often in films of pretty poor quality. Among the positive exceptions was Robert Aldrich's *The Last Sunset* (1961). In the '60s, Malone became famous as a star of the TV series *Peyton Place* (1964–69), although the role hardly challenged her as an actor. She continued to make movies, though fewer and fewer as time went on. Her last appearance to date was in a guest role in Paul Verhoeven's *Basic Instinct* (1992).

otherwise have been. The film seems almost to negate the very idea of objective knowledge, thereby reversing the pattern of the classical whodunit: here, the "story" is not so much a description of how a difficult case is solved, as the atmospheric evocation of a thoroughly criminal cosmos.

Murder, betrayal, perversion: Marlowe makes his way through this bleak film noir landscape with the loneliness of an existential hero. Quick-witted, sure-footed, crafty and tough, he's well-armed for the inhospitable terrain — yet his attractiveness resides not so much in his toughness as in his integrity. Bogart's Marlowe is the ideal

Vivian: "How did you find her?"
Marlowe: "I didn't find her."
Vivian: "Well then how did you ..."
Marlowe: "I haven't been here, you haven't seen me, and she hasn't been out of the house all evening."

Film quote: Vivian (Lauren Bacall) and Philip Marlowe (Humphrey Bogart)

1 Rise and shine: sleeping on the job can have fatal consequences.

2 Bestseller: Dorothy Malone's memorable performance won her many further Hollywood bookings.

3 Weeding through information: General Sternwood's (Charles Waldron, right) conservatory is as ominous as the concrete jungle where the majority of the film's investigation takes place.

4 Who's got the upper hand? If Marlowe isn't careful Vivian could leave him holding the check.

screen detective, a man with qualities undreamt of by Sam Spade, the cynical gumshoe in *The Maltese Falcon* (1941). More clearly than Chandler's novel, Hawks's film adaptation of *The Big Sleep* celebrates its hero's incorruptibility, while also establishing that this has at least as much to with an aesthetic attitude as with any real ethical principles. Marlowe is under no illusion that his actions can actually achieve very much, but he knows the power of a beautiful deed – and particularly, its effect on women.

That *The Big Sleep* is such a hugely entertaining movie has less to do with the kind of action scenes we expect from the hardboiled genre than with a series of witty verbal exchanges between Bogart and a whole host of self-assured beauties. It's almost worthy of a screwball comedy. Bogart's self-irony about his own star status only serves to make his character even more congenial. "You're not very tall," says the sultry Carmen; "I try to be," replies Marlowe.

5 The big bang: Martha Vickers, an actress in whom Hawks saw powder-keg potential, is simply stunning as the trigger-happy nymphomaniac.

6 Random acts of violence: Eddie Mars (John Ridgely, center) proves to be the culprit behind the wave of crime; his motives, however, remain a mystery.

7 Better you than me: the only way for Marlowe to avoid certain death is to remain still while lethal poison is administered to small-time snoop Harry Jones (Elisha Cook Jr., center).

"Brittle Chandler characters have been transferred to the screen with punch by Howard Hawks's production and direction, providing a full load of rough, tense action." *Variety*

> **"If only somebody had told us – the scriptwriters, preferably – just what it is that happens in _The Big Sleep_, we might be able to give you a more explicit and favorable report."** _The New York Times_

In Hawks's film, a woman's weapons include good old-fashioned guns. And indeed, what we're shown is not so much a fight between good and evil as a battle of the sexes. Not that this tussling for position rules out romance; on the contrary, it can easily provoke it, as is demonstrated by Bogart and Bacall, the dream team at the heart of the film. Just as in Hawks's _To Have and Have Not_ (1944), she's easily his match, and the powerful erotic charge between them is what holds the film together. When their coolness eventually dissolves, it's always one of the magic moments of the cinema.

Their most remarkable scene together was only added to the movie after filming had been completed. Arguing that too little use had been made of their star potential, the studio bosses pushed Hawks to remedy the deficit. So Hawks added some dialogue laced with double entendres: "I'm not sure how far you can go," says Bogart; "That depends on who's in the saddle," she answers. In the Hollywood of the '40s, that was as close to explicit sex as it was possible to get.

JH

BEAUTY AND THE BEAST

LA BELLE ET LA BÊTE

1946 - FRANCE - 96 MIN.

DIRECTOR

JEAN COCTEAU (1889–1963)

SCREENPLAY

JEAN COCTEAU, based on the story of the same name
by JEANNE-MARIE LEPRINCE DE BEAUMONT

DIRECTOR OF PHOTOGRAPHY

HENRI ALEKAN

EDITING

CLAUDE IBÉRIA

MUSIC

GEORGES AURIC

PRODUCTION

ANDRÉ PAULVÉ for DISCINA

STARRING

JEAN MARAIS (The Beast / The Prince / Avenant),
JOSETTE DAY (Belle), MARCEL ANDRÉ (Belle's Father), MILA PARÉLY (Felicity),
NANE GERMON (Adelaide), MICHEL AUCLAIR (Ludovic),
RAOUL MARCO (The Usurer)

**JEAN MARAIS
JOSETTE DAY**

dans

la **BELLE** *et la* **BÊTE**

HISTOIRE, PAROLES, MISE EN SCÈNE DE **JEAN COCTEAU** D'APRÈS LE CONTE DE MADAME **LEPRINCE DE BEAUMONT**

illustré par

CHRISTIAN BÉRARD

 avec **MILA PARELY, NANE GERMON, MICHEL AUCLAIR** et **MARCEL ANDRÉ**

CONSEILLER TECHNIQUE: **R. CLÉMENT**   MUSIQUE DE **GEORGES AURIC**   DIRECT. DE PRODUCT. **ÉMILE DARBON**

UNE SUPERPRODUCTION **ANDRÉ PAULVÉ**

Imp. S. A. COURBET, PARIS

"I have a good heart, but I am a monster."

While Belle (Josette Day) slaves away on the farm of her impoverished father (Marcel André), her two vain sisters (Mila Parély and Nane Germon) are busy looking for eligible princes. The charming Avenant wants to marry Belle, but she opts to stay with her father. One day, when returning home from yet another unsuccessful day, the father loses his way in the forest and spends the night in a strange and eerie castle. The following morning, he plucks a rose in the garden and arouses the ire of the owner: a beast appears (Jean Marais again), half-human, half-animal, and demands the life of the unlucky man – or that of one of his daughters. The father resolves to die, and is given three days to return home and bid farewell to his children. But before he can make his way back to the castle to pay his debt, Belle rides off to face the Beast in his place.

Jean Cocteau begins his version of *La Belle et la Bête*, the famous fairy tale written by Jeanne-Marie Leprince de Beaumont with the words, "Once upon a time …" It's an ancient storytellers' formula that encourages listeners to open themselves to the irrational. These four words also constitute a kind of promise, an assurance that we are capable of entering a simpler world, a place of extraordinary beauty and fathomless cruelty. Cocteau's film keeps its promise wonderfully by approaching the stuff of fairy tale with an entirely idiosyncratic and surreal imagination.

Even as a filmmaker, Cocteau saw himself essentially as a poet and as a surrealist. But in contrast to his

JEAN COCTEAU He designed stage sets, wrote poems and novels and plays, directed ballets, drew and painted. Jean Cocteau (1889–1963) saw the cinema as just one medium among many for a poet and a surrealist. And if his cinematic oeuvre is therefore comparatively thin, his versatility undoubtedly enriches his films. Cocteau's first surviving film, *The Blood of a Poet (Le Sang d'un poète,* 1930), clearly demonstrates how close he was to the artistic avant-garde of the time, and in many ways it resembles the early work of Luis Buñuel. In this movie, a bag of wonderful tricks, Cocteau has produced an intimate study of the artist's life and the origins of inspiration. He continued this study in the two later parts of the trilogy, *Orphée* (1949) and *The Testament of Orpheus (Le Testament d'Orphée,* 1959/60), his final film.
Beauty and the Beast (La Belle et la Bête, 1946) is undoubtedly Cocteau's most popular movie. Here, Cocteau succeeded brilliantly in bringing his surreal and poetic imagination to bear on a fairy tale everyone knows. He cast Jean Marais in the leading role. The actor was his lover and partner for many years, and appeared in every Cocteau film that followed, including the relatively little-known adaptations of Cocteau's stage plays, *The Eagle with Two Heads (L'Aigle à deux têtes,* 1948) and *The Storm Within (Les Parents terribles,* 1948). Cocteau also wrote screenplays for a number of excellent films, including Robert Bresson's *Les Dames du Bois de Boulogne* (1944/45), Jean-Pierre Melville's *Les Enfants terribles* (1950), and Georges Franju's *Thomas l'imposteur* (1964).

1 Rising above ill-fated shadows: Belle (Josette Day) proves herself as magnificent on the inside as she is on the outside.

2 Animal attraction: is it the beast (Jean Marais) that courts the beauty, or is he actually the incarnation of her unspoken desires?

3 Tale as old as time, song as old as rhyme: Jean Marais and Josette Day act out their own version of the Hephaestus and Aphrodite love story.

4 You stud, you: what some see as beastly, others might call unbridled masculinity.

previous film, *The Blood of a Poet (Le Sang d'un poète*, 1930), which was even more clearly influenced by the avant-garde of the '20s, *Beauty and the Beast* abides by the narrative conventions of "standard" cinema. Cocteau's unfamiliarity and relative unease with such forms of narrative storytelling may also explain the presence of René Clément as co-director.

One characteristic of Cocteau's visual poetry is the way it allows the supernatural to emerge from the everyday. In *Beauty and the Beast*, the quotidian is manifested with reference to Dutch genre paintings of the 17th century. For the look of the father's farm, Cocteau advised cameraman Henri Alekan to examine the work of Vermeer – not so as to cite these paintings directly, but in order to develop a feeling for the light, the space, and the positioning of the figures. And indeed, the results are clearly visible in Alekan's poetic camerawork. Other artworks provided the inspiration for the castle and its surroundings: Gustave Doré's somber illustrations of Perrault's fairy tales, as well as other "fantastic" artworks. Cocteau knew how to integrate his own film magic, his own surreal magic, into these weird and wonderful visual worlds. On several occasions, he uses film running backwards to astonishing effect. Just as simple, and just as effective, are the candelabra on the wall, which are held by human hands; or

"It is one of the most magical of all films. Before the days of computer effects and modern creature make-up, here is a fantasy alive with trick shots and astonishing effects, giving us a Beast who is lonely like a man and misunderstood like an animal." *Chicago Sun-Times*

5 Heart of darkness: Belle's sisters (pictured here, Mila Parély) are all alike and frighteningly beautiful.

6 Journey through Flanders: Cocteau's film reads like a homage to the Netherlands.

7 The enchanted forest: somehow it looks less sinister by day.

8 Ruffles and beaus: Jean Marais was director Jean Cocteau's dream prince – both on screen and off.

"Philosophically interpreted or not, this is a sensuously fascinating film, a fanciful poem in movement given full articulation on the screen." *The New York Times*

the living faces of the caryatids, whose eyes follow the characters as they pass. In one particularly beautiful sequence, Belle literally floats through the long corridors of the castle.

An awareness of the film's art-historical forebears also deepens our understanding of it, as exemplified by the scene in which Belle faints upon first seeing the Beast. As the Beast then carries her into her bedchamber, she has the physical posture of the sleeping girl in Fuseli's famous painting *The Nightmare*. The parallel makes us aware that Cocteau knows desire is also the property of women: the Beast himself may very well be seen as a manifestation of Belle's erotic imagination.

In the end, Avenant perishes: in his attempt to free Belle and steal the Beast's treasure, he has violated the principle of wonder. Simultaneously, the Beast dies, too; yet Belle's love transforms him into a prince, who bears a remarkably close resemblance to Avenant. It's a true fairy-tale ending, yet a vague air of melancholy suffuses the scene. For Cocteau allows us to feel that the Beast was Belle's true love, and that the prettiest of princes will never really take his place.

UB

NOTORIOUS

1946 - USA - 101 MIN.

DIRECTOR

ALFRED HITCHCOCK (1899–1980)

SCREENPLAY

BEN HECHT

DIRECTOR OF PHOTOGRAPHY

TED TETZLAFF

EDITING

THERON WARTH

MUSIC

ROY WEBB

PRODUCTION

ALFRED HITCHCOCK for RKO

STARRING

CARY GRANT (T. R. Devlin), INGRID BERGMAN (Alicia Huberman),
CLAUDE RAINS (Alexander Sebastian), LOUIS CALHERN (Paul Prescott),
LEOPOLDINE KONSTANTIN (Anna Sebastian),
REINHOLD SCHÜNZEL (Dr. Anderson),
MORONI OLSEN (Walter Beardsley), IVAN TRIESAULT (Eric Mathis),
ALEX MINOTIS (Joseph), WALLY BROWN (Mr. Hopkins)

CARY
GRANT
INGRID
BERGMAN
in **ALFRED HITCHCOCK'S**

Notorious!

with **CLAUDE RAINS**

LOUIS CALHERN · MADAME LEOPOLDINE KONSTANTIN

Directed by **ALFRED HITCHCOCK** *Written by BEN HECHT*

R K O
RADIO
PICTURES

"This is a very strange love affair." – "Why?" – "Maybe the fact that you don't love me."

As Humphrey Bogart and Ingrid Bergman proved in *Casablanca* (1942), the age-old adage that absence makes the heart grow fonder also applies to big-screen romances. Four years later, Alfred Hitchcock's psychothriller *Notorious* (1946) made it clear that Hollywood's love for Ingrid Bergman was here to stay. Like *Casablanca*, *Notorious* relies on war to provide the backdrop for a tragic love triangle. That, however, is where the resemblance ends, for here Bergman plays Alicia Huberman, the American-born daughter of a Nazi spy.

As her dossier suggests, Alicia is someone who often finds herself caught between two worlds. She agrees to marry someone she does not love for the sake of U.S. secret agent T. R. Devlin (Cary Grant), the man who holds her heart. At Devlin's request, this former party girl is to find out all she can about what goes on in the house of Alexander Sebastian (Claude Rains), a Nazi who has fled to South America.

Alicia's new life down south turns into a death trap when her husband discovers she has tapped into his little sideline in smuggling large quantities of uranium and suspects her of being a double agent. Profoundly disappointed, Alexander begins poisoning his better half with ever-increasing doses of arsenic. But just before he succeeds in ridding himself of Alicia, Devlin saves her life in an eleventh-hour rescue mission.

Notorious is a prime illustration of Hitchcock's "MacGuffin" theory. Here, weapons-grade uranium and its potential for mass destruction casts no cloud over the classic Hollywood love story; the fact that the director's 1944 script, penned one year before the atom bomb was dropped on Hiroshima, tapped into a top-secret war project was pure coincidence.

The film's brilliance is the product of Hitchcockian streamlining, and the drama draws on the structural similarities of spy capers and romances. General distrust sets

INGRID BERGMAN *Notorious* (1946) was the second of three pictures Ingrid Bergman shot with Alfred Hitchcock, the other two being *Spellbound* (1945), and *Under Capricorn* (1949). She was the first of Hitch's great leading ladies, preceding other famous repeat performers like the icy blondes Grace Kelly and Tippi Hedren. The Master of Suspense was devastated when she declared that their professional collaboration had come to an end, although she maintained her friendship with him until his death. It wasn't just Hitchcock, but rather the whole world that fell at the feet of this extraordinary Stockholm native. Her name was synonymous with natural beauty, noble grandeur, and a unique professionalism. When producer David O. Selznick brought Bergman to Hollywood in 1938, the Swedish starlet was permitted to shoot only one movie a year. The choices she made are astounding, for this was to be an era that included not only *Casablanca* (1942), but also *For Whom the Bell Tolls* (1943) and *Gaslight* (1944). Regrettably, her immaculate reputation became the subject of scandal shortly after she agreed to make *Stromboli (Stromboli, terra di Dio,* 1949): she abandoned her husband and children to start a life with the picture's director, Roberto Rossellini. The public shunned Bergman for nearly a decade, and it was only when she received her second Oscar for *Anastasia* (1956) that Hollywood symbolically forgave her. In the years that followed, the actress divided her time between American and European productions. She won further acclaim later on in her career for her work in Ingmar Bergman's *Autumn Sonata (Höstsonaten,* 1978) and her portrayal of the Israeli prime minister, Golda Meir, in the made-for-TV *A Woman Called Golda* (1982). Ingrid Bergman died in London at the age of 67. Her daughter, the actress Isabella Rossellini, was born out of her marriage to the Italian director.

the stage for tension time and again, while interludes of deceit and betrayal cross paths with secrets that must be kept at all cost, imbuing the story with intrigue and suspense. These conventions are our only clue as to Devlin's actual feelings for Alicia. Meanwhile, she suffers at the hands of two men. There's Sebastian, the man she sleeps with, who smothers her with his trust and devotion. And then there's the icy Devlin, who repays her patriotism with open sarcasm.

Ingrid Bergman delivers a stunning portrayal of someone held at the mercy of love and duty, a woman coerced into playing a passive role that makes her appear significantly weaker than she is. Grant's Devlin, on the other hand, is as tertiary as a MacGuffin, despite his being the film's alleged romantic lead. Sebastian, the Nazi who genuinely loves Alicia, and who is afflicted by her deceptions all the more for it, does a much better job of winning the audience's compassion. The role exemplifies the complexity Hitchcock gave his villains, as these were often the characters he sympathized with most. Yet the director wasn't the only person who could relate to twisted injustices: to match the physical stature of his Swedish co-star, Claude Rains was forced to act on platforms just as Bogart did in *Casablanca*.

Despite the complexity of the story, the film is told in a relatively transparent manner, although some aspects of

1 Take a deep breath: Cary Grant and Ingrid Bergman prepare to dive into Hollywood's longest kiss on record.

2 Pillow talk: Devlin steps in to save Alicia in the nick of time – but the situation might require some mouth-to-mouth resuscitation.

3 Spy versus spy: Devlin convinces Alicia to join the secret service.

4 Spellbound: Alicia is so taken with Devlin that she marries another man at his request.

> "Alfred Hitchcock's *Notorious* is the most elegant expression of the master's visual style, just as *Vertigo* is the fullest expression of his obsessions. It contains some of the most effective camera shots in his – or anyone's – work, and they all lead to the great final passages in which two men find out how very wrong they both were."
>
> *Chicago Sun-Times*

the cinematography have entered film history. The camera pairs the various liquids that Alicia drinks with her constant state of suffering – from her self-imposed alcoholism to the arsenic cocktails she is tricked into tippling. Among the film's finest special effects is a 180° pivoting shot taken from Alicia's point of view, expressing her drunkenness after a long night out with Devlin. The result is one of the few moments when Alicia's love for Devlin doesn't inhibit her from seeing his duplicitous and elusive side. Later on, Hitchcock relocates the main storyline to Sebastian's wine cellar where the uranium is hidden, providing the director with an opportune venue to stage the

5 Sworn to secrecy: the CIA pulls Devlin's strings and forces him to feign emotional indifference toward Alicia. Then again, she'd never complete her mission alive if she knew as much as he did.

6 Packs a wallop: Devlin and Alicia go looking for a good vintage and find one that's radioactive.

7 We're in this together: Ingrid Bergman appeared in three Hitchcock films, Cary Grant in four. *Notorious* was their only joint venture.

8 Must have been something I ate: Alicia gets sick to her stomach when she thinks about all the wicked things her husband Alex Sebastian (Claude Rains) is up to.

"longest filmed kiss of all time." For three minutes solid, Grant and Bergman are locked in an amorous embrace. Their lips, however, are not. In order to comply with Production Code stipulations, the actual kissing had to be kept to intervals of three seconds maximum.

Notorious is undoubtedly the most romantic of all Hitchcock's films. The picture's undercurrent of suppressed sexual tension would turn up time and again in his later works and come to be revered as part of his film-making style. This tension is at long last unleashed by a spectacular though inevitable ending that liberates Alicia and Devlin's hearts from a state of imprisonment, leaving the doomed Sebastian with no alternative but to take his own life.

PB

"We do not recall a more conspicuous – yet emotionally delicate – love scene on the screen than one stretch of billing and cooing that the principals play in this film. Yet, withal, there is rich and real emotion expressed by Miss Bergman in her role, and the integrity of her nature as she portrays it is the prop that holds the show."

The New York Times

THE TREASURE OF
THE SIERRA MADRE ⛹⛹⛹

1947 - USA - 126 MIN.

DIRECTOR

JOHN HUSTON (1906–1987)

SCREENPLAY

JOHN HUSTON, based on the novel
of the same name by B. TRAVEN

DIRECTOR OF PHOTOGRAPHY

TED D. MCCORD

EDITING

OWEN MARKS

MUSIC

MAX STEINER

PRODUCTION

HENRY BLANKE for WARNER BROS.

STARRING

HUMPHREY BOGART (Fred C. Dobbs), WALTER HUSTON (Howard),
TIM HOLT (Bob Curtin), BRUCE BENNETT (James Cody),
BARTON MACLANE (Pat McCormick), ALFONSO BEDOYA (Gold Hat),
JOHN HUSTON (American in a White Suit), ROBERT BLAKE (Boy with the Lottery Tickets),
JOSÉ TORVAY (Pablo), MARGARITO LUNA (Pancho)

ACADEMY AWARDS 1948

OSCARS for BEST DIRECTOR (John Huston), BEST SCREENPLAY (John Huston),
and BEST SUPPORTING ACTOR (Walter Huston)

They sold their souls for...

"THE TREASURE OF THE SIERRA MADRE"

STARRING

HUMPHREY BOGART

WARNER BROS.
hit a new high in high adventure...
bringing another great best-seller
to the screen!

AND WALTER HUSTON · TIM HOLT · BRUCE BENNETT

DIRECTED BY
JOHN HUSTON

PRODUCED BY
HENRY BLANKE

"Bye, mountain, thanks!"

Howard (Walter Huston), old and experienced, has no illusions: "Gold itself ain't good for nothin', except makin' jewelry with, and gold teeth." He's spent his life grubbing around in the dirt, hoping to strike it rich some day, and he's still very far from wealthy. In a lousy dive in Tampico, Mexico, he picks up with Dobbs (Humphrey Bogart) and Curtin (Tim Holt), two washed-up workers who are broke, yet again, after being cheated by McCormick (Barton MacLane), a crooked businessman: "Yeah, I know what gold does to men's souls." Yet Howard's eyes sparkle when he talks about prospecting … and that's why he leaps at the chance when Dobbs and Curtin, in sheer desperation, decide to form a partnership and go off in search of gold.

Together, the three of them make their way to the Sierra Madre, a remote, inaccessible corner of Mexico where Howard suspects there are immense riches waiting to be found.

Howard leads the group, for he's the only one with the necessary know-how; yet he's very anxious that everyone should get on well. He knows only too well that the success of their expedition depends on mutual trust, and that as soon as they lose that trust, every gold strike will become a murderous affair. It's as if the elusive substance were a drug capable of clouding a man's reason and driving him mad. Curtin is the most innocent of the three, but he also has a moral sense. The braggart Dobbs, by contrast, has a tendency to be excessively distrustful. He's

B. TRAVEN Who was the mysterious B. Traven? Even the textbooks aren't entirely sure. All we know for certain is that from the time of his earliest literary successes in the early 1930s until his death nearly 40 years later, he craved anonymity. "B. Traven" changed his name several times. The British journalist Woodrow Wyatt claimed to have proven that he was actually Albert Otto Maximilian Feige, a German born in Schwiebus near Frankfurt in 1882. Rolf Recknagel had another theory: in a biography first published in Leipzig in 1966, he argued that Traven was none other than Ret Marut, former publisher of the Munich-based socialist-anarchist journal *Der Ziegelbrenner*. (The name "Ret Marut" was also, it seems, a pseudonym.) What we do know is that Traven fled to Mexico by a roundabout route after the First World War. He did so under the name "Berick T. Torsvan," making good use of the opportunity to abandon his old identity. His career as a writer began in Mexico, where he allegedly became a Mexican citizen in 1941, under the name "Hal Croves." There, he wrote a series of compelling and socially critical novels, such as *Death Ship* (1926), *Rebellion of the Hanged* (1936), and *The Treasure of the Sierra Madre* (1927). These densely metaphoric works are characterized by a highly idiosyncratic voice, and the social criticism they embody has a decidedly existentialist flavor. They also speak out clearly against violence and inhumanity. While preparing to make his version of *The Treasure of the Sierra Madre* (1947), John Huston arranged to meet Mr. Hal Croves in Mexico. Croves said that he was Traven's agent, but Huston was later convinced he had been dealing with B. Traven himself.

After Traven's death on March 26, 1969, Traven's widow Rosa Elena Luján confirmed that he had indeed been none other than the German-speaking anarchist Ret Marut, who had played a significant role in the Munich "Räterepublik" (Council Republic).

1 24 carats a day, 7 days a week: Curtin (Tim Holt) experiences the round-the-clock burn of gold fever while seeking the mother lode.

2 That's the ticket: Dobbs (Humphrey Bogart) wonders whether buying a lottery ticket from a young boy is an easier route to fortune.

3 All for one and one for all: when it comes to mining, three musketeers Curtin, Dobbs and Howard (Walter Huston) are inseparable.

4 Thinking with his ass: the ongoing treasure hunt drives Dobbs to the brink of insanity.

5 Still got a ways to go: Curtin and Dobbs sense that age isn't the only respect in which Howard is further along than they are.

been taken for a sucker too often in life not to see a simple, friendly chat between his partners as proof of a plot against him. The three men do eventually find gold — lots of it — and that's when their troubles really start.

The mysterious B. Traven had published the original novel in 1927, and director John Huston (who makes three brief appearances in the film as a rich American dressed in white) had been wanting to film it since before World War II. The arrival of his call-up papers put his professional plans on hold for a while, but shortly after the Allied victory, the project began to take shape once more. It was important to Huston to make some changes to the

"More than a meditation on the vanity of all earthly ambition, it is a hymn to liberty, from John Huston to his father Walter – who plays Bogart off the screen quite effortlessly. The true hero of this film is the film itself." *Le Nouvel Observateur*

"**_Treasure of the Sierra Madre_** was one of the first American films shot almost completely on location outside the U.S. Tampico, Mexico, was the jumping off point, but Huston wanted his cast as far away from civilization as possible, which to Bogart was any place where you couldn't drive to Mike Romanoff's restaurant for a drink. 'John wanted everything perfect,' he said." *moviediva.com*

6 Holy frijoles! Mexican banditos get ready to give themselves something to celebrate this Cinco de Mayo.

7 Age before beauty: Dobbs and Curtin would be lost without Howard's wisdom. Director John Huston cast his father in the role of the old sage, and both men took home Oscars for their work that year.

literary model: the dialogue seemed too unwieldy, and the plot too loose and overloaded with metaphorical significance. He was mainly interested in exploring how the characters develop, and in depicting the murky depths that open up beneath and within them as they walk the tightrope between trust and suspicion. In Mexico, Huston went looking for suitable locations, as he wanted to film outdoors as much as possible.

The finished product powerfully evokes the sheer physical isolation of the three gold diggers. For months on end, these men are left to themselves and their imaginations. In an environment made up of rocks, dust, heat, and cacti, their clothes grow increasingly tattered and shabby. Huston's father Walter won an Oscar for his performance (while his son carried off two, for Best Director and Best Screenplay). The director had persuaded his dad to leave out his dentures in the cause of authenticity, yet Walter Huston still spoke his lines at breakneck speed and without fluffing a single one of them. His philosophical excur-

sions on the deadly effects of filthy lucre are worth their weight in gold.

Howard is the most human of the three characters, for he lives according to the principle that he can't expect more from life than it chooses to give him. When the tale has run its course, the gold dust they've sweated to acquire blows away in the wind, leaving not a trace behind, Howard bursts into raucous laughter: "The gold has gone back to where we found it!" Nature knows no morality, yet it doesn't stop Howard from seeing the drama of their terrible loss as a clever comedy penned by a higher power. His laughter liberates and rejuvenates, for it scorns death and puts life before profit. More essential to life than riches is the happiness achievable in a human community based on trust. "Hell is other people," wrote Jean-Paul Sartre in *No Exit* (*Huis Clos*, 1944); Huston had directed Sartre's play in New York only shortly before making this film.

SR

BICYCLE THIEVES ♦
LADRI DI BICICLETTE
1948 - ITALY - 88 MIN.

DIRECTOR
VITTORIO DE SICA (1902–1974)

SCREENPLAY
CESARE ZAVATTINI, ORESTE BIANCOLI, SUSO CECCHI D'AMICO,
ADOLFO FRANCI, GERARDO GUERRIERI, VITTORIO DE SICA,
based on the novel of the same name by LUIGI BARTOLINI

DIRECTOR OF PHOTOGRAPHY
CARLO MONTUORI

EDITING
ERALDO DA ROMA

MUSIC
ALESSANDRO CICOGNINI

PRODUCTION
VITTORIO DE SICA, GIUSEPPE AMATO
for PRODUZIONI DE SICA

STARRING
LAMBERTO MAGGIORANI (Antonio Ricci), ENZO STAIOLA (Bruno),
LIANELLA CARELL (Maria Ricci), GINO SALTAMERENDA (Baiocco),
IDA BRACCI DORATI (Signora Santona), VITTORIO ANTONUCCI (The Thief),
ELENA ALTIERI (The Charitable Lady), GIULIO CHIARI (The Beggar),
MICHELE SAKARA (Secretary of the Charity Organization),
FAUSTO GUERZONI (Amateur Actor)

ACADEMY AWARDS 1949
SPECIAL PRIZE to VITTORIO DE SICA from the
ACADEMY BOARD OF GOVERNORS, for the most outstanding foreign language film
released in the United States during 1949

Ladri di biciclette

PRODUZIONE P. D. S. UN FILM DI **VITTORIO DE SICA**

"You live and you suffer."

Only a miracle can help him now. Antonio (Lamberto Maggiorani) has trekked across Rome in search of his stolen bicycle. He has been to the police, rummaged around the flea markets, done everything he can; in vain. Antonio had literally sold his last sheet to buy the bike – and without it, he'll lose his job as a billsticker, forfeiting the wages that support him, his wife and his little son Bruno (Enzo Staiola). In his mounting distress, he has even struck the child, who's been at his side throughout this terrible odyssey. Now they're sitting in a trattoria, for even if he really can't afford it, Antonio feels they both deserve a treat. Then he has an idea.

They walk to a tenement in the Via della Paglia, where Signora Santona (Ida Bracci Dorati) has an apartment on the second floor. Around a dozen people are already waiting to see her. The lady is clad in a bathrobe and enthroned in an armchair beside her enormous bed. Her daughter hands her a cup of coffee; she takes the spoon and stirs; and little

VITTORIO DE SICA Comedies made him a star, and his career wound down with melodramas. In the period between, he shaped Italian neorealism with such movies as *Shoeshine (Sciuscià,* 1946), *Bicycle Thieves (Ladri di biciclette,* 1948), and *Umberto D.* (1951).
Vittorio De Sica was one of the most important protagonists of Italian cinema, both as an actor and as a director. He was born in 1902, and grew up in Naples. Although he discovered his talent for the theater at an early age, he trained as an accountant in order to support his family. In 1932, he played a lively young man in Mario Camerini's comedy *Gli uomini, che mascalzoni!* It was the kind of role that would typify his later acting career, and it marked his breakthrough from stage to screen. In the decade that followed, he would become one of the most popular actors in Italy. As the '40s began, he took up directing, and he financed his ambitious projects by acting in less ambitious films.
After his Neorealist phase, he was popular mainly as Sophia Loren's director: for her performance in his film *Two Women (La ciociara,* 1960), she received an Oscar as Best Actress; and for *Yesterday, Today and Tomorrow (Ieri, oggi, domani / Hier, aujourd'hui et demain,* 1963), with Loren in the female lead, De Sica won the Oscar for Best Foreign Film. This was his third Academy Award, after the honorary prizes for *Shoeshine* and *Bicycle Thieves.* In 1970, he received yet another, for *The Garden of the Finzi-Continis (Il giardino dei Finzi-Contini,* 1970). This German-Italian co-production told the story of a Jewish family during the Fascist period – a subject tackled repeatedly by De Sica.
Vittorio De Sica was a playboy and an idealist – a man who made conscious use of his popularity to draw attention to people on the edge of society. He appeared in more than 150 movies and directed more than 30 himself. In 1974, he died in France, his second home. He is remembered above all as a humanist, and as a man with a wonderful sense of humor.

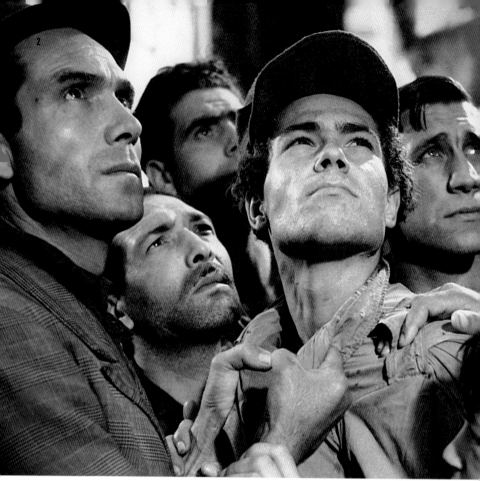

1 Putting the brakes on justice: it'll take more than positive identification for Antonio Ricci (Lamberto Maggiorani, right) and son Bruno (Enzo Staiola) to nab a bicycle thief.

2 One hit wonder: Lamberto Maggiorani worked in a weapons manufactory prior to starring in *Bicycle Thieves* and then returned to life as a laborer following several off-target acting attempts.

3 The wheels of progress: Antonio's wife Maria (Lianella Carell) suggests keeping the gears of family life greased with steady employment.

Bruno seizes the opportunity to push his hesitant father into the vacated chair beside her, ignoring the protests of the other supplicants who are standing patiently in line. Antonio whispers into the soothsayer's ear, and she answers with a puzzling prediction: either he will find his bicycle immediately, or it's lost for ever. Father and son leave the Signora's house … and just as they step onto the street, they see the thief they've been looking for all day. Showdown. It is the classical simplicity of *Bicycle Thieves* that explains its extraordinary beauty. This, at least, was the opinion of André Bazin, the great French film theorist. Writing in 1951, Bazin pointed out how the deliberate renunciation of a spectacular storyline opens the viewer's eyes to a different kind of spectacle: reality itself. A man walks along a street, alone, and the spectator is astounded by the sheer grace of his presence. Bazin saw *Bicycle Thieves*, therefore, as the definitive expression of Italian neorealism – the influential movement that revolutionized the cinema in the second half of the '40s.

The Neorealist filmmakers wanted to capture reality with the greatest possible authenticity by filming on location and employing amateur actors. Vittorio De Sica and his scriptwriter Cesare Zavattini went their own way. While some directors saw documentary films as their aesthetic and stylistic compass, De Sica and Zavattini used a kind of poetic hyperbole to reveal the underlying reality. Where other Neorealists tried to force the viewer to reflect by creating a distance between the audience and the events on screen, De Sica and Zavattini brought the audience closer by embracing emotion and empathy.

They approach the characters in their films with an almost tangible decency and sympathy. Take *Bicycle Thieves*:

"Much of the film's power resides in its relative silence – its lack of talking. Like the great films made before the coming of sound, it demonstrates the intensity of silent acting, here done by non-professionals." *Norton Resource Library*

"No other filmmaker has come close to matching De Sica's greatest achievement: his development of a cinematic dialectics capable of bridging the gulf between theatrical action and pure event. In this respect, *Ladri di biciclette* is one of the first examples of pure cinema. No more actors, no more story, no more mise-en-scène; in the complete aesthetic illusion of reality, this means, ultimately: no more cinema." *Esprit*

4

5

4 A bicycle built for two: Lamberto Maggiorani and Vittorio De Sica ride high with naturalistic performances that make this film what it is.

5 And many happy returns: despite being a relatively pricey undertaking for an economy recovering from war, *Bicycle Thieves* made a pretty penny and emerged as one of the few undisputed hits of neorealism.

although Antonio becomes increasingly desperate, he never loses his dignity – not even when he cries with shame. For Signora Santona's miracle brings him no more than a few minutes of hope: Antonio manages to catch the thief, but he never gets his bike back. As evening falls and he heads for home, exhausted, a soccer stadium presents him with an irresistible temptation: he chooses one of the countless bicycles parked outside, leaps onto the saddle and pedals away. He's caught immediately by the angry crowd, and only allowed to go free when the owner takes pity on him. As a tear rolls down Antonio's cheek, Bruno grasps his father's hand – for the first time in the entire film.

Thus, on a second level, *Bicycle Thieves* traces the relationship between a father and son brought closer by a shared task. De Sica attends to the details of family life with an intensity bordering on reverence. Some of the most beautiful scenes in the film take place in the first 15 minutes, as father and son prepare for work in the early morning hours: they are wearing almost identical work clothes, and each of them has a modest lunch package, prepared by the mother, in his left breast pocket. It's a moment of luminous intensity, as the family's undemonstrative warmth and their hope for the future form an oasis in the desert that is postwar Rome. There's almost no work, no solidarity at all, and the city's institutions have collapsed. When everyone is struggling to survive, even something as simple as a bicycle can become the object of an existential drama.

In the end, we lose sight of Antonio and Bruno in the vast crowd streaming from the football stadium: a man and a boy, mortified but unbroken, walking towards an uncertain future.

NM

THE THIRD MAN 🏆

1949 - GREAT BRITAN - 104 MIN.

DIRECTOR
CAROL REED (1906–1976)

SCREENPLAY
GRAHAM GREENE

DIRECTOR OF PHOTOGRAPHY
ROBERT KRASKER

EDITING
OSWALD HAFENRICHTER

MUSIC
ANTON KARAS

PRODUCTION
CAROL REED, ALEXANDER KORDA, DAVID O. SELZNICK
for LONDON FILM PRODUCTIONS, BRITISH LION FILM CORPORATION

STARRING
JOSEPH COTTEN (Holly Martins), ORSON WELLES (Harry Lime),
ALIDA VALLI (Anna Schmidt), TREVOR HOWARD (Major Calloway),
PAUL HÖRBIGER (Porter), ERNST DEUTSCH (Baron Kurtz),
ERICH PONTO (Doctor Winkel), SIEGFRIED BREUER (Popescu),
BERNARD LEE (Sergeant Paine), GEOFFREY KEEN (British MP)

ACADEMY AWARDS 1950
OSCAR for BEST CINEMATOGRAPHY (Robert Krasker)

IFF CANNES 1949
GOLDEN PALM (Carol Reed)

DAVID O. SELZNICK and ALEXANDER KORDA

PRESENT

THE 3RD MAN

by GRAHAM GREENE

STARRING **JOSEPH COTTEN · VALLI**
ORSON WELLES · TREVOR HOWARD
PRODUCED AND DIRECTED BY **CAROL REED**

A SELZNICK RELEASE

"Poor Harry!"

A corpse floats belly up in the picturesque blue Danube as a narrator's voice off-handedly remarks that postwar Vienna's black market economy is no place for amateurs. We're not more than a minute into the film, and yet already knee-deep in a story that capitalizes on the magic of place and period like no other film ever made. Closely following Graham Greene's script, British director Carol Reed shot *The Third Man* in occupied Vienna against a backdrop of romance and rubble. From these ashes rose a masterpiece of black comedy that is as much a thriller as it is melodrama. With spot-on accuracy, Reed captures the atmosphere of postwar mayhem as displaced persons wheel and deal in a many-tongued chatter, hoping to make a buck and praying to stay alive.

This world of black-market trade and unpredictable police raids couldn't be more foreign to American dime novelist Holly Martins (Joseph Cotten). Before he gets a chance to take in his surroundings, Holly is whisked off to attend the sudden funeral of his good friend Harry Lime (Orson Welles), his sole acquaintance in town. The sordid details Holly unearths while conducting his own impromptu investigation of Harry's allegedly accidental death unfold on screen in the deliciously macabre style of Alfred Hitchcock's earlier British films. Without warning, the scene flips

DAVID O. SELZNICK David O. Selznick (1902–1965) is one of the great Hollywood prodigies. He started running his own production company at the age of 34 (Selznick International Pictures, founded in 1936), following an immaculate record in top corporate positions at Paramount, RKO, and MGM. One could say that Selznick had a knack for discovering talent: during his time at RKO, he signed on Fred Astaire and furthered the careers of actress Katharine Hepburn and director George Cukor. Selznick was also responsible for wooing Europeans Ingrid Bergman and Alfred Hitchcock to Hollywood as well as securing the exclusive rights to film Margaret Mitchell's Southern epic novel *Gone with the Wind* – a deal that cost him 65,000 dollars. Though it's no secret that this little investment proved most lucrative in the end, getting the project off the ground was an arduous endeavor indeed. Years of pre-production saw numerous directors and even more scripts fall casualty to its mammoth demands. The product, however, is among the premier examples of the legendary Hollywood studio system at its finest: impeccably crafted entertainment which finds that perfect balance of intimate melodrama and sweeping epic.

It was no secret that Selznick's perfectionism and genuine interest in virtually all aspects of filmmaking prevented his being satisfied with the work of those around him – to this day, his production memos are as legendary as they are notorious. In the 1940s he took a fancy to actress Jennifer Jones – the future Mrs. Selznick – and devoted much of his time to the advancement of her career. In addition, Selznick often collaborated on co-productions with Italian and British filmmakers, although he never granted them full artistic license. This was also the case for *The Third Man* (1949), which he brought to American screens in a version ten minutes shorter than its British counterpart. Selznick produced his final picture *A Farewell to Arms* in 1957, and died of a heart attack in 1965.

1 The grapes of wrath: Major Calloway (Trevor Howard) is out to give penicillin racketeer Harry Lime a taste of his own medicine.

2 Freeze tag: Harry Lime (Orson Welles) does his best to blend in with the surroundings.

3 The river Stynx: in the labyrinthine tunnels of Vienna's sewer system, Calloway, Paine (Bernard Lee), and Holly Martins (Joseph Cotten) discover that Harry Lime is indeed the scum of the earth.

"**The music is particularly original and exciting. Like a leitmotif, the catchy and authentically popular zither melody accompanies the appearances of the mysterious Harry Lime, telling us of his presence even when he remains invisible or is represented only by his proxies and messengers.**" *Der Tagesspiegel*

from one locale to the next: Martins outruns a bloodthirsty mob who suspects him of having killed Lime's porter (Paul Hörbiger), but ends up getting shoved into the back of a taxi waiting for him at the gates of his hotel. When the ride is over, he surfaces as the guest of honor at a meeting of literary enthusiasts only to disappoint them when, as the author of *The Lone Rider of Santa Fé*, he has little to say about James Joyce. No sooner does he exit the function than he is tailed by a pair of hoods, bitten by a parrot, and forced to scale a mountain of rubble. It is a neverending fight for survival that culminates in a fluke encounter with none other than Harry Lime himself.

No one could paint villainy in as tragic a palette as actor-director Orson Welles, and the unscrupulous penicillin racketeer Harry Lime counts among his greatest roles. Despite a performance confined to the story's end and 15 minutes of screen time, Welles's character never budges from the center of the plot. While his disturbing and prolonged absence holds the audience in an indefinite state of suspense, this by no means eclipses Welles's actual performance. In the shadows of an entryway, we see a tomcat seated contentedly beside a man's pant leg. We recognize

the animal as the pet of Lime's lover Anna (Alida Valli), who informed us in a prior scene that the cat "only likes Harry." Light shoots in from a window on the opposite side of the street and confirms what we already suspect – from the perspective of a drunken and dumbfounded Holly Martins, we lock eyes with the supposedly dead Harry Lime. His wide-eyed baby face curls into a contemptuous grin that was quintessentially Welles. Then he vanishes. Later, when the smoke has cleared, he'll offer us this flippant justification for his insidious behavior: "In Italy for 30 years under the Borgias, they had warfare, terror, murder, bloodshed; but they produced Michelangelo, Leonardo da Vinci, and the Renaissance. In Switzerland they had brotherly love and 500 years of democracy and peace. And what did that produce? The cuckoo clock." Unlike the irresistible bounder he plays in *The Third Man*, Welles's contributions to the film were anything but elusive. Cameraman Robert Krasker's opulent, black-and-white photography works with the same Expressionist lighting and camera angles that Welles himself favored as a filmmaker.

As much as Krasker looked to Welles for guidance, the principal characters define themselves and their moral beliefs according to Harry Lime: the British Major Calloway (Trevor Howard) is determined to apprehend Lime in the name of all the children who lost their lives to the racketeer's contaminated penicillin; Anna, however, wouldn't denounce him no matter what the extent of his crimes, claiming that "a person doesn't change because you find out more." And then, of course, there's Holly Martins, a man who could never turn his pal over to the authorities, but still bestows the kiss of death upon him during the film's thrilling conclusion in the maze of Vienna's sewers. Beyond all this, Harry Lime's ubiquitous presence lingers in every note of this picture's score. The character has grown inseparable from Anton Karas's zither-based theme, which has found an additional home in popular music.

LP

4 Fan club: actress Anna Schmidt (Alida Valli) is the only person who believes in Harry's virtue. After all, he is the man responsible for falsifying her identity.

5 More than he bargained for: dime novelist Holly Martins is suddenly expected to take a stance on matters which are clearly over his head – James Joyce included.

ALL ABOUT EVE ♔♔♔♔♔♔

1950 - USA - 137 MIN.

DIRECTOR

JOSEPH L. MANKIEWICZ (1909–1993)

SCREENPLAY

JOSEPH L. MANKIEWICZ based on
the short story *The Wisdom of Eve* by MARY ORR

DIRECTOR OF PHOTOGRAPHY

MILTON KRASNER

EDITING

BARBARA MCLEAN

MUSIC

ALFRED NEWMAN

PRODUCTION

DARRYL F. ZANUCK for 20TH CENTURY FOX

STARRING

BETTE DAVIS (Margo Channing), ANNE BAXTER (Eve Harrington),
GEORGE SANDERS (Addison De Witt), CELESTE HOLM (Karen Richards),
GARY MERRILL (Bill Sampson), HUGH MARLOWE (Lloyd Richards),
THELMA RITTER (Birdie Coonan), MARILYN MONROE (Miss Caswell),
GREGORY RATOFF (Max Fabian), BARBARA BATES (Phoebe)

ACADEMY AWARDS 1950

OSCARS for BEST PICTURE (DARRYL F. ZANUCK), for BEST DIRECTOR (Joseph L. Mankiewicz),
for BEST ADAPTED SCREENPLAY (Joseph L. Mankiewicz),
for BEST SUPPORTING ACTOR (George Sanders),
for BEST COSTUMES (Edith Head, Charles Le Maire),
and BEST SOUND DESIGN (20th Century Fox Sound Department)

IFF CANNES 1951

BEST ACTRESS (Bette Davis),
SPECIAL JURY AWARD (Joseph L. Mankiewicz)

it's all about women... and their men!

"all about eve"

Darryl F Zanuck presents

BETTE DAVIS
ANNE BAXTER
GEORGE SANDERS
CELESTE HOLM
ALL ABOUT EVE

Gary Merrill · Hugh Marlowe
Thelma Ritter · Marilyn Monroe
Gregory Ratoff · Barbara Bates
Walter Hampden

Produced by DARRYL F. ZANUCK
Written for the screen and
Directed by JOSEPH L. MANKIEWICZ

"There comes a time that a piano realizes that it has not written a concerto."

It's just a matter of time before Margo Channing (Bette Davis), queen of the New York stage, will be twice the age of the 20-year-old ingénues she plays. Mere mention of her new show's title, *Aged in Wood*, is enough to remind her that she's fast becoming a vintage on the verge of souring. Then, one fateful night, a starstruck girl named Eve Harrington (Anne Baxter) is invited back to Margo's dressing room and revitalizes the diva like a veritable fountain of youth. It is Eve's moving stories about having never missed a Channing performance and her lifelong enthusiasm for the theater that appeal to the leading lady and her entourage. "Back home," she gushes, "I acted out all sorts of things. Make-believe began to fill up my life more and more; it got so that I couldn't tell the real from the unreal except that the unreal seemed more real to me."

Mesmerized and inspired by Eve's naïve candor, Margo hires her on the spot to be her Girl Friday – a decision she will live to regret. For it is only well after the new secretary establishes herself as loyal, trustworthy, and irreplaceable that the actress suspects her of having a hidden agenda. Scenes of cut-throat ambition, biting sarcasm, and backstage backstabbing soon replace the initial interludes of heartfelt sincerity. Director Joseph L. Mankiewicz shows us that there truly is "no business like

JOSEPH L. MANKIEWICZ Besides being the only person ever to win both the Best Director and Best Screenplay Oscar two years in a row, Joseph L. Mankiewicz had a career with a manifold impact on the cinema. Raised in the heartland of the Pennsylvania Dutch, Mankiewicz translated text stills for the UFA silents of the 1920s. He and his older brother Herman soon headed for Hollywood, where each enjoyed a successful screenwriting career. *All About Eve* (1950) showcases some of Mankiewicz's finest work in this field; in fact, playwright Edward Albee was so taken by the piece that he reappropriated a passage from the script for *Who's Afraid of Virginia Woolf?*

Although Herman initially helped Joseph get his career off the ground, the brothers suffered from endless sibling rivalry, with Joseph immediately getting pegged by the industry as the lesser talent. Nonetheless, Herman's early prestige, which included his Oscar-winning screenplay for *Citizen Kane* (1941), was soon eclipsed by that of Joseph, who enjoyed success as a producer with films like *The Philadelphia Story* (1940), and later as a director.

Oftentimes doubling as screenwriter on his filmmaking projects, Mankiewicz made movies that spanned nearly every genre from Westerns to musical comedies. His was a cinema that relied on sharp dialogue, puns, and clever stories, with staging, camera, and set design concerns kept to a minimum. Indeed, rather than experimenting in this department, he stuck to conventions that worked, resorting to flashbacks not only in *All About Eve*, but also in *A Letter to Three Wives* (1948) and *The Barefoot Contessa* (1954). Despite this, his storytelling genius made him one of Hollywood's hottest directing commodities during the '40s and '50s. This prominence lasted throughout the '60s and '70s and enabled him to work with A-list names like Laurence Olivier, Henry Fonda, and Kirk Douglas right up until the end of his career.

A further Oscar nomination came for his direction of the period epic *Cleopatra* (1963), starring Elizabeth Taylor. Unfortunately, the film was a financial disaster due to Hollywood's insistence that he turn it into an eye-dazzling spectacle that would outshine the competing medium of television. Mankiewicz had to direct his way around budget-cramping set pieces rather than being allowed to bank on his plot-point bravado. As François Truffaut said, "The studio subjugated his role to cleaning set pieces, when all he wanted to do was tear down walls." Joseph L. Mankiewicz died of heart failure in 1993.

show business" as he shines the spotlight on a pack of beasts who'll fight to the death to secure their place in the arena: there's the imperious Margo, her devoted lover-director Bill Sampson (Gary Merrill), her friend and yes-man scriptwriter Lloyd Richards (Hugh Marlowe), the fork-tongued theater critic Addison De Witt (George Sanders), the ailing producer Max Fabian (Gregory Ratoff), and, of course, Eve – the most venomous viper of them all.

All About Eve received an astounding 14 Oscar nominations, a record held for almost 50 years until Titanic one-upped it in 1997. While both of Eve's leading ladies received a nod from the Academy, Anne Baxter comes across as strangely wooden by today's standards. Davis, however, is anything but. An electrifying powerhouse, her Margo commands center stage from start to finish, refusing

to grow old gracefully and ready to go for broke to keep her younger beau. It's an all-consuming fight she nearly loses when she throws her beloved Bill a birthday party only to spend the festivities drowning her sorrows. During an endless string of melancholy ballads at the piano, Bill asks her in jest: "Many of your guests have been wondering when they may be permitted to view the body. Where has it been laid out?" The answer wafts back at him in an inebriated haze: "It hasn't been laid out, we haven't finished with the embalming. As a matter of fact, you're looking at it. The remains of Margo Channing." One-liners like these bear the Davis trademark to such an extent that it's hard to tell if she's even acting. Furthermore, the parallels between the actress's off-screen life just prior to filming and the character she plays are astounding: Davis's career had been

2

1 Taming of the shrew: it's no use trying. Margo (Bette Davis) doesn't do Shakespeare, not even for boyfriend Bill (Gary Merrill).

2 Aged in wood but not to perfection: Eve (Anne Baxter) thinks herself the perfect understudy but Addison De Witt (George Sanders) doesn't find her act at all convincing.

3 Party pooper: the hostess with the mostess had better be having a good time or rest assured no one else will.

> ### "A basically unconvincing story with thin characters is transformed by a screenplay scintillating with savage wit and a couple of waspish performances into a movie experience to treasure." *Halliwell's Film and Video Guide*

floundering for years and Mankiewicz's film supplied her with the comeback vehicle she'd been yearning for.

It was at just about this time that Billy Wilder also dived into the milieu of aging actresses, making *Sunset Boulevard* (1950) with silent-screen legend Gloria Swanson. Yet whereas Wilder and cinematographer John F. Seitz employed the insignia of 1930s Expressionist cinema, using severe lighting design, exaggerated gesticulation, angular shots, and decadent sets, Mankiewicz and Krasner's piece is a study in aesthetic subtlety. Here, the first-rate *mise-en-scène* lies hidden beyond the floodlights, where Eve first fronts her angelic aura as she embarks on a steady climb

to the top. During her acceptance of the Sarah Siddons Award for acting, we see beyond this image of purity to the resentment it awakens in everyone around her. As a wave of applause pours over Eve, Margo and her entourage watch on with expressionless indifference, as close-ups of old hat and new blood are tellingly intercut. One action sparks the next, with dramatic arches and conflict reaching a level worthy of Mankiewicz's sophisticated script. The dialogue doesn't miss a beat as it takes subtle stabs at Hollywood while dazzling the audience with cheeky exchanges, hard-hitting monologues, and philosophic voiceover.

4 And the winner is…: the award for this year's brightest young star is being presented by a bunch of has-beens – funny that Margo didn't want to do the honors herself.

5 Constructive criticism: a theater reviewer teaches an up-and-coming actress an age old lesson – don't bite the hand that feeds you.

6 Bedtime for Bonzo: the only time Margo doesn't feel like a laughing stock is when she has Bill's reassuring voice to fall back on.

"Fasten your seatbelts – it's gonna be a bumpy night."

Film quote: Margo Channing (Bette Davis)

Equally masterful is the way Mankiewicz views Eve through a series of ever-changing perspectives, finishing up with that of the narrator, theater critic Addison De Witt. In the movie's most stinging verbal attack, De Witt unmasks Eve, now a diva in her own right, and lets the audience in on all there really is to know about the shooting star: "You're an improbable person, Eve, and so am I. We have that in common. Also a contempt for humanity, an inability to love or be loved …" With these condemning words, he also alludes to their shared homosexual predilections, which are addressed more directly in this tirade than anywhere else in the film. In light of the values of the day, the characters become all the more morally reprehensible through their sexual deviance. And the manner in which the story comes to a brief halt whenever it questions their sexuality attests to this, be it when Addison lasciviously dangles a cigarette holder from his lips or when Eve escorts a young female fan into her bedroom after sizing her up.

The film concludes this non-stop grudge match between aging diva and bright young star with both parties caught in a deadlock. When all is said and done, Mankiewicz only lets the viewer come out on top. And clearly, it is for the benefit of the audience alone that the filmmaker has lifted the curtain to demystify what goes on backstage. What we see is a sensationalized display that makes the theater seem no less insidious than the cinema. Indeed, Mankiewicz reconciles Broadway and Hollywood in this film, allowing his alter-ego Bill, the on-screen director, to remark that "wherever there's magic and make-believe and an audience – there's theater." It is only fitting that as a hybrid of screen and stage, *All About Eve* was later adapted into a Broadway show with a movie star in the leading role. In 1970, the musical *Applause* took New York by storm with Lauren Bacall filling Bette Davis's shoes. And wouldn't you know it, when Bacall left the cast in 1973, Anne Baxter, the original Eve, stepped in to take her place.

OK

RASHOMON 🏆

1950 - JAPAN - 88 MIN.

DIRECTOR
AKIRA KUROSAWA (1910–1998)

SCREENPLAY
AKIRA KUROSAWA, SHINOBU HASHIMOTO, based on the stories
Rashomon and *Yabu no naka* by RYUNOSUKE AKUTAGAWA

DIRECTOR OF PHOTOGRAPHY
KAZUO MIYAGAWA

EDITING
AKIRA KUROSAWA

MUSIC
FUMIO HAYASAKA

PRODUCTION
JINGO MINORU for DAIEI STUDIOS

STARRING
TOSHIRÔ MIFUNE (Tajomaru, the Bandit), MASAYUKI MORI (Takehiro, the Samurai),
MACHIKO KYÔ (Masako, Takehiro's Wife), TAKASHI SHIMURA (Woodcutter),
MINORU CHIAKI (Monk), KICHIJIRO UEDA (Commoner),
DAISUKE KATÔ (Policeman), FUMIKO HONMA (Medium)

ACADEMY AWARDS 1951 HONORARY
OSCAR for BEST FOREIGN LANGUAGE FILM

IFF VENICE 1951
GOLDEN LION (Akira Kurosawa)

"It's human to lie. Most of the time we can't even be honest with ourselves."

Rain, relentless and never-ending. Three men – a wood-cutter (Takashi Shimura), a Buddhist monk (Minoru Chia-ki), and a third apparently a commoner (Kichijiro Ueda) – take shelter beneath the ancient, dilapidated city gate of Rashomon. The woodcutter and the monk make allusions to a horrifying incident that has recently taken place. The third man is all ears as the first two recount the testimo-nies given at the imperial trial they were summoned to attend. But the accounts they speak of do not add up to a conclusive whole, and there's no way to paint a clear pic-ture of the crime, let alone assess who was at fault.

Only two things are certain: a samurai (Masayuki Mori) died in the woods, and his wife (Machiko Kyô) was raped by a bandit named Tajomaru (Toshirô Mifune). Every-thing else remains a mystery. Did the bandit murder the

samurai? Did his wife do it? Or did he, in fact, take his own life? We listen to four possible accounts of the events that transpired in the forest as they unfold before our eyes in flashback: first we hear the bandit's version, then the wife's, then the dead samurai's through a medium (Fumiko Honma), and finally that of the woodchopper. Each time the tale is drastically different and each version presents a different view as to who was the honorable or dishonor-able party.

Rashomon was a sensation in three respects. When the picture played at the 1951 Venice Film Festival, Western audiences suddenly realized just what sort of spectacular filmmaking could come out of Japan, until then a country whose cinema had been given little international regard. There were several moments in Japanese history during its

KAZUO MIYAGAWA The severe Expressionist lighting style of the films of German cinema's silent era inspired Kazuo Miya-gawa (1908–1999) to pursue a career in cinematography. This same enthusiasm for stark visual contrasts is what powers *Rashomon's* (1950) photography. Well before getting his foot through the studio door, Miyagawa studied the traditional Japanese black ink painting technique of "sumi-e." He started off in film as a laboratory technician and worked his way up behind the scenes as a camera assistant to become a cinematographer.

His lifelong collaboration with Akira Kurosawa marks his career's official start and finish lines: his contribution to *Rashomon* won him and the filmmaker entry into the international film circuit; 30 years later vision impairment prevented him from completing his camerawork on *Kagemusha* (1980). What lies between is an exemplary oeuvre. Early on in his career, Miyagawa began experimenting with tracking shots and cranes as a means of making his camerawork more fluid (*Rashomon's* photography attests to this). He was inspired by traditional Japanese scroll paintings to employ long, slow-moving tracking shots to reveal the action in Kenji Mizoguchi's *Ugetsu monogatari* (1953). Kon Ichikawa's *The Temple of the Golden Pavilion (Enjo*, 1958) marked his initial encounter with the then state-of-the-art wide-screen format Daieiscope, which enabled him to cinematically depict ancient Japanese painting techniques by dividing up portions of the image and "framing" them within doors, etc. For another Kurosawa collaboration, the samurai film *Yojimbo the Bodyguard (Yojimbo*, 1961), Miyagawa shot battle scenes with a telescopic lens, giving his photography a surreal veneer.

centuries of isolation from Western culture, when Japan broke open gates to the West. *Rashomon* and the acclaim it won in Venice was one such moment, and ushered in a new era for Japan as an international cinematic force.

A personal stroke of destiny was also in store for director Akira Kurosawa (*The Seven Samurai, Shichinin no samurai*, 1954), who wasn't even aware that the film had been accepted for screening at the Venice festival. And given the skepticism and lack of understanding his film endured while it was still in production, Kurosawa believed it to be anything but prize-winning material. He couldn't

"Everyone seeing the picture will immediately be struck by the beauty and grace of the photography, by the deft use of forest light and shade to achieve a variety of powerful and delicate effects." *The New York Times*

4

1 He says, she says: bandit Tajomaru (Toshirô Mifune) has his way with Masako (Machiko Kyô), the samurai's wife. Whether or not she enjoyed it is anybody's guess.

2 Stop messing with my head! Tajomaru tries cutting a temptress down to size, but leaves the scene with his tail between his legs.

3 Gateway to the imagination: during a meeting of the minds at the Rashomon pavilion, three men try to sort out the sordid events that transpired in the forest.

4 Sweet nothings: Takehiro (Masayuki Mori) is unmoved by his wife's words after watching her test them on someone first.

have been more wrong. *Rashomon* was not only present- ed with the grand prize at one of the world's three major film festivals, but it also received a special honorary Acad- emy Award for Best Foreign Language Picture.

Beyond its significance for both Japan and Kurosawa, *Rashomon* was also an audience milestone. Never before had a picture depicting this many elements of a criminal investigation been so steadfast in its refusal to offer a solu- tion. At least three of the scenarios we see – if not all of them – are false, and the film ends without actually reveal- ing to us where the grain of truth lies. The deliberately un- satisfying outcome sent audiences through the roof in 1951 and continues to do so more than 50 years later. *Rashomon* adopts the structure of a mystery, obliging the viewer time

and again to piece together what actually happened in the forest. There is no official authority to be seen or heard in the flashbacks of the witnesses' official court testimonies. They speak directly into the camera and plead not with a judge so much as with the viewer, who has, in effect, been asked to stand in as a surrogate. But the real party on trial here is mankind, and the film emerges as a parable of human arrogance and our attempts at mastering the truth – a bitterly bleak tale. It's no coincidence that the film is set in 12th-century Japan, a time of feudal war lords and wide- spread decline in political and cultural life.

The film's formal technique continues to inspire au- diences to this day. The plot fans out across three temporal and spatial planes: playing in the present at the city gate,

in the immediate past at the trial, and three days previously in the woods. The clearly defined narrative structure springs to life through the highly stylized, high contrast black-and-white photography, which captures performances that are often reminiscent of great live theater. As exotic as it is alluring, *Rashomon* is a meticulously crafted masterpiece.

HJK

"**People are incapable of being honest to themselves. They cannot talk about themselves without trying to appear better than they are. This film is like a Japanese picture scroll; when unrolled, it reveals the human ego.**"

Akira Kurosawa

5 Playing both sides: Masako protects herself by turning a tricky situation into a cock fight.

6 I saw what I saw what I saw: caught with his hands tied, Takehiro must wait at the base of a tree while his wife pleasures herself with another man.

7 Anal thermometer: bandit Tajomaru and samurai Takehiro take each other's temperature.

THE YOUNG AND THE DAMNED

LOS OLVIDADOS

1950 - MEXICO - 80 MIN.

DIRECTOR

LUIS BUÑUEL (1900–1983)

SCREENPLAY

LUIS BUÑUEL, LUIS ALCORIZA

DIRECTOR OF PHOTOGRAPHY

GABRIEL FIGUEROA

EDITING

CARLOS SAVAGE

MUSIC

RODOLFO HALFFTER, GUSTAVO PITTALUGA

PRODUCTION

OSCAR DANCIGERS, SERGIO KOGAN, JAIME A. MENASCE for ULTRAMAR FILMS

STARRING

ALFONSO MEJÍA (Pedro), ROBERTO COBO (Jaibo),
ESTELA INDA (Marta, Pedro's Mother), MIGUEL INCLÁN (Don Carmelo, the Blind Man),
ALMA DELIA FUENTES (Meche), HÉCTOR LÓPEZ PORTILLO (The Judge),
FRANCISCO JAMBRINA (The Principal), JAVIER AMÉZCUA (Julian),
JESÚS NAVARRO (Julian's Father), JORGE PÉREZ (Pelon)

IFF CANNES 1951

BEST DIRECTOR (Luis Buñuel)

Ultramar Films, S.A.

Estela INDA
Miguel INCLAN
Alfonso MEJIA
Roberto COBO
Alma Delia FUENTES

DIRECCION
Luis BUÑUEL
PRODUCCION
Oscar DANCIGERS
FOTOGRAFIA
Gabriel FIGUEROA

Los OLVIDADOS

ARGUMENTO : LUIS BUÑUEL Y LUIS ALCORIZA

"Is there no mercy for a poor blind man?"

While the kids in the gang play bullfight with a jacket for a cape and two fingers as the bull's horns, their leader Jaibo (Roberto Cobo) strolls through the streets of Mexico City. Jaibo has a downy beard, and he wears his hair in a cool quiff; he's older than the others – and meaner. He encourages the kids to rob a blind beggar and musician (Miguel Inclán), and to pelt him with rocks, and he himself deals with a "traitor" by beating him to death with a stick.

Pedro (Alfonso Mejía) is also in the gang, but he's different from Jaibo. He lives with his mother (Estela Inda), who's raising him and his sisters all on her own. But Jaibo is always in his way: in the blacksmith's forge where Pedro works, Jaibo steals a dagger. Pedro is accused of the crime and lands in a home for juvenile delinquents. When the Principal (Francisco Jambrina) sends him off to buy cigarettes, Jaibo is waiting to pocket the money. To cap it all, Jaibo makes a play for Pedro's mother, a young widow who can't give Pedro the motherly love he craves. It's a story that will end, not just in tears, but in death.

As a caption at the beginning tells us, Los Olvidados is based on events that actually took place. It's a powerful and moving film, and the premiere audience was shocked by its atmosphere of sheer hopelessness. Even today, this is a disturbing movie; the kids are sly and aggressive – and Pedro, too, takes part in their nastiest adventures. The blind beggar is the children's adversary, yet he himself is far from "good": he misuses the Indian boy who helps him, and the girl who brings him donkey's milk has to sit on his lap and suffer his lecherous attentions. These two children are the only positive characters in the entire film. Otherwise, the life we see here is solitary, poor, nasty, brutish, and short.

In 1929, the Spanish director Luis Buñuel and his collaborator Salvador Dalí had caused a scandal with the

---

GABRIEL FIGUEROA Mexican cameraman Gabriel Figueroa (1907–1997) studied painting and worked in a photo studio before starting his movie career as a stills photographer. He learned his craft as a cinematographer in Hollywood, where he worked as an assistant to *Citizen Kane* cameraman Gregg Toland. After returning to Mexico in 1935, Figueroa began his own career behind the camera. In the 1940s, he became famous through his collaboration with the director Emilio Fernández, and together they developed a cinematic aesthetic strongly influenced by the culture and natural environment of Mexico. When he began working with Luis Buñuel, a different "look" was called for. (They made a total of seven films together, including *The Exterminating Angel / El ángel exterminador*, 1962). In his autobiography, Buñuel describes an incident during the filming of *Nazarin (Nazarín,* 1959): Figueroa had prepared a beautiful shot with the strange mountain of Popocatépetl in the background, but he found it *too* beautiful, and quickly turned the camera round to frame a scene of everyday banality. Hollywood directors working in Mexico frequently employed Gabriel Figueroa. For John Ford, he filmed *Two Mules for Sister Sara* (1969); for John Huston, *The Night of the Iguana* (1964) – which earned the cameraman an Oscar nomination, and *Under the Volcano* (1984). Gabriel Figueroa died in 1997 at the age of 90. His life's work comprised more than 220 films.

1 The pledge of allegiance: as the oldest member of the pack, Jaibo (Roberto Cobo, right) uses his fist at any hint of dissent.

3 Feeling is believing: the blind Don Carmelo (Miguel Inclán, right) would rather rub a human talisman than look into the future.

5 Gang bang: Jaibo (center) has no qualms about sending his younger soldiers to their deaths.

2 Gangbusters: Pedro (Alfonso Mejía, right) looks on in disbelief as Jaibo (left) clocks an ostensible traitor.

4 My little pony – grows up to be horse-meat.

short Surrealist film *An Andalusian Dog* (*Un chien andalou*), in which a girl's eye is sliced by a razor in startling close-up. From 1946 onwards, Buñuel worked in Mexico, for Franco's fascists refused to allow him back into Spain. *Los Olvidados* marked the beginning of his international breakthrough. It's a socially critical film, and at first glance it has something in common with the works of Italian neo-realism. Yet it's much more than this; the film's uncompromising quality and its intense visual language form a direct link to Buñuel's Surrealist masterpiece.

The superb cinematography of Gabriel Figueroa creates a world of claustrophobia and palpable decay. The boys move between miserable shacks and ruined buildings. The luminous sky and the vast countryside are practically absent in this film. Pedro and his family are squashed into a one-room apartment crammed with beds, and in the darkness, their frames cast weird, barred shadows on the walls. A nightmare sequence shows Pedro's mother handing him a piece of raw flesh – which Jaibo snatches away from him. The film is populated by chickens: aimless, indolent, and apathetic, they're living symbols that reflect the situation of the human protagonists. One cockerel gazes balefully at the battered, blind beggar; another pecks away at Pedro's corpse. In a vision of death, Jaibo, by contrast, is assigned a dog as his familiar. For the grimly malevolent gang leader, a proud and powerful hound; for poor Pedro, who has at least tried to be good, a feeble, flightless bird; until the bitter end, Luis Buñuel disturbs us with his radical refusal to draw a clear line between good and evil.

HJK

"Buñuel took a then popular genre, a major force in both Hollywood and Italian Neorealism – the liberal social conscience picture – and transformed it into a brilliantly acidic vision of human desires, fears and foibles." *Time Out*

SUNSET BOULEVARD ♟♟♟

1950 - USA - 110 MIN.

DIRECTOR

BILLY WILDER (1906–2002)

SCREENPLAY

CHARLES BRACKETT,
BILLY WILDER, D. M. MARSHMAN JR.

DIRECTOR OF PHOTOGRAPHY

JOHN F. SEITZ

EDITING

ARTHUR SCHMIDT

MUSIC

FRANZ WAXMAN

PRODUCTION

CHARLES BRACKETT for PARAMOUNT PICTURES

STARRING

GLORIA SWANSON (Norma Desmond), WILLIAM HOLDEN (Joe Gillis),
ERICH VON STROHEIM (Max von Mayerling), NANCY OLSON (Betty Schaefer),
FRED CLARK (Sheldrake), LLOYD GOUGH (Morino),
JACK WEBB (Artie Green), FRANKLYN FARNUM (Undertaker),
CECIL B. DEMILLE (Himself), BUSTER KEATON (Himself)

ACADEMY AWARDS 1950

OSCARS for BEST ORIGINAL SCREENPLAY (Charles Brackett, Billy Wilder,
D. M. Marshman Jr.), BEST MUSIC (Franz Waxman),
and BEST ART DIRECTION (Hans Dreier, John Meehan, Sam Comer, Ray Moyer)

A MOST UNUSUAL STORY
SUNSET
BOULEVARD
NOT SUITABLE FOR CHILDREN
HOLLYWOOD FROM THE INSIDE
WILLIAM HOLDEN · GLORIA SWANSON · ERICH von STROHEIM
A Paramount Picture

"I am big. It's the pictures that got small."

A dead man tells all. A chance encounter with silent-screen legend Norma Desmond (Gloria Swanson) has cost screenwriter Joe Gillis (William Holden) his life. Now he bobs face down in her swimming pool like debris waiting to be fished out by the Hollywood homicide detectives. Welcome to *Sunset Boulevard*, a movie that starts off at the end of the line.

Director Billy Wilder originally staged the above sequence, undoubtedly one of the most chilling openings on film, as a dialogue among corpses at the morgue. Test audiences laughed out loud. Infuriated that moviegoers could mistake his message for black humor, Wilder returned to the drawing board until he achieved the desired result: an unlikely purgatory, where the line separating life from death has been all but erased.

And truly it is in a dimension inhabited by the "living dead" in which Joe Gillis finds himself after successfully outrunning a band of debt collectors. Desmond is in the process of burying her dead monkey – one might deem it a premonition of Gillis's own grim fate. The scene is a spectacle of distilled rage that mirrors the feelings that drove Wilder to shoot this film – hatred of the Hollywood dream factory, where anyone who wishes to survive is obliged to make an ape of himself.

The has-been star and her butler Max von Mayerling (Erich von Stroheim) have made an equally perverse

---

WILLIAM HOLDEN   The Illinois native William Franklin Beedle Jr. won instant fame for his first serious role as a young boxer in *Golden Boy* (1939). That title also provided him with a nickname that would follow him throughout his career. Incidentally, the then unseasoned 20-year-old actor would have been thrown off the set had not co-star Barbara Stanwyck seen to it that he keep his job despite a rocky start. He served his country during the Second World War, managing to secure steady acting work in modest productions upon his return.

His popularity reached unprecedented heights in 1950 when he played down-and-out screenwriter playboy Joe Gillis in *Sunset Boulevard* (1950); critics agreed that the film had Holden's Oscar-nominated performance to thank for the fact that the almost surreal story came over so convincingly on screen. Still on a winning streak with director Billy Wilder, Holden went on to star in *Stalag 17* (1953), which won him the Academy Award for Best Leading Actor; a year later the two men joined forces once more for *Sabrina* (1954), another film that attested to Holden's tremendous acting potential. But despite this, he often took on roles far beneath his caliber. Film critic Leonard Maltin cites two reasons for this: his earlier career as a contract player for Columbia and Paramount probably stunted his artistic ambitions, and later, an insatiable desire to travel won out over his interest in taking on challenging screen roles. Despite this, Holden continued to turn out further exemplary performances in films like John Sturges's *Escape from Fort Bravo* (1953), David Lean's *The Bridge on the River Kwai* (1957), and Sam Peckinpah's epic Western saga *The Wild Bunch* (1969).

His later work is in keeping with the pattern of his career: he starred in a final Wilder film *Fedora* (1978), gained another Oscar nod for his work in Sidney Lumet's *Network* (1976), and contributed to a flop or two like *Ashanti* (1979), a project he signed onto mainly so that he could shoot in Africa. Holden died on November 16, 1981, from the effects of long-term alcohol poisoning.

"It is one of those rare movies which are so full of exactness, cleverness, mastery, pleasure, and arguable and unarguable choice and judgment, that they can be talked about, almost shot for shot and line for line, for hours on end." *Sight and Sound*

dreamland of the labyrinthine villa that serves as their present surroundings. Here, the screen queen's star continues to flourish and the imagined masses fall at her feet. In her seclusion, she feverishly writes a screenplay about the nubile seductress Salomé and deludes herself that she is on the verge of a comeback performance.

Gillis couldn't have arrived at a more opportune time for all involved. Given that money is no object, the penniless screenwriter is happy to try his hand at making Desmond's incoherent manuscript halfway passable. Despite the young man's initial contempt for the aging movie star, he is reeled into her nostalgic web of glamour and allure. Only when Gillis witnesses his hostess playing cards with the appari-

tions of other silent film greats like Buster Keaton and others (all of whom have cameos as themselves) does he realize that he has become an intrinsic part of Desmond's ghostly vortex. Later, when Betty Schaefer (Nancy Olson), Gillis's secret girlfriend and co-writer employed at Paramount, makes a failed attempt at rescuing him, it becomes painfully clear that not even love can get the upper hand over Norma's will. The incident, however, sends the diva into a fit of mania, and she shoots the screenwriter dead to prevent him abandoning her, as everyone else did long ago.

David Lynch, who counts *Sunset Boulevard* among his five all-time favorite films, described it as a "street to another world." The filmmaker was particularly fascinated

1 Silent music starts to play: screenwriter Joe Gillis (William Holden) dances with death when he takes up employment with screen legend Norma Desmond (Gloria Swanson).

2 Everything's as if we never said goodbye: Norma informs Cecil B. DeMille that it's time they throw her starved fans a few crumbs.

3 Comeback vehicle: Max von Mayerling (Erich von Stroheim, far left) is Norma's one-man band. By keeping her dreams alive, he supplies the drive she needs to persevere in a world that's forgotten her.

4 Don't call us, we'll call you: Norma Desmond tries to sell her screenplay to Hollywood. But, as always, nobody wants to hear what the silent-screen diva has to say.

by the black aura that shrouds the Desmond estate, and used it as a source of inspiration in pictures like *Eraserhead* (1974/77) and *Blue Velvet* (1985). In its original incarnation, the colossal dilapidated mansion was a metaphor for early Hollywood. It recalls a bygone era when the studio system produced screen gods who spoke in a language without words.

Insular in nature, the estate is also symbolic of the human mind and its tendency to create imagined, potentially imprisoning realities. Thus *Sunset Boulevard* can also be seen as a parable about the dark side of imagination. Desmond and von Mayerling are buried alive under their own unstable vision of Shangri-La, and Joe Gillis sells out to them to avoid facing the demands of the outside world.

Ironically, he turns his back on his ideals just as things begin to take shape with Betty Schaefer and success is a mere stone's throw away. As Gillis learns the hard way, there's no return to innocence for those who lose faith in themselves.

This existential reflection about the fear of change also serves as a sharp warning to the representatives of present-day Hollywood. As the film reminds us, the machinery that ran Old Hollywood was still all-powerful in the late 1940s. We need only look at the caricature studio boss set on financial gain, who puffs away at a cigar from atop a cushy sofa, or at the screenwriters he works to the bone. The subtext of Wilder's intentional typecasting is equally significant: Erich von Stroheim, a filmmaker who

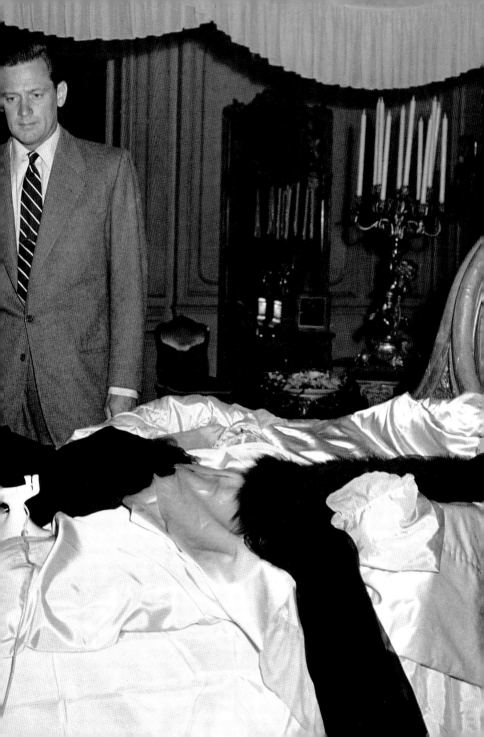

5 Alright Mr. DeMille, I am ready for my close-up: Norma finally gets the media attention she's been craving.

6 Betty droop: two screenwriters get so caught up with the villain that it ruins their own romance.

fell foul of the studios, plays a filmmaker who has been reduced to life as a butler; and silent starlet Gloria Swanson's performance reads like a ghastly self-portrait as both she and her character make a genuine attempt to reenter the spotlight that has shunned her. Their tragic fates are indicative of how the film industry is willing to treat its VIPs when they are suddenly deemed obsolete – never mind that without them studios like Paramount wouldn't have existed in the first place, as Desmond states.

Hollywood saw to it that Wilder got his just desserts for dragging the film industry through the mud. Despite being nominated for an astounding eleven Oscars, *Sunset Boulevard* was only awarded three; among them were Best Score, Best Art Direction for a black-and-white film, and Best Original Screenplay. MGM film mogul Louis B. Mayer exited a Paramount screening in an uproar, denouncing Wilder as a "bastard… who should be tarred, feathered and chased out of town." But even Mayer eventually had to concede the fact that the Dream Factory's golden age was a thing of the past – and that the television era was upon him.

SH

A STREETCAR NAMED DESIRE ♀♀♀♀

1951 - USA - 125 MIN.

DIRECTOR

ELIA KAZAN (1909–2003)

SCREENPLAY

OSCAR SAUL, TENNESSEE WILLIAMS,
based on Williams's play of the same name

DIRECTOR OF PHOTOGRAPHY

HARRY STRADLING SR.

EDITING

DAVID WEISBART

MUSIC

ALEX NORTH

PRODUCTION

CHARLES K. FELDMAN for CHARLES K. FELDMAN GROUP, WARNER BROS.

STARRING

VIVIEN LEIGH (Blanche DuBois), MARLON BRANDO (Stanley Kowalski),
KIM HUNTER (Stella Kowalski), KARL MALDEN (Harold "Mitch" Mitchell),
RUDY BOND (Steve Hubbell), NICK DENNIS (Pablo Gonzales),
PEG HILLIAS (Eunice Hubbell), WRIGHT KING (Cashier),
RICHARD GARRICK (Doctor), EDNA THOMAS (Mexican woman)

ACADEMY AWARDS 1951

OSCARS for BEST ACTRESS (Vivien Leigh), BEST SUPPORTING ACTRESS (Kim Hunter),
BEST SUPPORTING ACTOR (Karl Malden), and BEST ART DIRECTION
(Richard Day, George James Hopkins)

IFF CANNES 1951

BEST ACTRESS (Vivien Leigh)

WINNER OF
5
ACADEMY
AWARDS!

"A Streetcar
Named Desire"

AN ELIA KAZAN PRODUCTION · PRODUCED BY CHARLES K. FELDMAN

STARRING
VIVIEN LEIGH AND MARLON BRANDO

KIM HUNTER · KARL MALDEN   SCREEN PLAY BY TENNESSEE WILLIAMS

FROM THE PULITZER PRIZE AND CRITICS AWARD PLAY

BASED UPON THE ORIGINAL PLAY "A STREETCAR NAMED DESIRE"
BY TENNESSEE WILLIAMS
AS PRESENTED ON THE STAGE BY IRENE MAYER SELZNICK   DIRECTED BY ELIA KAZAN   DISTRIBUTED BY 20th CENTURY-FOX

"Hey, Stella!"

Film adaptations of stage plays have a bad reputation. Only one of them can be said to have given a new direction to the performing arts of the 20th century, including both theater and film: Elia Kazan's *A Streetcar Named Desire*, based on Tennessee Williams's play of the same name.

A blood-chilling yell pierces the sultry heat of a New Orleans summer night: "Hey, StellAAAH!" Stanley Kowalski (Marlon Brando) doesn't have to wait for long. Stella (Kim Hunter) will come into his strong arms, magically drawn by an animal virility that makes her forget all the times he hurt her. Another woman will be shipwrecked by this merciless love: Stella's sister Blanche DuBois (Vivien Leigh), who is driven mad by Stanley's coarse attacks. She's an aging Southern belle, and she hates the impoverished milieu of the Kowalskis. Blanche has lied to herself all her life, for she's convinced she deserves better. Stanley will drum the truth into her, expose her bitter past and (it is implied) ruin her life by raping her.

ELIA KAZAN When Elia Kazan (1909–2003) picked up his Lifetime Achievement Oscar in 1999, many guests and members of the Academy remained seated in protest. His statement to the House Un-American Activities Commission had made him the bad boy of Hollywood. Kazan, a former member of the Communist Party, had collaborated with McCarthy's witchhunters, and he had never publicly expressed any regret about it. In fact, the role of the outsider seemed to suit him: Elia Kazan, the son of Greek-Anatolian immigrants, was a socially critical realist whose films repeatedly examine the contradictions at the heart of American society.

In *Gentleman's Agreement* (1947), for example, he had already criticized the pervasive, latent anti-Semitism in the United States. But in the '50s, he found his best "material" in the plays of Tennessee Williams, a writer whose work excited huge controversy at the time. With *A Streetcar Named Desire* (1951) and *Baby Doll* (1956), Kazan started a veritable boom in Williams adaptations for the cinema. Kazan himself came from the theater. In 1947, he and Lee Strasberg had opened the famous Actors Studio together. The actors he discovered there included Marlon Brando and James Dean, both of whom played a huge role in Kazan's rise to fame. For *On the Waterfront* (1954), both he and Brando won an Oscar. Kazan's Steinbeck adaptation *East of Eden* (1955) marked his final departure from the visual and dramaturgical constraints of the theater. Though the '50s were Elia Kazan's great decade, he did make some remarkable films in later years, including *Splendor in the Grass* (1961), *America, America* (1963), and *The Arrangement* (1969).

2

"Brando's performance as Stanley is one of those rare screen legends that are all they're cracked up to be: poetic, fearsome, so deeply felt you can barely take it in. In the hands of other actors, Stanley is like some nightmare feminist critique of maleness: brutish and infantile. Brando is brutish, infantile and full of a pain he can hardly comprehend or express. The monster suffers like a man." *The Washington Post*

1 Treasure trove: Stanley Kowalski (Marlon Brando) holds the keys to the heart of Stella (Kim Hunter).

2 Wife beater: only Blanche (Vivien Leigh) is immune to Stanley's animal magnetism.

3 Fox and sable: Brando and Leigh are contradictory breeds – the former is Method, the latter Old Hollywood.

This is more than a battle of the sexes, though; it's a struggle between two fundamentally different styles of acting. The Method actor Brando, fresh from Lee Strasberg's Actors Studio, *is* Kowalski, with body and soul. This was the role that made him famous. In his proletarian directness, he seems wholly unaware of the camera's presence. He talks with his mouth full, he fills the entire room with his physical presence, and while he's at it, he makes the t-shirt fashionable. The tattered army-surplus item on his muscular torso was probably a major factor in the film's success.

What's meant by the "Method" is a little harder to say; classical actors suspected the Method was no more and no less than Marlon Brando himself. All we can say with any certainty is that Vivien Leigh's performance as Blanche is the opposite of Method acting; yet her nervous theatricality is the perfect embodiment of a woman who lives in a dream world and cannot survive reality. And there's something truly tragic in the casting of this former screen goddess as poor Blanche DuBois: 12 years after *Gone With the Wind* (1939), Scarlett O'Hara is finally blown away. By 1951, Old Hollywood was on its way out.

4 The end of the line: Stanley's friend Mitch (Karl Malden) backs Blanche into a corner and sees through her shadow and fog allure. Director Elia Kazan said that Method actor Malden was his brightest protégé.

5 For whom the "belle" tolls: Stanley pushes Stella to the limit and forces her to decide between him and her sister.

For director Elia Kazan, *Streetcar* also signified a transition to a new creative phase, as he moved away from the theater and into the movies. When one compares it to his later Tennessee Williams adaptations (*Cat on a Hot Tin Roof*, 1958, and *Sweet Bird of Youth*, 1962), *Streetcar* still looks very much like the work of a man of the theater. Most of his actors had already been acclaimed for their performances in his Broadway production of the play, while the English Vivien Leigh had played Blanche in London. Moreover, the film itself is basically theatrical in conception: Kazan keeps his focus narrow and concentrated, and evokes a claustrophobic atmosphere by means of short panning shots. Yet he does use cinematic means to create the impression of unreality so expressive of Blanche's worldview, making effective use of indirect light filtered through lanterns and the eerie shadows cast by ceiling fans. In New Orleans, the night belongs to the dead, and only the nocturnal loudmouth Stanley Kowalski is capable of bringing it to life. Brando's performance has often been copied, but never matched. At the time, many critics felt his acting was exaggerated, overstated, and simply *too much*. This was not just because Brando's style was so radical and unfamiliar. In fact, censorship had a lot to do with it, as was made clear by a reconstructed version of the movie released in 1992. Just a few brief sequences had been cut, but the effect was to rob the "animal" Stanley of his full humanity, while Stella's wild desire was carefully tamed for a '50s audience. The difference between the two versions is enormous. In 1951, apparently, the world was not yet ready for the full spectrum of human emotions. Reality would have to wait just a little bit longer.

PB

"The haunting performance of England's great Vivien Leigh in the heartbreaking role of the deteriorating Southern belle, and the mesmerizing moods Mr. Kazan has wreathed make this picture as fine, if not finer, than the play. Inner torments are seldom projected with such sensitivity and clarity on the screen." *The New York Times*

THE AFRICAN QUEEN 🏆

1951 - USA / GREAT BRITAIN - 105 MIN.

DIRECTOR

JOHN HUSTON (1906–1987)

SCREENPLAY

JAMES AGEE, JOHN HUSTON,
based on the novel of the same name by CECIL SCOTT FORESTER

DIRECTOR OF PHOTOGRAPHY

JACK CARDIFF

EDITING

RALPH KEMPLEN

MUSIC

ALLAN GRAY

PRODUCTION

SAM SPIEGEL for ROMULUS FILMS LTD., HORIZON PICTURES

STARRING

HUMPHREY BOGART (Charlie Allnut), KATHARINE HEPBURN (Rose Sayer),
ROBERT MORLEY (Samuel Sayer), PETER BULL (Captain of the *Louisa*),
THEODORE BIKEL (First Officer), WALTER GOTELL (Second Officer),
PETER SWANWICK (First Officer of the *Shona*), RICHARD MARNER (Second Officer of the *Shona*),
GERALD ONN (Petty Officer)

ACADEMY AWARDS 1951

OSCAR for BEST ACTOR (Humphrey Bogart)

"Could you make a torpedo, Mr. Allnut?"

Had things gone according to plan, this film as we know it today would have never been made at all. MGM had secured the rights to C. S. Forester's novel (which was based on a true story) 13 years before successfully producing it, having hoped for a screen adaptation starring Bette Davis and David Niven. But the pampered Miss Davis shuddered at the thought of an on-location shoot, especially in the most remote corner of the big bad African continent. She was a studio girl and that was that. The project was pushed back indefinitely on the MGM production schedule and nothing came of it until film noir great John Huston got hold of the script. Immediately clear about who would fit the bill for the unshaven, ornery, and usually sauced riverboat captain Charlie Allnut, Huston contacted old pal Humphrey Bogart. "The hero is a common Joe," the director told him, "and you're the commonest Joe this town's got."

A happy marriage was born. Bogey threw everything he had into the role, endowing it with dramatic virtuosity and sardonic wit, and walked away from the film with a much overdue Oscar – the only one of his entire career. Acting at his side was the equally brilliant Katharine Hepburn as the matronly Methodist missionary Rose Sayer. Credit must also be given to master of ceremonies John Huston, the man who dreamed up the best mismatched pairing in the history of romantic adventure. His vision proved to be box-office gold, and today the AFI rates The African Queen as the 17th best film of all time.

The story begins with Rose Sayer, a progressive-thinking, God-fearing Englishwoman who in 1914 finds

HUMPHREY BOGART Much has been written about New York City native Humphrey Bogart (born January 23, 1899, despite dissenting opinion). As time goes by, philosophies continue to spring up that try to pinpoint just what it was about his presence that set him apart. John Huston once made an indirect attempt at solving the mystery, remarking facetiously about his good friend and colleague that "the trouble with Bogart is he thinks he's Bogart." Having directed him in three films, Huston himself had a hand in creating the Bogey myth. When film noir was born with The Maltese Falcon in 1941, Bogart became the genre's foremost icon. From then on the name Bogart became synonymous with the image of detective Sam Spade's snugly belted trench coat and downward tilted fedora; and Sam Spade likewise was forever associated with Bogey's gestures, with hands that dug deep into his coat pockets and a mouth that turned up at one side as a snow-white Chesterfield cigarette dangled from his lips. Although portraying a rawer and more differentiated character in the 1948 adaptation of Traven's novel The Treasure of the Sierra Madre, Bogey's performance remained true to the image he'd created. In The African Queen (1951) indomitable humor added body to his rough-around-the-edges, no-nonsense persona. Different from the quick-quipped brand of humor he'd mastered in Michael Curtiz's Casablanca (1942), Allnut's rye humor mirrored Bogart's rather cynical take on himself. The actor summed up his approach to the character saying "I've got an image of someone in my mind who drove me to drink and cost me many a sleepless night." According to The African Queen's screenwriter James Agee, the secret to his success lay in his ability to "be always the same, and yet surprise us every time. He's naturally charming and doesn't waste any of his energy by trying to act … His facial expression never changes, whether he's looking at the woman he loves, the corpse of someone he killed, or an ordinary bug."

The bottom line is that Bogart was Bogart because he was an original. He lost his life to cancer in 1957. Although it wasn't as spectacular a departure as that of James Dean or Marilyn Monroe, it was just as jolting, if only because it was so premature.

"Well I ain't sorry for you no more, ya crazy, psalm-singing, skinny old maid!" *Film quote: Charlie Allnut (Humphrey Bogart)*

1 Oscar for a grouch: from eternal hangovers to devoted husband, the role of boatsman Charlie Allnut supplied Humphrey Bogart with his sole Academy Award.

2 Mission impossible: Rose Sayer (Katharine Hepburn) plays the organ, while her brother Samuel (Robert Morley) spreads the word of the Lord in the African jungle.

3 River regalia: the African Queen may not look like much, but she gives it her all against those nasty Germans.

4 Virgin forest deflowered: soldiers overrun a new population of imperial subjects in a war that knows no boundaries.

5 Prohibitionist: an old maid does a little housekeeping in an effort to keep Charlie sober.

her calling in German East Africa after imperialist troops kill her beloved brother (Robert Morley) and destroy a Methodist mission. She feels compelled to confront the evildoers face to face. Her only means of doing so is to board a rickety mail and transport steamboat called the *African Queen* and journey down the Ulanga River with the vessel's Canadian skipper, Charlie Allnut.

Surrounded by the enemy and somewhat distrustful of each other, Charlie and Rose seem to be headed on a one-way trip up the creek without a paddle. With the chips stacked against them, they flee downstream through a torrential rainstorm and past a German fort. The pair eventually arrive on a large lake patrolled by a German gunboat, which they intend to sink with two homemade torpedoes.

While acclimatizing to the endless obstacles of bush life, Rose gradually softens to Allnut's unconventional charm. About halfway into their odyssey, she blossoms with the gossamers of love, eclipsing the colors of even

the most tropical flowers Africa has to offer. Likewise, Allnut abandons the bottle at Rose's stern request and reforms himself from an incorrigible drifter into a courageous and responsible human being. Although Allnut can hardly believe it himself, he and Rose become a couple.

In terms of story line and acting styles, Katharine Hepburn and Humphrey Bogart complement each other perfectly. Both the actors themselves and the characters they portray represent opposing views on life that are drawn together over time. Huston gave the actors total freedom in developing the character dynamics as they saw fit, allowing for the relationship to veer into comic waters. The result was a love story that is neither forced nor far-fetched. The unique on-screen chemistry gave rise to one of the most beautiful and endearing romances ever to come out of Hollywood. In the original script the protagonists were to meet with an untimely demise; but the ending was changed to better suit the dramatic arc born out of the acting as well as to preserve

"Bogart ... does the best acting of his career as the badgered rumpot who becomes a man and a lover against his will. Katharine Hepburn is excellent as the gaunt, freckled, fanatic spinster. Their contrasting personalities fill the film with good scenes, beginning with Bogart's tea-table agony as the indelicate rumbling of his stomach keeps interrupting missionary Robert Morley's chitchat about dear old England." *Time Magazine*

6 Method to his madness: director John Huston pushed his leading actors to their limits. Particular demands were made of Bogart, who had to swim in crocodile-infested waters.

7 Bushwhackers: by the film's end, Charlie and Rose have ripped through the convictions that once confined them. At long last, their travels through the swamp are steered by common goals.

the dignity of Charlie and Rosie's love. Had they died in the jungle, the film's humor and the carefree nature of their affair would have perished along with them.

Instead, the characters succeed in the impossible. They triumph over the river and send the Germans packing. It is a metaphor for the cinema's own aptitude for having illusion emerge victorious over reality. The implicit message is that courage and love conquer all – no matter what the odds. The audience feels the power of this mystical princi-

ple in the exotic imagery of the river wild, which serves throughout the picture as a living mirror of Charlie and Rose's feelings for one another. And like any good odyssey, this heroic quest meets love story is actually an allegory for life itself. One can only imagine what sort of monsters might have inhabited the jungle had Bette Davis been a sun worshipper or nature lover and adhered to the terms of the MGM contract she so nonchalantly signed.   SR

HIGH NOON

1952 - USA - 85 MIN.

DIRECTOR

FRED ZINNEMANN (1907–1997)

SCREENPLAY

CARL FOREMAN, based on the short story
The Tin Star by JOHN W. CUNNINGHAM

DIRECTOR OF PHOTOGRAPHY

FLOYD CROSBY

EDITING

ELMO WILLIAMS, HARRY W. GERSTAD

MUSIC

DIMITRI TIOMKIN

PRODUCTION

STANLEY KRAMER
for STANLEY KRAMER PRODUCTIONS

STARRING

GARY COOPER (Marshal Will Kane), GRACE KELLY (Amy Kane),
THOMAS MITCHELL (Mayor Henderson), KATY JURADO (Helen Ramirez),
LLOYD BRIDGES (Harvey Pell), IAN MACDONALD (Frank Miller),
LEE VAN CLEEF (Jack Colby), LON CHANEY JR. (Martin Howe),
OTTO KRUGER (Judge Mettrick), JACK ELAM (Charlie)

ACADEMY AWARDS 1952

OSCARS for BEST ACTOR (Gary Cooper), BEST EDITING (Elmo Williams, Harry W. Gerstad),
BEST MUSIC (Dimitri Tiomkin), BEST SONG: “Do Not Forsake Me, Oh My Darlin’”
(Music: Dimitri Tiomkin; Lyrics: Ned Washington)

"A man's gotta do what a man's gotta do."

By 1880, the Wild West was taking it easy. Particularly on Sundays. But today is an exception: between 10:34 a.m. and 12:15 p.m., the life of Will Kane (Gary Cooper), Hadleyville's resident marshal, will be turned on its head. Just moments after marrying Amy Foster (actress Grace Kelly was incidentally 30 years younger than her on-screen husband Gary Cooper) and ending a career in law enforcement, he gets word that murderer Frank Miller (Ian MacDonald) is coming to town and decides to hold onto his badge just a bit longer. Miller, eager to settle a score with Kane, is scheduled to arrive on the noon train, and the outlaw's three old cohorts are already waiting at the station.

Kane's initial impulse is to leave with Amy, but having "never run away from anybody" he soon makes his way back to Hadleyville to face the bandit. He seeks out reinforcements, but the only men willing to help him are a half-pint, a half-ass, and a guy who's half-blind. And even they are prepared to ditch him. With no one to rely on but himself, Kane drafts a will, heads out to Main Street, and waits for the four outlaws to show up. The confrontation gets underway from behind the building, with Kane laying two of the posse to rest. Amy does away with a third, coming to her husband's aid just in the nick of time. She, in turn, is taken hostage by Miller, who is soon eating lead at Kane's hand. Peace is restored, and the town denizens

appear from their homes with a sigh of relief. Too little, too late; for Kane flings his badge to the ground and is off with Amy to venture into the proverbial sunset.

Within its first six minutes, *High Noon* hits just about every Western convention in the Hollywood bible. "Do Not Forsake Me, Oh My Darlin'", the title song performed by country music's Tex Ritter, establishes a link between Hadleyville's opposing forces as Miller's cronies mosey through town toward the train station, while Will Kane and his Quaker bride say "I do." The wedding and the marshal's shedding of his star take place with the audience fully aware that Will Kane has another law enforcement challenge lying in store. When he receives word of Miller's return, the newly retired Kane decides to stick it out one last time. 'Cause as the old saying goes, "A man's gotta do what a man's gotta do."

Shooting on the project began in 1951, coinciding with gung-ho efforts to combat sedition during the Cold War. Communist witch-hunter Republican Senator Joseph McCarthy and the House Un-American Activities Committee were smearing the dossiers of public figures who had anything resembling a pink past. And the Committee's efforts weren't lost on *High Noon*. Screenwriter Carl Foreman was called to disclose names, but refused to testify. His name was promptly blacklisted creating tension and discord on the project. Producer Stanley Kramer and leading

GARY COOPER Even those born well after Gary Cooper's relatively early death still readily recognize the name and the face of this legendary actor. An American film critic once dubbed Coop's angular face "a map of America," and Jean-Luc Godard viewed it as a timeless "geological artifact." Born in Montana, Cooper got his start in film around 1925, working as a stuntman in Hollywood Westerns. His rise to fame got underway in 1929, when he played the title role in *The Virginian*, a Western about life on a frontier devoid of judges and jail cells – and the Easterner who tried to change it all. In 1937, *The New York Times* reported Cooper to be the highest-paid American actor. He enjoyed a sterling career that included collaborations with Paramount's brightest directors and the industry's sultriest leading ladies, including Marlene Dietrich, Jean Arthur, and Claudette Colbert. Often playing characters in uniform, be it in military or Western garb, Cooper became the quintessential image of bygone America and traditional values. In 1947, he testified in front of the House Un-American Activities Committee, although he didn't speak out against any of his associates. He was awarded an Oscar for lifetime achievement in February 1961, which James Stewart accepted on behalf of the critically ill actor. Cooper lost his battle with cancer in Beverly Hills in May of that year.

1 Star couple: Amy Foster (Grace Kelly) and Marshal Will Kane (Gary Cooper) are forced to put love on hold when outlaw Frank Miller returns to town.

2 Model citizens: propriety gets a foothold in the West when Amy and Will tie the knot. No-one seemed to object to the fact that Grace Kelly was 30 years Cooper's junior.

3 Veto power: even the mayor (Thomas Mitchell) refuses to support the marshal's cause.

"Loaded with interest and suspense, *High Noon* is a Western to challenge *Stagecoach* for the all-time championship." *The New York Times*

actor Gary Cooper severed all ties to Foreman, whereas director Fred Zinnemann stood by him. Broader opposition formed throughout Hollywood when John Wayne organized a movement against the picture. As the president of the Motion Picture Alliance for the Preservation of American Ideals, he and others banded together against Foreman. A point of note: Wayne later signed onto Howard Hawks's *Rio Bravo* (1959), still referred to by Western buffs as the "anti-*High Noon* movie."

High Noon enjoys the distinction of being a classic Western with a message that transcends the story line. Political and moral yardsticks have inspired a wide range of critical interpretations. There's no overlooking the traditional debate of integrity, conscience, commitment, and duty pitted against opportunism, self-interest, easy outs, and cowardice. Some might go so far as to say that the film casts a critical eye on democracy, at least the form it has taken in the United States. Also striking is that Zinnemann's lifelong motto can be readily applied to *High Noon*'s under-lying philosophy: a man's character is his destiny. It was an endeavor steered by individualists, each of whom was a master in his own right: producer Stanley Kramer, Fred Zinnemann, screenwriter Carl Foreman, cinematographer Floyd Crosby (1931 Oscar recipient for Friedrich Wilhelm Murnau's *Taboo [Tabu]*), composer Dimitri Tiomkin, and editors Elmo Williams and Harry W. Gerstad. Sadly, the col-laborative efforts of these men came to a halt in the early 1950s; but each of them was instrumental in contributing to *High Noon*'s success. Still, the actors were the ones to thank for an enthusiastic audience. A stunningly silver Gary Cooper, aged 50, plays the stoic Will Kane, a former hero of the Wild West ready to reassume his duty for good

measure. He is beautifully countered by 21-year-old Grace Kelly as Amy Kane, the character that propelled Kelly on a lightning-speed career, however short-lived it was; a star-studded supporting cast with players like Thomas Mitchell as the mayor, Lloyd Bridges as the deputy, and Katy Jurado as Kane's former love gave the film its finishing touches. All of their roles economically serve the progression of the story; there is little hint of a private life beyond what we see, and no tinge of comic relief. Indeed, the film is earnest to the point of being bone dry – often a cinematic liability, but not here. Severe and laconic in style and narrative, its 100 minutes of action are compressed into an actual 85 minutes of celluloid. The magic of this documentary feeling and the acting talents of the cast gave *High Noon* its status

3

4 A woman's gotta do what a woman's gotta do: when this Quaker must decide between her life and her principles, she momentarily forgets what the Good Book says.

5 Death trap: Westerns are studies in masculinity and willpower; the first guy to flinch gets to push up the lilies.

"A man's character is his destiny." *Fred Zinnemann*

as a seminal Western. Kane is not a lonesome dove, he's socially isolated. His manner isn't cool, it's cautious and fear-ridden. He's on the verge of tears as he makes out his will. This aside, he's preyed upon and compelled to fight dirty for survival with all he's got.

Finally, mention must also be made of the breath-taking photography. Director and cameraman wanted the

film to have the aesthetic of a news broadcast. The coarse grain of the black-and-white imagery is set off by Dimitri Tiomkin's marvelous score; it doesn't push the story forward per se, but rather layers the film with a new rhythm altogether, making for a gripping viewing experience more than 50 years strong.

RV

SOLDIER OF LOVE/FANFAN THE TULIP

FANFAN LA TULIPE

1952 - FRANCE / ITALY - 105 MIN.

DIRECTOR

CHRISTIAN-JAQUE (1904–1994)

SCREENPLAY

HENRI JEANSON, RENÉ WHEELER, RENÉ FALLET, CHRISTIAN-JAQUE

DIRECTOR OF PHOTOGRAPHY

CHRISTIAN MATRAS

EDITING

JACQUES DESAGNEAUX

MUSIC

MAURICE THIRIET, GEORGES VAN PARYS

PRODUCTION

ALEXANDRE MNOUCHKINE for AMATO PRODUZIONE,
FILMSONOR S.A., LES FILMS ARIANE

STARRING

GÉRARD PHILIPE (Fanfan la Tulipe), GINA LOLLOBRIGIDA (Adeline),
MARCEL HERRAND (Ludwig XV), OLIVIER HUSSENOT (Tranche-Montagne),
NERIO BERNARDI (La Franchise), GENEVIÈVE PAGE (Marquise de Pompadour),
SYLVIE PELAYO (Henriette), NOËL ROQUEVERT (Fier-à-Bras),
JEAN-MARC TENNBERG (Lebel), HENRI ROLLAN (Marschall d'Estrees),
JEAN DEBUCOURT (Narrator, Original version), HIRAM SHERMAN (Narrator, English version)

IFF CANNES 1952

BEST DIRECTOR (Christian-Jaque)

IFF BERLIN 1952

SILVER BEAR (Christian-Jaque)

"Henriette, love me, quick!"

Why would a carefree young buck like Fanfan la Tulipe (Gérard Philipe) decide to join the army of Louis XV? Because the beautiful gypsy Adeline (Gina Lollobrigida) has predicted he will win the hand of the King's daughter. Things seem to be going to plan: on the way to join his regiment, Fanfan saves Princess Henriette (Sylvie Pelayo) and Madame Pompadour (Geneviève Page) from a gang of fearsome highwaymen. Adeline, it turns out, is a trickster, the daughter of a recruiting sergeant, but Fanfan never loses faith in her prophecy. He deserts from the army and sneaks into Henriette's bedchamber at night, where he is caught and sentenced to death. Adeline manages to wrangle a pardon for him, but when the King (Marcel Herrand) demands repayment in kind from the dark-eyed beauty, Fanfan realizes it's her he's really in love with. The King kidnaps Adeline, and in attempting to free her, Fanfan causes so much confusion behind the enemy's lines that they end up surrendering. In the meantime, the King has adopted Adeline ... and he's so grateful to Fanfan that he offers him her hand in marriage. Adeline's prophecy comes true at last.

Fanfan la Tulipe has a firm place in the hearts of French cinema-lovers. Like d'Artagnan and Cartouche, he was the hero of countless playground battles; every French boy wanted to be like Fanfan and free his own personal Adeline from the hands of the villains. Almost seven million people saw this movie, and it's also been shown innumerable times on TV. Its success was guaranteed by the presence of the young Gérard Philipe, who dances through the film with irresistible charm. In the cloak-and-dagger genre, his Fanfan represents a kind of counter-model to Douglas Fairbanks and Robin Hood: slower on the draw but faster with the mouth, and quite happy to indulge in a little philosophical repartee between two amorous rendezvous.

GÉRARD PHILIPE   He was one of the most popular actors in Europe, a legend in his own lifetime; and to many, he was the ideal romantic lover and man of action.

After acting lessons in Paris and years with traveling theaters in provincial France, Gérard Philipe had his first major movie role as Prince Myshkin in an adaptation of Dostoevsky's *The Idiot (L'Idiot,* 1946). Unhappy characters seemed to suit him. In Claude Autant-Lara's *Devil in the Flesh (Le Diable au corps,* 1946), his older mistress dies during childbirth. In Christian-Jaque's *The Charterhouse of Parma (La Chartreuse de Parme / La certosa di Parma,* 1947/48), he was sentenced to 20 years imprisonment in a tower.

The high points of his career were his appearances in *Fanfan the Tulip (Fanfan la Tulipe,* 1952) and in René Clair's comedy *Beauties of the Night (Les Belles de nuit / Le belle della notte,* 1952), both with Gina Lollobrigida. In 1955, he was named best French actor for his performance as a notorious heartbreaker in René Clément's *Knave of Hearts (Monsieur Ripois,* 1954). In 1956, he fulfilled a lifelong ambition by directing *Till Eulenspiegel / Bold Adventure (Les Aventures de Till L'Espiègle,* 1956), in co-production with the DEFA studios in East Germany. But although Philipe himself played the legendary joker, the film was not a success. In 1959, Roger Vadim made a spectacular adaptation of Laclos's *Dangerous Liaisons (Les Liaisons dangereuses / Relazioni pericolose),* in which Philipe starred alongside Jeanne Moreau. By the time it reached the cinemas, Gérard Philipe was dead: The "darling of the gods" had succumbed to cancer of the liver at the age of 36.

1 Prisoners of love: if Adeline (Gina Lollobrigida) can't spring "Fanfan the Tulip" (Gérard Philipe) from prison at least she can be close to him.

2 Children of the corn: the utterly charming Gérard Philipe won the hearts of audiences worldwide. The utterly buxom Gina Lollobrigida made a similar impact.

3 Kink: whisper sweet nothings in her ear and she's all yours.

4 Panty raid: night after night, Fanfan and Tranche-Montagne storm the most treasured parts of the castle.

5 Hi-ho, Silver! Tranche-Montagne (Olivier Hussenot) follows Fanfan places his shadow has yet to go.

"The perils of war and the perils of love!"

Film quote: Narrator

In another break with the conventions of the genre, the elegant hero is not an aristocrat (nor even an aristocrat in disguise). Fanfan — a mythical, swashbuckling figure with roots in the 18th century — is a soldier of love and by conviction, he's nobody's lackey and has no respect for authority. To him, there's no difference between a simple country girl and a pampered princess. If he can meet the former in the hayloft, he's happy to take a shortcut through the chimney for the latter. As it turns out, though, the princess wasn't worth getting his clothes sooty for.

Love and war were the 18th century's favorite occupations. Though anyone was free to join in, not every-one could take part on equal terms. *Fanfan the Tulip* is also an amusing satire on militarism and the aristocracy. King Louis XV designs his battles on the drawing board and calculates, with visible pleasure, the number of corpses to be expected. Yet his power doesn't reach as far as Adeline, who slaps his face when he tries to get fresh with her. Fanfan's greatest enemy, the sly and ugly Sergeant Fier-à-Bras (Noël Roquevert), is his favorite victim. He too has his greedy eye on Adeline — and naturally, he loses out against the charismatic ladies' man.

Fanfan the Tulip is a flawless costume drama — and it's tempting to describe "Miss Italia" Gina Lollobrigida as

the film's most fetching special effect. Her first French co-production is a splendid panorama of the Rococo Age, an epoch that will forever be associated with bursting bodices and flying skirts. Yet the diva-to-be contributed more than stunning looks to this intelligent mixture of adventure, comedy, and romance. This was the third film version of the Fanfan saga, and it's still the best. A decade later, Christian-Jaque, at that time one of the most successful directors in the commercial French cinema, did attempt to plagiarize himself, but *La Tulipe noire* (1963) never matched the success of its forerunner. In 2003, a remake of *Fanfan la Tulipe*, starring Vincent Pérez and Penélope Cruz, was the opening film at the Cannes Festival, where the original had triumphed decades previously. It was an utter embarrassment. The black-and-white 1953 version has now been re-released in a surprisingly successful colored version.

PB

THE WAGES OF FEAR

LE SALAIRE DE LA PEUR

1953 - FRANCE / ITALY - 156 MIN.

DIRECTOR

HENRI-GEORGES CLOUZOT (1907–1977)

SCREENPLAY

HENRI-GEORGES CLOUZOT,
JÉRÔME GÉRONIMI, based on the novel of the
same name by GEORGES ARNAUD

DIRECTOR OF PHOTOGRAPHY

ARMAND THIRARD

EDITING

HENRI RUST, MADELEINE GUG, ETIENNETTE MUSE

MUSIC

GEORGES AURIC

PRODUCTION

RAYMOND BORDERIE, HENRI-GEORGES CLOUZOT
for CICC, FILMSONOR S.A., FONO ROMA, VERA FILMS

STARRING

YVES MONTAND (Mario), CHARLES VANEL (Jo),
PETER VAN EYCK (Bimba), FOLCO LULLI (Luigi),
VÉRA CLOUZOT (Linda), WILLIAM TUBBS (O'Brien),
DARIO MORENO (Hernandez), JO DEST (Smerloff),
LUIS DE LIMA (Bernardo), ANTONIO CENTA (Camp Chief)

IFF CANNES 1953

GRAND PRIZE (Henri-Georges Clouzot)

IFF BERLIN 1953

GOLDEN BEAR (Henri-Georges Clouzot)

Filmsonor

UN FILM DE
H.G. CLOUZOT
YVES MONTAND
CHARLES VANEL

ROBERT
LÉVÊQUE

LE
SALAIRE DE LA PEUR

D'APRÈS LE ROMAN DE **GEORGES ARNAUD**
DIRECTEUR DE LA PHOTOGRAPHIE A . THIRARD . DÉCORS DE RENÉ RENOUX . DIRECTEUR DE PRODUCTION LOUIS WIPF

PETER VAN EYCK
CENTA · JO DEST · DARIO MORENO

CO-PRODUCTION
FILMSONOR · C.I.C.C
VERA FILM · FONO ROMA

WILLIAM TUBBS · VERA CLOUZOT ET **FOLCO LULLI**

PRODUCTEURS DÉLÉGUÉS : RAYMOND BORDERIE ET H.G. CLOUZOT

"Life is like a prison."

In the dusty heat of Las Piedras, a godforsaken hole in Venezuela, life has ground to a halt. Funerals are the liveliest things that ever happen here. While the U.S.-owned Southern Oil Company exploits the country's only real resource, lost souls from every country on earth wait in Las Piedras for a chance to escape their misery. The men are like caged animals dozing in the heat; the sun glows through Venetian blinds, casting barred shadows on faces and lives ravaged by hopelessness. For 30 merciless minutes, the film shows us images of failure, ennui, emptiness, "tristesse": in San Piedro, *rien ne va plus*. These men are shadows, living out the remainder of their time on earth.

And then one day, a glimmer of hope: an oil well has exploded, and only a second and even bigger explosion can quench the raging fires. Suddenly there's a job opportunity for men with nothing left to lose: candidates are being offered 2,000 dollars a head to drive two truckloads of highly explosive nitroglycerine across nearly 200 miles of bad roads and rocky terrain to the scene of the fire. Hundreds apply for the job.

The four lucky winners are a Corsican named Mario (Yves Montand), Jo the Parisian gangster (Charles Vanel), Luigi the Italian bricklayer (Folco Lulli), and a German called Bimba (Peter van Eyck). What follows is a cinematic *tour de*

CHARLES VANEL By the 1950s, Charles Vanel (1892–1989) was already a Grand Old Man of the French cinema. Born in Brittany, his original plans for a career at sea were dashed by his nearsightedness. So he became an actor, arriving at the movies via Sacha Guitry's traveling theater. In the '20s, he was a popular romantic leading man, as in René Clair's *La Proie du vent* (1926). In 1928, he played Napoleon in the German production *Waterloo*. In the '50s, he appeared in a number of socially critical thrillers, in which he embodied a range of shady, taciturn characters. For these compellingly understated performances, he received several acting awards. Towards the end of his working life, he delighted moviegoers and critics as the state prosecutor Varga in the silent sequences of the Mafia film *Illustrious Corpses*, a.k.a. *The Context (Cadaveri eccellenti / Cadavres exquis*, 1976). It was a return to the roots of the cinema. With over 150 films in a career spanning 70 years, Charles Vanel had stamped his name indelibly on the history of the movies.

force as the men face death at every turn, surviving narrow mountain paths, hairpin bends, potholes, falling rocks, and internal conflicts, until finally one of the trucks explodes. Only Mario and Jo are left, and time has altered the balance of power: the swaggering blowhard Jo is now a miserable wreck, while the greenhorn Mario is a man obsessed. He leaves Jo to perish, and arrives at his destination alone: but after all that, will he make it home?

Clouzot's dramaturgy is highly sophisticated, with the tension cleverly built up and characters who are precisely drawn and credibly developed. It's still miles ahead of most action movies, including William Friedkin's remake, *Sorcerer* (1977). Shot in cool black and white, *The Wages of Fear* avoids all sentimentality and thereby achieves a powerful emotional charge. While the early scenes are a compelling evocation of terminal stagnation, the rest of the film develops with the terrible precision and inevitability of death itself.

Filmed in the south of France (because it was cheaper), *The Wages of Fear* marks an early highpoint in a genre that didn't even exist until then: the road movie. Yet it's not a melancholy film, like many later examples of the genre, but a radically existentialist work. Disillusioned and defiant, lacking all hope and therefore ready to risk

"You haven't got a chance, so use it." *Neue Zürcher Zeitung*

1 Hotter than hell: the German Bimba (Peter van Eyck) enjoys one last cigarette before crossing the River Styx.

2 Next time, read the map more carefully.

3 Playing God: the Southern Oil Company claims any lives it wants.

4 Heat stroke: in the face of such unprecedented danger, even the level-headed Jo (Charles Vanel) can't keep his cool.

5 Running on empty: technology is always one step ahead of the common man.

6 A laugh among friends: Folco Lulli as the terminally ill Luigi.

everything, these four men never stand a chance; but they use that non-existent chance for all that it's worth. Mario has saved a Metro ticket for better days; when he dies, he'll be holding it in his hand. Jo has always wanted to know what's behind a certain fence in his corner of Paris, and he ultimately finds out: "There's nothing." Luigi has to change his life, or the dust in his lungs will kill him; his last job provides a quicker way out. Bimba (an officer in World War II, like his father) insists on shaving, even in the face of death; in the end, he's blown to smithereens. Mario is the only one who makes it through; and just as he

"The excitement derives entirely from the awareness of nitroglycerine and the gingerly breathless handling of it. You sit there waiting for the theater to explode."

The New York Times

7 Dropping like flies: with death at the door, it's hard for the men to show any humanity.

8 False idyll: life in Las Piedras ain't all it's cracked up to be. Anyone who

gets his hands on cash ships out before he's through counting it.

9 Take these broken wings: local hussy Linda (Véra Clouzot) sets her sights on Mario (Yves Montand), the only

man who doesn't treat her like the plague. In truth, she is the only person left who is capable of demonstrating genuine emotion.

"An existentialist road-movie avant la lettre."

The New York Times

celebrates his improbable triumph, Death comes calling to claim his dues. To the accompaniment of Strauss's "Blue Danube," we see images of the terrible journey crosscut with the victory celebrations in Las Piedras. The trucks

and the dancers are spinning to the rhythm of a Viennese waltz, and every single one of them is heading for the same final destination.

RV

THE SEVEN SAMURAI
SHICHININ NO SAMURAI
1954 - JAPAN - 206 MIN.

DIRECTOR

AKIRA KUROSAWA (1910–1998)

SCREENPLAY

SHINOBU HASHIMOTO, HIDEO OGUNI, AKIRA KUROSAWA

DIRECTOR OF PHOTOGRAPHY

ASAKAZU NAKAI

EDITING

AKIRA KUROSAWA

MUSIC

FUMIO HAYASAKA

PRODUCTION

SOJIRO MOTOKI for TOHO COMPANY LTD.

STARRING

TAKASHI SHIMURA (Kambei Shimada), TOSHIRÔ MIFUNE (Kikuchiyo),
YOSHIO INABA (Gorobei Katayama), SEIJI MIYAGUCHI (Kyuzo),
MINORU CHIAKI (Heihachi Hayashida), DAISUKE KATÔ (Shichiroji),
ISAO KIMURA (Katsushiro Okamoto), KEIKO TSUSHIMA (Shino),
KAMATARI FUJIWARA (Manzo), YOSHIO TSUCHIYA (Rikichi), BOKUZEN HIDARI (Yohei)

IFF VENICE 1954

SILVER LION (Akira Kurosawa)

THE SEVEN SAMURAI

"We won, and yet we lost."

The most celebrated of all samurai films is an epoch-making masterpiece, yet it's also a highly untypical example of this most Japanese of genres. Never before had a camera got so close to these proud warriors, and no previous filmmaker had burdened them with such a menial task as the defense of an impoverished village. So it's little wonder that Akira Kurosawa was decried in his homeland as a "Westernized" director. Such suspicions were apparently confirmed when John Sturges produced his celebrated Western remake, *The Magnificent Seven* (1960). For his own movies, Kurosawa himself had in fact borrowed from John Huston, a director he revered; and in using a modern film language understandable anywhere in the world, he had made a clean break with the strict formalism of Japanese cinema. The result, despite its enormous length, is an enthralling drama. The film builds up slowly, closely observing the complex society it depicts before climaxing in a thrilling extended battle scene. Almost in passing, Kurosawa invented the modern action movie.

This may also be the first film to show how a team of men is assembled in order to carry out a perilous mission. The poverty-stricken inhabitants of a rural village are being ruthlessly exploited by a gang of brutal bandits: year in, year out, they are robbed of the fruits of their labor as soon as the harvest is in. Clearly, they need help; but what could possibly motivate a proud samurai to risk his life for three bowls of rice a day? The village elder has a piece of advice for the desperate peasants: "Find some hungry samurai!" And here it becomes apparent that Kurosawa will submit the classical image of the samurai to a rigorous historical revision; for indeed, by the end of the 16th

THE WAY OF THE SAMURAI The samurai were members of a medieval warrior caste who gained enormous repute in the service of powerful warlords. Their code of honor, Bushido (The Way of the Warrior), demanded they show absolute loyalty and unshakeable resolve. In the 1930s, the samurai were first depicted in the Japanese cinema. After World War II, however, Bushido came to be associated with Kamikaze pilots and Japanese nationalism, and the American occupying forces instituted a temporary reduction in the number of historical dramas ("jidai-geki") produced there. With *Rashomon* (1950) and *The Seven Samurai (Shichinin no samurai*, 1954), Akira Kurosawa became a master of the genre, although his mythical dramas focused mainly on the "ronin," those vagabond samurai without a master who became such a social problem in 17th-century Japan. Kurosawa's international success led to a lively cross-pollination between the Japanese cinema and the American and European Western. Traces of the samurai can be found in *The Magnificent Seven* (1960) and *A Fistful of Dollars (Per un pugno di dollari*, 1964). Their technique of sword fighting also had a clear effect on George Lucas's Star Wars trilogy (1977, 1980, 1983); indeed, the very name of the Jedi Knights is derived from the word "jidai-geki." In the '70s, the samurai warrior transmogrified into the Yakuza, the Japanese gangster. Both figures were immortalized in countless B-movies, and these had a huge influence on Western directors. The most original appropriations of the samurai / yakuza motif are to be found in Jean-Pierre Melville's *Le Samouraï* (1967), Jim Jarmusch's *Ghost Dog: The Way of the Samurai* (1999), and Quentin Tarantino's *Kill Bill: Vol. 1 and Vol. 2* (2003, 2004).

1 Simply dashing: Takashi Shimura as the wise Kambei in one of the best action films of all time.

2 Crazy for you: Kurosawa favorite Toshirō Mifune as fearless funny-face Kikuchiyo.

3 Follow my leader: many directors picked up on Kurosawa's astonishing use of slow motion for battle and action scenes.

century, after a serious of grueling civil wars, the Japanese warrior class was clearly on its way out.

The villagers take enormous pains to find the right man, and eventually come up with Kambei (Takashi Shimura), an old warrior who has lost more battles than he's won. Five further samurai follow in their turn, each of whom has different abilities and different motivations for taking on the job. The last man to come on board is Kikuchiyo (Toshirō Mifune), a boastful drunk who joins the team without even being asked to do so.

As they prepare for battle, the tension grows inexorably. The director's modus operandi resembles that of the wise old warrior Kambei, who draws a map of the territory and starts to keep a tally sheet of the enemy's losses. In a series of calm, unhurried long shots, Kurosawa's camera measures out the village and the paths leading in and out of it. These sequences are complemented by some unforgettable close-ups – portraits of people determined to face the inevitable. As the samurai and the villagers interact and

quarrel, Kurosawa shows them in all their human strength and weakness. Here too, the film is wonderfully intelligent in the way it follows this complex, developing relationship. In the eyes of the warriors, the villagers are mean, cowardly, and distrustful; to them, in their turn, the samurai seem arrogant and capricious. The gulf between them has an almost tragic quality, and only Kikuchiyo is capable of bridging it occasionally: with his mad jokes, this trickster figure soon has the village youngsters on his side. Kikuchiyo is himself the son of a peasant, and only this enables any kind of interaction between the two castes. Yet although his humble origins make him the best man to train the villagers – who have no experience of fighting whatsoever – his lack of blue blood also means he can never become a real samurai. The role of Kikuchiyo is performed wonderfully by Toshirō Mifune, Kurosawa's favorite actor.

The battle is won, at enormous cost. Four samurai, men of the sword, have suffered the terrible indignity of being killed by guns. Kurosawa however – who was him-

"Many characters die in *The Seven Samurai*, but violence and action are not the point of the movie. It is more about duty and social roles. The samurai at the end have lost four of their seven, yet there are no complaints, because that is the samurai's lot. The villagers do not want the samurai around once the bandits are gone, because armed men are a threat to order. That is the nature of society." *Chicago Sun-Times*

self the scion of a renowned samurai family – achieves an unparalleled creative synthesis of the traditional and the modern. It's not just the exactness of the characterization that makes this film so memorable, but its sheer visual brilliance. The expressive power of the high-contrast black-and-white photography is amplified by its exceptional depth of focus; phases of quiet contemplation are perfectly balanced by dynamic, fast-cut scenes of wild squabbling and bloody battle. Kurosawa also filmed some particularly dramatic death scenes in slow motion, a technique that had a noticeable influence on Sam Peckinpah's seminal Western *The Wild Bunch* (1969).

Incidentally, Akira Kurosawa thanked John Sturges for *The Magnificent Seven* – by presenting him with a samurai sword.

PB

LA STRADA ♟

1954 - ITALY - 104 MIN.

DIRECTOR
FEDERICO FELLINI (1920–1993)

SCREENPLAY
TULLIO PINELLI, FEDERICO FELLINI, ENNIO FLAIANO

DIRECTOR OF PHOTOGRAPHY
OTELLO MARTELLI

EDITING
LEO CATOZZO

MUSIC
NINO ROTA

PRODUCTION
DINO DE LAURENTIIS, CARLO PONTI for
PONTI-DE LAURENTIIS CINEMATOGRAFICA

STARRING
GIULIETTA MASINA (Gelsomina), ANTHONY QUINN (Zampanò),
RICHARD BASEHART (Matto), MARCELLA ROVERE (Widow),
LIVIA VENTURINI (Nun), ALDO SILVANI (Colombiani)

ACADEMY AWARDS 1956
OSCAR for BEST FOREIGN FILM

IFF VENICE 1954
SILVER LION (Federico Fellini)

"Zampanò is here!"

When the decision was announced, the audience went crazy. One set of fans booed the other lot, and the whole thing culminated in a punch-up. Luchino Visconti's *Senso* (1954) had come away empty-handed, and Federico Fellini's *La strada* had won the Silver Lion. In the mid-'50 s, Italian cinema was divided into two camps: on the Left, the neo-realists, whose star was gradually waning; on the Right, the conservatives, who wanted a cinema that propagated the values of Catholicism. The neorealists around Visconti saw *La strada* as an act of betrayal by their former ally Fellini; they found it abstract, individualistic, and even tainted with religiosity. As these critics saw it, *La strada* did nothing to further the cause of educating and informing cinema audiences, nor did it accurately represent the real problems facing society.

It's true that *La strada* says nothing about the class struggle, and the film can indeed be interpreted religiously, as a parable about salvation. But Fellini rejected the accusation that his movie had nothing to do with reality. *La strada*, he said, most certainly did have a point to make about society, for it examined the shared experience of two individuals, and this was the very basis of any human community. Maybe it wasn't literally "a true story," said Fellini, but it was a product of his own personal reality, of his memories and feelings, which had conjured up this vision of two creatures bound together for life without ever knowing why.

"Gelsomina! Gelsomiiina! You've got to come home now!" Two girls on the beach are calling their blonde sister (Giulietta Masina), who's busy collecting driftwood in the dunes: Zampanò (Anthony Quinn) has come to take her away. He's bought her, for 10,000 lira, and his converted motorcycle sidecar will be her future home. Zampanò is a showman, a muscle-man, a one-man circus who performs his shabby show in the market squares of godforsaken villages. Gelsomina is to be his assistant, as a drummer, clown

---

GIULIETTA MASINA When Giulietta Masina visited her husband in Cinecittà, the studio workers gave a thunderous round of applause. A bunch of flowers appeared from nowhere, and work only resumed after she had taken her seat beside Fellini to watch the great man direct. Federico Fellini and Giulietta Masina were one of the most legendary couples in movie history. Under his direction, she became one of the greatest stars of Italian cinema. Her best-known roles included the naïve Gelsomina in *La Strada* (1954) and the plucky prostitute in *Nights of Cabiria (Le notti di Cabiria/Les Nuits de Cabiria*, 1957), for which she won the Best Actress award at the Cannes Festival. The critic François Truffaut was not pleased by the decision, but he was forced to agree that Giulietta Masina had marked a moment in cinema history, in a manner comparable to James Dean.

Giulia Anna Masina was born in 1920 in the province of Bologna and grew up mainly with her worldly, sophisticated aunt in Rome. She performed with theater groups and worked in radio. In 1942, she met Fellini there, and performed in a radio play he had written. She first attracted moviegoers' attention in a supporting role as a prostitute in Alberto Lattuada's *Without Pity (Senza pietà*, 1948); Fellini had co-written the script and also worked on the movie as an assistant. From then on, Masina worked mainly in her husband's films, from *Variety Lights/Lights of Variety (Luci del varietà*, 1950) to *Juliet of the Spirits (Giulietta degli spiriti / Juliette des esprits*, 1965). Then she retired from the movies, although she did continue to appear sporadically on TV. She later made a successful comeback in *Frau Holle (Perinbaba*, 1985) by Juraj Jakubisko, Fellini's *Ginger and Fred (Ginger e Fred / Ginger et Fred*, 1985) and *Aujourd'hui peut-être* (1991) by Jean-Louis Bertuccelli.

Giulietta Masina will go down in cinema history for her role as the puckish Gelsomina, a girl with a deep faith in the essential goodness of mankind. She died in 1994, only a few months after her husband had passed away.

"Signor Fellini has used his small cast, and, equally important, his camera, with the unmistakable touch of an artist. His vignettes fill the movie with beauty, sadness, humor and understanding." *The New York Times*

1 Screen-smart sweetheart: Giulietta Masina gained international acclaim as Gelsomina. But the greatest praise came from film legend Charles Chaplin.

2 Can I tickle your pickle? Utterly naïve Gelsomina is intrigued by the crude Zampanò (Anthony Quinn). All he's

interested in, however, are cheap women and fast wine.

3 Creatures of the night: she's a bat, he's a beast. But by the time Zampanò realizes just how attached he is to this fragile, kooky soul he will have missed his chance with her.

4 '54 Dodge Caravan: poverty hits the open road in postwar Italy.

5 Brute force: in his autobiography, Anthony Quinn wrote that no character he ever played came closer to the real him than Zampanò.

and money collector. So she leaves her impoverished seaside home, forever.

They're an odd couple, this small, childish, naïve, fun-loving young woman, who's looking forward to her life as a traveling artiste, and the crude, bear-like man who becomes her master, hardened by the streets and blind to the world around him. Years of grinding routine have made Zampanò's performances lifeless and mechanical; every time he bursts the chains on his massive, hairy chest, he utters the same tired patter for the crowd.

Gelsomina, by contrast, can't help clowning as soon as she dons her hat at the correct jaunty angle, and the mere sight of a trumpet enchants her. When first presented with a drum, she immediately starts pounding away freestyle, until she feels the sting of a blow to her

bare legs – Zampanò won't tolerate indiscipline. He drills Gelsomina until she can introduce his act just the way he wants.

Zampanò is a laborer who sees his body art as nothing more than a means of earning a crust and a bottle of wine. His attitude contrasts sharply with that of Matto (Richard Basehart), whom Gelsomina and Zampanò encounter repeatedly in the course of their travels. For Matto, his high-wire act is a carefree game, and his art is indistinguishable from his life. There's something unearthly about his witty, gravity-defying performances; indeed, on one occasion, we see him in the circus ring with a pair of angel's wings on his back. So it's no wonder that he and Zampanò are sworn enemies – a rivalry that the weaker of the two will not survive.

6 The main attraction: Gelsomina meets the "angelic" Matto (Richard Basehart) in the circus ring. But rather than running off with him, she runs herself into the ground.

7 Wrestle with the devil: Matto is Italian for loon, and this man's nature costs him his life.

"It's Gelsomina's sad clown face that remains the film's most haunting image, vividly photographed in black-and-white by Otello Martelli. As French critic André Bazin pointed out, 'The Fellini character does not evolve; he ripens.' And so do his movies." *The Washington Post*

Matto's death finally breaks Gelsomina. She could have gone with him, but she chose to stay with Zampanò, who never saw her as a wife or a woman, and who always brusquely rejected her shy attempts to support and understand him. In the dead of night, on the beach, his loneliness finally overcomes him; finally he can feel something, and understand that he has lost something priceless. Zampanò weeps, perhaps for the very first time in his life.

La strada is not merely a poetic social parable, not just a fairy tale in the form of a road movie. More than anything, it's a sad love story. Film critics the world over, and especially in France, celebrated this movie as "a lighthouse for the cinema" (Jacques Doniol-Valcroze), "a milestone in film history" (Georges Sadoul), "an encounter with an unknown world" (André Bazin). A world rejected by the Italian Marxists, because magic was not part of their world view. Fellini is not content to reflect reality: he wants transcendence. The surface of things is there to be penetrated, and he's determined to find the meaning that makes life worth living, however burdensome it may sometimes be.

"Everything in the world is good for something," says Matto to Gelsomina, when the humiliations heaped on her by Zampanò almost destroy her will to live. Even stones have their part to play in the grander scheme of things. Matto picks up a stone from the ground, and says: "If this is meaningless, then everything else is, too – even the stars." He gives it to Gelsomina – who nods, understands, and smiles.

NM

"I was enthralled by the film's resolution, where the power of the spirit overwhelms brute force." *Martin Scorsese*

REBEL WITHOUT A CAUSE

1955 - USA - 111 MIN.

DIRECTOR

NICHOLAS RAY (1911–1979)

SCREENPLAY

STEWART STERN, IRVING SHULMAN,
NICHOLAS RAY

DIRECTOR OF PHOTOGRAPHY

ERNEST HALLER

EDITING

WILLIAM H. ZIEGLER

MUSIC

LEONARD ROSENMAN

PRODUCTION

DAVID WEISBART for WARNER BROS.

STARRING

JAMES DEAN (Jim Stark), NATALIE WOOD (Judy),
SAL MINEO (John 'Plato' Crawford), JIM BACKUS (Frank Stark),
ANN DORAN (Mrs. Stark), COREY ALLEN (Buzz Gunderson),
DENNIS HOPPER (Goon), EDWARD PLATT (Ray Fremick),
FRANK MAZZOLA (Crunch), ROBERT FOULK (Gene)

The reception committee for the new kid on the block!

JAMES DEAN

The overnight sensation of 'East of Eden'

Warner Bros. put all the force of the screen into a challenging drama of today's juvenile violence!

"REBEL WITHOUT A CAUSE"

IN **CINEMASCOPE**
AND WARNERCOLOR

...and they both come from 'good' families!

"Want my jacket?"

It was a film that made history even before it hit the screens. On September 30, 1955, just four weeks prior to its premiere, its leading actor rammed into a limousine in his silver Porsche 550 Spyder and died on impact. It was as if 24-year-old James "Jimmy" Byron Dean intended to live out the role he played in *Rebel Without a Cause*, which is one of the only three films he made; the others were *East of Eden* (1955) and *Giant* (1956). *Rebel*, however, was the one that shaped Dean's image, making film and star into an inseparable whole.

The fused Dean-rebel unit is the product of Nicholas Ray's deft and compassionate directing. Ray allowed Dean and the other young actors plenty of room for improvisation. Dean's Method acting imbued the Jim Stark character with attributes above and beyond those inherent in the script, and the film became a cult classic overnight. Actor and role

NICHOLAS RAY He was immortalized as the man with free-flowing, cotton-white hair, clad in a fur-lined leather coat and a cowboy kerchief tied around his neck.

With a patch over his right eye and a cigarillo dangling from his lips, Nicholas Ray stood before the Manhattan skyline like a supernatural spirit returned from beyond as Derwatt the painter in Wim Wenders's *The American Friend (L'Ami américain,* 1977), a screen adaptation of Patricia Highsmith's thriller *Ripley's Game.* It was a role that also caught Ray in the final stages of cancer, just before he lost his life to the disease in the summer of 1979. His role in this film was an allegory of his own life's work, which encompassed some 30 filmmaking projects: Derwatt, a painter publicly declared dead, sees his artwork go up in value as a result of this media-propagated hoax. At the time, Ray's best directing years were more than a decade behind him, for he virtually withdrew from the movie industry at the beginning of the 1960s.

The man born Raymond Nicholas Kienzle was Hollywood's filmmaking rebel during the 1940s and '50s, emerging as a force that refused to be tamed by the studio system. He fought vigorously against the sensibilities of big-budget Hollywood, preferring to pursue his strongly narrative and visually overwhelming obsessions that resulted in such unmistakable films as: *Knock on Any Door* (1949), a non-linear social study about a young man whose life goes off track, and *In a Lonely Place* (1950), Ray's scathing critique of Hollywood. His diversity is also exhibited in works like the polarizing city-country drama *On Dangerous Ground* (1952/53) and the sumptuously colorful Western ballad *Johnny Guitar* (1954).

Ray's pictures are distinguished by their excellent sense of color, composition, and supreme mastery of the CinemaScope format. Their power had its greatest impact on voices that would rise to fame in the decade to come: the auteurs of the *Nouvelle Vague*, New British Cinema, and New German Cinema. They took Ray's individualistic, alienated heroes as a model for personal expression in cinema itself. As Jean-Luc Godard said of him, "If cinema hadn't existed, Nicholas Ray could have invented it himself."

1 Rebel, rebel: an actor with a lifestyle as fast and furious as the Jim Stark character he played. James Dean improvises his way into the hearts of world audiences in *Rebel Without a Cause*.

2 Forever in blue: jeans plus white t-shirt and red windbreaker gives you Jim Stark traipsing through the night in patriotic colors. By contrast, Stark's rival Buzz Gunderson (Corey Allen) only lets symbol-free leather caress his loins.

3 Drunk as a skunk: a night of binge drinking lands Jim Stark in the slammer.

4 The in-crowd: Buzz's gang gives Jim directions to school – via Albuquerque.

"*Rebel Without a Cause* is a reasonably serious attempt to show that juvenile delinquency is not just a local outbreak of tenement terror but a general infection of modern U.S. society." *Time Magazine*

were one and the same, and the rebel smoker in a red windbreaker and blue jeans became synonymous with the iconography of the off-camera Dean.

Even before the opening credits, the film presents us with one of Hollywood's all-time most touching moments. On an ordinary night in small-town America, a man in a drunken stupor loses his balance and lands flat on the asphalt. That man is Jim Stark, and beside him is a wind-up monkey, whose mechanical dance is coming to a halt. Smiling gently, he tends to the toy as if it were something more. He lovingly wraps it in a crumpled sheet of newspaper, lays it down on the street as if putting it to bed, and then curls up next to it. A triumph in improvisation, the scene is indicative of the tragic plight the film's teen characters are about to endure. And, oddly enough, it was an entirely unscripted sequence.

The story centers around a day in the life of three troubled adolescents living in the suburbs of Los Angeles. A Romeo and Juliet tale in a compact time frame, the characters meet, forge ties, fall in love and are separated by death before dawn. New to town, outsider Jim Stark lays eyes on gorgeous Judy (Natalie Wood) during his first day at school. Ignored by an uncaring father, Judy is a member of a gang of rebels led by Buzz (Corey Allen), who

"But it takes only a blink to visualize *Rebel Without a Cause* as a movie so audacious it can only be poetry, a kind of cinematic free verse whose tone saves it from caricature and the now disregarded sociological assertion that parents are entirely to blame for the alienation of kids." *San Francisco Chronicle*

5

"Ray's films refuse to become the stuff of cozy retrospectives, for they embody the great motive force of the era in which they were made. Only someone who lived through that period could do justice to it. This is all the more true because these films are content to be films, and the truths they express are only expressible in this form. It's the images themselves that move, and move us; palpable, visible, audible traumata. Ray's restlessness created films of feverish beauty, and they still have the power to disturb."

Süddeutsche Zeitung

5 Reckless abandon: the call of the wild ends in disaster when Buzz races over the edge of a cliff and loses his life. The incident incites a witch hunt and forever alters the lives of Judy (Natalie Wood), Jim, and Goon (Dennis Hopper).

6 Balancing act: Plato (Sal Mineo) performs a stunt above an empty swimming pool that reflects his precarious emotional state. He'd better watch his step, for he has neither friends nor family to break his fall.

does his best to make Jim feel unwelcome. Tagging along for the ride is the runty Plato (Sal Mineo), a child from a broken home as extraneous to his family as he is to the other kids at school, until the unbiased Jim takes him under his wing. Feeling Jim moving in on his turf, Buzz challenges him to a game of chicken that ends in the accidental death of the leader of the pack. When Jimmy turns himself in to the authorities, despite his parents' advice, his guilty conscience falls upon deaf ears.

Gang members Goon (Dennis Hopper) and Crunch (Frank Mazzola) decide to avenge Buzz's untimely demise. Things come to a head on an abandoned Hollywood estate, where Jim, Judy, and Plato live out the family life they lack at home. As the other gang members storm the premises, Plato shoots at them and flees the scene. Wanted by the police and utterly disoriented, he runs for cover at the local planetarium. Jim intends on smoothing things over for Plato, but catches up with him just as a cop shoots him down. In a

gesture that recalls the movie's introduction, Jim lays Plato to rest, covering his friend's body in the red windbreaker he lent him to protect him from the cold. "He's always cold," Jim says to a stunned crowd of bystanders.

"It's the story of a generation that grew up overnight," dialogue writer Stewart Stern once said of the film. *Rebel Without a Cause* is among Nicholas Ray's most outstanding pieces. Here, he addresses his audience with a blind confidence that makes for an arrestingly direct storytelling style, whose plot revolves around the character of his protagonists. Ray's heroes are grating individualists, and his films

"James Dean was so cool in the film that guys ached to be him and spent hours training their hair into messy pompadours. He's like a lost puppy being hunted by trouble. But he's also a cat stalking elusive prey, and he even seems at times a sinewy cool serpent ready to strike. But he's always lonely." *San Francisco Chronicle*

7 Chin up: Judy's father (William Hopper) tries to act impartially towards the womanly daughter who has replaced daddy's little girl.

8 Damned if you do, and damned if you don't: Jim contemplates whether he should take on Buzz at the drag race or stay at home like a sissy.

9 That's the concussion talking: Mrs. Stark (Ann Doran) just doesn't get her son these days. Why would Jim insist on turning himself in to the authorities when he hasn't technically committed a crime?

spotlight an indifferent, uncompromising reality. His is a ruggedly individual style of filmmaking, which was admired and emulated by French *Nouvelle Vague* greats Godard, Rivette, and Truffaut, as well as the German Wim Wenders.

Part of an attempt to win a new contingent of moviegoers, *Rebel Without a Cause* was one in a series of pictures that responded to the spirit of rebellion that characterized America's youth in a decade dictated by complacency. It is only fitting that movies like *Rebel Without a Cause*, Laszlo Benedek's *The Wild One* (1953) starring Marlon Brando, and Richard Brooks's *Blackboard Jungle* (1955) with Glenn Ford and Sidney Poitier captured the hearts and minds of audiences at the very moment that rock 'n' roll took the airwaves by storm.

SR

THE NIGHT OF THE HUNTER

1955 - USA - 93 MIN.

DIRECTOR

CHARLES LAUGHTON (1899–1962)

SCREENPLAY

JAMES AGEE, based on the novel of
the same name by DAVIS GRUBB

DIRECTOR OF PHOTOGRAPHY

STANLEY CORTEZ

EDITING

ROBERT GOLDEN

MUSIC

WALTER SCHUMANN

PRODUCTION

PAUL GREGORY for PAUL GREGORY PRODUCTIONS, UNITED ARTISTS

STARRING

ROBERT MITCHUM (Harry Powell), SHELLEY WINTERS (Willa Harper),
LILLIAN GISH (Rachel Cooper), EVELYN VARDEN (Icey Spoon),
PETER GRAVES (Ben Harper), BILLY CHAPIN (John Harper),
SALLY JANE BRUCE (Pearl Harper), JAMES GLEASON (Birdie),
DON BEDDOE (Walt Spoon), GLORIA CASTILLO (Ruby)

"I'll be back, when it's dark."

The actor Charles Laughton directed only one film, and there is nothing else like it. Darkly poetic and deeply moving, *The Night of the Hunter* is a work of horror and enchantment, a hypnotic fairy tale for grown-ups. Laughton's cinematic tableau distills the worst terrors of childhood into a beautiful fable about a brother and sister on the run from a demonic preacher. It's the very stuff of nightmare: two defenseless children pursued relentlessly by an unpredictable and pathologically violent adult.

America is in the grips of the Depression, demoralized and prey to hysterical religiosity. Two country children, John (Billy Chapin) and his younger sister Pearl (Sally Jane Bruce) watch helplessly as their father is arrested. He had murdered two people for the money to ensure his family's survival. But seconds before the cops catch up with him, he succeeds in handing over the booty to his son John. He makes the boy swear to protect his sister with his own life – and never to talk about the money. It's an almost mon-strous burden to place on a child's soul, and it's also the beginning of a nightmarish odyssey for John and Pearl. Their father is executed for murder; and a short time later, a sinister wandering preacher appears on the scene. Not content to woo the widow, he appears to know something about the kids and the carefully hidden loot …

Hollywood's most charismatic bad guy, Robert Mitchum, gives a brilliant performance as the mysterious Harry Powell, serial murderer and itinerant "man of God." With the words LOVE and HATE tattooed on his knuckles, Powell stages bizarre fights between his left and right hands, symbolizing the eternal struggle between Good and Evil. From the very start, he dominates every room he en-ters, every space he inhabits – an impression reinforced by some powerful and unorthodox framings and camera an-gles. Harry Powell is practically ubiquitous and seemingly inescapable. *Something wicked this way comes* – on a train, in a car, or on a horse. And to John and Pearl's

LILLIAN GISH Born in 1893, she is still regarded as "The First Lady of the Silent Screen." Lillian Gish came to fame through the good offices of Mary Pickford, another star of the day, who introduced her to the pioneering director David W. Griffith; and it was in Griffith's thriller *An Unseen Enemy* (1912) that Lillian Gish made her debut. She was an ideal protagonist for the sentimental Victorian world of Griffith's films, often playing deceptively fragile figures with a strong spiritual core. Under Griffith's aegis, she became perhaps the best actress of her day, appearing in movies such as *The Birth of a Nation* (1915), *Intolerance* (1916), and *Broken Blossoms* (1919). In the early '20s, after she and Griffith went their separate ways, Lillian Gish's career went into a slow decline. Nonetheless, she still enjoyed star status for some time to come. Thus the production company MGM allowed her to have a say in the making of *The Scarlet Letter* and *La Bohème* (both 1926).
In 1928, having been supplanted at MGM by Greta Garbo, Lillian Gish turned her back on Hollywood, returned to the theater and worked for radio and TV. Later, she received many awards for her life's work, including an Oscar in 1971 and an award from the American Film Institute in 1984. Lillian Gish died of heart failure on February 27, 1993.

1 Toying with her affections: Reverend
   Harry Powell (Robert Mitchum) takes
   advantage of little Pearl Harper's
   (Sally Jane Bruce) good nature
   without a morsel of shame.

2 As I lay dying: Harry Powell pulls an
   inconceivable con with fatal consequences for the children's mother
   (Shelley Winters).

3 Cheers and sneers: a diabolical mind
   lies behind this man's bright smile.

**"I can hear you whisperin' children, so I know you're down there.
I can feel myself gettin' awful mad. I'm out of patience children.
I'm coming to find you now."** *Film quote: Harry Powell (Robert Mitchum)*

4 The little man takes a stand: young John (Billy Chapin) launches a surprise attack on Harry Powell.

5 Bustin' out: the children orchestrate a plan for survival from the confines of their basement.

dismay, it seems Harry Powell is even capable of entering locked rooms. In short, he is a figure of almost mythical power, a manifestation of evil in human form.

And he's irresistible: Harry Powell marries the widowed mother (Shelley Winters) and crushes her spirit with talk of sin and salvation, before murdering her in cold blood to clear his way to her children. To make it look like an accident, he places her body in the driver's seat and rolls her car into the river. The underwater sequence that follows has since acquired an almost legendary status. We see the dead woman in the submerged automobile, her loose hair swaying softly above her like seaweed. Poetry and horror, beauty and terror, grace and decay: a fabulously melancholic sequence quite without parallel in the cinema.

Indeed, the whole film is unique in the way it combines an almost mannered Expressionist style with motifs from the realms of dream and nightmare. The result is a well-nigh Surrealist masterpiece, profoundly strange and subtly frightening.

The Night of the Hunter gives us a child's-eye view of the world, in which nocturnal terrors become manifest in the person of a monstrous man. At the moment of greatest threat, on the banks of the river, John and Pearl just manage to escape into a tiny boat; their pursuer, Harry Powell, scrambles after them in the shallows, howling like a beast as the boat drifts away from his grasping hands. The children's ordeal finally ends when they find refuge with Mrs. Cooper, a steadfast and warm-hearted woman who takes in and cares for the waifs and strays that come her way. As Rachel Cooper, the former silent-movie star Lillian Gish is another glory of this film. She is the antithesis of Harry Powell, the light that banishes his darkness, a kind of ideal mother, in fact. And it's Rachel Cooper who finally defeats the evil preacher and hands him over to the police. The circle closes when John, finally freed from his unbearable burden, reveals where the money had been hidden all along: in Pearl's rag doll. By the end of this film, the little girl's doll has come to symbolize far more than a stolen childhood. BR

GIANT ⍟

1956 - USA - 201 MIN.

DIRECTOR

GEORGE STEVENS (1904–1975)

SCREENPLAY

FRED GUIOL, IVAN MOFFAT,
based on the novel of the same name by EDNA FERBER

DIRECTOR OF PHOTOGRAPHY

WILLIAM C. MELLOR

EDITING

WILLIAM HORNBECK

MUSIC

DIMITRI TIOMKIN

PRODUCTION

GEORGE STEVENS, HENRY GINSBERG for
GIANT PRODUCTIONS, WARNER BROS.

STARRING

ELIZABETH TAYLOR (Leslie Lynnton Benedict), ROCK HUDSON (Jordan "Bick" Benedict),
JAMES DEAN (Jett Rink), CARROLL BAKER (Luz Benedict II.),
JANE WITHERS (Vashti Snythe), CHILL WILLS (Uncle Bawley Benedict),
MERCEDES MCCAMBRIDGE (Luz Benedict), DENNIS HOPPER (Jordan Benedict III),
SAL MINEO (Angel Obregon II), ROD TAYLOR (Sir David Karfrey),
JUDITH EVELYN (Mrs. Nancy Lynnton), EARL HOLLIMAN (Bob Dace),
ROBERT NICHOLS (Pinky Snythe), PAUL FIX (Doctor Horace Lynnton)

ACADEMY AWARDS 1956

OSCAR for BEST DIRECTOR (George Stevens)

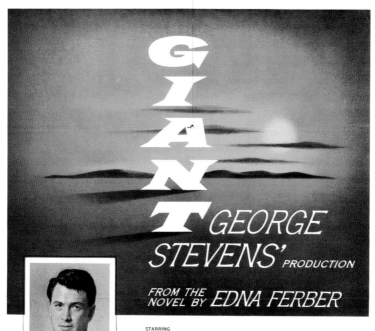

"Bick, you should have shot this fellow long time ago. Now he's too rich to kill."

Stripped of its stars, this picture would still be a cinematic giant. It is a tale of family lineage and legacy with epic magnitude, and the proud recipient of ten Oscar nominations, hailed by critics and audiences alike. But George Stevens's land baron saga became an instant classic for another reason altogether: it was James Dean's final movie. The 1950s Hollywood icon, whose fast and furious film career consisted of just two other features, *Rebel Without a Cause* (1955) and *East of Eden* (1955), died unexpectedly in a car crash on September 30, 1955 – a year before *Giant*'s official world premiere.

Dean plays cowboy Jett Rink, the third of his three big-screen rebels, and a man with an iron will tormented by eternal jealousy and unrequited love. Rink is what you might call *Giant*'s third wheel; for the two main characters are wedded couple Leslie and Jordan "Bick" Benedict (Eliz-

abeth Taylor and Rock Hudson). Their story begins in Maryland during the early 1920s. Bick, a rich Texas rancher, falls for sassy East Coast beauty Leslie while trying to acquire a horse from her father. It's love at first sight, so the two quickly tie the knot and Leslie follows her beau to Texas to live on his Reata ranch. But acclimatizing to her new environs proves a trial for the fragile flower of the East as Bick's sister Luz (Mercedes McCambridge) is harsher than the Texas sun. And being progressively minded, Leslie finds it hard to look the other way when her husband demeans Mexican immigrants or ruthlessly exploits his staff. This pressure cooker comes to a head when she befriends the introverted farmhand Jett Rink, and Bick gets a bad case of sour grapes. A full-blown marital crisis ensues when Leslie, continuing to press her luck, fights for the welfare of the Mexicans living in the neighboring town. Just as the

GEORGE STEVENS Although George Stevens (1904–1975) was responsible for classics like the comedy *Woman of the Year* (1941), the *Western Shane* (1953), and the Biblical epic *The Greatest Story Ever Told* (1964), Hollywood's upper echelons were forever to evade him. The son of actors Landers Stevens and Georgie Cooper, he was born in Oakland, California, and started off as a cameraman in what would amount to an extremely diverse career. In the 1920s, he served as cinematographer to Hal Roach on Laurel & Hardy comedies like *Big Business* (1929) and *Men O'War* (1929). It was Roach who gave the ambitious young cameraman a chance to shoot his own short films. Stevens then began to gain further experience at Universal and RKO, eventually shooting his first feature-length film, *The Cohens and Kellys in Trouble* (1933).

An important development in Stevens's life and artistic work came during the Second World War as cameraman for a U.S. army outfit, with whom he would film the Allied invasion of Normandy. His camera crew also documented the Dachau concentration camp, resulting in the film *Nazi Concentration Camps* (1945), which was first shown at the Nuremburg Trials. Over the course of his career, perfectionist George Stevens went from being a director of light comedies to a masterful genre chameleon, gradually gaining total control as producer on many of his filmmaking endeavors. He received his first Oscar nomination in directing for *The More the Merrier* (1943). His work as producer was recognized the previous year when *Talk of the Town* (1942) was nominated for Best Picture. *A Place in the Sun* (1951) marked his final departure from comedy – but earned Stevens his first Oscar in directing. His second came for his adaptation of Edna Ferber's *Giant* (1956). George Stevens died of a heart attack in March 1975.

"The performances by Dean, Taylor, Hudson, et al, remind us of the days when 'movie star' wasn't a dirty phrase." *E! Online*

1 A giant among men: he only made three films, but he left Hollywood a legend. James Dean as talk of the town, Jett Rink.

2 Cream of the crop: Leslie (Elizabeth Taylor) has a soft spot for pretty boy Jett Rink, but her heart belongs to handsome husband and cattle baron Bick.

3 Relationship derailed: Jordan "Bick" Benedict (Rock Hudson) can only sit and watch as his wife packs up with the children. He'll have to lay plenty of new track if he intends to win her back.

2

couple seem to be patching things up, Luz dies in a riding accident and leaves a dark legacy that will forever bear upon the Benedicts: she bequeaths the hard-working Jett a small piece of homestead, and it soon transpires that he's sitting on a fortune in black gold. Overnight, the young man becomes one of Texas's most powerful oil barons and Bick's most ruthless competitor.

Giant spans 25 years at Reata. The film chronicles Leslie and Bick's lives both as a married couple and as parents, documenting their personal crises on the ranch alongside those of the other members of the Benedict family and the farmhands. The story's second tier follows Jett's metamorphosis from dirt-poor laborer to super-rich tycoon, who will not rest until he either wins Leslie's hand

or drives Bick into the ground, going so far as to seduce their daughter (Carroll Baker) to achieve his ends. As the title suggests, Giant is a grand, sweeping film: well over three hours in length, and saturated with breathtaking shots of Texas landscapes as fertile as they are unforgiving. It is a film that delves into the complexities of racism, emancipation, and family; and its exceptional cast bring the minutiae of their world to life with razor-sharp accuracy and conviction. A generous amount of screen time is devoted to Bick's lifelong struggle with his own fatherly ambitions, for even at a young age the Benedict children defy the values of their father. A four-year-old Jordan breaks into tears when mounted on a pony. Disgusted at the sight before him, Bick snorts, "I could ride before I

"*Giant* is as intimate as a letter from home. A masterpiece." *The Chicago Daily News*

4 With the wind in their mares: Bick and Leslie Benedict take a morning ride across Reata and enjoy the advantages of private property.

5 South Fork meets Manderley: it's a good thing these walls can't talk, because we'd never hear the end of it.

6 Family foibles: after 25 years of hard work, Leslie manages to work some of the kinks out of her grassroots husband. Only now the hotheaded Bick picks fights with strangers rather than his loved ones.

could walk," never suspecting that this event is a premonition of the trajectory their relationship will take. As an adolescent, Jordan (Dennis Hopper) has already voiced his lack of interest in ranching, wishing instead to pursue a career in medicine. Adding insult to injury, he later weds a Mexican. But this act of defiance also becomes a turning point in Bick's life, as he finally overcomes his deepseated racism: when his daughter-in-law is refused service at a hotel beauty parlor during a reception honoring Jett Rink, Bick gives Jett a piece of his mind. However, this new mindset soon has negative repercussions in a separate incident at an eatery, when he tries to share his enlightened ways with a waiter unwilling to serve a Mexican family, and is beaten to a pulp.

Reforming his social views proves a long and arduous task, and time and again Bick falls victim to his own machismo and prejudice. Like a living cog in a cycle of

hate, he blindly sings the praises of the Lone Star State – just one example of how the Texan mentality emerges as an invisible supporting player within the drama – and internalizes its implicit mantras as he dismisses Mexicans as lesser mortals, or silences his spouse when she dares to contribute to an exclusively male discussion about politics. Leslie, meanwhile, is the personification of moral goodness. As *Giant's* sole Texas outsider and narrative counterpoint, actress Elizabeth Taylor subtly layers her character by displaying the undying devotion and patience of a loving wife, while astutely ridiculing the powers that be. While the Benedicts' repeated tiffs and lovers' quarrels never threaten to destroy their marriage, the brawl at the diner inadvertently renews their vows and reaffirms their relationship. By putting both his social status and his life on the line, Bick at long last wins his wife's respect.

ES

THE SEARCHERS

1956 - USA - 119 MIN.

DIRECTOR
JOHN FORD (1894–1973)

SCREENPLAY
FRANK S. NUGENT, based on the novel
of the same name by ALAN LE MAY

DIRECTOR OF PHOTOGRAPHY
WINTON C. HOCH

EDITING
JACK MURRAY

MUSIC
MAX STEINER, STAN JONES (Song: "The Searchers")

PRODUCTION
C. V. WHITNEY for C. V. WHITNEY PICTURES, WARNER BROS.

STARRING
JOHN WAYNE (Ethan Edwards), JEFFREY HUNTER (Martin Pawley),
VERA MILES (Laurie Jorgensen), WARD BOND (Reverend Captain Samuel Clayton),
NATALIE WOOD (Debbie Edwards), JOHN QUALEN (Lars Jorgensen),
OLIVE CAREY (Mrs. Jorgensen), HENRY BRANDON (Chief Scar),
WALTER COY (Aaron Edwards), DOROTHY JORDAN (Martha Edwards)

he had
to find
her...
he had
to find
her...

WARNER BROS. PRESENT
THE C.V. WHITNEY PICTURE STARRING

JOHN WAYNE
IN "THE SEARCHERS"

THE BIGGEST, ROUGHEST, TOUGHEST... AND MOST BEAUTIFUL PICTURE EVER MADE!

THE STORY THAT SWEEPS FROM THE GREAT
SOUTHWEST TO THE CANADIAN BORDER IN

VISTAVISION
MOTION PICTURE · HIGH-FIDELITY

COLOR BY
TECHNICOLOR

CO-STARRING
JEFFREY HUNTER · VERA MILES
WARD BOND · NATALIE WOOD
SCREEN PLAY BY FRANK S. NUGENT   EXECUTIVE PRODUCER MERIAN C. COOPER   ASSOCIATE PRODUCER PATRICK FORD
PRESENTED BY WARNER BROS.   DIRECTED BY JOHN FORD
4-TIME ACADEMY AWARD WINNER

THE SEARCHERS

"We'll find them in the end. We'll find them. I promise you."

The Searchers is a classic Western, but by no means a classical one. Good fails to defeat evil, and civilization certainly doesn't triumph over nature. Contradictions and mysteries remain, and most of them have to do with a man it's hard to call a hero.

Three years after the end of the Civil War, Ethan Edwards (John Wayne) visits the farm owned by his brother Aaron (Walter Coy) in Texas. It's a brief reunion. Ethan returns from an unsuccessful search for poachers to a scene of pure horror: Aaron and his wife Martha (Dorothy Jordan) have been murdered by Comanches, and their daughters Lucy and Debbie have been abducted. Ethan immediately organizes a search party and sets off in pursuit of the culprits. With them is young Martin Pawley (Jeffrey Hunter), the adopted son of the family, whom Ethan himself had once found wandering in the desert. Soon, they stumble upon Lucy's corpse. The rest of the search party give up. Ethan and Martin continue on their quest, alone. In the course of the following five years, a terrible suspicion will

form in Martin's mind: Ethan is less interested in finding his niece than in killing her, for her long captivity has now made Debbie a Comanche.

Without robbing the Western of its mythic power, John Ford shows that he is capable of keeping a distance from the genre with which he is identified. Ethan is a puzzling figure, a man surrounded by unasked and unanswered questions. What has he been doing since the Civil War ended? Was he a hero? A bandit? Is his deeply racist attitude really based only on a desire to avenge his brother's family? He hates the Indians, especially the Comanche tribe; yet it becomes increasingly clear that he has a profound knowledge of their customs and way of life. When the search party passes an Indian grave, Ethan shoots out the eyes of the corpse, so the deceased will have to "wander amongst the winds for all eternity." And when Ethan meets his deadly enemy Scar (Henry Brandon) – the demonic Comanche chief – it's as if he were looking into a mirror.

JOHN WAYNE America's most popular actor, indeed to this day, was born in Iowa in 1907 as Marion Michael Morrison. At the University of Southern California, "the Duke" was mostly known as a football player. From 1928 onwards, he played minor roles in films directed by his friend John Ford, until he finally made his breakthrough in Ford's classic Western *Stagecoach* (1939). The two of them would go on to make around 20 films together, including *She Wore a Yellow Ribbon* (1949), *Rio Grande* (1950), and *The Man Who Shot Liberty Valance* (1962). These were films that stamped his image as a Western roughneck: craggy, tenacious, tightlipped, and unwavering – the quintessential American hero, often in uniform. Wayne was thoroughly unfazed by the accusation that he only ever played himself. Ford's nostalgic Irish comedy *The Quiet Man* (1952), in which he partnered with Maureen O'Hara, featured Wayne in one of his few comic roles. Even in other genres, such as the safari adventure *Hatari!* (1962) or the war film *The Green Berets* (1968), Wayne remained true to himself and his image. A Hollywood strongman who never tried to conceal his reactionary views, John Wayne was nevertheless capable of treating his own myth with considerable irony. *El Dorado* (1967) and *Rio Lobo* (1970), two of Howard Hawks's famous late Westerns, featured the elderly Wayne as a washed-out gunslinger. For his performance as the drunken marshal in Henry Hathaway's *True Grit* (1969), he received his only Oscar. His last role was as a cancer-ridden gunslinger in Don Siegel's *The Shootist* (1976). John Wayne died of lung cancer in 1979. It's said that he wasn't averse to a little punch-up right up until the very end.

"A bitter racist, quick to anger and take offense, the implacable foe of all tribes but especially the Comanche, Edwards is one of the most astonishing portraits of unapologetic, unmotivated fury ever put on screen, an unvarnished, frightening glimpse of the darkest side of the men who subdued the plains." *Los Angeles Times*

Everything Ethan does makes one thing clear: this is a man without a tribe. In white society, he remains an outsider. The most famous shots are at the beginning and end of the film: they show him alone at the door of the farmhouse. This door marks the boundary between civilization and wilderness, and Ethan never goes through it. Nor did he even do so in the days when he and Martha were a couple, as we see from the few scenes in the family home.

Ford closes the door with a cut to the next scene: Ethan alone in the depths of Monument Valley. Like the dead Indian, Ethan will find no peace, for he is haunted and pursued by the demons of his own past.

Many years passed before Ford's film was accused of being racist; and it took even longer until people were ready to do justice to its unusually modern episodic structure. Ford's attitude is as hard to pin down as that of his

1 The search is over: searchers Martin (Jeffrey Hunter), Ethan (John Wayne), and the Reverend (Ward Bond) find themselves at a dead end when internal squabbles come to a head.

2 Monument Valley: the Grand Canyon excluded, John Ford and John Wayne are the cornerstones of the American West.

3 Some things never change: Ethan and Martin lose their posse and get stuck alone with one another yet again. Their quest to retrieve Debbie lasts five long, arduous, painful, and backbreaking years. How's that for a mouthful?

4 Elbow room: John Wayne strips himself of his Hollywood veneer to deliver a performance as awe-inspiring as it is repugnant.

protagonist, and can perhaps only be understood by viewing the entire film. We are never shown an Indian committing a murder; yet Ethan kills Indians as they flee – a senseless deed, which shocks even his thick-skinned companions. The U.S. Cavalry, the pride of many earlier Ford films, is also guilty of terrible crimes. Ethan is a stark contrast to the peaceable Martin, who is one-eighth Cherokee, and whom Ethan clearly rejects from their first meeting onwards. That he finally does accept this man effects a change within Ethan: when the searchers finally find Debbie (Natalie Wood), he is capable of embracing her. Not without scalping her husband, though, for she has indeed become Scar's squaw.

The Searchers is John Ford's darkest and most complex Western, its tragic weight barely lightened by a minor subplot concerning the Edwards' Swedish neighbors. The leading actor also described the movie as Ford's best, and it certainly features one of John Wayne's most impressive performances. His irrepressible strength and individuality lend this movie even more power. *The Searchers* became a milestone of American cinema, and motifs from the movie can be found in countless later films, including Martin Scorsese's *Taxi Driver* (1975) and George Lucas's *Star Wars* (1977).

PB

ELEVATOR TO THE SCAFFOLD

ASCENSEUR POUR L'ÉCHAFAUD

1957 - FRANCE - 88 MIN.

DIRECTOR

LOUIS MALLE (1932–1995)

SCREENPLAY

LOUIS MALLE, ROGER NIMIER,
based on the novel of the same name by NOËL CALEF

DIRECTOR OF PHOTOGRAPHY

HENRI DECAË

EDITING

LÉONIDE AZAR

MUSIC

MILES DAVIS (Miles Davis Quintet:
Miles Davis, Barney Wilen, René Urtreger,
Pierre Michelot, Kenny Clarke)

PRODUCTION

JEAN THUILLIER for NOUVELLES ÉDITIONS DE FILMS

STARRING

JEANNE MOREAU (Florence Carala), MAURICE RONET (Julien Tavernier),
GEORGES POUJOULY (Louis), YORI BERTIN (Véronique),
LINO VENTURA (Inspector Chérier), JEAN WALL (Simon Carala),
FÉLIX MARTEN (Christian Subervie), IVAN PETROVICH (Horst Bencker),
ELGA ANDERSEN (Frieda Bencker), CHARLES DENNER (Inspector Chérier's Assistant)

Présente:

LE
PRIX
LOUIS
DELLUC

La
plus
haute
récompense
Française
du
Cinéma

JEANNE MOREAU
et
MAURICE RONET

dans
un
Film
réalisé
par
LOUIS MALLE

Willy Mucha

Ascenseur pour l'échafaud

D'APRÈS LE ROMAN DE NOEL CALEF · ADAPTATION DE ROGER NIMIER ET LOUIS MALLE

DIALOGUE DE ROGER NIMIER

avec GEORGES POUJOULY · YORI BERTIN · JEAN WALL

et IVAN PETROVICH et FELIX MARTEN et LINO VENTURA

MUSIQUE DE MILES DAVIS

PRODUCTION NOUVELLES ÉDITIONS de FILMS · PRODUCTEUR DÉLÉGUÉ : JEAN THUILLIER

"I looked for you all night, but I couldn't find you."

Florence Carala (Jeanne Moreau) and her lover Julien Tavernier (Maurice Ronet) have planned the murder of Florence's husband right down to the last detail. The idea is to make it look as though the man has committed suicide in his office. Hardly has the deed been done when things start to go badly wrong: departing from the scene of the crime, Julien gets stuck in the elevator, and, as he struggles to find a way out, his car is stolen by a couple of kids. Florence, waiting outside for her lover, sees his convertible whizz past and begins to doubt her lover's feelings for her. She wanders the nocturnal streets of Paris in search of Julien, while he, marooned between floors, tries in vain to escape. Meanwhile, the two joyriders have knocked down and killed a couple of German tourists before fleeing the scene – and the cops have launched a major manhunt for the owner of the car … An adulterous couple, a burdensome spouse, an ingenious murder plan, and the destructive power of accident: it's the stuff of a thousand movies. What was new and exciting about Malle's film was the way he created an existential drama from the ingredients of a classical thriller. *Elevator to the Scaffold* was his directing debut, and he was only 25 years old at the time. Malle himself once said that he had been torn between his desire to emulate Hitchcock and his admiration for the philosophical films of Robert Bresson, with whom he had worked as an assistant director on *A Man Escaped/ The Wind Bloweth Where It Listeth (Un Condamné à mort s'est échappé/*

JEANNE MOREAU Orson Welles once called her "the greatest actress in the world." She had an astonishing ability to change her expression instantly from forbidding severity to irresistible joy, and she stamped her image on French cinema like no other actor. Jeanne Moreau (born 1928 in Paris) had already achieved fame in the theater before making her movie breakthrough with *Elevator to the Scaffold (Ascenseur pour l'échafaud*, 1957). Her second collaboration with Louis Malle was *The Lovers (Les Amants*, 1958), a film widely regarded as scandalous in its time. It brought her international fame and a lasting reputation as a "free-living" woman. Moreau had an important influence on the changing image of women in '60 s cinema, and she also demonstrated her independence in the way she chose her roles. For her performance in Peter Brook's *Moderato cantabile* (1960), she received her first major award, as Best Actress at the Cannes Festival. But her most famous performance was yet to come, as the strong-willed lover of two friends in François Truffaut's *Jules and Jim (Jules et Jim*, 1961); it made her an icon of the *Nouvelle Vague*. The media had a field day when she starred alongside Brigitte Bardot in Malle's Western parody *Viva María!* (1965). Jeanne Moreau went on to work with many famous directors, including Michelangelo Antonioni, Joseph Losey, Luis Buñuel, Jacques Demy, Tony Richardson, Paul Mazursky, André Téchiné, Elia Kazan, Marguerite Duras, Rainer Werner Fassbinder, and Wim Wenders. She also directed several movies herself, as well as pursuing a successful second career as a *chanson* singer.

2

1 Going up? While Maurice Ronet (1927–83) was undoubtedly one of the best French actors of his generation, he never achieved the status of A-listers like Alain Delon and Jean-Paul Belmondo.

2 Basket case: Florence (Jeanne Moreau, right) is left at a loss by what has proven to be a crummy plan. Meanwhile, beau Julien (Maurice Ronet) is indefinitely detained in an elevator jam.

3 Heavyweight: in 1957, former wrestler Lino Ventura (right) stepped into the acting arena, and ten years later he was knockin' 'em dead as a main attraction.

4 French cuts: unlike most hairdos, some actors never fall out of favor. Jeanne Moreau takes an *Elevator to the Scaffold* and remains at the top of French cinema for the rest of her acting career.

"**The debut from Louis Malle, *Elevator to the Scaffold* is a stylish noirish crime drama boasting, amongst other things, an improvised Miles Davis soundtrack.**"

Edinburgh University Film Society

Le Vent souffle où il veut, 1956). In fact, both influences are clearly detectable in Malle's film. After a suspenseful beginning, the plot gradually grinds to an almost complete halt, and Malle subjects his frantic protagonists to a near-clinical examination. While police investigations proceed apace, Florence and Julien seem almost incarcerated in their existential loneliness and despair. Like Bresson, Malle makes repeated use of apt metaphors: Julien is trapped in a kind of prison, but Florence too is lost in the labyrinth that is rain-soaked Paris. In Malle's film, the big city is a symbol of the modern world, and freedom is not what it promises. The surface glitter of the city's storefront windows only serves to emphasize the emotional barrenness of its denizens.

Although Malle has always taken pains to distance himself from the *Nouvelle Vague*, *Elevator to the Scaffold* was undoubtedly an important source of inspiration for the French *cinéma d'auteur* of the late 1950s. It might be grimmer in tone than anything by Godard or Truffaut, but it evinces the same enthusiasm for American B-movies as *Breathless* (*À bout de souffle*, 1959) or *Shoot the Piano Player* (*Tirez sur le pianiste*, 1959/60). Cameraman Henri Decaë creates a noir Paris in intense black and white, illuminated only by passing headlights and the garish neon of late-night cafés. It's a diffuse and formless environment, an abode of shades in which Florence is soon in danger of losing her soul. Though Malle takes a strictly detached view of his protagonists, he makes it clear that Florence is

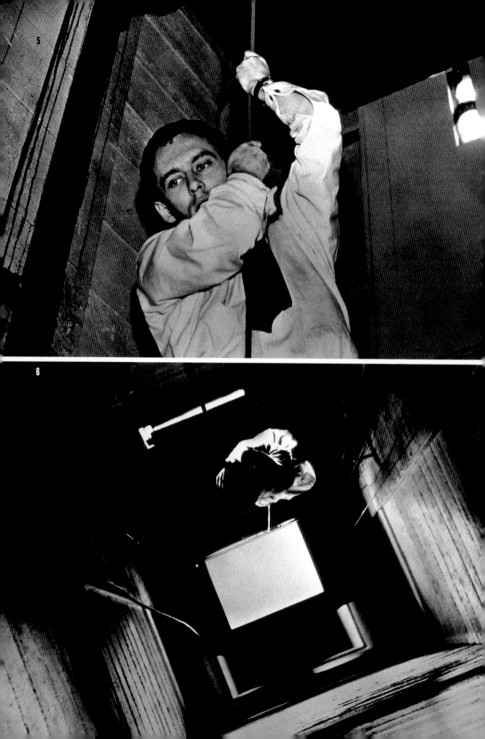

5 Hanging by a thread: the longer Julien remains trapped in the elevator, the clearer it becomes there is no such thing as the perfect plan...

6 ... no matter how bright the prospects.

7 Disconnected, or no longer in service? In *Elevator to the Scaffold* the telephone is both a means of instant communication and of keeping others at a distance.

8 Slice of life: Louis Malle's detached mise-en-scène is reminiscent of mentor Robert Bresson's directing style. No coincidence either, as Malle had assisted Bresson on one of his pictures the year before.

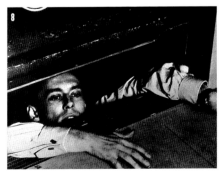

in a state of emotional crisis. As the camera focuses on the face of Jeanne Moreau, her beauty ravaged by tension and fatigue, we listen in on Florence's increasingly despairing interior monologue. Miles Davis's now-famous soundtrack makes her uncertainty almost palpable. The jagged aggressiveness of his trumpet transmits the character's anxiety straight to the moviegoer's bloodstream. All in all, *Elevator to the Scaffold* is a deeply pessimistic take on human nature. It now enjoys the status of an uncontested classic.

UB

WILD STRAWBERRIES
SMULTRONSTÄLLET
1957 - SWEDEN - 91 MIN.

DIRECTOR
INGMAR BERGMAN (1918–2007)

SCREENPLAY
INGMAR BERGMAN

DIRECTOR OF PHOTOGRAPHY
GUNNAR FISCHER

EDITING
OSCAR ROSANDER

MUSIC
ERIK NORDGREN

PRODUCTION
ALLAN EKELUND FOR SVENSK FILMINDUSTRI

STARRING
VICTOR SJÖSTRÖM (Professor Isak Borg), BIBI ANDERSSON (Sara),
INGRID THULIN (Marianne Borg), GUNNAR BJÖRNSTRAND (Evald Borg),
FOLKE SUNDQUIST (Anders), BJÖRN BJELFVENSTAM (Viktor),
NAIMA WIFSTRAND (Isak's Mother), JULLAN KINDAHL (Agda),
GUNNAR SJÖBERG (Sten Alman), GUNNEL BROSTRÖM (Mrs. Alman),
GERTRUD FRIDH (Karin, Isak's wife), ÅKE FRIDELL (Karin's lover),
MAX VON SYDOW (Åkerman), SIF RUUD (Aunt Olga),
YNGVE NORDWALL (Uncle Aron), PER SJÖSTRAND (Sigfrid Borg),
GIO PETRÉ (Sigbritt), GUNNEL LINDBLOM (Charlotta),
MAUD HANSSON (Angelica), LENA BERGMAN (Kristina), MONICA EHRLING (Birgitta)

IFF BERLIN 1958
GOLDEN BEAR (Ingmar Bergman)

INGMAR BERGMANS

Smultron-stället

VICTOR SJÖSTRÖM
BIBI ANDERSSON
GUNNAR BJÖRNSTRAND
INGRID THULIN

FOLKE SUNDQUIST
BJÖRN BJELVENSTAM
NAIMA WIFSTRAND

WILD STRAWBERRIES

"The question is no longer whether God is dead; the question is whether man is dead."

Dream, memory, and the present: in *Wild Strawberries*, Ingmar Bergman combines several narrative levels with admirable dexterity. Here, there is no clear line between imagination and reflection, fantasy and contemplation of the thing fantasized. A dream sequence right at the beginning states the basic theme: fear of death. In the glow of dawn, an old man walks through an abandoned city. He sees clocks without hands, faces without eyes – surrealist images, born of a private nightmare. Ingmar Bergman himself has encouraged us to see it as an autobiographical film: "A hearse crashes into a pole, the coffin falls out and the corpse is flung to the ground: I had dreamt this myself, many times."

Wild Strawberries tells the story of a single day. Isak Borg, a 76-year-old professor of medicine, drives from Stockholm to Lund, an ancient Swedish university town, where he plans to join the celebrations for the anniversary of his doctorate. The journey takes him back through many episodes of his past life, both real and imaginary: he visits his mother (Naima Wifstrand), who produces a case full of toys, and he thinks back on his marriage, his first love and his parents. He gives a lift to a young hitchhiker, who strongly resembles Sara, the girl he loved in his youth (both roles are played by Bibi Andersson). At the summer house, memory takes possession of him. Wild strawberries still grow here, as they did in his childhood and youth. In Swedish, *smultronstället* has two meanings: it denotes a place where wild strawberries grow, and it also signifies a *locus amoenus*, a secret garden, a place of magical serenity, outside of everyday existence. These wild strawberries

1 Dreams are my reality: although Sara (Bibi Andersson, left) confides in her cousin Charlotta (Gunnel Lindblom) that she'd much rather have Sigfrid than her fiancé Isak, we'll never know whether it's true or just a figment of an old man's imagination.

2 Eternal youth: Isak Borg (Victor Sjöström) picks up three hitchhikers at the side of the road. The woman of the bunch, Sara, bears an uncanny resemblance to Isak's former fiancée of the same name. Bibi Andersson in a scintillatingly callous double role.

3 Bearing fruit: Marianne (Ingrid Thulin) longs for a child, but her husband Evald (Gunnar Björnstrand) doesn't want to spoil yet another person's life.

4 Sweet dreams: by the end of his journey, Isak comes to amiable terms with the life he has led and the children who once shunned him.

5 Marianne Faithful: though the others wrongly suspect her of infidelity, Marianne places honesty above all other human virtues. Why else would she be so rude to her father-in-law?

> **"*Wild Strawberries*, scripted by Bergman himself with infinite delicacy and compassion, is a poem about old age that wanders through the borderland between the dream world of life and the real world of dreams. A richly rewarding expedition into the labyrinth of the soul."** *Newsweek*

appear in many of Bergman's films, and in *Fanny and Alexander* (*Fanny och Alexander*, 1982), for example, they symbolize paradise lost – youth, happiness, and pure unadulterated love.

In a second dream sequence, the failures and character defects of the dreaming man are listed: he is selfish, cold, and egotistical. As a basis for this character analysis, Isak Borg undergoes a kind of test: his teacher leads him

"Life as paradise lost." *Der Spiegel*

through a dream landscape to a place where he's forced to watch his wife commit adultery. The old man awakens, tormented but reconciled to the truth. Far from allowing Borg to "reap the harvest" of his life and work, the film depicts a journey into the interior: self-knowledge is the ultimate goal, even if it means facing some very bitter facts. The moral is clear: a life story is only worth telling if it refuses to sentimentalize the past.

"I imagined this man to be a jaded egotist who has broken every link to the world around him – just as I had done." Bergman claimed that *Wild Strawberries* had been an unconscious attempt to depict his difficult relationship with his parents. The final scene, he said, had been a projection of his own deepest yearnings: Sara takes Borg by the hand and leads him to a glade, where he sees his mother and father waving to him from the other side of the water.

6 Strawberry fields forever: the family sits down to the midday meal at their country house, where strawberries grow as wildly and intensely as human emotion. Indeed, this is to be the summer that the impassioned

Sigfrid (Per Sjöstrand, back row center) snatches Sara away from Isak, whose intellect is both his greatest attribute and fault.

7 One-way window: as he roams through his private dream world, Isak Bork sees characters from the past who cannot see him.

It's a highly personal film, but thanks to Victor Sjöström, a great Swedish actor who was famous even in the days of silent film, much of it depicts a more likeable character than Bergman had intended. Thirty-three years later, Bergman noted: "Only now have I realized that Victor Sjöström took the script of my life and made it his own, with his own torment, misanthropy, reclusiveness, brutality, grief, fear, loneliness, chilliness, warmth, asperity and ennui."

With this film, Ingmar Bergman established a new poetry of the cinema. Not unjustly, it's been described as a second Surrealism. Yet when Bergman sends his alter ego into the world of dreams, he still draws a line between dream and waking life. In the decade that followed, there would no longer be a clear distinction between the inner and outer worlds of the protagonists.

RV

VERTIGO

1958 - USA - 128 MIN.

DIRECTOR

ALFRED HITCHCOCK (1899–1980)

SCREENPLAY

ALEC COPPEL, SAMUEL A. TAYLOR, based on the novel *D'entre les morts*
by PIERRE BOILEAU and THOMAS NARCEJAC

DIRECTOR OF PHOTOGRAPHY

ROBERT BURKS

EDITING

GEORGE TOMASINI

MUSIC

BERNARD HERRMANN

PRODUCTION

ALFRED HITCHCOCK
for ALFRED J. HITCHCOCK PRODUCTIONS, INC., PARAMOUNT PICTURES

STARRING

JJAMES STEWART (John "Scottie" Ferguson), KIM NOVAK (Madeleine Elster / Judy Barton),
BARBARA BEL GEDDES (Midge Wood), TOM HELMORE (Gavin Elster),
KONSTANTIN SHAYNE (Pop Leibel), HENRY JONES (Coroner),
RAYMOND BAILEY (Doctor), ELLEN CORBY (Hotel Manager)

PARAMOUNT PRESENTS

JAMES STEWART
KIM NOVAK
IN ALFRED HITCHCOCK'S
MASTERPIECE

'VERTIGO'

CO-STARRING
BARBARA BEL GEDDES WITH TOM HELMORE · HENRY JONES · DIRECTED BY ALFRED HITCHCOCK · SCREENPLAY BY ALEC COPPEL & SAMUEL TAYLOR · TECHNICOLOR®
BASED UPON THE NOVEL 'D'ENTRE LES MORTS' BY PIERRE BOILEAU AND THOMAS NARCEJAC · MUSIC BY BERNARD HERRMANN

"Do you believe that someone out of the past – someone dead – can enter and take possession of a living being?"

The depths of a stairwell beckon from beyond. The ground vanishes, and the banister uncoils, and we are overcome by a sense of vertigo. Combining a forward zoom and reverse tracking shot (now sometimes called "contra-zoom" or "trombone shot"), director Alfred Hitchcock creates a dizziness that has gone down as the stuff of legends. As the stairwell springs in and out of proportion, we are thrust into the mind of the protagonist, John "Scottie" Ferguson (James Stewart), a man with a paralyzing fear of heights. A San Francisco police detective, Scottie turns in his badge following a rooftop pursuit that ends in the death of a fellow officer. He blames himself or rather his acrophobia for the incident, convinced that the fatal fall has left him half a man.

Several months pass. Months that for Scottie are a sea of contemplation. Then a phone call promises hope from out of the blue: an old college acquaintance and shipbuilding tycoon named Gavin Elster (Tom Helmore) wants to meet up and reminisce about old times. However, instead of losing themselves in nostalgic reverie, the businessman offers Scottie a job; Elster's wife, it seems, has been exhibiting signs of psychological instability and needs to be watched. Scottie initially refuses to get involved, but quickly changes his mind upon laying eyes on her: Madeleine Elster (Kim Novak) – a platinum vision of elegance – is supernaturally stunning, and Scottie just can't look away.

And so begins a hypnotic game of cat and mouse. The private detective discreetly follows Madeleine around San Francisco as she goes about her daily business and journeys to the city's furthest enclaves. Guided by music, these are sequences without dialogue and without contact, until one afternoon when Madeleine tries to take her life by jumping into the bay. Scottie dives in after her, but ultimately cannot abate her suicidal tendencies: just days later, a fit of hysteria sends Madeleine running up the stairs of a church bell tower and out of Scottie's life – for now.

Vertigo is the story of a man stricken by a debilitating handicap that prevents him from seeing clearly at higher elevations. The predicament is confounded when Scottie

JAMES STEWART *It's a Wonderful Life* (1946), *Winchester '73* (1950), and *Rear Window* (1954) are just three of more than 80 feature films starring James Stewart.(1908–1997). What these three masterpieces have in common is that their respective directors were instrumental in shaping Jimmy's career: he made three pictures with Frank Capra, eight with Anthony Mann, and four with Alfred Hitchcock. One of the most remarkable actors ever to grace the screen, Stewart very much deserves his own chapter in its history. At 6'3" he made an art form of lankiness and of never quite knowing what to do with his long limbs. This, however, didn't stop him from turning up in the musical *Born to Dance* (1936). Indeed, he felt at home in nearly all genres, appearing in comedies, romances, Westerns, war movies, and thrillers alike. He also portrayed his fair share of historical figures, including Glenn Miller and Charles Lindbergh. His list of co-stars is equally impeccable, topped off by names like Edward G. Robinson, John Wayne, Katharine Hepburn, Marlene Dietrich, and a six-foot-three-and-a-half-inch-tall invisible rabbit named *Harvey* (1950). Stewart had an incredible range, always managing to hit on something universal in his acting that was unmarred by histrionics. The son of a Pennsylvania hardware store owner, he got his start in pictures playing shy innocents – usually guys from the countryside – before establishing himself as a leading man in romantic comedies. He freely enlisted in the service during World War II and returned home a highly decorated pilot. From this point on, his screen work took on a darker edge, and his characterizations became more vulnerable and rich with internal conflict. Upon his passing in 1997, the German regional newspaper *Süddeutsche Zeitung* declared him "the last of the cinematic greats … and the greatest among them."

1 The fall of man: Scottie (James Stewart) is head over heels for a suicidal dream girl. Kim Novak as Madeleine, Hitchcock's ultimate blonde.

2 Image is everything: it's incredible what magic a gray dress suit and upswept hair can work when you've got all the right moves.

3 Dizzy dame: Scottie follows Madeleine to the most remote corners of the Bay Area and discovers nuts among the Sequoias.

4 Breaking the waves and the ice: when they kiss, the moon surrenders its command of the tides.

5 On shore and under the covers: Scottie fishes Madeleine out of the bay, but who will fish him out of the sea of delirium that threatens to drown him?

falls in love with an unattainable woman, and loses all sight of reality and literally the ground below. He's a loner and a dreamer, qualities we see heightened through his relationship with his pragmatic confidante Midge (Barbara Bel Geddes, later of *Dallas* fame, 1978–1990). And all these things make him the perfect pawn in this masterful Hitchcockian chess game.

It seems almost inconceivable that *Vertigo* met with overall disapproval at the time of its original release. The critics tore it apart and the *New Yorker* branded it "farfetched nonsense." Elements like the Saul Bass title and dream sequences most likely estranged the 1950s moviegoer. Both integrate animation and dissociative color schemes, and qualify as experimental pieces in their own right.

"Once this movie is under way, it's off into very deep waters. The desperation of Scottie's need to revive Madeleine is both disturbing and moving, a combination you don't expect from a Hitchcock film." *San Francisco Examiner*

"The female characters in Hitchcock's films reflected the same qualities over and over again: They were blond. They were icy and remote. They were imprisoned in costumes that subtly combined fashion with fetishism." *Chicago Sun-Times*

6 Role playing: Scottie convinces Madeleine to confront her nightmarish visions by acting them out. But she breaks character for a parting kiss in the carriage house.

7 39 steps to psychosis: a legendary scene that left cineastes suffering from acrophobia.

8 Dirty blondes play dirty tricks: she changes her hair color, removes her brassiere and voilà – she's a new woman. Kim Novak as brassy redhead, Judy Barton.

9 On a painful mission: Scottie gets a funny feeling that there's a lotta Carlotta lying around at Mission Dolores.

10 A dead end: Madeleine's grandmother, Carlotta Valdez, has come back from beyond to take possession of what is rightly hers – Madeleine's soul.

11 Do it for me, cookie: Scottie wants to transform Judy into the Madeleine he so lovingly remembers.

It was only in the '70s that *Vertigo* gained a second lease on life. Critics began to praise the film's sleek story, its beautifully composed shots, and it entered into the canon of great cinema. Although Alfred Hitchcock directed more than his share of masterpieces, *Vertigo* is beyond compare. With an impact as haunting and captivating as ever, the film exhibits all the laudable Hitchcockian themes and calling cards theorists once claimed it lacked: from the master's trademark suspense, where the audience knows more than the characters, via doppelganger motives, voyeurism, guilt complexes embodied by the hero, wry humor, all the way to obsessive love for a blonde woman.

It is with particular regard to this latter aspect that *Vertigo* emerges as the British filmmaker's magnum opus.

As Andreas Kilb argues, it's no secret that Hitchcock was forever molding his vision of the "aloof, mysterious blonde icon," evident in his work with actresses like Ingrid Bergman and Grace Kelly. Yet *Vertigo* takes this single-minded fetish to its zenith. Here, not only Hitchcock, but the characters themselves are doubly driven by the desire to create the perfect blonde. What one can say without robbing the piece of all its mystique is that Madeleine is trained to act as an alluring decoy; and that a woman named Judy turns up in the second half of the film who, apart from her hair color and makeup, is a dead ringer for Madeleine. And so, after losing the love of his life, Scottie is given the chance to recreate her – using Judy.

HJK

THE 400 BLOWS
LES QUATRE CENTS COUPS
1958/59 - FRANCE - 101 MIN.

DIRECTOR
FRANÇOIS TRUFFAUT (1932–1984)

SCREENPLAY
FRANÇOIS TRUFFAUT, MARCEL MOUSSY

DIRECTOR OF PHOTOGRAPHY
HENRI DECAË

EDITING
MARIE-JOSÈPHE YOYOTTE

MUSIC
JEAN CONSTANTIN

PRODUCTION
FRANÇOIS TRUFFAUT, GEORGES CHARLOT for
LES FILMS DU CARROSSE, SÉDIF PRODUCTIONS

STARRING
JEAN-PIERRE LÉAUD (Antoine Doinel), CLAIRE MAURIER (Gilberte Doinel, the mother),
ALBERT RÉMY (Julien Doinel, the father), GUY DECOMBLE ('Petite Feuille', the French teacher),
PATRICK AUFFAY (René Bigey), ROBERT BEAUVAIS (Principal),
PIERRE REPP (English teacher), LUC ANDRIEUX (Sports teacher),
DANIEL COUTURIER (Mauricet), RICHARD KANAYAN (Abbou)

IFF CANNES 1959

COCINOR présente

JEAN-PIERRE LÉAUD

dans

PRIX DE LA MEILLEURE
MISE EN SCÈNE
au FESTIVAL de CANNES 1959

les

Quatre Cents

coups

PRIX DE L'OFFICE
CATHOLIQUE INTERNATIONAL
DU CINÉMA

UN FILM DE
FRANÇOIS TRUFFAUT

avec **CLAIRE MAURIER** et **ALBERT RÉMY**

GUY DÉCOMBLE . **GEORGES FLAMANT** . **PATRICK AUFFAY**

SCÉNARIO DE **FRANÇOIS TRUFFAUT** _ ADAPTATION DE **M. MOUSSY** et **F. TRUFFAUT**

DIALOGUES DE **MARCEL MOUSSY**

DIRECTEUR DE LA PHOTOGRAPHIE: HENRI DECAE   MUSIQUE DE JEAN CONSTANTIN

PRODUCTION: LES FILMS DU CARROSSE . S.E.D.I.F

"Your mother, your mother ... Well? What's wrong with your mother?" "She's dead, Monsieur!"

When the *Nouvelle Vague* celebrated its breakthrough at the Cannes Film Festival in 1959, reporters and photographers flocked around the 14-year-old Jean-Pierre Léaud. His performance as a neglected kid in *The 400 Blows* had impressed the critics – and moved them. At his side was the director François Truffaut, himself only 27, but already a notoriously belligerent film critic for *Arts* and *Cahiers du cinéma*. A year previously, he had been barred from the festival because of his polemical writings; now he was there to pick up the prize as Best Director.

Moviegoers also reacted ecstatically to the film, Truffaut's first full-length feature. *The 400 Blows* approached its topic with unprecedented honesty, directness, and compassion. It tells the tale of an unhappy childhood in Paris; and essentially, it was Truffaut's own story. He did nothing to embellish that story, or to romanticize his protagonist.

Young Antoine Doinel is no more an angel than his parents are devils. He skips school and heads for the Pigalle to watch movies with his buddy René (Patrick Auffay). To avoid the teacher's wrath, he forges notes and invents ever more drastic excuses; once, he even claims his mother has died. Antoine's parents are mainly preoccupied with themselves. Bored with her life as a housewife, his mother (Claire Maurier) has taken a lover. Antoine's father (Albert Rémy) tolerates this for the sake of a quiet life, and devotes all his time to his hobby: rally racing. This leaves little room for Antoine, who has in any case long since seen through the adults' hypocrisy. When he simply functions, he's ignored; when he misbehaves, he's punished. It's not just that the adults fail to understand Antoine, it's that they are loveless. Truffaut's film depicts a boy who is quite painfully alone.

CAHIERS DU CINÉMA Probably no other film journal has had such a decisive influence on the history of the movies: *Cahiers du cinéma*, founded in Paris in 1951 by Jacques Doniol-Valcroze, Lo Duca, and André Bazin, was not just a major contributor to the development of modern film criticism and theory, but also played a key role in the development of the cinema itself. In the '50s, uncompromising young critics such as François Truffaut, Jean-Luc Godard, Jacques Rivette, and Claude Chabrol made the *Cahiers* the leading voice for a renewal of the French cinema. Calling for a *politique des auteurs*, these so-called Young Turks demanded a cinema of personal artistic expression; they wanted to see films that reflected the filmmaker's own unique vision. As examples of what an *auteur* looked like, the *Cahiers* critics pointed to Hollywood directors such as Howard Hawks and Alfred Hitchcock, or to French individualists such as Jean Renoir and Robert Bresson – and they lambasted the respected representatives of the established French cinema. This *cinéma de qualité* they found sterile, clichéd, unoriginal, and fixated on the script.

Several *Cahiers* authors regarded their critical writings as a necessary prelude to their own filmmaking activity. And so, at the end of the '50s, Truffaut, Godard, Chabrol, and others exchanged the desk for the director's chair, and the *Nouvelle Vague* was born. Since then, the journal has gone through numerous changes. After May '68, the *Cahiers* was heavily influenced by Marxist ideas for a number of years. Now more docile politically, and with a smart new look, the *Cahiers du cinéma* has maintained its reputation as an intellectual forum for passionate cinéastes.

Catastrophe strikes when Antoine steals a typewriter from his father's office, intending to sell it for cash. His dad catches him and calls the cops. Antoine spends the night in a police cell, shoved in amongst crooks and hookers. Eventually he lands in a reform school for juvenile delinquents, somewhere out in the sticks.

For all the bitterness of the events it depicts, *The 400 Blows* is an astonishingly optimistic film. The tone of the movie oscillates between melancholy and exuberance. Like a secret ally, the camera accompanies Antoine and René on their adventures in Paris, and it succeeds almost

"The boy actor, who had never faced a movie camera before Truffaut found him, plays faultlessly and with pure, unsentimental appeal, mostly in his own unrehearsed words and gestures." *Time Magazine*

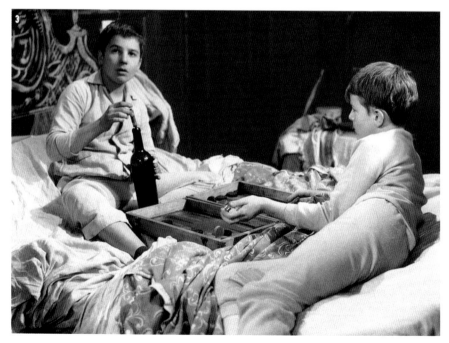

1 Kennel club: in his first feature-length film, François Truffaut recounts his isolated childhood.

2 A child star with staying power: Jean-Pierre Léaud (age 14) won instant accolades for his portrayal of Truffaut's alter ego, Antoine Doinel.

3 Extended slumber party: Antoine says good riddance to his neglectful parents and sets up camp with his friend René (Patrick Auffay).

4 Out of line: following in the footsteps of young Truffaut, Antoine endures a regimented life in a reform school. Even here, he sticks out like a sore thumb.

miraculously in capturing the specific flavor of what it feels like to be young. These black-and-white Dyaliscope images convey the luminous intensity of adolescent experience, a vital spontaneity and innocent curiosity that most adults have lost forever.

Though *The 400 Blows* was a key film of the *Nouvelle Vague*, most present-day viewers will agree that it's far less radical in its form than – for example – the work of Jean-Luc Godard. What was new about this movie was the unforced episodic narrative structure and the unprejudiced view of its characters, who are always more than mere marionettes of the screenplay. Above all, it was the autobiographical aspect of this film that would ensure its seminal influence on the *cinéma d'auteur*. The movie's final scene

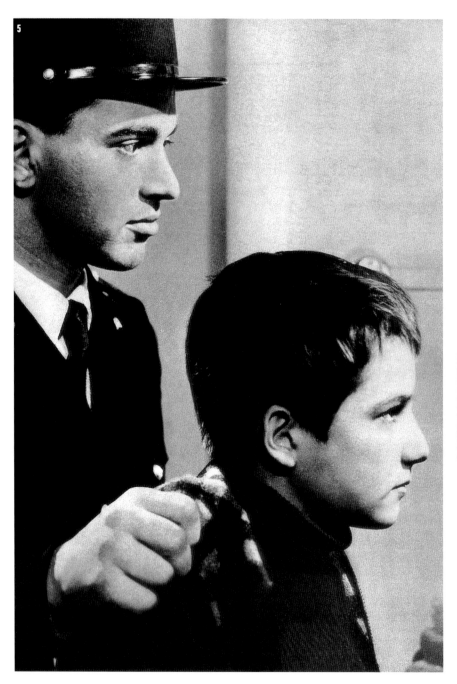

has also inspired a host of filmmakers. In the middle of a soccer match, Antoine manages to escape from the reformatory. He runs and runs until he reaches the sea, then suddenly turns to the camera and pauses. The frame freezes, and the film ends with a close-up of the boy gazing straight out at us. Not that this was to be audiences' last encounter with Antoine Doinel: over the 20 years that followed, Léaud went on to play Truffaut's alter ego no fewer than four times. It was a collaboration that would eventually go down in the history of cinema.

JH

"Truffaut has responded to his doubters and detractors in the only way that carries conviction: by offering us a very fine film."

Le Monde

5 Civil servant: when Antoine's father hands him over to the authorities, the boy learns that a man's first and foremost duty is to the state and not to his family.

6 Clouds in my coffee: this is the closest Antoine will ever come to having anything handed to him on a silver platter.

7 French fashion trends: Antoine tries to avoid taking an additional 400 blows by sporting a tough-guy fedora. The film was the first big hit of the *Nouvelle Vague* and started a major cult of its own.

SOME LIKE IT HOT ♟

1959 - USA - 120 MIN.

DIRECTOR

BILLY WILDER (1906–2002)

SCREENPLAY

BILLY WILDER, I. A. L. DIAMOND,
suggested by a short story by ROBERT THOEREN and M. LOGAN

DIRECTOR OF PHOTOGRAPHY

CHARLES LANG JR.

EDITING

ARTHUR P. SCHMIDT

MUSIC

ADOLPH DEUTSCH

PRODUCTION

BILLY WILDER for THE MIRISCH CORPORATION, ASHTON PRODUCTIONS

STARRING

MARILYN MONROE (Sugar Kane Kowalczyk), TONY CURTIS (Joe / Josephine),
JACK LEMMON (Jerry / Daphne), JOE E. BROWN (Osgood Fielding III),
GEORGE RAFT ("Spats" Colombo), PAT O'BRIEN (Mulligan),
NEHEMIAH PERSOFF (Little Bonaparte), JOAN SHAWLEE (Sweet Sue),
GEORGE E. STONE (Toothpick Charlie), EDWARD G. ROBINSON JR. (Johnny Paradise)

ACADEMY AWARDS 1959

OSCAR for BEST COSTUMES (Orry-Kelly)

MARILYN MONROE
and her bosom companions

TONY CURTIS

JACK LEMMON

in a BILLY WILDER production

"SOME LIKE IT HOT"

GEORGE **RAFT** · PAT **O'BRIEN** · JOE E. **BROWN**

SCREEN PLAY BY **BILLY WILDER** and **I. A. L. DIAMOND** · DIRECTED BY **BILLY WILDER**

An ASHTON PICTURE · A Mirisch Company Presentation Released thru United Artists

SOME LIKE IT HOT 259-90

SOME LIKE IT HOT

Josephine: "You're NOT a girl! You're a GUY! Why would a guy wanna marry a guy?" Daphne: "Security!"

Chicago, 1929. After accidentally witnessing a mob massacre, fly-by-night musicians Jerry (Jack Lemmon) and Joe (Tony Curtis) decide that a change of scenery might be good for their health. They get a gig with an all-girl band headed south for Florida, shave their legs to blend in with the crowd, and say *arrivederci* to the city's trigger-happy hoods.

Life as the weaker sex presents each of the boys with unforeseen snags: Joe alias "Josephine" loses his heart to a liquor-loving, ukulele-strumming singer named Sugar Kane (Marilyn Monroe) and wants nothing more than to liberate himself of both dress and drawers. Jerry, on the other hand, takes to his feminine side a little too well: calling himself "Daphne" and exuding natural charm, Jerry catches the eye of octogenarian tycoon Osgood Fielding III (Joe E. Brown), and can't shake the aging playboy off his skirt. But when murderous Chicago mafioso "Spats"

Colombo (George Raft) turns up on the scene, there's suddenly one beau too many in what was supposed to have been a "ladies only" club.

You might wonder what prompted Billy Wilder to shoot the picture many consider to be his best comedy in black and white. For wouldn't Technicolor's dazzling effects do better in bringing out the contours of a story about men caked in rouge? Perhaps, but *Some Like It Hot* is more than just a drag comedy; it's a salute to the dawn of cinema, Hollywood gangster pictures, screwball comedies of the 1940s, and that special brand of Marx Bros irreverence. These old-fashioned ingredients, when shaken up in the Wilderian cocktail mixer, make for a high-octane concoction that strips us of all inhibitions and has us laughing ourselves silly over its overtly sexual subtext.

If your last viewing of *Some Like It Hot* predates puberty, be prepared for a real eye-opener: racy double-

TONY CURTIS His candid autobiography tells of a Jewish kid born in 1925 in the Bronx who didn't have it easy, but managed to soar to the top thanks to his natural good looks. Indeed, Hollywood wholeheartedly opened its gates to Bernard Schwartz's winning appearance, and the name his Hungarian immigrant parents bestowed on him quickly fell by the wayside. Curtis's initial successes in low-caliber period pieces like *Son of Ali Baba* (1952) had him pigeonholed as the Hollywood Dream Factory's first teen idol, and presented James Dean with a bit of competition. But Curtis was seldom cast as the heartthrob, acting instead in epics like *Spartacus* (1960) and *Taras Bulba* (1962) as the on-screen son to stars like Kirk Douglas, Burt Lancaster, Yul Brynner, and Cary Grant. Stanley Kramer's racial drama *The Defiant Ones* (1958) gave him his first break at character acting, and *The Boston Strangler* (1968) was his second and last attempt at making headway in that field. His knack at comedy was responsible for the greatest hits and most regrettable misses of his circa 120 films.

And when he wasn't in front of the camera, the tabloids kept Tony Curtis in the public eye: his numerous marriages to actresses like *Psycho's* Janet Leigh and Germany's Christine Kaufmann as well as his long battle with drug addiction were highly publicized. His notoriety as a playboy and lover of fast cars was poked fun at in the cult TV series *The Persuaders!* (1971–72). Tony Curtis, father of actress Jamie Lee Curtis, died in 2010 from complications of chronic lung disease.

"Both Curtis and Lemmon are practicing cruel deceptions – Curtis has Monroe thinking she's met a millionaire, and Brown thinks Lemmon is a woman – but the film dances free before anyone gets hurt. Both Monroe and Brown learn the truth and don't care, and after Lemmon reveals he's a man, Brown delivers the best curtain line in the movies." *Chicago Sun-Times*

1 Last tango in platforms: Jerry alias Daphne (Jack Lemmon) celebrates his engagement to Osgood Fielding III (Joe E. Brown) with the dance of death.

2 You're blocking my sun: while posing as the shortsighted heir to the Shell Oil fortune, Joe (Tony Curtis) tries to

get Sugar (Marilyn Monroe) to share her own special set of riches with him. Her chaperone, however, is a real drag.

3 How's about a little goodnight kiss? Now, nighty night and don't let the Chihuahuas bite.

4 Girls will be girls: nothing like sneaking a slug of whisky when mother hen isn't looking.

entendres about free love, homosexuality, and impotence – as fresh today as they were 50 years ago – pop up throughout the film's seemingly innocent dialogue. The film censors must have been deaf, dumb, and blind to miss the connotations of remarks like Sugar's demure "I-always-get-the-fuzzy-end-of-the-lollipop." And no less audacious is how Wilder pits glaring opposites like sex and money, life and death, appearance and reality, as well as mobsters and music against one another.

It is, without question, a comedy born out of contradiction and role-reversal. The virile Joe, for example, must dress up as an allegedly impotent and near-sighted oil baron to strike it big with Sugar; but rather than putting the moves on her, he lets an intimate evening on board

Osgood's yacht inspire her to do the job for him. And thus by seeing to it that his protagonists are constantly compelled to don various disguises, Wilder transforms what should be a fight for survival into a never-ending laugh attack. It is a dynamic that waxes doubly ironic when the prospects of a honeymoon with Osgood *à la* "he wants to go to the French Riviera but I'm kinda leaning towards Niagara Falls" make Jerry / Daphne wish he were dead.

Some Like It Hot was a legendary endeavor from start to finish; from the shimmering sheer dress Marilyn wears while singing "I Wanna Be Loved By You" right up until Osgood's unfazed "Nobody's perfect" in reaction to Daphne's true identity. And the long journey to this immortal last line was even more of an adventure than the fittings

"When we talked about it we decided that they should join the girls' band as an absolute question of life and death. Otherwise it would seem that at any point in the picture they could remove their wigs and skirts and say to the girls that they love 'Look, no problem, we're guys and you're gals and we love you.'" *Billy Wilder*

5 I wanna be loved by you: Sugar Kane does some field research to help find a cure for impotence.

6 The Great Depression hits home: like so many other qualified men, Jerry and Joe are out of work and flat out

of luck. Looks like Santa Claus might not be the only one putting those old Christmas stockings to good use.

7 Rock candy: Joe can barely keep his mind on his sax with all that sweetness kicking about on stage.

8 In hot water: to look at the two of them, who would believe that Tony Curtis compared locking lips with this blonde to kissing Hitler? Not Curtis, that's for sure. Later he denied ever having said it.

with Academy Award–winning costume designer Orry-Kelly; for working with Marilyn Monroe entailed a crazy shooting schedule that supplied Billy Wilder and Tony Curtis with a lifetime of anecdotes. There was simply no telling whether she'd show up on the set, and when she would, she'd need 40 takes for a single line of dialogue like "Where's that bourbon?" At her mercy, Curtis and Lemmon were left standing for hours on end in high heels, and Wilder himself claimed to have suffered a nervous breakdown as a result of his leading lady's unreliable work ethic. Years later, the director was singing a very different tune, deifying Monroe for her electric presence and the perfect sense of comic timing she demonstrated here.

Be it scripted subtext or revisionist interpretation, *Some Like It Hot* can also be seen as a commentary on the tragic sex goddess's off-screen life: misguided by

romantic ideals and driven to drink by irresponsible partners, Sugar longs to find a sensitive, understanding man. Was it just coincidence that the spectacled heir to Shell Oil she falls in love with resembled Monroe's real-life intellectual husband Arthur Miller? For indeed a sentimental heart-note lies beyond the picture's general lunacy and Wilder's cynical overtones: pouring her heart out in song, Sugar is granted the magical kiss she's been yearning for all along, when Joe, dressed as a woman, marches across the stage and reveals his true feelings for her. Now that Joe has gained insight into how "the other half lives," he can no longer toy with Sugar's emotions.

Marilyn Monroe's tragic death in 1962 was far removed from the celluloid happy endings so many of her characters knew. But her story and her appeal transcend them all. PB

BEN-HUR ♛♛♛♛♛♛♛♛♛♛♛

1959 - USA - 213 MIN.

DIRECTOR
WILLIAM WYLER (1902–1981)

SCREENPLAY
KARL TUNBERG, based on the novel *Ben-Hur:
A Tale of the Christ* by LEW WALLACE

DIRECTOR OF PHOTOGRAPHY
ROBERT SURTEES

EDITING
JOHN D. DUNNING, RALPH E. WINTERS

MUSIC
MIKLÓS RÓZSA

PRODUCTION
SAM ZIMBALIST for MGM

STARRING
CHARLTON HESTON (Judah Ben-Hur), JACK HAWKINS (Quintus Arrius),
HAYA HARAREET (Esther), STEPHEN BOYD (Messala),
HUGH GRIFFITH (Sheik Ilderim), MARTHA SCOTT (Miriam),
CATHY O'DONNELL (Tirzah), FRANK THRING (Pontius Pilate),
FINLAY CURRIE (Balthasar), MINO DORO (Gratus), CLAUDE HEATER (Jesus),
SAM JAFFE (Simonides)

ACADEMY AWARDS 1959
OSCARS for BEST PICTURE (Sam Zimbalist), BEST DIRECTOR (William Wyler),
BEST LEADING ACTOR (Charlton Heston), BEST SUPPORTING ACTOR (Hugh Griffith),
BEST CINEMATOGRAPHY (Robert Surtees), BEST EDITING (Ralph E. Winters, John D. Dunning),
BEST MUSIC (Miklós Rózsa), BEST ART DIRECTION (William A. Horning,
Edward C. Carfagno, Hugh Hunt), BEST COSTUMES (Elizabeth Haffenden),
BEST VISUAL EFFECTS (A. Arnold Gillespie, Robert MacDonald),
BEST SOUND EFFECTS (Milo B. Lory), and BEST SOUND (Franklin Milton)

THE ENTERTAINMENT EXPERIENCE OF A LIFETIME!

METRO-GOLDWYN-MAYER
presents

A Tale of the Christ
by GENERAL LEW WALLACE

Directed by
WILLIAM WYLER

Starring

CHARLTON HESTON · JACK HAWKINS

HAYA HARAREET · STEPHEN BOYD

HUGH GRIFFITH · MARTHA SCOTT with CATHY O'DONNELL · SAM JAFFE

Screen Play by   Produced by
KARL TUNBERG · SAM ZIMBALIST

TECHNICOLOR®   FILMED IN
CAMERA 65

"I tell you, the day Rome falls there will be a shout of freedom such as the world has never heard before."

In the 26th year of our Lord, the Roman province of Judea is in turmoil. The winds of revolt stir up the empire, and the sermons of an awe-inspiring rabbi in the little village of Nazareth are drawing ever-larger crowds.

Suspicious of any hint of subversion, Rome sends reinforcements to Jerusalem. Messala (Stephen Boyd), the man appointed commanding officer of the Roman legions, grew up in the Jewish holy city as the son of a high-ranking official. The first person to welcome his homecoming is a childhood friend named Judah Ben-Hur (Charlton Heston), a well-respected and influential businessman. Sadly, the years have made strangers of them: Messala wants nothing more than to serve the Emperor Tiberius and implores Judah to disclose the names of the rebel ringleaders;

Judah's allegiance, however, is to his people, and he refuses to betray them.

Messala doesn't have to wait long to act against the Jews and spite Ben-Hur. The day after their encounter, proconsul Gratus (Mino Doro) arrives in Jerusalem and a dislodged roof tile from Judah's palatial home injures the official as he rides by. Messala has Judah's family arrested in a flash: his mother Miriam (Martha Scott) and sister Tirzah (Cathy O'Donnell) are incarcerated, and Judah is sentenced to the slave galleys with little prospect of survival. Miraculously, he survives his excruciating labors. Tormented by a blistering thirst, he and the other prisoners are hauled through Nazareth, where a carpenter's son lets Judah drink from the elixir of life …

MIKLÓS RÓZSA In 1934, 27-year-old Miklós Rózsa received some friendly, career-shaping advice from well-established composer and colleague Arthur Honegger, who convinced him that his future lay in scoring motion pictures. The son of a Budapest entrepreneur, Rózsa started off writing orchestra and chamber music. He went to London, where he landed his first job in cinema, composing the score to *Knight Without Armour* (1937) directed by Jacques Feyder and starring Marlene Dietrich. The film's producer, fellow Hungarian Alexander Korda, was so taken by his work that he put him under contract. The Korda production *The Thief of Bagdad* (1940) sent both men to Hollywood, and Rózsa was soon working for some of the industry's largest studios. It wasn't long before he'd rooted himself as one of the premier fixtures in his field, earning his first of three Oscars in 1945 for Alfred Hitchcock's *Spellbound*. His scores were the first to be pressed and sold as records – a further testament to his greatness. The flip side to his success is that Rózsa thought he had been pegged as a specialist in the scoring of period pieces. And considering some of the highlights of his resumé, including *Quo vadis?* (1951), Richard Thorpe's *Ivanhoe* (1952), and Joseph L. Mankiewicz's *Julius Caesar* (1953), there was little question as to who would be asked to compose *Ben-Hur* (1959) when MGM announced their intention to remake it. Full-orchestra scores went out of fashion in Hollywood during the earlier 1960s, and Rózsa put his academic roots to good use, becoming a music professor at the University of Southern California. The last picture he worked on was Carl Reiner's detective caper comedy *Dead Men Don't Wear Plaid* (1981). Rósza died in Los Angeles in 1995.

Three years go by, and Judah finds himself chained to the oars of a slave-powered Roman warship under the command of consul Quintus Arrius (Jack Hawkins). Stationed in the Mediterranean, the vessel's mission is seek out and destroy Macedonian pirates. When battle is joined with some pirates on the open water one day, the imperial ship is rammed, and Judah slips his chains, escapes from the galley and saves Quintus Arrius. To show his gratitude, the Roman consul adopts Judah as his son. Galley slave number 41 is reborn as Roman citizen Ben-Hur, raising himself up from hard laborer to star chariot driver.

"And then the furious chariot race! The cameras are so close to the horses and charioteers that it simply takes one's breath away. Seldom before has any film scene achieved such a heartstopping tempo, such active suspense. This is pure cinema, at the height of technical perfection." *Die Welt*

1 Your own personal Jesus: Charlton Heston as the godly Coliseum chariot driver Judah Ben-Hur.

2 Battleship Potemkinus: a countless number of men will lose their lives slaving away in these galleys. But not to worry, Hollywood can always replenish them with another round of extras.

3 Pony express: Judah challenges his arch-enemy to a Roman-style drag race. Heston trained for months to pull off the spectacular sequence without a stuntman. His competitor obviously trained less.

4 Manischewitz makes *meshuggah*: behold a set of Jews who are about to mix some ancient traditions with some newer ones this high holiday season. From right: Judah's right-hand man Simonides (Sam Jaffe), Judah's mother Miriam (Martha Scott), Simonides's daughter Esther (Haya Harareet), and Judah's sister Tirza (Cathy O'Donnell).

After several years of fame and fortune in the capital city, Ben-Hur heads home to settle scores with Messala.

With a reputation that precedes him, the undefeatable charioteer from the great circus at the Roman arena challenges Messala to a race: nine laps in battle chariots, with four horses harnessed to each cart. It is a deadly competition without rules, and not everyone makes it home in one piece. Messala dies trying, but a sadistic bit of glory is left to be his: just as the consul takes his final breath, he tells the victorious Ben-Hur that although Tirzah and Miriam have survived the Roman dungeons, they have both contracted leprosy, a then incurable disease.

Judah finds Miriam and Tirzah living as outcasts in the Valley of the Lepers, but Tirzah's days are numbered. Ben-Hur now realizes that avenging his enemy did not afford him the peace of mind he had anticipated. But stories once again abound of the miraculous rabbi who preaches of love and forgiveness on the hill outside the city. Miriam and Tirzah want to hear one of the sermons, but the Roman Pontius Pilate robs them of the chance when he sentences the man called Jesus of Nazareth to death by crucifixion. Death, however, cannot stifle the man's message, and as Jesus's mortal life comes to an end, thunder and lightning tear across the sky bringing forth a downpour that cures Miriam, Tirzah, and

5 Chalice from the palace: Messala (Stephen Boyd) and Judah have no idea what damage drinking can do to a friendship.

6 Jesus Christ Superstar: or is it a precursor to Woodstock? To maintain

the sense of mystery, director William Wyler only shows Jesus (Claude Heater) from his best side – the rear.

7 I work and I slave and what thanks do I get? Messala sentences loyal subject Ben-Hur to hard labor aboard

the war galleys. His survival will require nothing short of a miracle.

all the lepers of their ailments. The miracle also has a cathartic effect on Judah, who at last finds inner peace.

By 1959, Hollywood's own empire was faltering. Television was the enemy, and the number of its disciples was increasing rapidly. Ready to do whatever it took to get audiences to return to the cinema, the big-name studios planned a counterattack that promised to deliver a larger-than-life moviegoing experience flooded with dazzling images, wide-screen dimensions, exotic locales, a host of stars, and sets and costumes of unprecedented opulence. With its 365 speaking parts, 50,000 extras, and 15-million-dollar budget, *Ben-Hur* was not only the most ambitious of this wave of epic films (which also included Mervyn LeRoy's *Quo vadis?* (1951), Henry Koster's *The Robe* (1953), and, in 1956, Cecil B. DeMille's *The Ten Commandments*), but also

the most acclaimed. It was one of the box-office sensations of the decade and became the first picture to win a total of 11 Oscars, a record not matched until James Cameron's *Titanic* (1997). Unfortunately, *Ben-Hur*'s gold standard was far costlier than anticipated: while shooting was still in progress, producer Sam Zimbalist died of what is widely believed to have been a stress-induced heart attack. At the time, the movie's enormous budget had threatened to send the failing Metro Goldwyn Mayer filing for bankruptcy, but its enormous popularity with audiences supplied the studio with a manifold return on its investment. Still, *Ben-Hur* would end up being the zenith of such spectaculars, for there was no denying that the inordinate effort productions like these demanded made them an unviable means of saving the studio system.

On the other hand, *Ben-Hur*'s story was already a proven cinematic success. Lew Wallace's novel of the same name was an instant bestseller when it was published in 1880. The piece was subsequently adapted for the stage and then resurrected in 1925 as a sensational silent film by director Fred Nibo. Banking on the "you can never have too much of a good thing" Hollywood mentality, the 1959 remake drew from all the magic of the original and enhanced it by means of the 65 mm Technicolor camera, a stereo soundtrack, and all imaginable technical innovations of the day.

"Great credit goes to producer Zimbalist, scenarist Tunberg and director Wyler, but the greatest belongs to Wyler. His wit, intelligence and formal instinct are almost everywhere in evidence, and he has set a standard of excellence by which coming generations of screen spectacles can expect to be measured." *Time Magazine*

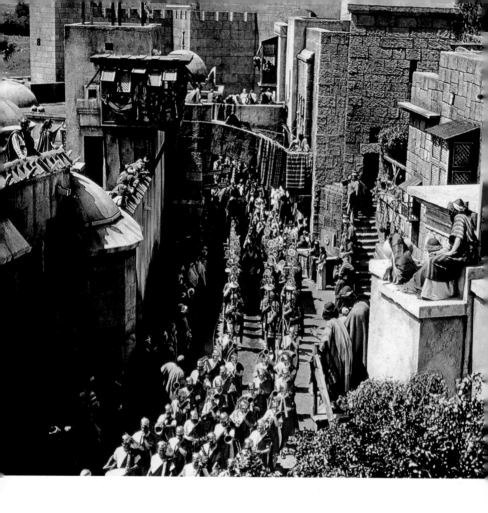

"Although many viewers tend to believe that this is a fact-based story, it is a quintessentially American fiction that could as easily have been set in the American Revolutionary War as in the Holy Land during the time of Christ." *Apollo Movie Guide*

8 March of dimes: rest assured, they're marching for a good cause – world domination.

9 Live from Las Vegas: after a brief stint on the stage of the MGM Grand, Messala packs up his things and moves on to bigger and better projects at Caesar's Palace.

A filmgoing experience that supplies everything the eye could possibly want, *Ben-Hur*'s chariot race in Jerusalem remains one of the cinema's most recognized and revered sequences. An entire year was required to bring the nine-minute scene to the screen. One of the great ironies of this meticulously organized filmmaking endeavor is that director William Wyler, awarded an Oscar for his work, wasn't responsible for the sequence's staging. The job was the task of Andrew Marton and Yakima Canutt. The latter also served as the picture's stunt director and had risen to screen fame for his death-defying pass beneath director John Ford's moving *Stagecoach* (1939).

Several uncredited names on the *Ben-Hur* production team went on to become some of the industry's movers and shakers: second unit director Sergio Leone is known today for his own Ancient World epics; and set designer Ken Adam, on staff with the production's art department, ventured off to more covert arenas, waging war as the most prominent art director of the 007 series.

EP

LA DOLCE VITA – THE SWEET LIFE 🏆

LA DOLCE VITA

1959/60 - ITALY / FRANCE - 177 MIN.

DIRECTOR

FEDERICO FELLINI (1920–1993)

SCREENPLAY

FEDERICO FELLINI, TULLIO PINELLI,
ENNIO FLAIANO, BRUNELLO RONDI

DIRECTOR OF PHOTOGRAPHY

OTELLO MARTELLI

EDITING

LEO CATOZZO

MUSIC

NINO ROTA

PRODUCTION

GIUSEPPE AMATO, ANGELO RIZZOLI for
RIAMA FILM, PATHÉ CONSORTIUM CINÉMA, GRAY-FILM

STARRING

MARCELLO MASTROIANNI (Marcello Rubini), ANITA EKBERG (Sylvia),
ANOUK AIMÉE (Maddalena), YVONNE FURNEAUX (Emma), ALAIN CUNY (Steiner),
WALTER SANTESSO (Paparazzo), ADRIANO CELENTANO (Singer),
LEX BARKER (Robert), ALAIN DIJON (Frankie Stout),
ANNIBALE NINCHI (Marcello's Father), NADIA GRAY (Nadia), NICO (Partygoer)

ACADEMY AWARDS 1961

OSCAR for BEST COSTUMES (Piero Gherardi)

IFF CANNES 1960

GOLDEN PALM (Federico Fellini)

FEDERICO FELLINI

LA DOLCE VITA

DISTRIBUZIONE
CINERIZ

MARCELLO MASTROIANNI * ANITA EKBERG

ANOUK AIMEE * YVONNE FURNEAUX * ALAIN CUNY * ANNIBALE NINCHI
WALTER SANTESSO e MAGALI NOEL * LEX BARKER * JACQUES SERNAS e con NADIA GRAY

UNA CO-PRODUZIONE RIAMA FILM, ROMA
PATHE CONSORTIUM CINEMA, PARIGI

TOTALSCOPE
MARCHIO DEPOSITATO DALL'A.T.C.

REALIZZATA DA GIUSEPPE AMATO

"Rome is simply marvelous. A kind of jungle – humid and beautiful, loud at times, peaceful at others – it's a place where you can hide behind the foliage."

"Scandalous!" The cries of the Italian press were heard far and wide: *La dolce vita* was a wanton, permissive, blasphemous piece of celluloid and nothing short of appalling. The Vatican condemned it to the last circle of hell, and the in crowd turned up their noses. Federico Fellini was spat at and even challenged to a duel. With *La dolce vita*, the filmmaker immersed himself in a world of stars and hopefuls, artists and intellectuals, and supplied his audience with superficiality and decadence instead of the traditional content and good morals. As Fellini saw it, desire had won out over reason, speechlessness over communication, and filth over purity …

A stone-carved Jesus glides over the rooftops of Rome, sanctifying arms outstretched. Suspended by cables, the gigantic statue is being flown to the Vatican via helicopter, followed by a second chopper in which reporter Marcello (Marcello Mastroianni) and photographer Paparazzo (Walter Santesso) keep a close eye on the action. The two men are tabloid journalists, riff-raff propagators of the flashbulb storm that hits the city whenever a movie star struts down a runway. Their notebooks are always within arm's reach in case they spot an aristocrat canoodling with his mistress at a nightclub. Paparazzo chomps at the bit for a potential photo opportunity of Rome's A-listers – preferably with their pants down. The suave Marcello, however, is discrete in his approach, offhandedly ensnaring his quarry while he shadows them from one haunt to the next. The chic cafés of the Via Veneto are his second home, the

NINO ROTA It all started with a bus stop. This was the site where Fellini was to happen upon a fellow caught up in his own thoughts and waiting for a line that normally took a totally different route. Fellini wanted to inform him of his error, but the gentleman's desired bus stopped right in front of them before he got the chance. The event left a lasting impression on Fellini, who was convinced that he had met someone capable of performing magic. Although the particulars of the account vary – sometimes the director placed the bus stop at Rome's Via Po, sometimes in front of Cinecittà Studios – this is allegedly how Fellini got to be friends with composer Nino Rota just after the end of World War II. Their genial relationship gave rise to many a magical moment in cinematic history. Be it Gelsomina's lament in *The Road (La strada*, 1954) or the circus march in *8½ (8½ / Otto e mezzo*, 1962) Nino Rota's music was, as one critic wrote, very much an invisible player within a film's narrative. Nino Rota Rinaldi was born into a Milano family of musicians in 1911. It wasn't long before he was deemed a prodigy and schooled in classical music throughout Italy and abroad in American conservatories. He started out composing orchestra and choir pieces, before trying his hand at film scoring in the early 1940s. By the time he scored Alberto Lattuada's *Without Pity (Senza pietà*, 1948) it became clear just what the distinguishing factors of Rota's music were: he had a knack for pursuing known melodies, transforming them, and integrating existing snippets here and there. Later, for example, he was awarded an Oscar for scoring Francis Ford Coppola's *The Godfather – Part II* (1974), a project largely inspired by the musical compositions he created for Eduardo de Filippo's *Fortunella* (1957).

Rota produced dozens of readily recognizable melodies. His music seesawed between pathos and irony, and it was not unheard of for melancholy bars to suddenly switch into something snappier, or for a loud note to subside into an extended undertone. He collaborated with big name directors like Luchino Visconti, King Vidor, and René Clément. Nonetheless, his lifelong partnership with Fellini is the stuff of legend. Starting with *The White Sheik (Lo sceicco bianco*, 1952), Rota wrote the music to all Fellini's pictures for the remainder of his life. The two men would sit together at the piano with Rota composing and testing out combinations, while Fellini provided feedback. This was to be the birthplace of some of the cinema's most magical music. *The Orchestra Rehearsal (Prova d'orchestra*, 1978) was the last project they would work on together. Nino Rota died in Rome the following year. He was one of the 20th century's most influential film composers.

1 Couldn't aspire to anything higher: the statuesque Anita Ekberg soaks up the sweet life during a midnight bath in Rome's Trevi Fountain.

2 Passing up the paparazzi: and wouldn't you know it, the man that coined the term "paparazzi" was none other than former tabloid journalist turned film director Federico Fellini.

3 Sweets for the sweet: within minutes, this sober pair will be utterly drunk on life and ready to brave the shallows.

"This sensational representation of certain aspects of life in contemporary Rome, as revealed in the clamorous experience of a free-wheeling newspaper man, is a brilliantly graphic estimation of a whole swath of society in decay and a withering commentary upon the tragedy of the over-civilized." *The New York Times*

heart of the action and a breeding ground for young ladies itching to get discovered.

Marcello is not an impartial observer, more an active member of the lofty company he keeps tabs on. Accompanied by Maddalena (Anouk Aimée), a local billionaire's daughter, he gallivants through the night until sunrise, then rushes off to the side of a Hollywood glamour girl (Anita Ekberg), giving her a personal tour of all Rome has to offer … He'll attend a palace soirée, and promenade with blue bloods across the expanse of the princely estate. At an outdoor party where starlets and movie producers fill the dance floor, Marcello's the one who puts a sizzle in their step, only to watch from the sidelines as the night nearly ends in an orgy. Sunset comes and goes, and he completes the circle at a gathering hosted by his intellec-

tual buddy Steiner (Alain Cuny), bringing a tone of calm to the evening while rediscovering his calling in life as a writer – only to let it slip through his fingers once more.

By openly depicting sexuality to an extent that had been virtually unheard of until then – from a barefooted Anita Ekberg getting down and dirty to the sound of young Adriano Celentano's wild rock 'n' roll stylings to Nadia Gray baring it all at a party to the pack of hungry eyes – Fellini's film was immediately the target of a heated debate. The outcome: even in the more remote provinces, audiences lined up in their thousands to see a three-hour picture that would normally have only run in arthouse cinemas. *La dolce vita* instantly became Federico Fellini's greatest hit, regardless of its episodic narrative structure and the absence of an exciting story line. Marcello is the film's sole connecting

4 Wiggle and jiggle your way across the dance floor: Fellini's depiction of high society's decadence-till-dawn mentality awakens images of the Fall of Rome.

5 Caught up in the glamour: an ordinary woman loves the unexpected media attention she is showered with. Little does she suspect her husband's suicide and the murder of their children is the reason for it. Without a doubt, Fellini's criticism of the media has even more force today.

6 Undulating Undine: a former "Miss Sweden," the real life Anita Ekberg also lost her heart to Italy's capital city. Shortly after the shoot of *La dolce vita* wrapped up, she relocated there permanently.

"... an allegory, a cautionary tale of a man without a center."

Chicago Sun-Times

8

7 Va-va-va-voom! A woman, dressed in her own version of the holy cloth, awaits Marcello at the top of the cathedral. It was one of the many scenes that shocked the Vatican, especially considering that St. Peter's

Square can be spotted in the background.

8 Maestro Mastroianni: *La dolce vita* marked the beginning of a collaboration between Mastroianni and Fellini

that spanned several decades and six films. As the director's on-screen alter ego, the suave actor plays Marcello Rubini, a man desperately trying to escape the frustrations of life as a tabloid journalist.

thread, leading us through a labyrinth of nightly escapades across Rome.

The film's opulent visuals meant that it was often compared to a painting, deemed either a "portrait of society" or "Baroque fresco." Much of that in fact is the result of Swedish actress Anita Ekberg's performance. Her nighttime dip in Rome's Trevi Fountain is one of the most illustrious images ever to grace the screen; her viewing of St. Peter's Dome in a slinky priest-like garment created a furor among the Catholic churchmen sensitive to the use of symbols. Ekberg, in fact, was a sensation throughout Rome even before shooting commenced, and Fellini made shrewd use of her celebrity status. He drew from actual tabloid anecdotes – the slap Ekberg takes from her on-screen husband (Lex Barker) was directly lifted from a public incident with her real-life spouse – and shamelessly blurred the distinctions between real-life people and film characters. Likewise, he

had numerous aristocrats and models portray themselves, thus hoping to get the episodes to play as naturally and authentically as possible. His choices paid off. The German newspaper *Die Welt* wanted to know why there was so much controversy surrounding the film, claiming that Fellini had simply spliced together a chronicle of scandals to unmask Rome's nitty-gritty demi-mondes.

What *La dolce vita* does succeed in unmasking is the interdependency of the media and media sensations, and journalists and stars. The former needs material to write about, and the latter needs the publicity in order to exist at all. Long before this habitual feed-off became the focus of public attention, Fellini began to ask himself whether an event without media coverage can be regarded as an event *per se*. It is precisely this question which still makes the film read like something hot off the press.

NM

L'AVVENTURA / THE ADVENTURE

1960 - ITALY / FRANCE - 145 MIN.

DIRECTOR
MICHELANGELO ANTONIONI (1912–2007)

SCREENPLAY
MICHELANGELO ANTONIONI,
ELIO BARTOLINI, TONINO GUERRA

DIRECTOR OF PHOTOGRAPHY
ALDO SCAVARDA

EDITING
ERALDO DA ROMA

MUSIC
GIOVANNI FUSCO

PRODUCTION
LUCIANO PERUGIA, CINO DEL DUCA, AMATO PENNASILICO for CINO DEL DUCA,
PRODUZIONE CINEMATOGRAFICHE EUROPEE, ROBERT & RAYMOND HAKIM COMPANY,
SOCIÉTÉ CINÉMATOGRAPHIQUE LYRE

STARRING
GABRIELE FERZETTI (Sandro), MONICA VITTI (Claudia), LÉA MASSARI (Anna),
DOMINIQUE BLANCHAR (Giulia), JAMES ADDAMS (Corrado),
RENZO RICCI (Anna's Father), ESMERALDA RUSPOLI (Patrizia),
LELIO LUTTAZZI (Raimondo), GIOVANNI PETRUCCI (Goffredo), DOROTHY DE POLIOLO (Gloria)

"The thought of losing you kills me. But I no longer feel your presence."

This film needs some effective defenders, such as the famous Spanish director Pedro Almodóvar, who said: "When I first saw *L'avventura*, I was shaken. I felt just like Monica Vitti in the film. Like her, I could say: 'I don't know what to do … Good, let's go to a nightclub … I think I have an idea … I've forgotten it already …'" Or the great American film critic Pauline Kael, who wrote (in *Film Quarterly*): "*L'avventura* is, easily, the film of the year, because Antonioni demonstrated that the possibilities for serious, cultivated, personal expression in this medium have not been exhausted."

The reason why *L'avventura* needs some persuasive advocates is simple: at first glance, it looks forbidding, unfocused, and long-winded. At the premiere in Cannes, the audience made its feelings very clear, with some people shouting "Cut!" during scenes that seemed too protracted. Others disliked the characters' strange behavior. The ending was even greeted with mocking laughter, which is hard to understand, given the symbolic power of the final image: a panorama platform in the light of dawn; on the left, in the distance, the snowcapped peak of Mount Etna; in the middle, with his back to the camera, a man in a suit, sitting hunch-shouldered on a park bench. Standing beside him, also with her back to us, a blonde woman in a dark skirt and sweater; she strokes his head, but says nothing. The right half of the frame is filled with the windowless wall of a house. The man and the woman are in some kind

---

SICILY IN FILM Lanterns dangle from the bows of little boats as they row across the sea in the darkness: night after night, the fishermen of Acitrezza, a small village near Catania, perform the same hard work for starvation wages. Luchino Visconti's *The Earth Trembles* (*La terra trema*, 1948) was not the first film about Sicily, its sometimes rough people, and its idiosyncratic language; but it was the first great one. As someone says: "only the rich speak Italian here." *The Earth Trembles*: exploitation, tradition, rebellion, and pride on a stunningly beautiful island. The film is based on a novel by Giovanni Verga, a native of Catania. As the most important writer of the Italian realist tradition, he had a huge influence on Italian cinema. His novel of Sicilian jealousy, *I Malavoglia*, was published in 1881, and formed the basis of *The Earth Trembles*. Even more successful still was the short story "Cavalleria rusticana," adapted for the first time in 1916 by Ugo Falena, and remade many times. The Mafia made its movie debut no later than 1949, in Pietro Germi's *In the Name of the Law* (*In nome della legge*), a neorealist movie depicting a young judge's struggle against entrenched corruption. His next movie, *Il cammino della speranza* (1951), also focused on the miserable social conditions so prevalent in the south of the country, showing unemployed miners from Sicily forced to seek work in France. *Divorce Italian-Style* (*Divorzio all'italiana*, 1961) was a humorous satire on absurd marriage laws, and it cast an ironical eye on Sicilian ideas about honor and manliness.

One Sicilian in particular was an object of fascination for filmmakers: the bandit Salvatore Giuliano, whose heyday was in the '40s. Variously presented as a nationalist, a freedom fighter, or a would-be politician, he was always seen as a victim, either of society as a whole, or of powerful individuals pulling the strings from behind the scenes. Towards the end of the 20th century, the bloody wars against the Mafia took pride of place in cinematic portraits of the Italian island, resulting in films such as Francesco Rosi's *The Palermo Connection* or *To Forget Palermo* (*Dimenticare Palermo / Oublier Palerme*, 1989) or Ricky Tognazzi's *The Escort* (*La scorta*, 1993). A warmer take on Sicily was crafted by Giuseppe Tornatore in his films about the cinema such as *Cinema Paradiso* (*Nuovo cinema Paradiso*, 1989) and *The Star Maker* (*L'uomo delle stelle*, 1995), idyllic views of a past and so much more appealing island in the sun.

"Director Michelangelo Antonioni has given this a good beginning as he incisively blocks out the characters and the lack of roots in a life where emotion and love have been lost in an almost meaningless chain of attempts at love." *Variety*

2

1 It's nothing personal: Claudia (Monica Vitti) doesn't take to serious discussions first thing in the morning. Or could it just be that she wants to avoid talking about love with the man she's bedding (Gabriele Ferzetti as Sandro)? Director Michelangelo Antonioni once said of his films,

"You can't know what's really going on in a film unless you surrender yourself to its logic."

2 Lacking content? There are times when Claudia finds patterned wallpaper more interesting than her beau.

3 Nancy Drew ventures abroad: Giulia (Dominique Blanchar) and Claudia go off in search of Anna. It won't be long before Claudia finds herself assimilating aspects of the missing woman's character; in this scene, she's already wearing her clothes.

of limbo, or purgatory, or no-man's land; they are caught between the dense presence of the architecture and the vast distances of the natural world, between prison and escape. It's a powerful metaphor for the state of their relationship, as they are about to decide whether or not they will part. The film ends before we learn their decision.

The blonde woman is Claudia (Monica Vitti), a girlfriend of Anna (Léa Massari). Anna comes from a wealthy family, and she has a relationship with Sandro (Gabriele Ferzetti), though his work as a structural engineer means they rarely see each other. Together with some friends, they take a trip to the Liparian islands on a small private yacht. They are a typical bunch of Roman bohemians: vain, jaded, and cynical. When they stop off at a rocky island near Panarea, Sandro suddenly mentions marriage, but Anna no

longer wants this as she no longer has any feelings for him. A short time later, she disappears – and we never see her again.

Sandro and Claudia go off in search of her. Separately, then together, they follow vague clues across the island of Sicily, from Milazzo to Messina to Noto, and finally to Taormina. Though they never succeed in finding Anna, they do develop an interest in each other, and eventually they're a couple. Then Sandro meets an American starlet at a party ... and Claudia runs away, deeply hurt. On that terrace above the sea, he catches up with her. Both of them are crying; he, perhaps, out of regret, or because he realizes he is actually incapable of love.

Perhaps. In the world of Michelangelo Antonioni, things are seldom clear and simple. This is partly because

4 Gone with the wind? After Anna vanishes, Giulia and Claudia look for clues near her last known location – the rocky island, Lisca Bianca. As can be seen in numerous Antonioni films, the director was partial to the seaside.

5 I'll be at the office if you need me: whereas the Italian filmmaker consistently made pushovers of his male characters …

6 … he made sure his female leads always had a lot going on upstairs. And indeed, most of them gave new meaning to the term "women's lib."

the viewer is thrown in at the deep end, and told very little about the characters' past history. They seem impulsive and unpredictable, always acting on the spur of the moment. *L'avventura* was the first film in Antonioni's so-called *Italian Trilogy*, which continued with *La notte* (1960) and *Eclipse* (*L'eclisse*, 1962). These movies reflect the fragmentation of experience in the modern world. People have lost all orientation, traditional values have grown questionable, and there is no longer any real connection between the individual and society or between man and the natural world. Everything is growing more and more complicated, and more and more abstract.

L'avventura sketches this progress towards abstraction. After 25 minutes of the film, its main character simply vanishes, after a conversation in which she rejects the time-honored identity of a bourgeois wife. She is replaced by Claudia, an equally self-confident woman who is unsure of the role she will adopt in life. Then there's Sandro, whose new job as a structural engineer pays him a lot more money than his creative work as an architect. And finally we have the Sicilian ghost town, possibly the result of property speculation, whose empty houses may be seen as a symbol of the vacuum at the heart of the protagonists. *L'avventura*, then, is a study of the social abyss between the old world and the new, between the Roman sophisticates and the rooted Sicilians, who greedily eye any unaccompanied woman.

It may well be Antonioni's best work. Certainly, few other films have examined their time with such elegance and acuity, from such a distance and yet with such emotional power.

NM

PSYCHO

1960 - USA - 109 MIN.

DIRECTOR

ALFRED HITCHCOCK (1899–1980)

SCREENPLAY

JOSEPH STEFANO,
based on the novel of the same name by ROBERT BLOCH

DIRECTOR OF PHOTOGRAPHY

JOHN L. RUSSELL

EDITING

GEORGE TOMASINI

MUSIC

BERNARD HERRMANN

PRODUCTION

ALFRED HITCHCOCK for SHAMLEY PRODUCTIONS INC.

STARRING

ANTHONY PERKINS (Norman Bates), JANET LEIGH (Marion Crane),
VERA MILES (Lila Crane), JOHN GAVIN (Sam Loomis),
JOHN MCINTIRE (Al Chambers), MARTIN BALSAM (Milton Arbogast),
LURENE TUTTLE (Mrs. Chambers), SIMON OAKLAND (Doctor Richmond),
PATRICIA HITCHCOCK (Caroline), MORT MILLS (Policeman)

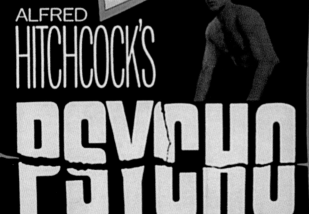

"Mother, she's just a stranger!"

It's what you might call a *twisted* fate. Marion Crane's (Janet Leigh) illicit affair with the married Sam Loomis (John Gavin) awakens deviant impulses within her. Entrusted with 40,000 dollars in company funds, she promptly invests in the future, making off with a sum that will allow her to start a new life with Joe. But the cops are on to her, and Marion thinks twice about executing her plan. The choice, however, isn't hers: a storm forces Marion to seek sanctuary at a remote motel, where a relaxing shower ends as a blood-bath. The murderess, it seems, suspected the overnight guest of making advances toward her son, the motel's introverted manager Norman Bates (Anthony Perkins), and decided to nip danger in the bud. Attempting to cover up his mother's regrettable actions, Bates wipes the scene clean, stuffs Marion's corpse into her car, and sinks the vehicle in a swamp – 40 grand and all.

Then the real investigation begins. Despite all their hard work, the gruesome twosome don't get to close shop

JANET LEIGH Jeanette Helen Morrison (1927–2004), born in Merced, California, was just 15 years old when she finished high school and began her studies in music and psychology. Her rise to fame is something of a Hollywood fairy tale: actress Norma Shearer apparently saw her while vacationing at a ski resort where Janet's father was working. Soon the young woman was cast in films opposite some of the industry's biggest names, including Robert Mitchum in *Holiday Affair* (1949), James Stewart in *The Naked Spur* (1953), John Wayne in *Jet Pilot* (1957), and both Charlton Heston and Orson Welles in *Touch of Evil* (1958). With *Psycho* (1960), Alfred Hitchcock supplied her with her most memorable role: Marion Crane, a heroine who is murdered before the first half of the picture is over. The part earned Leigh an Oscar nomination. John Frankenheimer's classic political drama *The Manchurian Candidate* (1962) proved to be one of the last high-caliber Hollywood films she would appear in; playing the girlfriend of the brainwashed Bennett Marco (Frank Sinatra), Leigh relies on her particular brand of aloof understatement to help him get his life back on track. From 1951 to 1962, the actress was married to favorite co-star Tony Curtis. They had two daughters, Kelly and Jamie Lee Curtis, both of whom followed in their parents' professional footsteps. Janet made an appearance in front of the camera at the side of daughter Jamie Lee in *Halloween H20 – 20 Years Later* (1998), the eighth installment in the horror film series made popular by Janet Leigh's world-famous child.

1 Who? *Moi?* Mama's boy Norman Bates (Anthony Perkins) fears the gaze of stranger's eyes – especially when they belong to his attractive hotel guests.

2 Heartbreak hotel: the Bates Mansion, a set-piece replica of an existing building, is among the most readily recognizable homes ever to grace the screen. The original is located in the 6th circle of hell.

3 Behind bars and closed doors: all the conniving Marion Crane (Janet Leigh) ever wanted in life was to elope with lover Sam Loomis (John Gavis). And she would have, had it not been for one little, but fatal, mistake. But then you only get to make one now darling, don't you?

just yet. Sam, Marion's sister Lila (Vera Miles), and a private detective named Arbogast (Martin Balsam) come in search of the missing woman and the stolen funds. Sticking his nose in the wrong place, Arbogast is also disposed of by the deranged old lady, who apparently resides in the seclusion of the familial estate overlooking the motel. After Sam and Lila wise up to the horrors of the Bates mansion,

they are dumbfounded to learn from the authorities that Mrs. Bates has been dead for a good ten years …

Psycho is undoubtedly Hitchcock's boldest film – although the critical uproar of the time, fixated on a close-up of a toilet bowl, seemed to miss the point. Tauntingly, the master of suspense plays with the viewer's expectations time and again: mercilessly killing off his leading lady in the

3

"After Hitchcock's suspense pictures and romantic adventure stories could he come up with a shocker, acceptable to mainstream American audiences, which still carried the spine-tingling voltage of foreign presentations such as *Diaboliques*? The answer is an enthusiastic yes. He blended the real and the unreal in fascinating proportions and punctuated his film with several quick, grisly and unnerving surprises." San Francisco Chronicle

first third of the picture, and introducing plot elements like the suitcase of money that amount to nothing more than red herrings. Arguably, the entire plot is a network of setups and visual suggestions meant to keep the audience unnerved until the curtain falls. And the seamless manner in which these subversive images undermine the story and suck it into the background makes *Psycho* more reminis- cent of an experimental arthouse piece than a Hollywood blockbuster. The most striking example of this is the shower scene, where a total of 70 camera shots fill 45 seconds of scream time – the hard cuts between shots and Bernard Herrmann's screeching score viscerally tuning us to each stab of the killer's knife. The scene was so shocking Hitchcock abstained from the further inclusion of

"What makes *Psycho* immortal, when so many films are already half-forgotten as we leave the theater, is that it connects directly with our fears: Our fears that we might impulsively commit a crime, our fears of the police, our fears of becoming the victim of a madman, and of course our fears of disappointing our mothers." *Chicago Sun-Times*

4 Drowned out screams: how many cuts does it take to kill Marion Crane? Hitchcock used approximately 70. Urban legend would have you believe that renowned cinema graphic artist, Saul Bass, staged Psycho's shower scene. But it's a bloody lie!

5 Don't tell mama: Mother will be livid if she finds out who's been sleeping in one of Norman's beds.

similarly violent displays in the rest of the film for he clearly already had the audience just where he wanted them.

Equally remarkable is how ingeniously the filmmaker and cinematographer John L. Russell come up with excuses not to reveal the face of Norman's mother until just before the end. We never suspect that Arbogast's stairwell death is shot from a bird's eye for anything other than artistic reasons.

Psycho's narrative takes just as many experimental liberties. Much like in a television drama, lengthy dialogue clarifies plot and subtext. Of prime importance is Norman and Marion's conversation at the motel, in which a bond is established between the killer and his victim. It is here that the viewer learns of Norman's interest in taxidermy, with the stuffed birds themselves acting as an eerie congress of witnesses: no amount of money can make them divulge the grizzly acts they've seen. These petrified beasts, and the peephole that Norman uses to spy on Marion as she undresses, are reminders of the camera's voyeuristic nature.

Everywhere we turn, *Psycho* confronts us with visual analogies of watching and being watched: from the eyelike shower drain into which Marion's blood disappears, to the smirking toilet seat that stares us down in one of the final shots. And there is no misunderstanding the accompanying dialogue: "They're probably watching me. Well, let them. Let them see what kind of person I am. I hope they are watching. They'll see. They'll see and they'll know."

It's more than just a coincidental choice of words Hitchcock placed in Bates's mouth. In truth, the soliloquy is as much a personal confession on the part of the director as of its speaker. At the peak of his career, Hitch couldn't have picked a more poignant moment to make it. For beyond the façade of terror, what is *Psycho* if not a great master's artistic manifesto?

SH

BREAKFAST AT TIFFANY'S ♟♟

1961 - USA - 115 MIN.

DIRECTOR

BLAKE EDWARDS (1922–2010)

SCREENPLAY

GEORGE AXELROD, based on the novella
of the same name by TRUMAN CAPOTE

DIRECTOR OF PHOTOGRAPHY

FRANZ F. PLANER

EDITING

HOWARD SMITH

MUSIC

HENRI MANCINI

PRODUCTION

MARTIN JUROW, RICHARD SHEPERD for PARAMOUNT PICTURES

STARRING

AUDREY HEPBURN (Holly Golightly), GEORGE PEPPARD (Paul "Fred" Varjak),
PATRICIA NEAL (2-E), BUDDY EBSEN (Doc Golightly), MICKEY ROONEY (Mr. Yunioshi),
MARTIN BALSAM (O. J. BERMAN), JOSÉ LUIS DA VILLALONGA (Villalonga),
JOHN MCGIVER (Tiffany's Sales Clerk), ALAN REED (Sally Tomato),
DOROTHY WHITNEY (Mag Wildwood)

ACADEMY AWARDS 1961

OSCARS for BEST MUSIC (HENRI MANCINI), BEST SONG: "MOON RIVER"
(Music: Henry Mancini; Lyrics: Johnny Mercer)

"You know those days when you've got the mean reds?"

Night dissolves into day over an all but empty Fifth Avenue. As the rest of New York brushes the sleep from its eyes, a willowy figure, still fragrant with dreams of yesterday, is reflected in the front window of the world's most famous jewelry store. Hidden behind tortoiseshell sunglasses, a slinky black cocktail dress, and a mane of upswept hair, she is a vision of aloof elegance softened only by the croissant and paper coffee cup she holds. This is Holly Golightly (Audrey Hepburn) as we best remember her: a lone and radiant gem amongst so many lesser diamonds as she indulges in an unforgettable breakfast at Tiffany's.

Unlike her clients, Holly herself is not a member of the upper echelons of New York society who patronize her beloved jewelry store. Although it's toned down in the movie, Truman Capote made it clear in his original novella that the 18-year-old powder room princess, described as "a creature of chic thinness with a face beyond childhood... yet this side of belonging to a woman," is indeed a professional call girl.

Holly has bolted from her May-December marriage to a Dust Bowl veterinarian without so much as a kiss goodbye for a stab at happiness in the Big Apple. This, naturally, involves pushing her luck on the Bohemian circuit, trying to make ends meet (or maybe even a fortune) amongst playboys and snobs in a world of masks, affectations, and countless mirrors. Whenever this party girl tires of the whole scene, she stays up all night with a case of the "mean reds," only to seek sanctuary and a glimmer of self-reflection the next morning in the Tiffany's storefront.

Sharing a Manhattan brownstone apartment with her nameless cat, she is utterly alone in the presence of countless aging millionaires, who look after her financial welfare in exchange for a bit of companionship. There are, however, several men who expect nothing in return, at least not

AUDREY HEPBURN Edda Hepburn van Hemmstra was born into a wealthy, influential family in Brussels, Belgium, on May 4, 1929. Her mother was a Dutch baroness and her father a British banker. After several years at a London boarding school, 12-year-old Edda headed to Amsterdam with her mother, who had severed ties with her husband because of his affiliation with English fascists. From their new home base, mother and daughter were active in Resistance efforts against the Nazi occupation. A fairy-tale career followed the war. Hepburn had her first small speaking part as a cigarette girl in Mario Zampi's *Laughter in Paradise* (1951), in which she could be heard saying "I'm not a lady, I'm a girl" to numerous elderly gentlemen. It wasn't long before French writer Colette cast her as the lead in the Broadway adaptation of her novel *Gigi*. The European ingénue played the courtesan 217 times until director William Wyler took her on a Hollywood-style *Roman Holiday* (1953). Wyler's film starred Audrey Hepburn as an inexperienced young princess eager to sow her wild oats at Gregory Peck's side. The doe-eyed actress became an instant postwar icon, a new type of woman which replaced the blonde bombshell. Hollywood approved wholeheartedly and Tinsel Town's infatuation with Audrey earned her a Best Actress award for her debut performance as Princess Ann in *Roman Holiday*.

Hepburn's designer, Givenchy, quickly transformed her into a trendsetting sensation and, together they succeeded in wiping the slate clean of the buxom female ideal. Tastes shifted from the full blonde mane to the pageboy or ponytail, from pumps to flats, from form-fitting sweaters to draping gowns.

Audrey Hepburn went on to shoot 26 more features and became an ambassador for Amnesty International in her later years. Indisputably, her final role in Steven Spielberg's *Always* (1989), four years prior to her passing, couldn't have been more fitting: Audrey Hepburn left Hollywood an angel.

2

1   Looking for a girl's best friend: Holly Golightly (Audrey Hepburn) sizes men up to make sure they can support the lifestyle she's grown accustomed to – and hopefully move her up a notch.

2   Nine lives: despite being penniless, Paul (George Peppard) tries to land on his feet with Holly.

3   Nickel and diming: in Holly's hands even a little nightshade can be a deadly weapon.

on the surface. She visits imprisoned drug-runner Sally Tomato once a week in Sing-Sing, thinking he just wants someone to talk to and never suspecting that he's really using her as an illegal messenger pigeon.

It's just as well – he's not her idea of relationship material anyway. And so she continues to seek out a man, preferably a millionaire under 50, who can fill the ever-increasing void in her life. The person she eventually turns to, neighboring tenant and penniless writer Paul Varjak (George Peppard), hardly fits the bill. Nonetheless, these two lost souls have a few things in common. Much like Holly, Paul's precarious existence is financed by a married benefactress who expects a little sugar for supporting the arts.

It's only a matter of time before floozy and gigolo warm to one another and set off on a relationship full of highs and lows. They establish a rare and precious sense of trust, gradually revealing themselves to one another

while discovering moments of clarity in a superficial and mixed-up world.

Deviating from Capote's literary work, in which Holly continues the search for her Mr. Right Millionaire in Brazil, the film's conclusion leaves us with one of the most poignant happy endings Hollywood has ever put forth. We are left witnessing an emotional storm in the streets of New York as Holly chooses Paul over money. They kiss and then the cat nestles in between their embrace and somehow completes a spectacularly unorthodox image of family. Rain pours down in sheets, as if the heavenly banks of "Moon River," had overflowed and spilled onto earth. The tune that accompanied the lovers throughout the entire picture (and won Oscars for composer Henry Mancini and lyricist Johnny Mercer) crescendos as Holly and Paul arrive at their train's final destination – simple happiness. These two drifters' days of running on empty, fleeing reality, and blindly chasing rainbows are over. Theirs is a distinctly urban quest for

meaning, which Woody Allen would pick up again in his New York stories some 20 years later.

Two things in particular make *Breakfast at Tiffany's* a Hollywood standout to this day. The first is the film's feel for fashion. It wasn't Marilyn Monroe who was cast in the role of 18-year-old Holly Golightly, but rather 32-year-old Audrey Hepburn, a former model for French designer Hubert de Givenchy, who used her to create a new style of dress and a new type of woman. For Hepburn made the busty blonde bombshell of the 1950s obsolete. Cultivated, reserved, tender, and somewhat girlish, Audrey Hepburn became the 1960s Hollywood trademark for the worldly and refined female, an image perfectly assimilated by Jacqueline Kennedy.

The picture's other characteristic is its utterly self-contained moments, celluloid snapshots that have become as famous as paintings. Be it Holly stowing her shoes in a fruit bowl or using her 20-inch-long cigarette holder to maneuver through a packed crowd of partiers – they are images that remain emblazoned in our mind. Nonetheless, the most memorable of these moments is the one the picture is named after, in which a traveling girl reflects on where she really belongs.   RV

4 A little sugar in his bowl: Holly finds out that she and Paul are in the same line of work. Patricia Neal as 2-E.

5 Two drifters off to see the world discover a little magic in their own backyard.

6 Bohemian rhapsody: partygoers in need of a nice cold shower.

7 Timber! Hostess plays lumberjack and clears the way for drunken partygoers.

"Audrey Hepburn didn't go to acting schools, she didn't hear the word Strasberg, she did not repeat in front of the mirror. She just was born with this kind of quality and she made it look so unforced, so simple, so easy." *Billy Wilder*

LAWRENCE OF ARABIA ♟♟♟♟♟♟♟

1962 - GREAT BRITAIN - 222 MIN.

DIRECTOR
DAVID LEAN (1908–1991)

SCREENPLAY
ROBERT BOLT, MICHAEL WILSON

DIRECTOR OF PHOTOGRAPHY
FREDDIE YOUNG

EDITING
ANNE V. COATES

MUSIC
MAURICE JARRE

PRODUCTION
SAM SPIEGEL for HORIZON

STARRING
PETER O'TOOLE (Thomas Edward Lawrence), ALEC GUINNESS (Prince Feisal),
ANTHONY QUINN (Auda Abu Tayi), JACK HAWKINS (General Allenby),
OMAR SHARIF (Sherif Ali Ibn El Kharish), ANTHONY QUAYLE (Colonel Harry Brighton),
CLAUDE RAINS (Mr. Dryden), ARTHUR KENNEDY (Jackson Bentley),
JOSÉ FERRER (Turkish Governor), DONALD WOLFIT (General Murray)

ACADEMY AWARDS 1962
OSCARS for BEST PICTURE (Sam Spiegel), BEST DIRECTOR (David Lean),
BEST CINEMATOGRAPHY (Freddie Young), BEST EDITING (Anne V. Coates),
BEST MUSIC (Maurice Jarre), BEST ART DIRECTION (John Box, John Stoll, Dario Simoni),
BEST SOUND (John Cox)

From the creators of "The Bridge On The River Kwai."
Columbia Pictures presents The SAM SPIEGEL · DAVID LEAN Production of

LAWRENCE OF ARABIA

"I deem him one of the greatest beings alive in our time.
...we shall never see his like again. His name will live in history.
It will live in the annals of war...It will live in the legends of Arabia!"
—WINSTON CHURCHILL

STARRING
ALEC GUINNESS · ANTHONY QUINN
JACK HAWKINS · JOSE FERRER
ANTHONY QUAYLE · CLAUDE RAINS · ARTHUR KENNEDY
AND INTRODUCING
PETER O'TOOLE as 'LAWRENCE' WITH OMAR SHARIF as 'ALI'
SCREENPLAY BY
ROBERT BOLT · SAM SPIEGEL · DAVID LEAN · TECHNICOLOR®

PHOTOGRAPHED IN
SUPER PANAVISION 70®

"The best of them won't come for money. They'll come for me!"

"I'm different," announces Thomas Edward Lawrence (Peter O'Toole) right at the start of the film. He's trying to explain to a Bedouin what distinguishes him from the rest of his compatriots in "a fat country with fat people." Different … yes. But in what way? Who was this British officer from Oxford, who led the Arab tribes to rebel against their Turkish rulers during the First World War? An idealistic dreamer? A narcissistic megalomaniac? A homosexual sadomasochist? He died young after a motorcycle accident, and his acquaintances and superior officers answered as one: we don't know who he was – we hardly knew him at all.

Indeed, T. E. Lawrence hardly knew himself, and the more he made his own acquaintance, the more he recoiled from what he saw. This is one major theme of David

Lean's monumental film biography, which shows various facets of this strange character without ever really solving the mystery that surrounds the man.

Lawrence of Arabia is not so much a film about war, politics, and British colonial history as a visually splendid record of one man's trip to the limits of sanity in the hope of finding himself. Only the most impossible challenges are enough for Thomas Edward Lawrence. He crosses deserts no one has ever ventured into; he plans surprise attacks on seemingly impregnable Turkish positions; he forges fragile alliances amongst bitterly opposed tribes; and eventually, he takes Damascus with his Arab army. Lawrence was once asked what he liked so much about the desert, and he replied, "its cleanliness." But far from achieving the purified soul he longed for, he paid for his

PETER O'TOOLE In 1962, the title role in David Lean's *Lawrence of Arabia* shot the unknown 29-year-old Irishman Peter O'Toole (1932–2013) into the major league of international movie stars. Previously, he had only played a few minor roles, such as a bagpiper in Robert Stevenson's *Kidnapped* (1959). In Britain, however, he had already made a name for himself on the stage, thanks to his appearances with the Royal Shakespeare Company in Stratford-upon-Avon. The '60s were to be O'Toole's great decade, in which he would be nominated for the Academy Award on several occasions, but without ever winning it. With his Irish charm, his piercing blue eyes, his impish sense of humor, and his faintly ironical air, he was perfectly cast in eccentric comedies such as *What's New, Pussycat?* (1965) and *How to Steal a Million* (1966). He had less luck with later roles, apart from his appearance as Robinson Crusoe in Jack Gold's *Man Friday* (1975), a new take on Defoe's tale that depicted the "native" Friday as the cleverer of the two men. By this time, O'Toole's problems with alcohol were gradually becoming noticeable.

Among other film appearances, O'Toole played Priam in Wolfgang Petersen's *Troy* (2004), based on Homer's *Iliad*, and starred as an aging romantic in the multiple award-winning *Venus* (2006). In 2003, Peter O'Toole was given an Honorary Academy Award for lifetime achievement – against his initial opposition – for he announced in no uncertain terms that he reckoned he still had a chance of winning a Best Actor Oscar in fair competition with his peers. Peter O'Toole died in London on 14 December 2013.

"In his performance, O'Toole catches the noble seriousness of Lawrence and his cheap theatricality, his godlike arrogance and his gibbering self-doubt; his headlong courage, girlish psychasthenia, Celtic wit, humorless egotism, compulsive chastity, and sensuous pleasure in pain." *Time*

2

3

1 Hitchcock mirage: director David Lean and cinematographer Freddie Young reeled in the Oscars for their desert magic.

2 Desert Storm: Omar Sharif emerged from the Arabian sands as Sherif Ali Ibn El Kharish and rose to international stardom.

3 Eagle eyes: Major Lawrence (Peter O'Toole) is a singular force and sees what he wants to see.

self-torturing expeditions with a loss of innocence. Originally inspired by the ideal of helping the Arabs to achieve their independence, Lawrence was eventually forced to recognize that his masters, the British, would never allow it. This is why, at the end of the film, Mr. Dryden (Claude Rains) calls him "a man who tells half-lies." Dryden is a British government representative in Arabia, and in his view, such "half-lying" is worse than mouthing complete falsehoods in the interests of political expediency. By this time, however, Lawrence is barely concerned with political considerations anymore. His courage and willpower have so impressed the Arabs that they have honored him with a new name, and Lawrence, with his tendency to narcissism, luxuriates in his popularity and the splendor of his triumphs. As his megalomania grows, he behaves increasingly as if he were the Messiah to the Arab people.

What's more, in the course of his military campaigns, he has learned to kill, and the power he feels while doing so is a source of genuine pleasure. On one occasion, he is captured, tortured, and raped by the Turks; and the film hints discreetly that even this is a somewhat ambivalent experience for Lawrence. Speaking to Jackson Bentley, the American reporter (Arthur Kennedy), the Englishman's comrade-in-arms Prince Feisal (Alec Guinness) sums him up as follows: "With Major Lawrence, mercy is a passion; with me, it is merely good manners. Judge for yourself which motive is the more reliable."

Lawrence certainly has reasons to be worried about his enthusiasms. When his desperate application for an "ordinary job" is turned down, his next mission ends in the insane butchery of an exhausted Turkish regiment, and in the course of the massacre Lawrence works himself into an ecstasy of bloodlust.

Before *Lawrence of Arabia* Peter O'Toole was an almost completely unknown actor, yet his portrayal is one of his greatest-ever performances. The background to

"Lean and cameraman Young have brought out the loneliness and pitiless torment of the desert with an artistic use of color, and almost every take is superbly framed and edited." *Variety*

4 Taking out the big guns: aristocrat Sherif Ali shows his impatient friend Lawrence that he is a man be reckoned with.

5 Head in the sand? Lawrence mobilizes the Arabs against a Turkish attack.

6 At a loss for words: lawmaking and bureaucracy are certainly not among Lawrence's strengths. His patience wears thin as disputes between the Arab tribes sour the spirit of new-found liberty.

7 Listening to his inner clock: Auda Abu Tayi (Anthony Quinn) fears that Lawrence is acting out of self-interest.

that portrait is almost equally spectacular: using Techni-color and Super Panavision 70, director David Lean and cameraman Freddie Young created astonishing panoramas of the beautiful and pitiless desert, with its fiery sun, its sand-storms, and a horizon like a line drawn through the world. Filming took two years, and ten months alone were spent filming exteriors in Jordan. At one surreal moment, we see a ship sailing through the sands: Lawrence has arrived at the Suez Canal. Equally impressive is the first meeting between Lawrence and Sherif Ali Ibn El Kharish (Omar Sharif): a shim-mering mirage that suddenly materializes into a real figure.

For all its beauty, the film is never merely interested in "strong images" for their own sake. Despite the over-whelming landscapes and the dynamic battle scenes, this is an actors' film performed by an outstanding ensemble, and its fascinating central character is always the main focus of interest. *Lawrence of Arabia* is one of the biggest *and* best movies ever made. LP

TO KILL A MOCKINGBIRD ♟♟♟

1962 - USA - 129 MIN.

DIRECTOR
ROBERT MULLIGAN (1925–2008)

SCREENPLAY
HORTON FOOTE, based on the novel
of the same name by HARPER LEE

DIRECTOR OF PHOTOGRAPHY
RUSSELL HARLAN

EDITING
AARON STELL

MUSIC
ELMER BERNSTEIN, MACK DAVID

PRODUCTION
ALAN J. PAKULA for PAKULA-MULLIGAN, BRENTWOOD PRODUCTIONS,
UNIVERSAL INTERNATIONAL PICTURES

STARRING
GREGORY PECK (Atticus Finch), MARY BADHAM (Jean Louise "Scout" Finch),
PHILLIP ALFORD (Jeremy "Jem" Finch), ROBERT DUVALL (Arthur "Boo" Radley),
JOHN MEGNA (Dill Harris), BROCK PETERS (Tom Robinson),
FRANK OVERTON (Sheriff Tate), ROSEMARY MURPHY (Maudie Atkinson),
RUTH WHITE (Mrs. Dubose), ESTELLE EVANS (Calpurnia),
COLLIN WILCOX (Mayella Ewell), JAMES ANDERSON (Bob Ewell),
ALICE GHOSTLEY (Stephanie Crawford)

ACADEMY AWARDS 1962
OSCARS for BEST ACTOR (Gregory Peck), BEST ADAPTED SCREENPLAY (Horton Foote),
and BEST ART DIRECTION (Alexander Golitzen, Henry Bunstead, Oliver Emert)

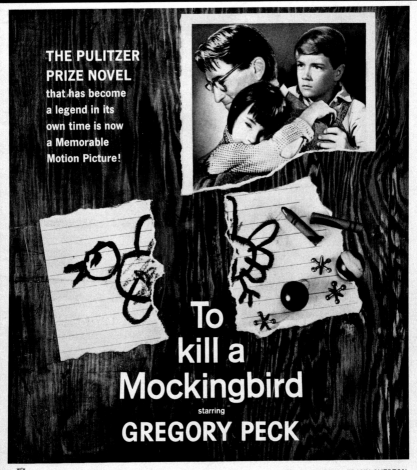

THE PULITZER
PRIZE NOVEL
that has become
a legend in its
own time is now
a Memorable
Motion Picture!

To
kill a
Mockingbird
starring
GREGORY PECK

WITH MARY BADHAM · PHILLIP ALFORD · JOHN MEGNA · RUTH WHITE · PAUL FIX · BROCK PETERS · FRANK OVERTON
ROSEMARY MURPHY · COLLIN WILCOX   Screenplay by HORTON FOOTE · Based upon Harper Lee's novel "To a Mockingbird"
Music by ELMER BERNSTEIN · Directed by ROBERT MULLIGAN · Produced by ALAN PAKULA · A Pakula-Mulligan, Brentwood Productions Picture · A UNIVERSAL RELEASE

THEATRE

Universal
Release

Ad Mat No. 602—6 Col.x14½"—1200 Lines

MAT No. 602

"I was to think of those days many times. Of Jem and Dill and Boo Radley, and Tom Robinson, and Atticus."

America is a land of unlimited optimism and perilous incongruity, and the history of the United States is also the history of its hopes, its fears, and its myths. Amongst the great tales of all the races and generations that have inhabited this country is *To Kill a Mockingbird* – written by Harper Lee and filmed by Robert Mulligan. Indeed, perhaps only Tom Sawyer and Huckleberry Finn have etched themselves into the collective unconscious as indelibly as this novel and this movie.

The story is set in the Depression years. The southern States are particularly hard-hit by the crisis, and countless idyllic small towns are threatened by poverty, racial hatred, ignorance, and bigotry. Yet for the children of the widowed lawyer Atticus Finch (Gregory Peck), life is one big adventure. To ten-year-old Jem (Phillip Alford) and his kid sister Scout (Mary Badham), everything is a source of wonder: an old car tire becomes an exciting toy; a box containing nothing but a few chalks, a broken clock, and a pocketknife is their jealously guarded treasure chest; and they have a burning interest in the house of the mys-

terious Boo Radley (Robert Duvall). It's been years since anyone saw him; and in the children's imagination, every step they take towards his scary, dilapidated house is a terrifying test of their courage. Yet their father's latest case also captures their attention: a black man, Tom Robinson (Brock Peters), has been accused of raping a white woman – and Atticus, bravely, is defending him. The case for the prosecution, and the trial itself, are outrageously unfair; but Jem and Scout gradually learn some lessons for life from their father, who looks evil in the eye and stands up firmly against it. And it's Atticus's tolerance and sympathy that finally enables the children to overcome their greatest fear: the fear of Boo Radley.

As the tomboy Scout, Mary Badham captured the hearts of generations of moviegoers, big and small. Her inimitable mixture of cheek and innocent curiosity disarms everyone she meets; and at the end of the film, she need only speak two words to build a bridge across an abyss: "Hey, Boo." A deathly pale Robert Duvall also gives a touching performance as Boo Radley. To prepare himself

GREGORY PECK He embodied the American ideal of modest integrity like no other actor – not even Gary Cooper, whose role in *High Noon* (1952) he had politely declined. Just a couple of years previously, he had played a dignified cowboy in *The Gunfighter* (1950), and he didn't want to be typecast. Yet the big man with the piercing eyes always remained true to himself, however varied the actual roles he played, from a dedicated journalist in *Gentleman's Agreement* (1947) to a New York office worker in *The Man in the Grey Flannel Suit* (1956) and a hard-bitten general in *The Guns of Navarone* (1961). Even ambivalent characters such as the innocently guilty lawyer in *Cape Fear* (1962) had a touch of quiet nobility about them. In *Moby Dick* (1956), his Captain Ahab bore a strong resemblance to Abraham Lincoln, with whom Peck himself had often been compared. Despite chalking up successes in *Roman Holiday* (1953) and *Arabesque* (1966), he never really felt comfortable playing comedies. But those who regarded him as the biggest bore in Hollywood not only failed to notice his immense charisma; they also overlooked the fact that he lived out his ideals, and not merely on screen. He was a committed worker for many charities, he took part in protest marches alongside Martin Luther King, and in 1970, he seriously considered standing as a candidate against the governor of California, Ronald Reagan. Gregory Peck died in 2003 at the age of 87. His funeral eulogy was given by Brock Peters, the actor who played Tom Robinson in *To Kill a Mockingbird* (1962).

1 The walls have ears: Scout (Mary Badham), Jem (Phillip Alford), and neighborhood friend Dill Harris (John Megna) get caught eavesdropping at the door.

2 Growing pains: the children follow the proceedings from the landing above the court-room and learn that the grown-up world isn't always fair. Scout begins to wonder whether her father has any chance of getting his innocent client off the hook.

for this tiny but unforgettable role (his film debut), he stayed indoors for six weeks, avoiding the sun. And then, of course, there is Gregory Peck as Atticus Finch, father and lawyer. An ideal combination of gentleness, intelligence, and strength, he became something of a model for all the fathers (and lawyers) who came after him. Peck's Atticus Finch is the very image of integrity.

What really made this quiet film such a huge success was its faithful adherence to a basic tenet of the novel: the story is told exclusively from the children's perspective. Each of their daily adventures is a journey into the shadow world that lies between Good and Evil. When they encounter the terrors of the adult world, they're armed with the power of their imagination and an absolute trust in the strength of their father; and so they're capable of moving mountains. Nowhere is this clearer than in the scene at the jailhouse, where a lynch mob demands that Atticus hand

over the prisoner Tom Robinson. Though Scout is barely even aware of the crowd's aggression, she manages to defuse the situation merely by asking a few simple questions. The lengthy trial scene is also attended by Scout and Jem, and it ends in a moving demonstration of support for Atticus by the entire black population of the town. *To Kill a Mockingbird* is studded with such minor high points, and quite free from the melodramatic tendentiousness of many films with a political or antiracist "message."

This is in every respect an extraordinary film – and it was nominated for no fewer than eight Academy Awards, including Best Film Music. Elmer Bernstein's remarkable score is an assemblage of simple melodies, of the kind a child might produce while tinkering around on the piano. But this sensitive literary adaptation was up against the mighty desert epic *Lawrence of Arabia* (1962) ... and ultimately, the only Oscars it received were for Horton Foote's

3 Hostile witness: Bob Ewell (James Anderson) is more fired up than a loose cannon. But his fervor leaves defense attorney Atticus Finch (Gregory Peck) cold.

4 In the hot seat: a simple parlor room trick proves that the allegations are false. The defendant, Tom Robinson (Brock Peters), is right-handed.

5 Taking a stand: in the name of the truth, Atticus and Tom combat latent racism in their small Southern town.

"If you just learn a single trick, Scout, you'll get along a lot better with all kinds of folks. You never really understand a person until you consider things from his point of view... Until you climb inside of his skin and walk around in it." *Film quote: Atticus (Gregory Peck)*

6 Rabid gunfire: with a steady hand and the eye of a marksman, Atticus silences a mad dog terrorizing the neighborhood.

7 Is there no justice? Despite presenting a compelling case, Atticus couldn't sway the jury from finding him guilty.

8 Ominous shadows: Dill and the other children may still be young innocents. However, a day will come when they'll have to ward off the darkness themselves.

> **"*To Kill a Mockingbird* is, first and foremost, a re-creation of a children's world, and a rather grizzly, ghoulish world at that: where the main center of local interest is a lunatic reputed to be dangerous."** *Sight and Sound*

reworking of the novel (which the novelist, unusually in the movie business, thoroughly admired); for the Art Direction, a loving reconstruction of Harper Lee's home town Monroeville on the premises of Universal Studios; and for Gregory Peck, as Best Actor. Till the day he died, he described *To Kill a Mockingbird* as his favorite among all the films he had made, and he maintained a friendship with Harper Lee for many years. In 2003, the American Film Institute voted Atticus Finch the greatest film hero of all time. Among the runners-up were Indiana Jones, James Bond – and Lawrence of Arabia. PB

8

DR. STRANGELOVE OR: HOW I LEARNED TO STOP WORRYING AND LOVE THE BOMB

1963 - GREAT BRITAIN - 93 MIN.

DIRECTOR

STANLEY KUBRICK (1928–1999)

SCREENPLAY

STANLEY KUBRICK, PETER GEORGE,
TERRY SOUTHERN, based on a novel by PETER GEORGE

DIRECTOR OF PHOTOGRAPHY

GILBERT TAYLOR

EDITING

ANTHONY HARVEY

MUSIC

LAURIE JOHNSON

PRODUCTION

STANLEY KUBRICK for HAWK

STARRING

PETER SELLERS (Capt. Lionel Mandrake / President Merkin Muffley / Dr. Strangelove),
GEORGE C. SCOTT (General "Buck" Turgidson), STERLING HAYDEN (General Jack D. Ripper),
KEENAN WYNN (Colonel "Bat" Guano), SLIM PICKENS (Major T. J. "King" Kong),
TRACY REED (Miss Scott), PETER BULL (Ambassador de Sadesky),
JAMES EARL JONES (Lieutenant Lothar Zogg)

"Gentlemen, you can't fight in here! This is the War Room!"

The story was meant to be taken very seriously indeed – and it was written by a man who knew what he was talking about. In the 1950s, Peter George, a former officer of the Royal Air Force, published a thriller under the pseudonym Peter Bryant. Its title: *Two Hours to Doom* (in the U.S.: *Red Alert*). Stanley Kubrick had been considering making a film about the nuclear threat for quite some time, and when George's book was recommended to him, he knew he'd found what he was looking for.

Together with Peter George, he started working on the script. At first, they stuck with the dramatic tenor of the original novel, but as time went on, Kubrick was struck by the comic potential of the military subject matter, and he changed his initial plans. *Dr. Strangelove* became an absurd coal-black comedy about the end of the world. It united the exceptional visual gifts of this brilliant director with the witty writing of the satirist Terry Southern – who was hired to work on the dialogue – and the unique pres-

ence of the comedian and character actor Peter Sellers, who improvised many of his own lines. Sellers's importance to this movie can hardly be overestimated: not only did Kubrick entrust him with three roles; he even shifted filming to England (where he himself would eventually settle), because Sellers was in the throes of a divorce case and couldn't leave the country. In *Dr. Strangelove*, Kubrick sets out to thwart all our usual expectations. Right at the start, most moviegoers will miss the customary musical accompaniment, as a disclaimer announces: "It is the stated position of the United States Air Force that their safeguards would prevent the occurrence of such events as are depicted in this film. Furthermore, it should be noted that none of the characters portrayed in this film are meant to represent any real persons living or dead."

The opening titles show a sea of clouds and a bomber being refueled in midair. And then we hear the music: "Try a little tenderness." In combination with the selection

GEORGE C. SCOTT General "Buck" Turgidson is the hard-bitten antithesis to Peter Sellers's soft-spoken President Muffley. He is played by an actor whose "unique qualities" Kubrick once testified to in an interview. George Campbell Scott was born in 1927. After serving in the Marines for four years, he worked in a variety of provincial and college theaters before enjoying his first successes on Broadway. His appearances in the TV series *East Side / West Side* (1963–64) made him famous coast-to-coast. Scott made his film debut in 1956, in a small, uncredited part in *Somebody Up There Likes Me* before going on to work with directors such as Otto Preminger, John Huston, and Mike Nichols. He himself directed the TV production *The Andersonville Trial* (1970) and the feature films *Rage* (1972) and *The Savage Is Loose* (1974). Scott had a reputation for being "difficult": one of his greatest successes was the film biography *Patton* (1969) – but although he was awarded an Oscar for his performance, he refused on principle to accept it. George C. Scott, a father of six, died in 1999. His son Campbell Scott, born in 1961, followed his father into the acting trade; moviegoers will know him from box-office hits like *Singles* (1992) and *The Amazing Spider-Man* (2012).

and editing of the images, this tender foxtrot melody transforms a complex military docking maneuver into a bizarre and comical act of love.

The actual story begins at Burpelson Air Base. The paranoid Commander-in-Chief, General Jack D. Ripper (Sterling Hayden), sends a squadron of bombers to the Soviet Union, seals off his airbase from the outside world and activates a special code that makes it impossible to communicate with the pilots. British contact officer Mandrake (Peter Sellers) has no success with his attempts to exercise a moderating influence. Meanwhile, a crisis team

"Dr. Strangelove's humor is generated by a basic comic principle: People trying to be funny are never as funny as people trying to be serious and failing."

Chicago Sun-Times

1 Watch the hand: scientist Dr. Strangelove's (Peter Sellers) prosthetic appendage has a mind of its own. Don't go pressing any buttons now.

2 Oral fixation: General Jack D. Ripper (Sterling Hayden) mutters bizarre incantations about the mixture of bodily fluids and exhibits a fondness for phallic symbols.

3 Knights of the round table: President Merkin Muffley (Peter Sellers) causes an uproar amongst his generals by inviting red sheep de Sadesky (Peter Bull) to graze among his herd in the top-secret war room.

4 Practice what you preach.

chaired by President Muffley (Peter Sellers) is meeting at the Pentagon. Despite the protests of Air Force Chief of Staff Buck Turgidson (George C. Scott), the Soviet ambassador Alexi de Sadesky (Peter Bull) is also permitted to enter this military Holy of Holies. When de Sadesky and Muffley inform the president of the Soviet Union that his country is in danger, they learn to their horror that the Communist state is in possession of a "Doomsday Machine," which reacts automatically to a nuclear attack and cannot be switched off.

Muffley has no choice but to reveal the target coordinates to the Soviets, in the hope that the bombers can

"Once again, Peter Sellers demonstrates his versatility and fine comedy sense with three widely varied portrayals: A mild-mannered British liaison officer, the calm, serious President of the U.S. and the heavily accented crippled German scientist, who gives the film its title (certainly the longest ever)."

Box Office Magazine

8

5 Bollocks! British group captain Mandrake (Peter Sellers) goes into a frenzy upon hearing of mad U.S. general Jack D. Ripper's (Sterling Hayden) plan to launch World War III.

6 All very hush, hush: the Pentagon's phone call reaches General Buck Turgidson (George C. Scott) after

wrapping up a flagrante delecto session with secretary Miss Scott (Tracy Reed).

7 Nothing like a little personality to brighten a place up.

8 Gripping the joystick: "King" Kong opts for a cowboy hat rather than flying helmet for his final mission in pioneering the great frontier.

"Stanley Kubrick's nightmare comedy – the extraordinary story of a psychotic American general who triggers off a mass nuclear attack on Moscow!" *Film Review*

be intercepted in time. Mandrake manages to decipher the codeword and communicate the solution to Washington, and all the bombers are recalled – with the exception of one. The Russians have fired a missile at the B52 of Major T. J. "King" Kong (Slim Pickens) and destroyed his communications equipment. He is now unreachable, and still on his way. Though the damage to the plane is con-

siderable, Kong is determined to accomplish his deadly mission. When the release mechanism refuses to function, he climbs down personally into the bomb bay. Sitting astride an atom bomb, he sets to work on the electronics. Sparks fly, the bay doors open and the bomb falls free – and Kong, happily whooping and waving his Stetson, rides off into the sunset of the world.   HK

GOLDFINGER ♟

1964 - GREAT BRITAIN - 106 MIN.

DIRECTOR

GUY HAMILTON (*1922)

SCREENPLAY

IAN FLEMING, RICHARD MAIBAUM, PAUL DEHN

DIRECTOR OF PHOTOGRAPHY

TED MOORE

EDITING

PETER R. HUNT

MUSIC

JOHN BARRY

PRODUCTION

ALBERT R. BROCCOLI, HARRY SALTZMAN for
EON PRODUCTIONS and UNITED ARTISTS

STARRING

SEAN CONNERY (James Bond), HONOR BLACKMAN (Pussy Galore),
GERT FRÖBE (Auric Goldfinger), SHIRLEY EATON (Jill Masterson),
TANIA MALLET (Tilly Masterson), HAROLD SAKATA (Oddjob),
BERNARD LEE (M), MARTIN BENSON (Martin Solo),
CEC LINDER (Felix Leiter), LOIS MAXWELL (Miss Moneypenny)

ACADEMY AWARDS 1964

OSCAR for BEST SOUND EFFECTS (Norman Wanstall)

THE
ONE
AND
ONLY...

ALBERT R. BROCCOLI & HARRY SALTZMAN PRESENT
SEAN CONNERY AS JAMES BOND 007
IN IAN FLEMING'S

GOLDFINGER A

HONOR BLACKMAN   GERT FROBE
AS PUSSY GALORE   TECHNICOLOR   AS GOLDFINGER

SHIRLEY EATON TANIA MALLET HAROLD SAKATA BERNARD LEE AS 'M'

SCREEN PLAY BY   PRODUCED BY
RICHARD MAIBAUM & PAUL DEHN   HARRY SALTZMAN & ALBERT R. BROCCOLI
DIRECTED BY GUY HAMILTON   EON PRODUCTIONS LTD

United Artists
Entertainment from
Transamerica Corporation

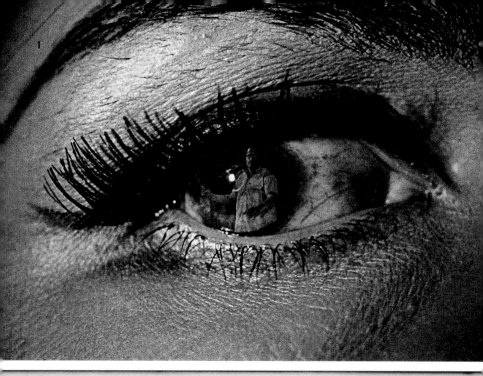

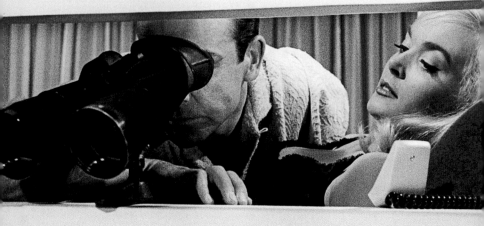

"This heart is cold – he loves only gold."

Sixties siren Shirley Bassey sings presciently of a man's stone-cold heart and his affinity with a certain precious metal; fragmented images of a female figure dipped in gold flash against a pitch-black screen: we are bid welcome to the world of Goldfinger, a scoundrel with a singular fixation.

Fireballs, high-speed chases, and love scenes hint at the action about to explode in this early James Bond thriller. The third picture in the British secret agent series – Bond spoof *Casino Royal* excluded – *Goldfinger* is a shrine to Cold War hysteria. This time around, 007 (Sean Connery) is out to stop unscrupulous German super-criminal Auric Goldfinger (Gert Fröbe) from monopolizing the metal that shares his name and which was associated with so much economic and political power in the 1960s. To succeed, this modern-day Midas has come up with a diabolical scheme...

For Mr. Goldfinger intends no less than to wipe out the Western world's economy by detonating an atomic bomb inside Fort Knox, home to the United States' gold reserve and democracy. With the entire supply of American gold radioactive and worthless, the value of his own resources would skyrocket. A piece of cake, except James Bond tails Auric Goldfinger to the States and wises up to the despicable plan. However, 007's attempts to fill his colleagues in on the matter are foiled by Goldfinger's right-hand man, a *femme fatale* known as Pussy Galore (Honor Blackman). Not to worry; after a night of spiritual cleansing with our favorite secret agent, she awakens a new woman, switching sides and informing the American authorities of her ex-employer's machinations.

In *Goldfinger*, female characters are all too readily seduced by gold's luster. There are even a few who meet an untimely demise as a result of its sparkle. Jill Masterson (Shirley Eaton), for example, suffocates when coated with an ever-so-fine layer of gold paint. Evidently, regardless of what form it takes, this high-carat poison can reduce women to little more than paper dolls and film decor. Pussy Galore is the only exception. She too is initially transfixed by the lure of its immeasurable wealth and power, but her

BOND GIRLS With the exception of Miss Moneypenny (played throughout the '60s and '70s almost exclusively by Lois Maxwell), most female characters who appear at Bond's side since the '60s readily bare all for the British secret agent (played by the likes of Sean Connery). Teasing monikers that play up the hanky panky like Honey Ryder (Ursula Andress) and Pussy Galore (Honor Blackman) take the edge off the fact that all of Bond's beautiful love interests and – less often – antagonists succumb to his charms without knowing the slightest thing about him. That's not to say that there's no price to pay for being a bad girl. Rosie (Gloria Hendry), Tiffany (Jill St. John), Kissy (Mie Hama), Bambi (Lola Larson), Tilly (Tania Mallet), Bonita (Nadja Regin), and many others all got the kiss of death after shagging 007. It almost makes one wonder whether it's more than just coincidence: for as everybody knows – all of James's actions are performed in the service of her Majesty. How else can we explain why 007 goes for someone as subversive as Pussy – a lesbian in the Ian Fleming novel *Goldfinger* (1964)? Too bad that Honor Blackman didn't get a chance to explore this aspect of her character in the movie. Still, much like her literary counterpart, it is a sexual awakening *à la* Bond that represents Ms. Galore's about-face and shift towards conformity with proper society. It was only in the 1990s that the sexual tables began to turn in the super spy series. Ever since *Golden-Eye* (1995) Judi Dench has stood at the MI6 helm as Bond's no-nonsense superior. And newer Bond girls like Jinx Johnson (Halle Berry) and especially Vesper Lynd (Eva Greene) have won us over with their distinctly self-confident presence.

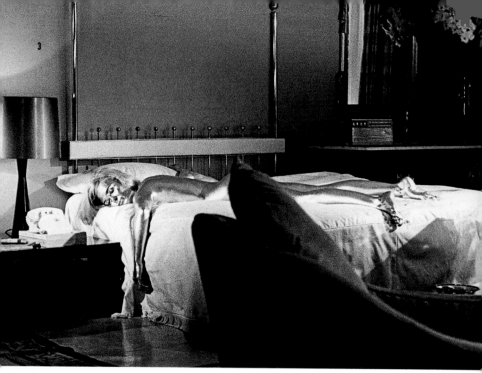

1 The evil eye: someone's watching 007's (Sean Connery) every move.

2 Rear window, revisited: even during a stakeout, there's always time for a little hanky panky.

3 The Midas touch: Jill Masterson's (Shirley Eaton) body has increased in value.

4 Nights in white satin: Bond is guaranteed more than just a few steamy rendezvous if he sports threads like these.

5 Into the fire: Bond doesn't know which of these guys is the worse of two evils – German Goldfinger (Gerd Fröbe) or Oddjob (Harold Sakata).

6 Cracker jack: whenever he's in a jam, James counts on Q's nifty gadgets for a novel rescue.

encounter with 007 changes all that. As the agent's prim secretary Miss Moneypenny (Lois Maxwell) might put it, after a girl lays eyes on James, the only golden trinket of any interest is a wedding band. To the picture's male leads, gold is a means to an end, and to Auric Goldfinger that end is world domination. He enlists the aid of North Korean communists and is willing to put the lives of thousands of innocent bystanders on the line. His idea of a hostile takeover is gassing the opposition – literally. More central to the film's plot, however, is Goldfinger's intention to hoard as much gold as he possibly can and paralyze the global cash flow in the process. But James Bond, like Moses tempted by the golden calf, does not let all that glitters get the best of him. Instead, the secret agent is intrigued by the practical value of bullion which, during the showdown in Fort Knox, proves a vital tool in the struggle to defuse Goldfinger's atomic bomb. Considering the era in which it was made, the film races across the screen at top speed, fueled by countless audio-visual effects and the simmering sex appeal of its cast. The same can't be said of its one-time extravagant set, which today looks more like a relic that could use a good dusting.

The picture's undisputed saving grace is its funny bone – especially with regard to its hero. James Bond may appear to be acting in the name of God, but, in truth, he is a servant of her Majesty's economy. By current standards, his character's impeccable playboy veneer and compliance to passé gender stereotypes read like a highly entertaining persiflage of what was intended to be taken seriously – very seriously. PLB

"There is an assumption – which you find, at quite the other end of the spectrum, in the Godard films – that we all know the clichés and can have a little fun with them." *Sight and Sound*

DOCTOR ZHIVAGO ♟♟♟♟♟

1965 - USA - 200 MIN.

DIRECTOR
DAVID LEAN (1908–1991)

SCREENPLAY
ROBERT BOLT, based on the novel
of the same name by BORIS PASTERNAK

DIRECTOR OF PHOTOGRAPHY
FREDDIE YOUNG

EDITING
NORMAN SAVAGE

MUSIC
MAURICE JARRE

PRODUCTION
CARLO PONTI for MGM

STARRING
GERALDINE CHAPLIN (Tonya), JULIE CHRISTIE (Lara),
TOM COURTENAY (Pasha Antipova / Strelnikov), ALEC GUINNESS (Gen. Jevgraf Zhivago),
SIOBHAN MCKENNA (Anna), RALPH RICHARDSON (Alexander Gromeko),
OMAR SHARIF (Yuri Zhivago), ROD STEIGER (Victor Komarovsky),
RITA TUSHINGHAM (The Girl), ADRIENNE CORRI (Amelia)

ACADEMY AWARDS 1965
OSCARS for BEST ADAPTED SCREENPLAY (Robert Bolt), BEST CINEMATOGRAPHY (Freddie Young),
BEST MUSIC (Maurice Jarre), BEST ART DIRECTION (John Box, Terry Marsh, Dario Simoni),
BEST COSTUME DESIGN (Phyllis Dalton)

A LOVE CAUGHT IN THE FIRE OF REVOLUTION

Turbulent were the times and fiery was the love story of Zhivago, his wife... and the passionate, tender Lara.

METRO-GOLDWYN-MAYER PRESENTS A CARLO PONTI PRODUCTION

DAVID LEAN'S FILM OF BORIS PASTERNAK'S

DOCTOR ZHIVAGO

STARRING

GERALDINE CHAPLIN · JULIE CHRISTIE · TOM COURTENAY
ALEC GUINNESS · SIOBHAN McKENNA · RALPH RICHARDSON
OMAR SHARIF (AS ZHIVAGO) ROD STEIGER · RITA TUSHINGHAM

WINNER OF 6 ACADEMY AWARDS!

SCREEN PLAY BY
ROBERT BOLT · DAVID LEAN

DIRECTED BY

IN PANAVISION* AND METROCOLOR

MGM

"The personal life is dead in Russia. History has killed it."

Love, affection, and sentimentality did not color the rainbows of Social Realism – at least not officially. As Soviet commander Strelnikov (Tom Courtenay) tries to impress upon poet and physician Yuri Zhivago (Omar Sharif), Russia's new social order has been painted a uniform tone: a grand, uncompromising red, which has turned his once-admired verse into meaningless displays of formalism. Though fired by the same fanatic idealism that made a general of him, the bloodthirsty Bolshevik's commentary on art and politics leaves the good doctor unfazed. Enslaved by distant echoes of individualism, Zhivago retreats to what has become a taboo private life, losing himself in his literary craft and the freedoms of the countryside. Yet the revolutionary goings-on that surround him cannot be ignored, and soon he is plunged into the throes of war and away from Lara (Julie Christie) – his mistress and the inadvertent cause of his undoing.

Based on a novel with a background as intriguing as the content of its pages, David Lean's film adaptation of Boris Pasternak's *Doctor Zhivago* was the inevitable conclusion of what had ballooned into a widely publicized East-West political scandal. First brought into the public eye by an Italian publisher in 1957, *Doctor Zhivago* became a run-

away literary hit throughout Western Europe and the United States within a year of its appearance. But success proved hollow for Pasternak, whose work remained banned in the Soviet Union for the next 30 years. Although he was recognized with the Nobel Prize for Literature in 1958, his government coerced him to decline the honor. Two years later, the author was dead.

These events were still very much alive in the collective consciousness of the West when David Lean decided to take on the film adaptation as the project to succeed his critically acclaimed *Lawrence of Arabia* (1962). Pasternak's tale about the fate of a nonconformist, whose only desire is to avoid being engulfed by the overwhelming backdrop of a new social order, seemed perfectly suited to Lean's cinematic style. Based on his track record, the self-proclaimed "sensualist of spectacle" promised to deliver yet another intricate character portrait that luxuriated in the contours of absolutely lavish scenery. And indeed, the stunning visuals of Lean's picture leave audiences breathless. Under the guiding hand of masterful production designer John Box, a crew of approximately 800 worked for two years straight at reconstructing the streets of Moscow on a lot located just outside Madrid. These are the resplendent, broad stretches of

OMAR SHARIF Omar Sharif (*1932) made a name for himself throughout the Western world with his role as Sherif Ali Ibn El Kharish in *Lawrence of Arabia* (1962). Nonetheless the actor, born Michael Shalhoub on April 10, 1932, in Alexandria, was already a big-screen heartthrob in his native Egypt, and had founded a thriving production company by the time international acclaim rolled around. His next move was to win the hearts of women worldwide with his role as the daydreaming poet Yuri in David Lean's adaptation of Boris Pasternak's *Doctor Zhivago* (1965). The role of Yuri as a boy was played by Sharif's son Tarek. The handsome actor's career flourished throughout the 1960s, and he had the great fortune of being cast in a breadth of roles alongside *Lawrence* and *Zhivago*. He played the war-faring Sohamus in *The Fall of the Roman Empire* (1963), a priest in *Behold a Pale Horse* (1964), and a jealous husband whose suspicious nature ends up destroying his marriage in Sidney Lumet's *The Appointment* (1969). Sharif's popularity began to dwindle in the 1970s, but his reputation as an international playboy ensured that his face would at least be in the tabloids. Sharif is a world-class bridge player and in later life enjoyed a steady career in made-for-TV movies and miniseries, with his César-winning turn as a sentimental shopkeeper in François Dupeyron's *Monsieur Ibrahim* (2003) showing a marked return to form.

1 Somewhere, my love: Yuri (Omar Sharif) holds onto antiquated ideals and chases a rainbow named Lara (Julie Christie).

2 Waltz with the wicked: the opportunistic Victor Komarovsky (Rod Steiger) offers Lara his experience and protection.

3 Cold front: the merciless Russian winter is indifferent to politics.

4 Love without passion: Yuri demonstrates tenderness and compassion for wife Tonya (Geraldine Chaplin), but denies her the fires of his soul.

> **"The bitter cold of winter, the grime of Moscow, the lush countryside, the drabness of life in a dictatorship, the brutality of war, and the fool's paradise of the declining Czarist era are forcefully conveyed in full use of camera, color, sound and silence."** *Variety*

promenade we cast our eyes upon, from the loggia adjoining the apartments of Zhivago's surrogate parents (Ralph Richardson, Siobhan McKenna), while the Czar's cavalry march upon a sea of Bolshevik demonstrators.

Together with his returning cinematographer Freddie Young, Lean again succeeds in delivering spectacular landscape shots, making superb use of the Panavision widescreen format to capture the snow-covered masses fighting desperately against the brutal Russian winter (these sequences were actually filmed in eastern Finland near the Soviet border).

In opposition to these monumental scenes and to Lean's larger-than-life protagonist in *Lawrence of Arabia*, Yuri Zhivago emerges as an unassuming character, who peers dreamily out his window while the rest of the world comes crashing down around him. Omar Sharif endows the role with an air of naïveté that plays up the reluctant hero's indecisiveness and lack of moral fiber as he traverses the many historical events he is powerless to influence. Zhivago's passivity provides other members of the ensemble, like his half-brother Jevgraf (Alec Guinness), with an opportunity to take the helm. A Bolshevik officer with the secret police, Jevgraf uses his influence to bail Yuri out of numerous impossible entanglements, just as he does with the entire film whenever a narrator

is required to bridge scenes separated by years. There's no doubt about who is the picture's most spellbinding character. Komarovsky (Rod Steiger), a cynical womanizer and color-blind political opportunist, is a shifty businessman who caters to the highest bidder, successfully negotiating one deal after the next with whomever he considers the man of the hour. He's flawed, but not entirely despicable, and his steady concern for Yuri and Lara win him the sympathies of the audience, even though the central couple despise him. Manifesting neither Strelnikov's fanaticism nor Yuri's introspection, he is high-spirited and resilient, and therefore Lara's true male counterpart. This would explain why before allowing Lara to become Strelnikov's wife or Zhivago's mistress, Pasternak had Komarovsky

4

deflower her himself. Indeed, Lara's character is of significance to those around her. To Komarovsky, she is a mere plaything to be enjoyed – a view he expects her to accept as a simple matter of fact, but which she doesn't take lightly. Yuri, of course, only sees the muse in her, and even his understanding wife Tonya (Geraldine Chaplin) deems the once-virtuous nurse a truly fine woman. In truth, Lara is a composite of all their assessments, but is first and foremost a survival artist.

Beyond the characterizations, Lean's unmistakable symbolism does a brilliant job communicating the struggle for individual and artistic survival in times of sheer adversity, and each merciless winter is followed by a spring bloom of daffodils. Likewise, a steadfast belief in legacy and greater meaning appears throughout the film in the form of Yuri's balalaika, the sole heirloom and recollection he has of his mother, who was a great musician. Although he cannot play the instrument himself, he carries it with him for most of his life, until finally passing it on to Lara, who in turn leaves it to their daughter – a child Yuri never meets, but who, nonetheless, inherits his mother's great gift for music.

5 Red, white and dead: the October Revolution according to Hollywood.

6 Gen. Yevgraf Zhivago (Alec Guinness) wonders if the girl before him

7 Yuri and family take refuge in what used to be the servants' quarters of

(Rita Tushingham) is indeed Lara and Yuri's lost child.

their summer residence, but without Lara, Zhivago can't write poetry.

8 Healing with dreams: Dr. Yuri Zhivago treats patients.

Russia never looked this glamorous, but then again, with its predominantly British cast and Egyptian leading man speaking what Lean must have taken to be the Czarina's English, *Dr. Zhivago* never looks quite like Russia. Screenwriter Robert Bolt cut major portions of Pasternak's book, relying on voice-overs to tie together his somewhat sporadic three-and-a-half-hour tragic love story. It is therefore hardly surprising that this triumph of schmaltz and romance was eaten alive by the critics but it went on to become one of the biggest box-office smashes of the entire decade! Eager moviegoers stood in lines that wrapped around blocks to get a glimpse of Soviet snuggling, and some theaters ran the film for years on end.

Cynics attribute *Zhivago*'s popularity to Maurice Jarre's score and the folkloric balalaika melody that flows through the film. So what? It's evidence that music lovely enough to fill the harsh Siberian winter with jingling bells can warm even the coldest of hearts.   LP

PIERROT LE FOU

1965 - FRANCE / ITALY - 110 MIN.

DIRECTOR
JEAN-LUC GODARD (*1930)

SCREENPLAY
JEAN-LUC GODARD

DIRECTOR OF PHOTOGRAPHY
RAOUL COUTARD

EDITING
FRANÇOISE COLLIN

MUSIC
ANTOINE DUHAMEL, BORIS BASSIAK,
JEAN-BAPTISTE LULLY, ANTONIO VIVALDI

PRODUCTION
GEORGES DE BEAUREGARD for ROME PARIS FILMS, SOCIÉTÉ NOUVELLE DES CINÉMATOGRAPHIE,
DINO DE LAURENTIIS CINEMATOGRAFICA

STARRING
JEAN-PAUL BELMONDO (Ferdinand "Pierrot" Griffon), ANNA KARINA (Marianne Renoir),
GRAZIELLA GALVANI (Ferdinand's Wife), DIRK SANDERS (Fred),
PASCAL AUBIER (Second Brother), PIERRE HANIN (Third Brother),
JIMMY KAROUBI (Dwarf), ROGER DUTOIT (Gangster),
HANS MEYER (Gangster), KRISTA NELL (Madame Staquet), SAMUEL FULLER (Himself)

LA SOCIÉTÉ NOUVELLE DE CINÉMATOGRAPHIE
présente **JEAN-PAUL BELMONDO**

DANS UN FILM DE
JEAN-LUC GODARD

AVEC
ANNA KARINA
GRAZIELLA GALVANI
DIRK SANDERS
ROGER DUTOIT
AVEC LA PARTICIPATION EXCEPTIONNELLE DE
RAYMOND DEVOS
DIRECTEUR DE LA PHOTOGRAPHIE RAOUL COUTARD
MUSIQUE ANTOINE DUHAMEL ÉDITIONS HORTENSIA

Pierrot LE FOU

SNC

EASTMANCOLOR TECHNISCOPE

PRODUCTION GEORGES DE BEAUREGARD – S.N.C. (PARIS) – DINO DE LAURENTIIS (ROME)

ATELIERS LALANDE – MITRY (XXXX) G.4.F 65.11 R

"If you're gonna be crazy, then be really crazy!"

Disgusted by his bourgeois existence, Ferdinand (Jean-Paul Belmondo) runs off with Marianne (Anna Karina). She's been involved in the shady business carried out by her brother Fred (Dirk Sanders), an arms dealer, and now there's a body and several guns lying around her flat. There's also a suitcase full of dollars there ... so the couple head south with the money, pursued by gangsters with political connections. When their car goes up in flames along with the cash, the couple are forced into a series of petty thefts in order to make it to the Mediterranean. For a while, they live in perfect freedom in a lonely house on the beach; but eventually differences arise, and their criminal past catches up with them.

With a plot like this, *Pierrot le fou* might well have been a thoroughly average American-style thriller. Naturally, the name of Jean-Luc Godard ensures that it isn't. Even his legendary debut *Breathless* (*À bout de souffle*, 1959) was much more than a mere variation on a familiar genre; indeed, it was one of the most brilliant works of the *Nouvelle Vague*, subverting the conventions of narrative cinema with playful ease. With *Pierrot le fou*, the French director continued the tradition he had initiated.

Godard did without a script and relied on free improvisation, producing a strikingly spontaneous movie that follows its own associative logic. Structurally, it is a kind of collage rather than a classical film narrative, and it manages to hold a number of very disparate elements in equilibrium. Paintings, advertising billboards, and comic strips are edited into the flow of images alongside quotes from various films and books, and the movie changes its tone

JEAN-PAUL BELMONDO He acquired his trademark as a young boxer: a very conspicuously broken nose. Jean-Paul Belmondo was born in Paris in 1933 and both his parents were artists. By the time he made his cinema debut in the mid-'50s, he had acquired a solid acting training and some experience on stage. In 1959, he became famous practically overnight with his performance as the cheeky but romantic crook in Godard's *Breathless* (*À bout de souffle*). From then on, Belmondo bore the nickname "Bebel," and French sociologists pondered the phenomenon of "le belmondisme" – a wave of imitation among the country's youth.

François Truffaut described Belmondo as the best French actor of his generation, and there's no denying his screen presence in a whole series of outstanding '60s films. These included Godard's comedy *A Woman is a Woman (Une femme est une femme*, 1961) and Truffaut's adventure movie *Mississippi Mermaid (La Sirène du Mississippi*, 1969), in which he gave a convincing performance in a romantic role – just as he had done in *Pierrot le fou* (1965). Jean-Paul Belmondo made three films with Jean-Pierre Melville, including the brilliant gangster movie *L'Aîné des Ferchaux / Lo sciacallo* (1963). He also appeared in some of the biggest box-office hits of the '60s and '70s. Of these, Philippe De Broca's *That Man from Rio (L'Homme de Rio / L'uomo del Rio*, 1963) best displayed his charm, temperament, and athletic physique. In the '70s, Belmondo concentrated increasingly on action-oriented thrillers and comedies that provided a more or less ironical take on his incomparably virile image. One exception was Alain Resnais's *Stavisky* (1974), which Belmondo himself produced. From then on, he mainly cropped up in run-of-the-mill entertainments. In the late '80s, however, with his pulling power at the movies in decline, he attracted a lot of attention with a successful comeback in the theater.

3

1 Death of Marat: guess again. 1960s French heartthrob and superstar Jean-Paul Belmondo plays Ferdinand a.k.a. "Pierrot le fou" (*Crazy Pete*) – slave to circumstance and dumb luck.

2 Fleeing south for the winter: Marianne (Anna Karina) seduces Ferdinand into abandoning his bourgeois existence.

3 Sand sculptures: Anna Karina and Jean-Paul Belmondo indulge in a bit of the *Nouvelle Vague's amour fou*.

4 Hard eight: Danish-born Anna Karina filmed a total of eight films under the direction of ex-husband Jean-Luc Godard.

5 Climb aboard, we're expecting you: Ferdinand, the vulnerable *homme faible*, falls for an adventuress and succumbs to her every whim. Just a few years later, Belmondo would play a similar role in François Truffaut's *Mississippi Mermaid (La Sirène du Mississippi,* 1969).

and style abruptly, seeming at various moments to be a thriller, a musical, a melodrama, or a grotesque comedy. It has room for a satirical mime show on the Vietnam War and a guest appearance by Sam Fuller, who provides Ferdinand with his personal definition of the cinema: "Film is like

a battleground," he explains: "Love, hate, action, violence, death. In one word: emotion."

Fuller's statement doesn't just anticipate the tragic development of the plot; it also indicates the extent to which *Pierrot le fou* reflects on its own making. For Godard's movie is also a confrontation with the cinema, a piece of film criticism in the form of a film. The regular shattering of the "realistic" illusion – the actors often speak directly to the camera, for instance – is typical of Godard, and such moments are of course also a challenge to follow the film with open eyes and a clear head. Those who do so experience *Pierrot le fou* as a fascinating attempt to approach reality in all its complexity. Godard shows the private, economic, cultural, and political influences that have made his film what it is. In the process, he proves himself to be a more skillful chronicler of his times than any of the other French New Wave's *auteurs*.

Not least, *Pierrot le fou* is a memorably beautiful love story that gave two stars the opportunity to exploit their enormous acting potential to the full. Anna Karina, at that time still married to Godard, imbues Marianne with emotional depth and anarchic charm. And Belmondo, for all his nonchalance, reveals a vulnerability that was already discernible behind the tough brittleness of the wise guy he played in *Breathless*. His Ferdinand – Marianne calls him "Pierrot," the clown – is a melancholy brooder in search of the truth. It's a mission that can only collide with Marianne's sensual and concrete approach to the world.

"Two or three years ago, I had the impression that everything had already been done, that there was nothing left to do that hadn't been done before. In short, I was a pessimist. Since *Pierrot*, I no longer have this feeling at all. Yes, one has to film everything, to talk about everything. Everything remains to be done." Jean-Luc Godard

Raoul Coutard's gently roaming camera luxuriates in the radiant Mediterranean light and captures the intoxicating freedom of the lovers in the widescreen Cinemascope format. But the promise of happiness contained in these images will eventually turn out to be deceptive. When Ferdinand realizes that Marianne has been lying to him – that Fred is not her brother but her lover – he shoots the two of them, paints his face blue, wraps two dynamite belts around his head and blows himself to pieces.

JH

ANDREI RUBLEV
STRASTI PO ANDREJU

1966 - USSR - 205 MIN.

DIRECTOR

ANDREI TARKOVSKY (1932–1986)

SCREENPLAY

ANDREI TARKOVSKY,
ANDREI MIKHALKOV-KONCHALOVSKY

DIRECTOR OF PHOTOGRAPHY

VADIM YUSOV

EDITING

LYUDMILA FEIGINOVA, T. YEGORYCHYOVA,
O. SHEVKUNENKO

MUSIC

VYACHESLAV OVCHINNIKOV

PRODUCTION

MOSFILM

STARRING

ANATOLI SOLONITSYN (Andrei Rublev), IVAN LAPIKOV (Kirill),
NIKOLAI GRINKO (Daniil), NIKOLAI SERGEYEV (Feofan Grek),
IRMA RAUSCH (Idiot Girl), NIKOLAI BURLYAYEV (Boriska),
YURI NAZAROV (Grand Prince), ROLAN BYKOV (The Jester), IGOR DONSKOY (Christ),
MIKHAIL KONONOV (Foma), YURI NIKULIN (Patrik)

· FILM RADZIECKI NAGRODZONY NA MFF W CANNES ·   · REŻYSERIA: ANDRIEJ TARKOWSKI ·

ANDRIEJ RUBLOW

W rolach głównych: Anatolij Sołonicyn, Iwan Łapikow,   Nikołaj Grińko, Nikołaj Burlajew.   Produkcja: MOSFILM

EROL V/73

"You found bells, I paint icons – what a feast day for mankind!"

A peasant stares flabbergasted as he watches a man slowly rise up into the air. "Now you're going to heaven!" he shouts, as the patchwork hot-air balloon drifts ever higher across a bizarre winter landscape. The makeshift aircraft reaches a dizzying height, when the whistling wind and the groaning rope make us fear the worst; and seconds later, the journey's over and the balloon crashes to the ground.

In this allegorical opening sequence, Andrei Tarkovsky anticipates the central theme of *Andrei Rublev*. By showing us the rise and fall of a man who reached for the sky, the Russian director illustrates a yearning for freedom and the desire to overcome humanity's limitations. On the surface, *Andrei Rublev* is a biopic about a 15th-century Russian icon painter. In essence, however, it's a reflection on the nature of art itself, and the eight episodes of this three-hour black-and-white masterpiece amount to a panoramic vision of the Russian nation under the heel of the Tatars.

On an epic scale, yet without a trace of nationalistic pathos, director Andrei Tarkovsky portrays a world in which the line between good and evil is impossibly blurred. Despite all the horrors of earthly existence, monk and painter Andrei Rublev (Anatoli Solonitsyn) is convinced of the essential goodness of mankind, and he regards art as a source of comfort and power for change. But his idealistic worldview collapses as the Tatars storm into his homeland: Russians fight Russians, slaughtering each other like cattle, and he is forced to kill a would-be rapist. Shaken to the core, he loses faith in art, lays down his brush and retreats into silence.

His faith in life and art is finally restored by a young man called Boriska (Nikolai Burlyayev). In an unforgettable sequence, Rublev observes how the young man gives his all to cast a colossal bell for the local prince. Deeply impressed by the joy this heroic endeavor gives to the people, Rublev takes up his work once again. He now realizes that the artist, like anyone else engaged in the struggle for existence, must fight to achieve his destiny.

Many critics have pointed out that Rublev, the monk, was a kind of cinematic avatar of Tarkovsky himself – the Russian title is *The Passion of Andrei* – and that the film's true subject was contemporary reality. So it's no surprise that, in 1966, the Soviet authorities weren't prepared to release the completed movie as it stood. The censors objected to some particularly harrowing torture scenes, and to an allegedly unpatriotic rendering of Russian history.

FILM BIOGRAPHIES OF ARTISTS A well-established subgenre of the biopic examines the lives of artists, both real and fictional, including painters, musicians, and writers. Although they occasionally verge on the didactic, these "artist films" have often been highly successful. Artists frequently lead spectacularly interesting lives, and the processes and techniques of creation are fascinating themes in themselves. Most of these movies deal with the life, work, and reputation of artists already reasonably familiar to the general public. Great pains are therefore taken to recreate the settings, characters, and costumes with a maximum of historical accuracy. Only a few films break with this tradition, preferring a timeless or contemporary look instead (as in Derek Jarman's *Caravaggio*, 1986).

In popular mythology, the artist is a lonely genius, suffering for his art and generally neglected by a philistine public. The movies are an ideal platform for variations on this theme, from Michelangelo as "divino artista" (*The Agony and the Ecstasy*, 1965) to Goya as a useful member of society (*Goya*, 1971), from the crazed creator as social outcast (*Vincent & Theo*, 1990) to the modern "mad and tragic hero" (*Pollock*, 2000).

1 Brothers in arms: the Grand Duke's brother (Yuri Nazarov in a dual role) enjoys the benefits of influence, but would prefer to occupy the prestigious position himself. Flexing his military muscle, he leads troops to pillage Vladimir's cathedral.

2 The passion: the jester (Rolan Bykov) and the painter Andrei Rublev (Anatoli Solonitsyn) fight for more humanity.

3 Sacred spaces: Andrei's meeting with the mighty grand duke is set in an eerie, vacuous church, echoing the emptiness in his heart.

4 I don't mean to shock anyone: Rublev explains his view of art and turns his back on the power-hungry.

5 Borscht bully: Kirill (Ivan Lapikov) is the sly counterpart to the woeful Andrei.

Tarkovsky stood his ground and refused to tolerate the mutilation of his work, which was originally 220 minutes long. Finally, though, he did agree to shorten a few scenes, without, however, affecting the film's essential content and meaning. It was February 1969 before *Andrei Rublev* received its first "semi-official" showing, but this was enough to capture people's attention. In the same year – though the film had still not been officially approved for showing abroad – *Andrei Rublev* was screened at Cannes, where it received the International Critics' Prize. Only in 1973 was it finally released for public distribution.

By this time, *Andrei Rublev* was recognized as one of the most serious, important and multifaceted films ever made about art. The episodic narrative structure allows Tarkovsky to incorporate a wide range of positions and perspectives. This enables him, not least, to deliver a variety of answers to the difficult question: "What is a work of art?" In the very first episode, the jester's jokes about popes and potentates broach the issue of the relationship between art, politics and social criticism. Several episodes contrast the quiet and thoughtful Andrei with his talentless but striving apprentice Kirill (Ivan Lapikov), who eventually suffers the consequences of his own excessive ambition. Kirill is pre-pared to betray both himself and Andrei if it will gain him the public recognition he so desperately craves. This is a clear allusion to Judas and Christ, and it implicitly assigns a redemptory function to the creation of true art.

In Tarkovsky's work, non-linear narrative plays a central role, and in this film his use of the technique reached its maturity. The camera meditates at length on the natural world behind and beyond humanity: snow-covered hills and swampy forests, wild horses and endless rain. It's as if the director were looking for a primary visual language, concealed within nature yet pointing to a dimension outside it.

AZ

"A violently poetic film, Dostoyevskyan in its furious intensity, yet breathtakingly precise and at times almost shockingly calculating." *Die Welt*

BONNIE AND CLYDE ♟♟

1967 - USA - 111 MIN.

DIRECTOR
ARTHUR PENN (1922–2010)

SCREENPLAY
DAVID NEWMAN, ROBERT BENTON

DIRECTOR OF PHOTOGRAPHY
BURNETT GUFFEY

EDITING
DEDE ALLEN

MUSIC
CHARLES STROUSE, LESTER FLATT & EARL SCRUGGS
(Song: "Foggy Mountain Breakdown")

PRODUCTION
WARREN BEATTY for TATIRA-HILLER PRODUCTIONS,
SEVEN ARTS, WARNER BROS.

STARRING
WARREN BEATTY (Clyde Barrow), FAYE DUNAWAY (Bonnie Parker),
MICHAEL J. POLLARD (C. W. Moss), GENE HACKMAN (Buck Barrow),
ESTELLE PARSONS (Blanche), DENVER PYLE (Frank Hamer),
DUB TAYLOR (Ivan Moss), EVANS EVANS (Velma Davis), GENE WILDER (Eugene Grizzard)

ACADEMY AWARDS 1967
OSCARS for BEST SUPPORTING ACTRESS (Estelle Parsons), and
BEST CINEMATOGRAPHY (Burnett Guffey)

Clyde was the leader, Bonnie wrote poetry.

C.W. was a Myrna Loy fan who had a bluebird tattooed on his chest. Buck told corny jokes and carried a Kodak. Blanche was a preacher's daughter who kept her fingers in her ears during the gunfights. They played checkers and photographed each other incessantly. On Sunday nights they listened to Eddie Cantor on the radio. All in all, they killed 18 people.

They were the strangest damned gang you ever heard of.

WARREN BEATTY
FAYE DUNAWAY

BONNIE *and* CLYDE x

MICHAEL J. POLLARD · GENE HACKMAN · ESTELLE PARSONS

WRITTEN BY DAVID NEWMAN and ROBERT BENTON · MUSIC BY Charles Strouse · PRODUCED BY WARREN BEATTY · DIRECTED BY ARTHUR PENN

TECHNICOLOR® FROM WARNER BROS. · RELEASED THROUGH WARNER-PATHE

"Now Mrs. Parker, don't you believe what you read in all those newspapers. That's the law talkin' there."

Faces of country folk unfold in a sequence of black-and-white photographs, yellowed by time. We hear the camera click, as it captures one image after the other of hunger and despair, and we could easily believe we're watching a documentary by Dorothea Lange, the most honest chronicler of the age. Then the final image appears, a photo of a young man and a thin blonde woman. The confusion disappears and the connection is explained: these were America's poor during the Great Depression, and among them were Bonnie and Clyde.

Back in 1967, it was probably fair to say that the public memory of Bonnie Parker and Clyde Barrow had accumulated as much dust as the photos we are shown. But when the cobwebs vanish, the tired faces of the amo-rous outlaws are replaced by a close-up of luscious ruby lips. The camera pulls back, revealing their owner, Bonnie Parker (Faye Dunaway), a woman thoroughly bored with her mundane existence as a waitress in some podunk Texas diner. Half-dressed, she undulates atop her bed, disturbed by the reflection of her body in the mirror and fit to burst with sexual frustration. The attractive young man in the front yard presents a welcome diversion. Bonnie is clearly taken by the swanky affectations of Clyde Barrows (Warren Beatty), a self-proclaimed crook in a suit and fedora. Before long Clyde robs a mom-and-pop store, giving some clout to his big talking ways. Tailed by the state cops and powered by adolescent giddiness, the couple blaze across the Texas border on "hot" wheels. These bandits quickly adopt

DEDE ALLEN *Bonnie and Clyde* (1967) presents an almost endless spectrum of dynamically innovative cinematic elements. This is firstly due to the screenplay by Robert Benton, who went on to direct films of his own, and David Newman. Both writers had worked with *Nouvelle Vague* director François Truffaut in the earlier stages of his career. Nonetheless, Arthur Penn's unconventional directing of *Bonnie and Clyde*, the achievement of a great *auteur*, benefited hugely from the film editing by Dede Allen (1923–2010). Her first high-profile job came with Robert Wise's drama on racism, *Odds Against Tomorrow* (1959), produced almost entirely in New York. She reached a milestone in the art of film montage with Robert Rossen's *The Hustler* (1961). Her editing endowed the Hollywood veteran's film with a feel as fresh as a Truffaut or Godard picture. Allen continued to play a crucial role in creating new film styles in the '60s and '70s, collaborating with directors Arthur Penn and Sidney Lumet on several occasions. Despite three Oscar nominations for her work on Warren Beatty's mammoth undertaking *Reds* (1981), Sidney Lumet's *Dog Day Afternoon* (1975), and, most recently, Curtis Hanson's *Wonder Boys* (1999), Allen has never received an Academy Award. Lighter entertainment flicks like *The Breakfast Club* (1984) and *The Addams Family* (1991) are also indebted to Allen for some of their sparkle. Her final project was Jordanian director Omar Naim's highly acclaimed sci-fi thriller *The Final Cut* (2003).

a charming, anarchic attitude toward the law and, stripped of their innocence, earn a much-publicized reputation as serial killers.

Parting studio head Jack Warner harbored serious reservations about *Bonnie and Clyde*. To his mind, the film was an all-too-explicit example of how the Hollywood system had changed in the 1960s. This was a project that an actor had produced with an independent production company, with a renegade artist in the director's chair. It was a sign of the studio's dwindling influence and of its relegation to the realm of marketing and financial sponsorship.

With its point-blank depiction of sex and violence, *Bonnie and Clyde* proved that the so-called production code could be nullified at a major studio. For decades, the code had ensured that Hollywood movies contained only "morally harmless" content and the film's no-holds-barred visuals ruffled the feathers of several highly regarded film critics. Premiering at the 1967 Montreal Film Festival, it was branded a tasteless display of ostentatious violence. After a poor initial run, the picture returned to theaters thanks to a massive counteroffensive launched by another set of film critics, including the then little-known Pauline Kael.

"The excellent script, with its strong characterizations, telling dialogue and gripping suspense, has benefited from the fresh and original directorial touch of Arthur Penn." *Herald Tribune*

2

1 Killer style: Faye Dunaway's public deified her far beyond anything the real Bonnie Parker had ever known. Dunaway's 1930s-inspired costumes took 1960s fashion by storm and her performance transformed her into an equal-rights icon.

2 Two gunslinging lovers: Clyde's (Warren Beatty) impotence could force Bonnie to put a pistol to her own head, if the police don't beat her to it.

3 Fireworks: robbing banks used to be more fun than being a kid at Christmas.

Although the movie's protagonists were rooted in the past, it was primarily young viewers who identified with the outlaws. Their forays into crime were regarded as anti-establishment acts of rebellion. The international and national political crises of the 1960s had shaken the public's trust in political authority, and created a need for critical reflection. *Bonnie and Clyde* allowed U.S. audiences to recognize themselves in the commoners of the Depression era, who had also lost a great deal of faith in the government. This is no minor aspect of the film, and may explain its unpopularity with hostile critics.

Bonnie and Clyde is sometimes reproached for being a romanticized gangster ballad, but its depictions of death are undeniably blunt. The bullet the bank teller takes in the face is as gruesome as the killing of Clyde's brother Buck (Gene Hackman), who dies like a flailing animal hours after being shot in the head. Still, the most poignant moment of violence undoubtedly comes at the film's conclusion as Bonnie and Clyde are riddled with bullets by the authorities. It is a scene that becomes surreally macabre as a result of slow motion photography, constantly changing camera angles, and the prolongation of the act itself. Their bodies convulse in a terrifying dance of death as they are shot through with enough lead to wipe out a small town. The execution transforms them into the stuff of legend, but it doesn't cleanse them of their sin or turn them into martyrs.

The final shot shows the man who carried out these official orders of police brutality. He looks on in total disgust until the screen goes blank, leaving nothing in its trail but anguish. DG

THE GRADUATE ♟

1967 - USA - 105 MIN.

DIRECTOR
MIKE NICHOLS (1931–2014)

SCREENPLAY
CALDER WILLINGHAM, BUCK HENRY,
based on the novel of the same name by CHARLES WEBB

DIRECTOR OF PHOTOGRAPHY
ROBERT SURTEES

EDITING
SAM O'STEEN

MUSIC
DAVE GRUSIN, PAUL SIMON

PRODUCTION
LAWRENCE TURMAN for EMBASSY PICTURES CORPORATION,
LAWRENCE TURMAN INC.

STARRING
ANNE BANCROFT (Mrs. Robinson), DUSTIN HOFFMAN (Benjamin Braddock),
KATHARINE ROSS (Elaine Robinson), WILLIAM DANIELS (Mr. Braddock),
MURRAY HAMILTON (Mr. Robinson), ELIZABETH WILSON (Mrs. Braddock),
BUCK HENRY (Hotel Desk Clerk), WALTER BROOKE (Mr. McGuire),
ALICE GHOSTLEY (Mrs. Singleman), NORMAN FELL (Mr. McCleery)

ACADEMY AWARDS 1967
OSCAR for BEST DIRECTOR (Mike Nichols)

JOSEPH E. LEVINE
PRESENTS
A
MIKE NICHOLS
LAWRENCE TURMAN
PRODUCTION

This is Benjamin.

He's a little worried about his future.

THE GRADUATE

STARRING
ANNE BANCROFT AND **DUSTIN HOFFMAN** · **KATHARINE ROSS**
SCREENPLAY BY
CALDER WILLINGHAM AND **BUCK HENRY** SONGS BY **PAUL SIMON**
PERFORMED BY
SIMON AND **GARFUNKEL** PRODUCED BY **LAWRENCE TURMAN**
DIRECTED BY
MIKE NICHOLS TECHNICOLOR® PANAVISION®

THE GRADUATE

"Mrs. Robinson – you are trying to seduce me ... aren't you?"

"I just want to say one word to you, Benjamin. Just one word ..." At a welcome home party on his parents' Beverly Hills estate, recent college graduate Benjamin Braddock (Dustin Hoffman) can't mask his bewilderment as business associate, Mr. McGuire (Walter Brooke) rants and raves about the wonders of ..."plastics!"

Plastics may be the wave of the future, but the new miracle substance has yet to corner a market with young Braddock – emerging voice in the next generation of American consumers. The young man has too many other things on his mind to be concerned with the "revolutionary" business propositions of his father's crowd. Actually, no one's really sure just what Benjamin wants from life – least of all him. Until now his future has fallen into his lap thanks to his parents, his social circle, and his class. He himself has no idea about the person he'd like to become, except that he doesn't want to end up like his well-dressed, superficial parents. That's one thing he knows for sure.

Taking cover in his room, he sits down beside his old aquarium, where a figurine diver floats about aimlessly. Then Mrs. Robinson (Anne Bancroft) sails onto his horizon, and suddenly things start to look up ...

What follows is one of the most suggestive seduction scenes in all Hollywood history. Mrs. Robinson has Ben drive her home in his new candy-apple red Alfa Romeo. A sultry siren in her mid-40s, she is the wife of his father's most trusted business associate, and one of his mother's dearest friends. After coming up with an array of pretexts, she manages to lure Ben up to her bedroom. And before he knows it, there she is standing stark naked in front of him, making a proposal that no one could misunderstand. At that instant, Mr. Robinson's (Murray Hamilton) car pulls into the driveway, and Ben bolts from the scene in a panic.

But it's not over yet. For those who are granted this sort of audience with Mrs. Robinson can't easily shake her off. Two days pass, and suddenly Ben is ready to take her up on the offer. He rings his seducer from a secluded hotel

ANNE BANCROFT When Anne Bancroft made her grand entrance at the hotel bar, clad in a tiger-striped coat and black tights, she was supposed to be a woman in her mid-40s. Provocatively removing both blouse and bra back at *The Graduate's* hotel room, after teasing herself out of her mile-long hose, she has no difficulty unpeeling the 21-year-old like a ripe banana. Indeed her domineering brass exudes the experienced air of a much older woman. But in truth Anne Bancroft had just turned 36 at the time she was cast as Mrs. Robinson – a wife on the prowl. Her severe, angular face, set-off by the silver highlights in her raven hair, a reminder of her trademark chain-smoking, imbued her character with a vampish vitality. Combined with her talent, it made for a virtuoso performance that went on to define eroticism for an entire generation.
Still, the acting range of the woman born Anna Maria Italiano on September 17, 1931, in New York City can hardly be measured by this role alone. A veteran of the theater, she triumphed in many roles on Broadway including Brecht's *Mother Courage*. Raised in the Bronx, Bancroft was always a pro at integrating her upbringing into her artistry. In Arthur Penn's *The Miracle Worker* (1961) she lit up the screen as Annie Sullivan, Helen Keller's visually impaired teacher and mentor, and won herself the Best Actress Oscar for breathing life into an uncompromising character. She exhibited her prowess again in David Lynch's *The Elephant Man* (1980), playing a stage diva who voices her admiration for the deformed John Merrick before her theatrical public. It was a cinematic spectacle as unforgettable as her ruthless seduction of Benjamin Braddock. Anne Bancroft died in 2005 in New York City.

485

1 Would you like me to seduce you?
Mrs. Robinson (Anne Bancroft) is on
the prowl and about to deflower the
newly graduated Benjamin Braddock.

2 Too funky: as Benjamin (Dustin
Hoffman) builds up his ego he begins
to turn his back on the persistent
Mrs. R.

3 Hello darkness my old friend:
Benjamin is fed up with being an
obedient son and rejects the com-
forts of his existence. But it is only
after meeting Mrs. Robinson's
daughter, Elaine, that his life really
begins to take on meaning.

4 Trying to stay afloat: even at what
should be a relaxing poolside
gathering, Benjamin's prospective
employers try to drown him with
responsibility.

5 A little R & R: Mrs. Robinson wants
to lock lips, but poor Benjamin is
tongue-tied.

room. Two hours later, the deed has been done. It may have
been Ben's first time, but from then on not a day goes by
without them meeting. In seamless cross-fades, the film
deftly fans out the progression of these days as one continuous cycle between hotels and Ben's childhood bedroom; from a firm white bed to a flimsy air mattress. Mrs.
Robinson doesn't make many demands of him, but she
does make one. Ben is to never meet with her daughter
Elaine (Katharine Ross). However, Ben cannot resist temptation, and suffers dire consequences as a result. He
embarks on a crusade of love and rebellion, leading to a
pathetic stalking and, finally, a spectacularly romantic rescue at the wedding altar. After a comic beginning, Mike

Nichols's second feature climaxes as a melodrama, turning
a fresh-faced Dustin Hoffman into an overnight sensation.

The film maps Benjamin Braddock's rite of passage
from aimless graduate to self-sufficient young man. With
zoom shots and practically invisible cross-fades, which elegantly mirror the spirit of the changes in Ben's life, the
film masterfully matches content and form. It is in this way
that *The Graduate* bridges temporal gaps with the greatest of ease, and relays the sense of time experienced by
the characters. Simon and Garfunkel's *Sounds of Silence*
album emerges as the cinematic ballad that enables Benjamin's maturation to unfold as a gradual realization of his
own feelings and desires. It's not by chance that watery

images appear throughout the film – shots of aquariums, the familiar swimming pool as well as the sequence meant to be seen from behind a set of diving goggles.

These visions are constant reminders of Benjamin's odyssey, sense of drifting, and need to give direction to his life. It is an arduous awakening to adulthood in a fractured, uncertain environment. Yet we always see light at the end of *The Graduate*'s tunnel in the form of vibrant imagery and the bright, carefree superficiality of an utterly decadent milieu.

SR

"Simon & Garfunkel's score fills *The Graduate* with a gloominess and somber quality. 'Sounds of Silence,' 'Scarborough Fair,' and 'Mrs. Robinson' are great songs and while, inside the movie they sound a bit like elevator music, they do add a sort of quiet in an otherwise pungent movie." Andrew Chan, Filmwritten Magazine

2001: A SPACE ODYSSEY ♀

1968 - GREAT BRITAIN - 141 MIN.
(ORIGINAL VERSION 160 MIN.)

DIRECTOR
STANLEY KUBRICK (1928–1999)

SCREENPLAY
STANLEY KUBRICK, ARTHUR C. CLARKE,
based on a short story by ARTHUR C. CLARKE

DIRECTOR OF PHOTOGRAPHY
GEOFFREY UNSWORTH, JOHN ALCOTT (additional shots)

EDITING
RAY LOVEJOY

MUSIC
ARAM KHACHATURYAN, RICHARD STRAUSS,
JOHANN STRAUSS, GYÖRGY LIGETI

PRODUCTION
STANLEY KUBRICK for POLARIS, HAWK, MGM

STARRING
KEIR DULLEA (David Bowman), GARY LOCKWOOD (Frank Poole),
WILLIAM SYLVESTER (Dr. Heywood Floyd), LEONARD ROSSITER (Smyslov),
DANIEL RICHTER (Moonwatcher), ROBERT BEATTY (Halvorsen),
FRANK MILLER (Mission Controller), MARGARET TYZACK (Elena),
SEAN SULLIVAN (Michaels), BILL WESTON (Astronaut)

ACADEMY AWARDS 1968
OSCAR for BEST SPECIAL EFFECTS (Stanley Kubrick)

An epic drama of adventure and exploration

...taking you half a billion miles from Earth...
further from home than any man in history.
Destination: Jupiter.

MGM PRESENTS A STANLEY KUBRICK PRODUCTION

2001
a space odyssey

CINERAMA Super Panavision and Metrocolor

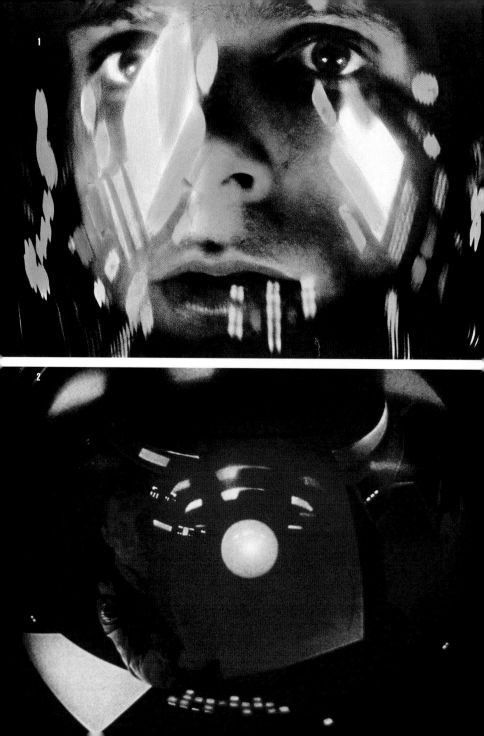

"What are you doing, Dave?"

A gate of light opens and swallows up the space capsule with its pilot Dave Bowman (Keir Dullea). He flies through a corridor of light: rays, flecks, waves and nets of luminosity, constantly dissolving and reforming into new patterns and shapes. He flies over crevices riddled with burning rivers, through shimmering mists, over glittering oceans. His mouth opens in a silent scream. His staring eye reflects a fireworks display of exploding colors. He sees what no one has ever seen. And suddenly, the journey ends, in a white room sparingly furnished with antiques. The astronaut looks out from his capsule: he sees a man in a space suit – himself, several years older; he discovers an old man eating at a table – himself again; he throws a glass to the floor, where it breaks, and he glimpses a decrepit bedridden figure – himself. At the end of the bed stands the black monolith that has led him here, beyond Jupiter. And now there's an embryo in the bed. Reborn as a star-child, he floats through space towards the earth in an amniotic sac.

The final sequence of *2001: A Space Odyssey* is a cinematic wonder, a baffling and visually overwhelming passage to another dimension where space and time are meaningless. The famous psychedelic trip through the corridor of light, made even more marvelous by the music of György Ligeti, is the crowning glory of Stanley Kubrick's masterpiece. Moreover, this virtuoso piece of special effects, a team effort, was created entirely without computers, using only models and light. There is still nothing to match this film in its quest for authenticity and sheer visionary power. It's a monolith of the science-fiction genre, and all questions about its meaning rebound off its smooth black surface.

In three separate episodes, Kubrick describes the emergence of new forms of existence: the development from ape to man; the leap from artificial intelligence to real, emotional life; and the transition from our own dimension to something entirely strange. The witness to these changes – and perhaps their cause – is a black monolith from God-knows-where. One day it's simply there, standing in the savannah amidst a horde of apes. In the shade of this monolith, one of the apes abruptly understands that a bone can be used as a weapon. The

MATCH CUT Triumphantly, the ape stands up. In its right hand it holds the animal bone it has just used to kill another ape. It seems to understand just how much power it has gained by discovering how to use the bone as a weapon. The hairy arm swings back, and the creature hurls the bone into the air. The camera follows this bone in close-up as it rises, turning, towards the sky; and as it drops back towards the earth – there's a sudden cut: the blue of the sky has become the blackness of interplanetary space, and instead of a bone, we see a spaceship. A single cut surmounted millions of years and millions of miles, linking the prehistoric past to the distant future. It's a cut that contains all of human history. This sequence, from *2001: A Space Odyssey* (1968) is perhaps the most famous "match cut" in movie history. The term describes a cut between two shots that may be far apart spatially or temporally, yet contain striking visual similarities. Identical plot elements, a similar movement or the same person can create a connection between these two shots, thus preserving a feeling of continuity. A match cut may cause a moment of surprise or uncertainty, yet it is an important element in the economy of film narrative, for it can leap over barriers of space and time.

1 Space – the final frontier: special effects designer Douglas Trumbull helped blast 2001 into cinematic history. Within just a few light years later, he gathered speed and took the helm of *Silent Running* (1972).

2 "Good afternoon, gentlemen. I am a Hal 9000 computer. I became operational at the H-A-L lab in Urbana, Illinois, on the 12th of January, 1992. I am completely operational and all my circuits are functioning perfectly." Although film co-writer Arthur C. Clarke insisted that HAL stood for Heuristic Algorithmic Computer, there's no denying that if all three letters were shifted a notch, you'd get I B M.

"I tried to create a visual experience, one that bypasses verbalized pigeonholing and directly penetrates the subconscious with an emotional and philosophical content."

Stanley Kubrick

3 Small sacrifices: Mama Hal is ready to severe the umbilical cord if need be. Meaning that astronaut Frank Poole (Gary Lockwood) had better gain independence fast if he intends to survive.

4 It can only be attributable to human error: Keir Dullea as astronaut David Bowman, the last human member of the Jupiter mission crew.

apes kill other animals and start eating meat, and their technological superiority enables them to defeat a rival horde. It's the first stage in the conquest of nature, and the birth of humankind. Several evolutionary stages later, an American scientist is traveling to the moon on a secret mission. Beneath the surface of the earth's satellite, a black monolith has been discovered, and the mysterious object is transmitting a powerful signal in the direction of Jupiter. Scientists are in no doubt: the monolith is four million years old, and it was buried deliberately.

The spaceship *Discovery* is on the way to the moon. Only the computer HAL knows the true reason for the journey – the search for extraterrestrial life. Three of the crewmembers are in hibernation while two others take care of

5

6

5 I can see you're really upset about this. I honestly think you ought to sit down calmly, take a stress pill and think things over: an ape (Dan Richter with a flawless makeup job) takes one bold step for his kind and discovers the benefits of organized violence.

6 The dark side of the moon: an artifact whose "origin and purpose is still a total mystery," is discovered on the earth's sleeping satellite.

7 Pulling the plug: just what do you think you're doing? Poole and Bowman revolt against technology.

the flight. HAL, the most complex electronic brain ever constructed, makes an error, and the men consider switching it off; but the machine starts fighting for its life, and kills the crew. Only Bowman manages to escape, and he succeeds in shutting down the computer. Outside the spacecraft, a black monolith is floating. Bowman boards a space capsule and follows it to Jupiter …

The film doesn't make things easy for the spectator. It follows no conventional narrative pattern, it makes enormous leaps in time and space, and the figures in it are mere functions rather than characters. Technically and formally perfect, *2001: A Space Odyssey* offers us nothing and nobody we can identify with. It is a cool and somewhat forbidding film. Only around one quarter of its 160 minutes are taken up with dialogue: Kubrick lets his pictures do the talking.

The film wasn't just an incredible enrichment of the science-fiction genre, but also changed the way we look at the universe. The dazzling sun, its rays reflected from the snow-white body of the spaceship, while the dark side is sunk in inky blackness; the fountain pen floating through the cabin, dropped by a sleeping passenger on the way to the moon; the ghostly silence enveloping a dead astronaut in his yellow spacesuit, as he spins eternally through space; the circular space station turning like a gyroscope on its own axis; the blue, shimmering planet Earth. Outer space is Stanley Kubrick's invention. Never before and never since has a film so brilliantly succeeded in conveying an impression of infinity.

A few years later, the pictures of the Apollo missions showed that Kubrick's vision was also highly realistic – much to the director's relief, incidentally. NM

ONCE UPON A TIME IN THE WEST
C'ERA UNA VOLTA IL WEST

1968 - ITALY / USA - 165 MIN.

DIRECTOR

SERGIO LEONE (1929–1989)

SCREENPLAY

SERGIO DONATI, SERGIO LEONE, based on a story by
DARIO ARGENTO, BERNARDO BERTOLUCCI, SERGIO LEONE

DIRECTOR OF PHOTOGRAPHY

TONINO DELLI COLLI

EDITING

NINO BARAGLI

MUSIC

ENNIO MORRICONE

PRODUCTION

FULVIO MORSELLA for RAFRAN,
EURO INTERNATIONAL, PARAMOUNT

STARRING

CLAUDIA CARDINALE (Jill MacBain), HENRY FONDA (Frank),
CHARLES BRONSON ("Harmonica" / The Man With No Name),
JASON ROBARDS (Cheyenne), GABRIELE FERZETTI (Morton),
FRANK WOLFF (Brett MacBain), KEENAN WYNN (Sheriff),
PAOLO STOPPA (Sam), LIONEL STANDER (Barkeeper),
WOODY STRODE (Gang member), JACK ELAM (Gang member)

C'ERA UNA VOLTA IL WEST con HENRY FONDA CLAUDIA CARDINALE JASON ROBARDS
NEL RUOLO DI ARMONICA
REGIA DI SERGIO LEONE GABRIELE FERZETTI CHARLES BRONSON PAOLO STOPPA
UNA PRODUZIONE
RAFRAN·S.MARCO
E IN ORDINE ALFABETICO
TECHNICOLOR®TECHNISCOPE® JACK ELAM LIONEL STANDER WOODY STRODE FRANK WOLFF KEENAN WYNN

"What's he waiting for out there? What's he doing?" "He's whittlin' on a piece of wood. I've got a feeling when he stops whittlin' ... somethin's gonna happen."

Three men in long coats are waiting at a lonely railroad station. A pinwheel creaks in the wind. A droplet from a water tank plops onto one man's (Woody Strode) hat; it's followed by another, and another. A fly buzzes around the unshaven face of the gang's leader (Jack Elam); the insect lands on his lip, he drives it away, it buzzes back again. Eventually, he catches the fly in the barrel of his Colt, and listens to the trapped creature with a smile on his face. We hear the distant sound of a train whistle. The men get ready. The train arrives – no sign of any passengers disembarking – and departs again. Suddenly, a doleful tune: on the other side of the tracks stands a man playing a mouth organ. He puts his bags down, and a dialogue ensues. Harmonica: "And Frank?" – The gang leader: "Frank sent us." – "Did you bring a horse for me?" – "Well ... looks like we're ...

looks like we're shy one horse." – "You brought two too many." They draw their guns, open fire, and collapse to the ground.

This incredibly slow beginning lasts a quarter of an hour, ending abruptly in a shoot-out that leaves only one man alive (but slightly injured): the man with the harmonica (Charles Bronson). It's a sequence that displays all the stylistic elements of the Spaghetti Western: extreme close-ups that reveal every pore in a man's face; warped perspectives, with characters shot from below; the sudden transition to panoramic views of a vast, empty landscape; terse dialogue; time stretched unbearably, then shattered in an eruption of gunfire. "Harmonica" – we never discover his real name – has come to avenge the death of his brother. Two and a half hours of the film will pass before

ENNIO MORRICONE The success of *Once Upon a Time in the West* (*C'era una volta il West*, 1968) was due not least to the music of Ennio Morricone. For each of the main characters, he composed a signature melody: the plangent harmonica for Charles Bronson, the female choir for Claudia Cardinale. It's for this reason that the film has often been compared to an opera; each of the themes functions independently of the others, and the music is highly effective even in the absence of the film. This is one of the most celebrated soundtracks in the history of the cinema, and it made the composer world famous. Leone and Morricone had known each other since childhood. Born in Rome in 1928, Morricone studied music from the age of 12, and later worked as a nightclub musician. He wrote his first film scores in the early '60s, and first attracted attention with the catchy soundtrack to *A Fistful of Dollars* (*Per un pugno di dollari*, 1964). This was followed by equally memorable music for *The Good, the Bad and the Ugly* (*Il buono, il brutto, il cattivo* 1966) and *The Sicilian Clan* (*Le Clan des Siciliens*, 1969). He worked with Bernardo Bertolucci on his mammoth project *1900* (1976), with Brian De Palma on *The Untouchables* (1987), and with Roman Polanski on *Frantic* (1987).

Though nominated for the Oscar several times – for example, for *The Mission* (1986) – Morricone has yet to win it. However as the recipient of an Honorary Academy Award in 2007 his position as one of the most important and versatile film composers of the 20th century was recognized. He has written more than 400 scores. Even if only around one-tenth of them were for Westerns, the name Ennio Morricone – much to his regret – will remain inseparably associated with the Spaghetti Westerns of the 1960s.

1 Play dead for me: like in opera, Ennio Morricone had individual theme music composed for each of his main characters. Charles Bronson as Harmonica.

2 O. Henry: Sergio Leone looks his characters straight in the face and makes villains like Frank (Henry Fonda) break out in a cold sweat.

3 Still life: Bernardo Bertolucci hangs 'em high and turns glorified violence into visual masterpieces. The film's script was a joint effort between Bertolucci, director of *Ultimo tango a Parigi (The Last Tango in Paris,* 1972) and horror flick aficionado Dario Argento.

"Sergio Leone ... seems to have improved as he has gone along, and *Once Upon a Time in the West* I consider his masterpiece, even surpassing *The Good, the Bad and the Ugly,* which is actually more efficient if less ambitious. Indeed, I am convinced that Sergio Leone is the only living director who can do justice to the baroque elaboration of revenge and violence in *The Godfather.*" *The Village Voice*

he finally encounters the man who didn't have time to meet him at the station. Frank was busy – massacring an entire family of defenseless settlers, including a little boy who'd looked right in his cold blue eyes.

As the face of the killer Frank was revealed for the first time, American moviegoers allegedly gasped in dismay – for it was none other than Henry Fonda. The living embodiment of Good as the face of pure Evil … This shocking casting-against-type was a straight declaration to the audience: What you're watching here has absolutely nothing to do with the classical Hollywood Western. That's why Woody Strode and Jack Elam, familiar faces from countless Westerns of the past, got blown away right at the start. What you're watching here is the myth of the Wild

West turned on its head; no more shining heroes, not an honorable motive in sight. Sergio Leone later stated that he had wanted to sweep away all the lies that had been told about the colonization of America. *Once Upon a Time in the West* tells of the blood and the dirty money that lubricated the wheels of "civilization."

Besides the revenger's tale, Leone also tells us of the building of the railroad and the passing of the old-style gunslinger. Frank is the right-hand man of a sickly entrepreneur who dreams of reaching the Pacific with his railroad line. It's Frank's job to remove any obstacles in the path of this project. The settler and his kids had to die because their land contained the only water source for miles around. The guy knew this, and dreamed of being

4 Death Valley: Jill (Claudia Cardinale) arrives at her new home on the frontier only to find that her entire family has been assassinated. Save for Jill's thought-provoking journey to the farm – filmed in the California desert – the picture was shot exclusively in Spain.

5 Sweetwater: Jill is set on the idea of founding an oasis town. It's a commentary in itself that Leone picked a whore to serve as mother of the civilization that grew out of the Wild West.

"They wanna hang me! The big, black crows. Idiots. What the hell? I'll kill anything. Never a kid. Be like killin' a priest."

Film quote: Cheyenne (Jason Robards)

the stationmaster and founder of a new town. What Frank doesn't know is that the widowed settler had previously married a high-class whore (Claudia Cardinale) in New Orleans. It takes her a while to grasp what a valuable piece of real estate she's inherited in the desert, but with the help of Harmonica and the desperado Cheyenne (Jason Robards), she sets out to realize her dead husband's plans.

With the three films that made up his "Dollar Trilogy" – *A Fistful of Dollars*, *For a Few Dollars More*, and *The Good, The Bad and The Ugly* – Sergio Leone became the most innovative director of European Westerns (along with Sergio Corbucci). Today, these three films look like preliminary studies for his ultimate masterpiece: *Once Upon a Time in the West*. It is perfect, in more ways than one: in its casting, its relentless build-up of suspense, and in its sheer visual power. Each shot is meticulously composed, and its use of zooms, complicated camera moves and slow motion in the flashback sequences give it the quality of a bold formal experiment. Some accused Leone of mannerism; other critics and colleagues such as Wim Wenders were appalled because the movie represented "the ultimate Western," and was therefore "the end of the road." It may well be the most breathtaking Western ever made.

NM

EASY RIDER

1969 - USA - 95 MIN.

DIRECTOR
DENNIS HOPPER (1936–2010)

SCREENPLAY
PETER FONDA, DENNIS HOPPER, TERRY SOUTHERN

DIRECTOR OF PHOTOGRAPHY
LÁSZLÓ KOVÁCS

EDITING
DONN CAMBERN

MUSIC
STEPPENWOLF, ROGER MCGUINN, THE BYRDS, THE BAND,
THE JIMI HENDRIX EXPERIENCE

PRODUCTION
PETER FONDA for PANDO, RAYBERT PRODUCTIONS, BBS,
COLUMBIA PICTURES CORPORATION

STARRING
PETER FONDA (Wyatt), DENNIS HOPPER (Billy),
JACK NICHOLSON (George Hanson), LUKE ASKEW (Hitchhiker),
LUANA ANDERS (Lisa), SABRINA SCHARF (Sarah),
TONI BASIL (Mary), KAREN BLACK (Karen),
WARREN FINNERTY (Rancher), ROBERT WALKER JR. (Jack)

THIS YEAR IT'S EASY RIDER

"This used to be a helluva good country. I can't understand what's gone wrong with it."

Freedom… and the impossibility of freedom in a country where people are scared to be free. Billy (Dennis Hopper) is sitting at the campfire with the lawyer George Hanson (Jack Nicholson). The legal eagle is no longer perfectly sober, and Billy is a little slow-witted because he's permanently stoned. But George is doing his best to clarify a few matters for Billy: why the motel owner slammed the door on him and his buddy Wyatt (Peter Fonda); why the girl behind the bar in the one-horse town refused to serve them; why the mob and their sheriff chased them out of town instead. The lawyer explains that these people are not scared of Billy personally; they're scared of what he represents: an easy, unforced existence outside of society – a life in which the only things that matter are self-realization and life itself.

Billy and Wyatt ran into the lawyer in a jail cell, where he'd been sleeping off his latest bout with the bottle. Now he's joined them on their motorcycle odyssey, all the way from Los Angeles to Mardi Gras in New Orleans. They cruise down endless empty highways, through stunningly beautiful landscapes, rarely stopping before the sun goes down. Wyatt has spurs on his boots and a star-spangled banner on the back of his leather jacket; Billy wears suede pants, and he sports a Stetson on his long, matted hair. They're two 20th-century cowboys on a quest for space and freedom, chasing an ideal America that disappeared many moons ago.

Easy Rider cost only $400,000 to make, but it quickly became one of the cult movies of the '60s. It's a piece of celluloid that evokes an entire generation's outlook on life, a road movie about youth, drugs, and the dream of revolution, with a soundtrack as hugely successful as the movie that spawned it. Far from merely accompanying the pictures, songs by the Byrds, the Band and Fraternity of Man provide

DENNIS HOPPER "I'll fuck anything that moves!" As Frank Booth in David Lynch's *Blue Velvet* (1985), he celebrated his unforgettable comeback – as an obscenely violent psychopath horribly dependent on an unnamed gas. During his career, Dennis Hopper (1936–2010) often embodied the unpredictable, the explosive, and the insane. He played variations on these themes in *Red Rock West* (1992) by John Dahl, *Speed* (1994) by Jan de Bont, and *Waterworld* (1995) by Kevin Reynolds and Kevin Costner. All told, Hopper appeared in over 100 films, more than 40 of them made in the '90s alone. "I no longer wait to be offered great roles," said Hopper in an interview with the German newspaper *Süddeutsche Zeitung*: "I just work. I make sure I'm always busy, because I love doing what I do."

Dennis Hopper came to Hollywood at the age of 18. Just a year later, after a few TV jobs, he appeared alongside his role model James Dean in Nicholas Ray's *Rebel Without a Cause* (1955) and George Stevens's *Giant* (1956). But Hopper acquired a reputation for being "difficult," and after studying at the Actors' Studio in New York he worked mainly in the theater. In 1969, with *Easy Rider*, he returned to Hollywood as director and protagonist of his own movie. The film's enormous success took its toll on him, however, as he embarked on a wild life marked by excessive drug use. After the failure of *The Last Movie* (1969/71), Hopper disappeared from view for a while, before returning in European films such as Wim Wenders's *The American Friend (Der Amerikanische Freund*, 1977) and Roland Klick's *White Star* (1982). He also worked as a photographer and collected artworks, including some important pieces of Pop art.

Later, he began making his own films, such as the mesmerizing *Colors* (1988), a police movie set in L.A. But the decisive turning point in his career was undoubtedly *Blue Velvet*. With this film, he began his *third* career, after his successes in the '50s and '60s; and the words of Frank Booth seemed to encapsulate Dennis Hopper's situation yet again: "Let's hit the fuckin' road!"

1 Made in the shades: Peter Fonda as the reflective and easygoing Wyatt.

2 Fireside chats: the erratic and eccentric Billy (Dennis Hopper) just loves chewin' the fat – no matter who's listening. It's no coincidence that the film's two main buddies share their first names with legendary cowboys Wyatt Earp and Billy the Kid.

3 The thrill of the open road: attorney George Hanson (Jack Nicholson) heads down south to New Orleans. Good thing his mom kept his football helmet of his high school glory days intact for him.

4 Road hogs: and hog wild at that. Peter Fonda was already an experienced biker at the time of the shoot – a clue as to why his cycle got more souped up than Dennis Hopper's.

a running commentary on the film. "Born to Be Wild," Steppenwolf's hymn to freedom, is a programmatic opening number; and Roger McGuinn's cover version of Bob Dylan's "It's Alright Ma (I'm Only Bleeding)" paves the way for the sober and melancholy conclusion. Producer and protagonist Peter Fonda reported that Dylan had refused to allow the original version to be used because he felt the movie offered too little hope. For Wyatt and Billy are ultimately blown out of existence by a reactionary hick with a rifle; they're on their bikes and he's in his truck, and he kills them just for the hell of it.

This pessimistic ending casts doubt on the whole freewheelin' on-the-road adventure. In an interview with the German magazine *Filmkritik*, Peter Fonda commented:

"We knew there couldn't be any more heroes, yet we still tried to *live* like heroes. This yearning is there in the film – along with the disillusionment." The project began with the simple desire of two real-life friends, Hopper and Fonda, to travel through the country by motorbike, and the end result was this movie. All the various episodes took place on the road, from the visit to a hippie camp in New Mexico to the meeting with a farmer whose entire extended family lived off the land. Like the characters they play, Hopper and Fonda were verbally abused by rednecks – and even threatened with guns – while filming. They also smoked a lot of grass.

In a cemetery in New Orleans, the two protagonists team up with a couple of hookers and embark on an acid

"*Easy Rider* is a Southern term for the whore's old man, not a pimp, but the dude who lives with a chick. Because he's got the easy ride. Well, that's what happened to America, man. Liberty's become a whore, and we're all taking an easy ride."

Peter Fonda

trip that turns completely nightmarish. Hopper shoots the drug experience not as a cleansing of the doors of perception, but as a splintering of reality, a kaleidoscope of terror and despair. A short time later, the thoughtful Wyatt comments to Billy: "We're duds." They've reached New Orleans but missed their true goal. A drug deal has brought them several thousand dollars, which Wyatt hides in the tank. It's this money that's supposed to guarantee their freedom. But anyone who wants a free life beyond bourgeois society must break their dependence on its symbols and material values – like that farmer, reaping the fruits of his honest labor, far from the snares of civilization.

Hopper and Fonda seem to feel an almost religious sense of connection to their native country, and this is evoked in gorgeous, panoramic views of the American landscape. In truth, they're in mourning, for they know that the America they revere has long since passed way. If God didn't exist, you'd have to invent him, says Wyatt, as the original duo arrive in New Orleans. George didn't make it with them; in the middle of the night, he was beaten to death by a mob. And in a sudden moment of vision, Wyatt sees his own approaching end.

NM

4

MIDNIGHT COWBOY ♟♟♟

1969 - USA - 113 MIN.

DIRECTOR

JOHN SCHLESINGER (1926–2003)

SCREENPLAY

WALDO SALT, based on the novel of the
same name by JAMES LEO HERLIHY

DIRECTOR OF PHOTOGRAPHY

ADAM HOLENDER

EDITING

HUGH A. ROBERTSON

MUSIC

JOHN BARRY, FLOYD HUDDLESTON, FRED NEIL

PRODUCTION

JEROME HELLMAN for FLORIN PRODUCTIONS, JEROME HELLMAN PRODUCTIONS

STARRING

DUSTIN HOFFMAN (Enrico Salvatore "Ratso" Rizzo), JON VOIGHT (Joe Buck),
SYLVIA MILES (Cass), JOHN MCGIVER (Mr. O'Daniel),
BRENDA VACCARO (Shirley), BARNARD HUGHES (Towny), RUTH WHITE (Sally Buck),
JENNIFER SALT (Annie), GILMAN RANKIN (Woodsy Niles),
PAUL MORRISSEY (Party Guest), VIVA (Gretel McAlbertson)

ACADEMY AWARDS 1969

OSCARS for BEST PICTURE (Jerome Hellman), BEST DIRECTOR (John Schlesinger),
and BEST ADAPTED SCREENPLAY (Waldo Salt)

A JEROME HELLMAN–JOHN SCHLESINGER PRODUCTION

DUSTIN HOFFMAN
JON VOIGHT

"MIDNIGHT COWBOY"

BRENDA VACCARO · JOHN McGIVER · RUTH WHITE · SYLVIA MILES · BARNARD HUGHES

Screenplay by WALDO SALT Based on the novel by JAMES LEO HERLIHY Produced by JEROME HELLMAN Directed by JOHN SCHLESINGER

Music Supervision by JOHN BARRY "EVERYBODY'S TALKIN'" sung by NILSSON ORIGINAL MOTION PICTURE SCORE AVAILABLE ON UNITED ARTISTS RECORDS

COLOR by DeLuxe

PERSONS UNDER 17 NOT ADMITTED

50 GO United Artists

Entertainment from Transamerica Corporation

"Frankly, you're beginning to smell and ... that's a handicap."

Midnight Cowboy is a portrait of urban life that can also be read as a revisionist Western. For beyond this bittersweet tale of the concrete jungle lies a melancholy ballad that bids adieu to the ideals of the American West. An ode to innocence lost, the movie follows the story of young Joe Buck (Jon Voight), the last urban cowboy, as he tries to hold onto a rapidly disappearing dream in the 1960s. A strapping Texan, Buck has come to the Big Apple to fulfill the sexual fantasies of the city's affluent lonely hearts. What he finds is a world with little need for such services. And soon, after a series of empty encounters with homosexuals, junkies, and religious fanatics, he's down and out as a second-rate male prostitute on 42nd Street. Stripped of everything but a fading dream, all that accompanies Buck on his travels is a transistor radio emitting a hollow stream of promises, and a TB-stricken runt in a tattered dress suit known as Rico "Ratso" Rizzo (Dustin Hoffman).

As his dubious name suggests, Ratso is quick to scam the bright-eyed cowboy in the hopes of running off with his money. Mr. Buck however seems too caught up in his polished appearance to take any notice, preferring instead to steal prideful glances in the mirror before hitting the town. In fact, all the Texan can think about is how his cowboy getup is sure to be all the rage of the New York penthouse scene. Hearing opportunity knock, the hobbling Ratso appoints himself the kid's manager and sets him up on "dates" with women and men alike – sordid little encounters that slowly but surely rub the shine off the cowboy's illusions.

Ratso and Joe soon become partners in crime, living hand to mouth as small-time crooks and spending most of their waking hours in a squat without electricity and running water. Their cohabitation is dominated by fantasies of a better life, where they would move to Florida and mingle with the rich and famous. And tragically, the men only realize how much they mean to each other when it is too late.

Transcending the picture's wretched ending, their curious love story is a tender message that still strikes a chord with contemporary audiences. Wistfully under-

DUSTIN HOFFMAN Dustin Hoffman (*1937) is among the world's best-known actors and one of the few to gain international acclaim through character roles. His striking features, nasal voice, and seeming lack of self-confidence virtually preordained him for difficult parts. A Los Angeles native, he studied music at Santa Monica City College and acting at the Pasadena Playhouse before gaining admission to Lee Strasberg's Actors Studio in 1958. His big break in Hollywood came at the age of 30 with Mike Nichols's timeless classic *The Graduate* (1967) in which he played Benjamin Braddock, a character ten years his junior. The part brought him his first Oscar nomination.

It took two years and much persistence before the allegedly "difficult" actor delivered his next incomparable performance as the sickly Ratso in *Midnight Cowboy* (1969). It was the beginning of a sterling career, and soon he was cast as a 121-year-old Western pioneer in *Little Big Man* (1970), a title that incidentally became the 5'5" tall actor's nickname. He went on to play a prisoner opposite Steve McQueen in *Papillon* (1973) and claim the stage all for himself as scathing satirist Lenny Bruce in *Lenny* (1974).

A master of disguise, he dazzled audiences in *Tootsie* (1982), one of his few blockbuster romantic comedies, playing an actor who has to dress up like a woman to get work. Hoffman also shone in the political thriller *Marathon Man* (1976) and in the sensitive divorce drama *Kramer vs. Kramer* (1979), which won him his first Oscar. After poignantly portraying an autistic *Rain Man* (1988), his reputation as an insufferable perfectionist started to get the better of him and great roles became more of a rarity. Be that as it may, Hoffman is still a box-office favorite and has continued to impress audiences in more recent productions like *Billy Bathgate* (1991), *Outbreak* (1995), and *Barney's Version* (2010).

"This is obviously the sort of film in which people argue endlessly about which of the principals steals it, and the argument is irresistible, if pointless. Both are very good, in different ways. Against Mr. Voight's unnoticeable acting Mr. Hoffman has a field day with all the fireworks – ugly, crippled eccentric, and dying by degrees, he is always at the very edge of his being, which, as we all know, is a very comfortable place for an actor. He does it very well, but finally I think Mr. Voight has the more difficult part, and carries it off impeccably." *The Times*

1 Bridge over troubled waters: Don Quixote and Sancho Panza are reincarnated in 1960s New York as Joe Buck (Jon Voight) and Rico Salvatore Rizzo (Dustin Hoffman).

2 Cry me a river: Dustin Hoffman made fans see just how sexy a black sheep can be.

3 Pop goes the weasel: Rico "Ratso" Rizzo has killed time long enough and is ready to turn his know-how into a moneymaking scheme as Joe Buck's manager.

4 Life's little fetishes: Joe gets to know a couple of gay guys really well and

finds out what life in the big bad city is really all about.

5 Back off. I'm contagious: Ratso is the kind of guy who'd think up anything to get out of danger's path, and so Joe doesn't realize just how ill he really is.

scored by "Everybody's Talkin'" (performed by Harry Nilsson), the strength of this paean to friendship lies in John Schlesinger's ingenious visuals and the astonishing talent of the movie's two principal actors. The interaction between a then virtually unknown Jon Voight and his co-star Dustin Hoffman inspires immediate empathy. Whereas Joe's

6 Flim flam man: Ratso doesn't want anyone's compassion; he'd much rather have a meal ticket and a cash cow.

7 Hopalong Cassidy: all that's missing to complete this image of American naivety is a broomstick pony. Jon Voight as Joe Buck, the sexy innocent, a role which made the actor an overnight sensation.

unfaltering optimism in a world where raw need overshadows all emotion is the only ray of hope, Ratso's tenacious pride is no less impressive. No scene encapsulates the nature of their struggle to survive so dramatically as Ratso's unforgettable outburst when a taxi nearly runs him over in the midday traffic. Screaming "I'm walking here! I'm walking here!" he claims his and Joe's stake to life with these words of retaliation. This unscripted moment came about when a real New York City cab driver recklessly motored onto the scene and nearly shut down the shoot. Rather than breaking character, Hoffman spontaneously ad-libbed an already difficult take.

It is scenes like this that attest to the extraordinary precision of British director John Schlesinger's gutsy experimental techniques and give the film such undeniable urban authenticity. Yet somehow *Midnight Cowboy*'s nightmarish images accurately capture the darkness and violence of 1969 New York without losing sight of the era's underlying hopefulness. For even though the only remnants of the utopia once promised by flower power and the sexual revolution are the pornography and prostitution beckoning at every corner, Joe Buck goes through life shielded by a diehard innocence.

The cowboy's naïve sexuality, played up by his childish misconceptions, is undoubtedly the picture's major riddle. While sex is peddled on the city streets like any other commodity, Joe Buck inexplicably regards physical intimacy and its sale as the most natural thing on earth. No less unsettling are the chilling flashbacks that tell of the Texan's traumatic childhood marked by abuse and rape. But even so, this leaves us far from a psychological diagnosis.

In awarding *Midnight Cowboy* the Oscar for Best Picture, mainstream cinema paid homage to an innovative form of filmmaking that would go on to shape New Hollywood and Indie Cinema. From a contemporary standpoint, it is hard to understand that several of the movie's scenes were considered extreme enough to warrant the X rating usually reserved for pornography.   PB

THE WILD BUNCH

1969 - USA - 145 MIN.

DIRECTOR
SAM PECKINPAH (1925–1984)

SCREENPLAY
WALON GREEN, ROY N. SICKNER,
SAM PECKINPAH

DIRECTOR OF PHOTOGRAPHY
LUCIEN BALLARD

EDITING
LOU LOMBARDO

MUSIC
JERRY FIELDING

PRODUCTION
PHIL FELDMAN for WARNER BROS.,
SEVEN ARTS

STARRING
WILLIAM HOLDEN (Pike Bishop), ROBERT RYAN (Deke Thornton),
ERNEST BORGNINE (Dutch Engstrom), EDMOND O'BRIEN (Sykes),
WARREN OATES (Lyle Gorch), BEN JOHNSON (Tector Gorch),
JAIME SANCHEZ (Angel), EMILIO FERNÁNDEZ (Mapache),
STROTHER MARTIN (Coffer), L. Q. JONES (T. C.), ALBERT DEKKER (Pat Harrigan)

"We all dream of being a child again, even the worst of us. Perhaps the worst most of all."

To judge by their faces, the men riding slowly into town have done some serious living. Their path takes them along a railroad line, where some kids are laughing and playing. The men stare at them sullenly as they pass. Only the close-up shows the cruelty of the children's game. While two scorpions struggle in vain to avoid being eaten by a horde of red ants, the kids are using sticks to block the tormented animals' escape route.

Under a tarpaulin, a traveling preacher is fulminating against the evils of drink. A little later, the Temperance Union sets off on a parade, accompanied by a brass band. By this time, Pike Bishop (William Holden) and his men have reached their destination: they're in the wages office of the railroad company, and they're quietly robbing it while holding the customers at gunpoint. Then one of Bishop's men spots the rifles on the roof... There are some pretty rough-looking men positioned all around them, and they're hungry for the bounty on the Wild Bunch's heads. In cold blood, Bishop organizes the breakout. Though the streets are filled with innocent passers-by, the bounty hunters

ERNEST BORGNINE He was born Ermes Effron Borgnino and over the course of his lengthy career, he got to know every aspect of the acting trade. Ernest Borgnine (1917–2012), as he later became known, appeared in provincial theaters, B-movies, and prestigious big-budget productions. And just once, in 1956, he stood in front of his peers at the Academy Awards ceremony, when he received the Oscar for his performance in Delbert Mann's *Marty* (1955). The quiet butcher Marty was one of the few leading roles Borgnine played, and the film was exceptionally good. But his unmistakable physiognomy – gap-toothed smile, bushy brows, and boxer's nose – was never going to make him a matinee idol. Nonetheless, in the '50s and '60s he soon became a familiar face to keen moviegoers.
Borgnine, who spent ten years in the army, gave a rambunctious performance as the sadistic Sergeant Judson in Fred Zinnemann's *From Here to Eternity* (1953). After appearing as the titular hero in the TV series *McHale's Navy* (1962–66), he also co-starred in two well-known movies directed by Robert Aldrich: *The Flight of the Phoenix* (1966) and *The Dirty Dozen* (1967). He also acted in several Westerns and historical epics, as well as turning up in the odd obscure European production. Though he often played the burly bad guy, he was just as memorable playing the rough diamond or the buddy with a heart of gold. Moviegoers liked the warmth and energy he brought to such roles, and when he played Dominic Santini in the TV adventure series *Airwolf* (USA, 1984–86), these qualities won him a whole new generation of fans.

1 King of the wild frontier: Pike Bishop (William Holden) isn't going to let renegade leader Mapache pull the wool over anyone else's eyes.

2 Following the leader: Dutch (Ernest Borgnine) has his reservations about Bishop's motives but joins up with him just the same.

3 White bishop takes black queen – check: Bishop and his men storm Mapache's headquarters, where the dastardly gaucho is being serviced with a smile.

4 Tending to a paper cut: despite a gaping wound, Bishop refuses to give up the fight against his mighty opponents. But his impassioned battle can only end in defeat.

open fire and start shooting wildly into the crowd. Bullets whine, horses whinny, people panic while others die. The bandits know no mercy, but use the crowd and the Temperance parade for cover. Only four members of Bishop's gang survive the massacre, and one of them is so badly wounded that he can't ride a horse. When he asks to be shot, Bishop doesn't hesitate. There is no time for a burial.

These first scenes already contain the essence of Sam Peckinpah's film. Noble heroes like John Wayne or Randolph Scott are nowhere to be found in this Western, and the law has no claim to moral superiority. The sleazy gunmen hired by railroad boss Harrigan (Albert Dekker) are a bunch of trigger-happy fools and money-grabbers. Only their leader Deke Thornton (Robert Ryan) demonstrates a certain amount of backbone, but even he is driven by self-interest: he's been promised amnesty for his crimes if he manages to hunt down his former friend Pike Bishop.

Peckinpah disposes ruthlessly of the old Western cliché that conflicts like these can be solved cleanly, in a heroic dual of individuals. His protagonists and their henchmen are fighting a filthy miniature war. Across the border, in Mexico, where the militias of General Mapache (Emilio Fernández) have established a reign of terror, life is even more brutal: soldiers move through Indian villages, raping, torturing, and killing – and are hunted in turn by the troops of Pancho Villa. The violence makes no exception of women and children. With unsparing exactness, Peckinpah shows us what bullets are really capable of: he shows us how blood spurts, and how human bodies are torn and tossed around by flying metal. In Peckinpah's

"Violent, thoughtful and authoritative, it keeps Peckinpah out on his own among the Western directors of his generation."

Sight and Sound

vision, the moment of death is extended, as the victims perform a horrible slow-motion dance.

The Wild Bunch can only be understood in the context of the late '60s. For the first time, the mass media were bringing uncensored images of warfare to the attention of the public and it was becoming impossible to ignore the dreadful suffering of civilian populations. Even if some of Peckinpah's interviews reveal a sneaking sympathy with the doomed desperadoes of his *Wild Bunch*, he never left us in any doubt that these were ruined men, souls in hell.

Although the film's outstanding artistic quality was almost universally recognized, its outrageously realistic depiction of violence led to some heated discussions. Peckinpah himself was furious at his producers, who released an allegedly more marketable shortened version of the film without his consent. In some countries, including Germany, further passages were cut, with the result that several different versions were in circulation worldwide. In 1982, a so-called director's cut lasting the originally planned 145 minutes was finally released.   HK

DEATH IN VENICE

MORTE A VENEZIA

1970 - ITALY - 135 MIN.

DIRECTOR

LUCHINO VISCONTI (1906–1976)

SCREENPLAY

LUCHINO VISCONTI, NICOLA BADALUCCO,
based on the novella *Der Tod in Venedig* by THOMAS MANN

DIRECTOR OF PHOTOGRAPHY

PASQUALE DE SANTIS

EDITING

RUGGERO MASTROIANNI

MUSIC

GUSTAV MAHLER

PRODUCTION

LUCHINO VISCONTI
for ALFA CINEMATOGRAFICA

STARRING

DIRK BOGARDE (Gustav von Aschenbach), SILVANA MANGANO (Tadzio's Mother),
BJÖRN ANDRESEN (Tadzio), ROMOLO VALLI (Hotel Director),
MARK BURNS (Alfred), MARISA BERENSON (Frau von Aschenbach),
FRANCO FABRIZI (Hairdresser), ANTONIO APPICELLA (Vagabond),
SERGIO GARFAGNOLI (Polish Boy), NORA RICCI (Gouvernante)

LA WARNER BROS. PRESENTA

UN FILM PRODOTTO E DIRETTO DA

LUCHINO VISCONTI

DIRK BOGARDE

MORTE A VENEZIA

DAL RACCONTO DI **THOMAS MANN**

CON BJORN ANDRESEN E MARK BURNS

E CON LA PARTECIPAZIONE STRAORDINARIA DI

SILVANA MANGANO

"Your music is stillborn."

Venice, in the early 20th century. Gustav von Aschenbach (Dirk Bogarde), an aging German composer, is visiting the city of canals, hoping to recover from a nervous breakdown. He moves into an exclusive hotel facing the beach, where his fellow guests include an aristocratic Polish lady (Silvana Mangano) with her children and servants. Aschenbach immediately notices her son Tadzio (Björn Andrésen), a pale, slender boy with long blond hair. Soon, Aschenbach is so fascinated by this beautiful youth that his daily schedule is increasingly dominated by the need to observe him. This obsession leads to a resolve to make contact with the boy – despite the threat posed by the cholera epidemic that is spreading through the city. Aschenbach ultimately succumbs to the disease and dies.

Few film adaptations of literary classics manage to surpass the original. Luchino Visconti's *Death in Venice* is one of the few exceptions, not least because the director refused to be intimidated by Thomas Mann's famous novella. His film version is strikingly different from the book, and he made these changes in order to realize his own cinematic vision.

In the course of his career, Visconti directed opera as well as films, and it shows. The importance of music to *Death in Venice* can be judged by the fact that Visconti made Aschenbach a composer; in Thomas Mann's novella, Aschenbach was a writer, though the character was in fact based on Gustav Mahler. Mahler's music is of essential importance to the film. His *Fifth Symphony* is heard over

LUCHINO VISCONTI He was the scion of a noble Italian family, and he described himself as a Marxist – though his politics didn't stop him enjoying the best that life had to offer. The apparently disparate sides of Luchino Visconti's personality left their traces in his filmography. After learning his trade with Jean Renoir, he made his directing debut while Mussolini's Fascist regime was still in power: the naturalistic style of *Obsession (Ossessione*, 1943) was the starting point for Italian *neorealismo*. Visconti's *The Earth Trembles (La terra trema*, 1948), the story of a fisherman exploited by wholesale merchants, is regarded as one of the masterpieces of the neorealist movement. His sympathy for ordinary people is also evident in later films: see *Rocco and His Brothers (Rocco e i suoi fratelli*, 1960), which shows the disintegration of a family that moves from southern Italy to Milan in search of work.

With *Senso (Senso*, 1954) however, he created the first of the splendidly operatic color films that would dominate his later career. Of these major productions, many critics feel the best was *The Leopard (Il gattopardo*, 1963), based on a novel by Giuseppe Tomasi di Lampedusa. This spectacular epic about a family of Sicilian aristocrats in the 19th century won him the Palme d'Or at Cannes and made him an international star director. He sustained his reputation with films such as *Death in Venice (Morte a Venezia*, 1970) and *Ludwig (Le Crépuscule des dieux*, 1972), the latter a biography of the eccentric king of Bavaria. In parallel to his work in the cinema, Visconti was also a successful theater and opera director. The career of Maria Callas was closely linked to his own.

1 Angel of death: frail aesthete Gustav von Aschenbach is overtaken by youth's fleeting beauty when he lays eyes on Tadzio (Björn Andrésen).

2 Eternal flame: much like Visconti, Silvana Mangano's (left) film career rode the wave of post-war Italian neorealism. She was one of the movement's shining stars.

3 Music to our ears: the role of composer Gustav von Aschenbach was the crescendo of Dirk Bogarde's acting career.

4 Phoenix from the ashes: Visconti and cameraman Pasquale de Santis masterfully translate Thomas Mann's prose to the screen with sensuous visuals, gliding cinematography, and seamless zoom-ins.

the opening titles, and it accompanies Aschenbach's arrival in Venice on a steamship emerging into the light of dawn. This musical motif recurs throughout the film, and the elegiac gravity of the piece is mirrored in the almost lethargic rhythm of the images. The drama is contained, and develops, in a series of slow zooms and meticulous tracking shots that capture the morbid and sensual atmosphere of Venice, in the strong but subdued colors of the sultry summer and in the broad Cinemascope format. There is a remarkably serene quality to Visconti's film, strengthening the impact of the music, which is used very sparingly. The film has no narrator, Aschenbach is allowed

"A film to be savored and one to be enjoyed and studied more than once." *Variety*

no internal monologues, and indeed, no one says very much at all. Instead, the camera feels its way around the story discreetly, and Dirk Bogarde's expressive acting does the rest. Thomas Mann's polished descriptions and the fine irony of the text are perfectly translated into a purely visual language. Visconti traces the beginnings of Aschenbach's downfall in a series of flashbacks: the destruction of a happy family, sexual frustration, and, above all, failure as an artist. In his ambition to express a pure, absolute beauty through his music, Aschenbach is not merely an anachronism; he is also in fatal rebellion against the claims of the body. When his friend Alfred (Mark Burns) insists on the dual nature of music, Aschenbach resists desperately. These are the moments in which Visconti interrupts the tranquil flow of his narrative and allows the

past to erupt into the sluggish present like a feverish memory. The lie that has ruled Aschenbach's life catches up with him in Venice: for in recognizing that Tadzio embodies both perfection *and* sensuality, the noble aesthete is thrown back upon his own physical desire, which is more clearly homosexual in Visconti than in Mann.

By the time Aschenbach realizes what's driving him, it's too late: he's an elderly man with a decaying body. With the bitterest of irony, Visconti shows us how the composer attempts to regain his youth in the hairdresser's salon. At the end of the film, a cadaverous Aschenbach lies slumped in his deckchair on the beach, with black hair-dye trickling down his sweat-soaked face. Tadzio, standing on the shore, turns towards him and points off into the distance: it's a last greeting from an angel of death.   JH

A CLOCKWORK ORANGE

1971 - GREAT BRITAIN - 137 MIN.

DIRECTOR

STANLEY KUBRICK (1928–1999)

SCREENPLAY

STANLEY KUBRICK, based on the novel of
the same name by ANTHONY BURGESS

DIRECTOR OF PHOTOGRAPHY

JOHN ALCOTT

EDITING

BILL BUTLER

MUSIC

WALTER CARLOS

PRODUCTION

STANLEY KUBRICK for POLARIS PRODUCTIONS,
HAWK FILMS LTD., WARNER BROS.

STARRING

MALCOLM MCDOWELL (Alex), PATRICK MAGEE (Frank Alexander),
MICHAEL BATES (Chief Guard Barnes), WARREN CLARKE (Dim),
JOHN CLIVE (Stage Actor), PAUL FARRELL (Tramp),
ADRIENNE CORRI (Mrs. Alexander), CARL DUERING (Doktor Brodsky),
CLIVE FRANCIS (Joe), MICHAEL GOVER (Prison Governor),
MIRIAM KARLIN (Miss Weatherly)

Being the adventures of a young man whose principal interests are rape, ultra-violence and Beethoven.

STANLEY KUBRICK'S
CLOCKWORK ORANGE

A Stanley Kubrick Production "A CLOCKWORK ORANGE" Starring Malcolm McDowell • Patrick Magee • Adrienne Corri and Miriam Karlin • Sceenplay by Stanley Kubrick • Based on the novel by Anthony Burgess • Produced and Directed by Stanley Kubrick • Executive Producers Max L. Raab and Si Litvinoff • **WARNER BROS** A WARNER COMMUNICATIONS COMPANY

"Viddy well, little brother, viddy well."

A Clockwork Orange was banned in England until Stanley Kubrick's death in 1999. The director himself had withdrawn it in 1974, and the motive behind this self-imposed censorship remains obscure. Perhaps he had simply grown tired of being blamed for glorifying violence, but it's possible he had actually been threatened. This is not as outlandish a suggestion as it may seem, for the film had occasioned a great deal of heated debate. No film before *A Clockwork Orange* had depicted violence in such an aestheticized manner, and with such a laconic refusal to justify itself. The critics accused Kubrick not merely of fomenting an appetite for extreme brutality, but of failing to challenge or even question that appetite. The violence on screen, they felt, was crying out to be imitated in real life. But Kubrick is no moralist, and no psychologist ei-ther; he doesn't explain what he shows. The audience is forced to decide for itself what it wants to see in his film, and the price we pay for this freedom includes accepting the risk that Nazi skinheads will love it.

. Black bowler and bovver boots, white shirt and pants, tastefully topped off with an eyecatching, fortified codpiece: this is the uniform of Alex (Malcolm McDowell) and his droogs, a teenage gang in constant search of some real "horrorshow" action. On a particularly enjoyable night out, they start off with a few drinks in the Korova Milkbar before going on to kick a drunken bum to a pulp, indulge in a rumble with a rival gang, and play "road hogs" in a stolen car. Having warmed up, they proceed to break into the country house of a successful author and take turns at raping his wife, making very sure that the elderly writer – bound and gagged – gets a first-class view of her lengthy ordeal. Back at the bar, "feeling a bit shagged and fagged and fashed," they chill out with a "moloko plus" (milk with a little something added) before heading "bedways."

It's not so much the brutality that makes *A Clockwork Orange* such a haunting experience: it's the choreography. Alex above all, adoring fan of Ludwig Van, celebrates and savors his own "appearances" like works of performance art. In the writer's villa, he parodies Gene Kelly in "Singin' In The Rain," keeping time to the music with a series of kicks to his victim's guts. In contrast to his three mates, who expect to pick up some booty on their raids, he has little

MALCOLM MCDOWELL *A Clockwork Orange* (1971) would not have been made without him. For Stanley Kubrick, Alex simply had to be Malcolm McDowell. At that time, the 27-year-old had almost nothing to show for himself. He had just made his very first major film, the impressive *If...* (1968), set in an English boarding school and directed by Lindsay Anderson. But Kubrick was convinced of the qualities of the young, unknown actor, for he saw in him the human being in a natural state. And so Malcolm McDowell became a star. His instant success was also a kind of curse, for his face came to stand for everything evil, incalculable, and dangerous, and he has rarely been permitted to play anything but the villain.
Born in Leeds in 1943, McDowell worked as a coffee salesman before going to drama school in London. Later, he acted with the Royal Shakespeare Company. After *A Clockwork Orange*, he went on to make two more films with Lindsay Anderson, both of them intelligent satires: *O Lucky Man!* (1973) and *Britannia Hospital* (1982). In 1979, he caused another stir, this time as the notorious dictator in Tinto Brass's controversial *Caligula*. He then disappeared from view, showing up almost only in B-movies, although he did have some interesting supporting roles in movies such as Paul Schrader's *Cat People* (1982). In the '90s, however, MacDowell was a very busy man, making around 50 appearances in movies or TV series, for example in *Star Trek: Generations* (1994), where he faced off Captains Kirk and Picard, and in Paul McGuigan's *Gangster No.1* (2000).

1 Here comes Alex (Malcolm McDowell) – the personification of brutality.

2 Doomed to look: Alex undergoes the Ludovico therapy.

3 Mmmm… milk plus vellocet (or is it synthemesc?): Dim (Warren Clarke) tanks up for a night of the old ultra-violence.

4 "That was me, that is Alex, and my three droogs, that is Pete, Georgie and Dim. And we sat in the Korova Milkbar, trying to make up our razu-doks what to do with the evening."

interest in money. To show them who's "Master and Lead-er," he beats them up. This will turn out to be a fateful dif-ference of opinion. For later, when Alex inadvertently kills a woman with an *objet d'art* (a giant phallus), his disgruntled and mutinous droogs smash a bottle in his face and leave him to be found by the police. He is sentenced to 14 years in jail, but thanks to a new resocialization program and a revolutionary therapeutic technique, he is granted an early

release. From now on, Alex will be violently sick whenever he's tempted to indulge in "a bit of the old ultra-violence." But though he can't hurt a fly, his past is inescapable: the world is full of people who suffered under his rule, and who will now exact revenge on their helpless ex-tormentor.

A Clockwork Orange is a complex discourse on the connections between violence, aesthetics, and the media. The film gives no answers, it merely asks questions, and it calls some assumptions into doubt: for example, that violence in the cinema will inevitably lead to violence in the world. Alex's therapy consists of forced viewings of brutal films. The longer he's bound to his seat with his eyes propped open, the worse he feels – an effect reinforced by the drug he's been given. Alex the Doer is transformed into Alex the Watcher. For the former hoodlum, it's a terrible torture; for the average moviegoer, it's a regular delight: to become a mere seeing eye, with no obligation to act; to watch, entranced, happily "glued to the seat." Kubrick almost literally pulls the audience into the film. Alex often

"**In my opinion, Kubrick has made a movie that exploits only the mystery and variety of human conduct. And because it refuses to use the emotions conventionally, demanding instead that we keep a constant, intellectual grip on things, it's a most unusual – and disorienting – movie experience.**" *The New York Times*

5 "A truly Satanic cinematic satire, made with almost unimaginable perfection," said *Der Spiegel*. In this scene, Kubrick himself operated the hand-held camera.

6 The writer Alexander (Patrick Magee), a victim of Alex and his droogs. But he'll wreak his revenge.

7 Pop art: Alex batters a woman to death with a giant phallus.

"Objectively, it has to be said that there has seldom been a film of such assured technical brilliance." *Der Tagesspiegel*

6

looks straight into the camera, apparently addressing the spectators. Before he rapes the writer's wife, he kneels down before her on the floor: "Viddy well," he says to the captive woman, and to the captivated audience in the argot of the droogs: "take a good look." The real scandal of *A Clockwork Orange* is that we catch ourselves looking forward with excitement to whatever is going to come next. It's not what Kubrick shows us that shocks, but how we react as spectators, fascinated by a masterly and unforgettable film. NM

DELIVERANCE

1972 - USA - 105 MIN.

DIRECTOR

JOHN BOORMAN (*1933)

SCREENPLAY

JAMES DICKEY,
based on his novel of the same name

DIRECTOR OF PHOTOGRAPHY

VILMOS ZSIGMOND

EDITING

TOM PRIESTLEY

MUSIC

ERIC WEISSBERG, STEVE MANDEL

PRODUCTION

JOHN BOORMAN for
ELMER PRODUCTIONS, WARNER BROS.

STARRING

JON VOIGHT (Ed Gentry), BURT REYNOLDS (Lewis Medlock),
NED BEATTY (Bobby Trippe), RONNY COX (Drew Ballinger),
ED RAMEY (Old Man), BILLY REDDEN (Lonny),
SEAMON GLASS (First Griner), RANDALL DEAL (Second Griner),
BILL MCKINNEY (Mountain Man), HERBERT "COWBOY" COWARD (Toothless Man),
LEWIS CRONE (First Deputy), JAMES DICKEY (Sheriff Bullard)

This is the weekend they didn't play golf.

Deliverance

A JOHN BOORMAN FILM Starring **JON VOIGHT · BURT REYNOLDS** in "DELIVERANCE"
Co-Starring NED BEATTY · RONNY COX · Screenplay by James Dickey Based on his novel · Produced and Directed by John Boorman
PANAVISION® · TECHNICOLOR® · From Warner Bros., A Warner Communications Company **R** RESTRICTED Under 17 requires accompanying Parent or Adult Guardian

DELIVERANCE

"That's the game, survival."

A river winds softly through a pristine landscape of craggy cliffs and dense virgin forest. Four men from the city are here to relax while exploring the area by canoe. Lewis (Burt Reynolds), Ed (Jon Voight), Bobby (Ned Beatty), and Drew (Ronny Cox), are paddling downriver in two fragile boats. They've paid some farmers to drive their cars to the final destination, which they expect to reach two days later; but this is an adventure holiday that will turn into pure terror.

The first day is idyllic, a boy scouts' paradise for four grown men: paddling boats, pitching tents, fishing with bows and arrows, and playing guitar round the campfire. On the second day, the horror begins. Ed and Bobby have gone on ahead in their canoe, and a welcoming party is waiting for them: two of the farmers, ugly rednecks with very bad teeth. After tying Ed to a tree, they beat, rape, and humiliate Bobby. As they turn their attentions to Ed, one of them keels over, pierced by an arrow; Lewis and Drew

have caught up with their friends. The other attacker flees, and the four friends bury the corpse. They're sick of adventures and hungry for home, and the canoes are their only means of transport. But down on the river, between the sheer cliffs, they're as open to predators as a hamburger on a plate …

With its breathtaking journeys through whitewater rapids and overwhelming images of natural splendor, *Deliverance* is a wonderful action and adventure film. Director John Boorman, his editor Tom Priestley (both of whom received Oscar nominations) and the cameraman Vilmos Zsigmond (who got an Oscar for *Close Encounters of the Third Kind*, 1977) created a visual language of great beauty, combining careful composition with a directness and immediacy that pulls the audience right into the story. The immensity and indifference of the natural world and the threat of sudden attack are almost physically present.

JOHN BOORMAN Civilized human beings forced to come to terms with barbarism: this is as good a summary of *Deliverance* (1972) as any, and it's also the groundplan for many of John Boorman's films. In the science-fiction movie *Zardoz* (1973/74) Sean Connery struggles against a terroristic slave system; in *The Emerald Forest* (1985), the son of an engineer (Boorman's own son, Charley) falls into the hands of an archaic forest-dwelling tribe.
England's John Boorman (*1933) has made highly idiosyncratic films in a wide range of standard genres. In *Hope and Glory* (1987), he called on his own childhood memories to tell the story of the war from a boy's perspective. The gangster in *The General* (1998) behaves like the gangsters he's seen in the movies. And in *The Tailor of Panama* (2001), Boorman portrays his "hero" (sex symbol and 007 Pierce Brosnan) as a deeply repellent character. Boorman made his cinema debut in 1965 with the Dave Clark Five pop vehicle *Catch Us If You Can (Having a Wild Weekend)*. The big break came in 1967 with his second film, the gangster drama *Point Blank*.

1 Hell bent over: Ed (Jon Voight) gets a close-up view of prison in the wild.

2 "The voyage down the river echoes the journey of Conrad's demonic Mr. Kurtz to the Congo's heart of darkness." (*The New York Times*)

3 A grassroots movement: Ed hunts his attackers with a bow and arrow.

"A repugnant but fascinating portrait of human beings out of their environment, forced to defend themselves where the laws of civilization no longer apply." *Motion Picture Guide*

"It's the best film I've ever done. It's a picture that just picks you up and sends you crashing against the rocks. You feel everything and just crawl out of the theater."

Burt Reynolds, in: Motion Picture Guide

4 Bobby (Ned Beatty), Lewis (Burt Reynolds), Drew (Ronny Cox), and Ed are looking forward to some male bonding – two days in virgin nature.

5 The men park their cars in a tiny hamlet – and sacrifice a link to civilization.

Boorman also demonstrates a fine feeling for effective but inconspicuous symbolism: In a famous scene, early on in the film, Drew and a retarded farmer's boy begin a tentative musical dialogue on guitar and banjo. The game of question-and-answer develops into a regular duet – or duel – in which the city dweller is eventually defeated by the sheer speed and skill of the hillbilly kid. In a beautifully understated manner, this joyful encounter anticipates the deadly power struggle to come.

The film's surface is brilliant, and the depths below it are multilayered and hard to fathom. With a screenplay by the poet James Dickey, who adapted it from his own novel of the same name (1970), the film resists any easy interpretation. "Man Against Nature" won't do, for the dumb-but-crafty hillbillies can hardly be seen as symbols for a state of unspoilt nature. "Arrogant City Slickers versus Disadvantaged Rural Population" is an equally unusable model, for neither the canoeists nor their antagonists can be reduced to this kind of cliché. What remains is the story of four men in an alien environment, defending their lives with alien methods; solid citizens far from civilization, struggling to survive with the aid of bows and arrows. Events take their course inexorably, and we are granted no comforting explanations. Lewis, the fittest of the four, is quickly incapacitated by an injury, while the cerebral pipe-smoking Ed is forced to kill in self-defense. When the survivors finally reach safety, they're still far from peace; the Sheriff (author James Dickey in a guest appearance) is a highly skeptical interrogator, and their dreams will long be haunted by memories of their hellish ordeal.   HJK

6 Sneak attack: Ed resorts to archery.   **7** Concealing evidence: Lewis hides the corpse of a redneck he's just neutralized. The men think their nightmare is over, but it's only just begun.

CABARET 𝕏𝕏𝕏𝕏𝕏𝕏𝕏𝕏

1972 - USA - 124 MIN.

DIRECTOR

BOB FOSSE (1927–1987)

SCREENPLAY

JAY PRESSON ALLEN, based on the Broadway musical of the same name by JOE MASTEROFF,
JOHN KANDER and FRED EBB, the drama *I Am a Camera* by JOHN VAN DRUTEN,
and the collection of short stories *The Berlin Stories* by CHRISTOPHER ISHERWOOD

DIRECTOR OF PHOTOGRAPHY

GEOFFREY UNSWORTH

EDITING

DAVID BRETHERTON

MUSIC

JOHN KANDER, RALPH BURNS

PRODUCTION

CY FEUER, HAROLD NEBENZAL; MARTIN BAUM for ABC PICTURES CORPORATION,
and EMMANUEL WOLF for ALLIED ARTISTS

STARRING

LIZA MINNELLI (Sally Bowles), MICHAEL YORK (Brian Roberts),
HELMUT GRIEM (Maximilian von Heune), JOEL GREY (Master of Ceremonies),
FRITZ WEPPER (Fritz Wendel), MARISA BERENSON (Natalia Landauer),
ELISABETH NEUMANN-VIERTEL (Fräulein Schneider), HELEN VITA (Fräulein Kost),
SIGRID VON RICHTHOFEN (Fräulein Mayr), GERD VESPERMANN (Bobby)

ACADEMY AWARDS 1972

OSCARS for BEST DIRECTOR (Bob Fosse), BEST ACTRESS (Liza Minnelli),
BEST SUPPORTING ACTOR (Joel Grey), BEST CINEMATOGRAPHY (Geoffrey Unsworth),
BEST MUSIC (Ralph Burns), BEST FILM EDITING (David Bretherton),
BEST ART DIRECTION (Rolf Zehetbauer, Hans Jürgen Kiebach, Herbert Strabel),
and BEST SOUND (Robert Knudson)

LIFE IS A

Allied Artists and ABC Pictures Corp. present An ABC Pictures Corp. Production **Liza Minnelli Michael York Helmut Griem** in A Feuer & Martin Production **Cabaret** with **Marisa Berenson** and **Joel Grey** as "Emcee" Based on the Musical Play "Cabaret" Book by **Joe Masteroff** Music by **John Kander** Lyrics by **Fred Ebb** Based on the Play by **John Van Druten** and Stories by **Christopher Isherwood** Produced on the New York Stage by **Harold Prince** Dances and Musical Numbers Staged by **Bob Fosse** Screenplay by **Jay Allen** Music by **John Kander** Lyrics by **Fred Ebb** Produced by **Cy Feuer** Directed by **Bob Fosse** Technicolor® Distributed by Allied Artists

CABARET

"Divine decadence, darling!"

Berlin 1931. Despite a severe economic crisis, the German metropolis is determinedly cosmopolitan and exudes sensuality. Leave your worries at the door and come on into the Kit Kat Club, a dazzling nightclub where evening after evening an enthusiastic emcee greets you in three languages: "Willkommen, Bienvenue, Welcome!" His diabolically painted white face is reflected on the shimmering stage. And like a funhouse mirror, the film presents the cabaret to movie audiences as a caricature of the outside world. "Life is a cabaret!" exclaims Liza Minelli in an unforgettable song that is meant to be taken at face value.

Like so many other foreigners, British student Brian (Michael York) feels drawn to this thriving urban center. Arriving at a boarding house, he quickly makes the acquaintance of American Sally Bowles (Liza Minnelli), who works as a singer at the Kit Kat Club and dreams of making it big one day as a movie star. She's not only willing to capitalize on her charisma to get there, but will readily exploit her body too if need be. Sexually uninhibited with a taste for luxury, Sally is a hedonistic modern girl whose deep-seated, hidden desire is to find true happiness. Beneath her decadent exterior we are shown more and more of the

LIZA MINNELLI The extent to which her image was shaped by one single film is itself a Hollywood phenomenon. Her belting voice and touching yet extravagant flair breathed so much life into *Cabaret's* (1972) nightclub singer Sally Bowles that from then on world audiences viewed Liza Minnelli as virtually inseparable from the role she had played. The daughter of Hollywood legend Judy Garland and director Vincente Minnelli was literally born into show business in 1946. She made her first appearance in front of a Hollywood camera when she was just two years old. Be it on Broadway, in film, in TV movies, or in the music industry, her work has always met with instant success. She received a Tony in 1965 for her performance in the Broadway musical *Flora, the Red Menace*. Her first Oscar nomination came for her portrayal of the eccentric Pookie in *The Sterile Cuckoo* (1969). Another nomination followed in 1970 for Otto Preminger's *Tell Me That You Love Me, Junie Moon*, and in 1973 she won the Best Actress Academy Award for *Cabaret*. She became more popular with audiences than ever before, and in 1972, NBC aired the award-winning television special *Liza with a Z*. Liza Minnelli, who describes herself as both "hopeful and cynical," is a star to this day, even though not all her films are smash hits. She collaborated with her father Vincente Minnelli on *A Matter of Time / Nina* (1976). Images of her superstar mother, who died in 1969, pop up in many of her movies, including Stanley Donen's *Lucky Lady* (1975) and most prominently in Martin Scorsese's musical drama *New York, New York* (1977). She experienced one of her greatest commercial successes in 1981 with *Arthur*. Shortly thereafter, her film career started to dry up. She disappeared completely from the public eye for several years. Alcohol and prescription drug addictions contributed to her personal downfall. In 1984 she sought professional help. She staged a comeback in 1985 in the form of an NBC made-for-TV movie *A Time to Live*, winning the Golden Globe for her performance. She then went on a star-studded tour at the end of the '80s with Frank Sinatra and Sammy Davis Jr. and even recorded a single with the Pet Shop Boys entitled "Losing My Mind" that reached number six on the U.K. charts. In 1997, Liza Minnelli was celebrated on Broadway in Blake Edwards's *Victor/Victoria*, yet another great comeback after a 12-year absence.

1 Cigarette, lipstick, and a voice that won't quit: the role of Sally Bowles made Liza Minelli an international superstar.

2 "Life is a cabaret": the stage as a world of entertainment and politics.

3 Babe in the woods: when Brian (Michael York) comes to Berlin, he's a shy young writer. Sally's attempts to seduce him are initially unsuccessful.

4 A pink-tinted love triangle: only later does Sally discover that Brian and Maximilian (Helmut Griem) have been playing house.

childish, vulnerable woman she really is. Brian, who at first seems immune to her erotic advances, eventually falls madly in love with her. It is a happy romance until the wealthy, young, and rather attractive Baron Max von Heune (Helmut Griem) enters their world. Sally, mesmerized by his charms and riches, becomes more impractically minded with each passing day. Brian is jealous and turned on at the same time. Their love triangle is only spoken of in jest initially, but it soon becomes reality. Both of them have slept with the affluent baron, and Sally, it turns out, is pregnant. While Sally and Brian are busy tackling their personal catastrophes, the Nazis take to the streets of Berlin in preparation for their rise to power. It seems the couple's lifestyle is doomed, for the epidemic of fascism spreading throughout the nation seeks to extinguish all that is urban and modern. In its place, the Nazi movement prescribes conservative and provincial values for the German people. Brian decides to return to England. Sally, however, stays on in Berlin to try her luck at acting.

Cabaret was one of last great Hollywood musicals. (Eat your heart out *Chicago* [2002]!) It was awarded an astounding eight Oscars at the Academy Awards. The movie version was based on John Kander and Fred Ebb's Broadway musical, which premiered in 1966. This, likewise, drew heavily from the short stories "The Last of Mr. Morris" and "Goodbye to Berlin" by Christopher Isherwood, which were published in a volume entitled *The Berlin Stories*. Unlike the

"*Cabaret* is dance routines and hit songs. It's a murky tale inspired by the novels of Christopher Isherwood. It's the myth of '30s Berlin. And above all, it's Bob Fosse. He has a marvelous grasp of the world of cabaret, its pathos and its poetry: fleeting, illusory, and poignantly authentic." *Le Monde*

"*Cabaret* may make a star out of Miss Minnelli, but it will be remembered as a chilling mosaic of another era's frightening lifestyle." *Films in Review*

majority of Hollywood musicals, such as *An American in Paris* (1951) or *Singin' in the Rain* (1952) there is nothing anachronistic about *Cabaret* even today. This is due to its songs, as popular as those of Kurt Weill's *Three Penny Opera (Dreigroschenoper)*, and to the then 25-year-old Liza Minnelli, whose image is more intrinsically linked to *Cabaret* than almost any other actress has ever been to a single production. Yet above all else, it is the film's narrative structure that plays the decisive role in its timelessness. Deviating from the traditional Hollywood musical format, *Cabaret* markedly separates its musical numbers from its plot. In other words, none of the characters in the film burst into song for no given reason. Instead, director and choreographer Bob Fosse brilliantly let the stage acts at the nightclub serve as commentary on both the surrounding political situation and the lives of characters themselves. In particular, the stage appearances of the emcee (Joel Grey), whose character doesn't exist within the framework of the plot outside the nightclub, do a poignant job of this.

Plot elements and musical numbers are occasionally brought together through the ironic use of parallel montage. Such is the case when a scene of a staged Bavarian folk dance is intercut with images of Nazis brutally beating up the Kit Kat's manager elsewhere. This sequence feeds violence into the musical number and choreography into the street fight. *Cabaret*, with its strikingly dark palette, is

5 Tomorrow belongs to… whom? It remains unclear how fascism will change Sally's wild and extravagant lifestyle.

6 Mirror, mirror on the wall, *Cabaret* was Liza's best picture of all.

highly reminiscent of the 1920s, as is the music inspired by Kurt Weill and Bob Fosse's stylized dance numbers, which clearly draw from that era's Expressionist tradition. Commendably, it does this without trying to ignore the cinematic conventions of the 1970s. The overall impact of the film is born out of its song and dance sequences which, with one exception, all take place on stage.

The only time we witness music outside the cabaret setting is when a young blond boy begins to sing what is meant to sound like a traditional German folk song at a beer garden. We just see his face at first, but soon the camera pulls back to show us his swastika armband. One beer garden patron after the next joins in his chant. The rhythm of the piece transforms into a military march and by the end, all have their hands extended in a Hitler salute. It may sound ludicrous, but at the time of the picture's European premiere, this scene was to be removed for German audiences. Only after a number of critics were up in arms about the decision was the sequence restored.

KK

THE GODFATHER ♟♟♟

1972 - USA - 175 MIN.

DIRECTOR
FRANCIS FORD COPPOLA (*1939)

SCREENPLAY
FRANCIS FORD COPPOLA, MARIO PUZO, based on his novel of the same name

DIRECTOR OF PHOTOGRAPHY
GORDON WILLIS

EDITING
MARC LAUB, BARBARA MARKS, WILLIAM REYNOLDS,
MURRAY SOLOMON, PETER ZINNER

MUSIC
NINO ROTA

PRODUCTION
ALBERT S. RUDDY for PARAMOUNT PICTURES

STARRING
MARLON BRANDO (Don Vito Corleone), AL PACINO (Michael Corleone),
DIANE KEATON (Kay Adams), ROBERT DUVALL (Tom Hagen),
JAMES CAAN (Santino "Sonny" Corleone), JOHN CAZALE (Frederico "Fredo" Corleone),
RICHARD S. CASTELLANO (Peter Clemenza), STERLING HAYDEN (Captain McCluskey),
TALIA SHIRE (Constanzia "Connie" Corleone-Rizzi), JOHN MARLEY (Jack Woltz),
RICHARD CONTE (Don Emilio Barzini), AL LETTIERI (Virgil Sollozzo),
AL MARTINO (Johnny Fontane), GIANNI RUSSO (Carlo Rizzi),
SIMONETTA STEFANELLI (Appollonia Vitelli-Corleone)

ACADEMY AWARDS 1972
OSCARS for BEST FILM (Albert S. Ruddy), BEST ACTOR (Marlon Brando),
and BEST ADAPTED SCREENPLAY (Mario Puzo, Francis Ford Coppola)

PARAMOUNT PICTURES PRESENTS

The Godfather

AN
Albert S. Ruddy
PRODUCTION

STARRING

Marlon Brando

AND

Al Pacino   James Caan   Richard Castellano   Robert Duvall
Sterling Hayden   John Marley   Richard Conte   Diane Keaton

PRODUCED BY   DIRECTED BY   SCREENPLAY BY
Albert S. Ruddy   Francis Ford Coppola   Mario Puzo AND Francis Ford Coppola
BASED ON
Mario Puzo's NOVEL "The Godfather"   MUSIC SCORED BY Nino Rota   Color By Technicolor® A Paramount Picture

R   RESTRICTED   SOUNDTRACK ALBUM AVAILABLE ON PARAMOUNT RECORDS

"I'll make him an offer he can't refuse."

The unmentionable words are never heard. No one dares speak of the "Mafia" or the "Cosa Nostra" in this film, despite the fact that it tells a tale whose roots are at the heart of organized crime. The contents are categorized by another word: family. "It's a novel about a family, and not about crime," said its author, Mario Puzo. Francis Ford Coppola initially rejected the offer to direct the film after reading the book overhastily and dismissing it as just another Mafia vehicle. He eventually changed his mind for a number of reasons, principally because he discovered the family aspect of the story and was fascinated by it.

It is no coincidence that the film begins and ends with traditional family celebrations – a wedding and a baptism. The marriage of Connie Corleone (Talia Shire) and Carlo Rizzi (Gianni Russo) is the occasion for an enchanting celebration. An orchestra plays in the Corleone's garden, filled with a mass of dancing guests. Feasting and joking, children run wild and glasses are repeatedly raised to toast the bride.

During the festivities, FBI agents mill outside the gates of the villa and scrawl down license plate numbers of the guests. The father of the bride, Vito Corleone (Marlon Brando) is one of the five Dons of the Italian community in the New York area and the guest list is accordingly illustrious. According to old Sicilian tradition, the father of the bride cannot refuse any favor on his daughter's wedding day. Surrounded by his sons and confidantes he aristocratically sits in his darkened reception room, glowing in a golden brown light, the perfect expression of dignity and power. He patronizingly receives the supplicants, listens to their dilemmas, accepts congratulations, and basks in the respect offered from all sides.

Like every scene with Marlon Brando in the role of the Godfather Vito Corleone, these scenes are filled with warmth. The colors fade when his son Michael (Al Pacino) flees to the family's ancestral home in sunny Sicily after committing two murders. Later Michael, who once strived

MARLON BRANDO Among the many curiosities surrounding the legendary film *The Godfather* (1972) is that its success sprung from a series of coincidences and imponderabilities. Mario Puzo was unhappy writing the screenplay, Francis Ford Coppola initially didn't want to direct the film, and the studio had problems with the choice for the male lead. At this time, Marlon Brando (1924–2004) was at a low point in his career, which began in the 1940s in the theaters of New York City. In 1947, his portrayal of Stanley Kowalski in *A Streetcar Named Desire* was a triumph and in 1951 he played the character in Elia Kazan's film adaptation. Schooled in "method acting," Brando graduated to Hollywood big-time – four Oscar nominations in a row speak for themselves. Initially he was repeatedly cast as the youthful rebel, but he soon proved his versatility in costume films and musicals. In the 1960s, his notorious moodiness and a string of flops caused him to fall from grace with Hollywood producers. In 1972 he made his comeback with *The Godfather* and *Last Tango in Paris (Ultimo tango a Parigi / Le Dernier Tango à Paris)*, receiving Oscar nominations for both films. Though he was awarded an Oscar for his role as Vito Corleone in *The Godfather*, he refused to accept it for political reasons.

"Like practically no other Hollywood film of recent years, the tale of the New York Mafia clan Corleone reflects the divisions, the compulsions and the fears afflicting American society. Damaged by Vietnam and shaken by a profound crisis of faith in the nation, America's hallowed norms of good and evil are looking more beleaguered than ever." *Kölner Stadt-Anzeiger*

2

3

1 A man who won't take "no" for an answer: Marlon Brando takes life in his stride as Don Corleone.

2 In sickness and in health: making a deal with Don Corleone is more than a business transaction – it's a life-long bond.

3 One wedding for fifty funerals: *The Godfather* opens with the Corleone family renewing its vows, while Carlo (Gianni Russo) and Connie (Talia Shire) take theirs.

for an honorable life and distanced himself from his family, will become the ringleader of a blood bath: the images change with him, slowly acquiring a cold, bluish tinge.

The cause of the violent clash is Vito Corleone's decision to deny his backing to Virgil Sollozzo's (Al Lettieri) plans to branch out in the drug dealing business. Vito's temperamental son Sonny (James Caan) seems to disagree with his father, which inspires Sollozzo to try and topple the patriarch. Five shots bring Corleone down, but the old tiger survives. Michael, who to this point has held himself out of the family business, is shaken. His outsider role makes him seem unsuspicious, and he is therefore sent to the negotiation table. Michael promptly uses the opportunity to murder both Sollozzo and the corrupt police captain McCluskey (Sterling Hayden), and flees to Sicily. His unsuspecting girlfriend Kay (Diane Keaton) remains behind.

In Sicily, Michael's hardening process continues. He falls in love and – with old-fashioned etiquette – asks the bride's father permission for his daughter's hand. But the long arm of vengeance stretches to Italy – his young wife, Appollonia is killed in a car bomb that was meant for Michael. In New York, the war between the families rages on. Michael's brother Sonny is the next victim. The slowly recovering Vito Corleone is devastated, but forgoes his right to vengeance in an attempt to put an end to the killing. Michael returns to the United States and marries Kay, who has become a teacher. But his eyes now have a cold, hard expression; he knows that the old feud is not over and plans a large liberating coup. While he is in church at his nephew's baptism, and is solemnly named as the child's godfather, the enemies of the Corleones are killed off one by one. Among them is Connie's husband Carlo, who lured Sonny into a deadly trap.

Connie has become a nervous wreck and Kay begins to ask critical questions. Michael coldly denies responsibility and Kay is forced to experience her utter exclusion from the

4 European vacation: a hunted man, Michael Corleone (Al Pacino) decides it's time to go back to his roots.

5 Like father like son: after some initial stumbling, Michael learns how to fill his father's shoes.

6 Deadlock: Michael Corleone and bride-to-be, Kay (Diane Keaton).

7 The emissary wore black: Michael holds out a Sicilian olive branch to Virgil Sollozzo (Al Lettieri).

8 When in Rome: during his time in Sicily, Michael samples the local cuisine and develops a taste for Appollonia (Simonetta Stefanelli).

"And all the while, we think we're watching a Mafia crime story; but we're actually watching one of the great American family melodramas."

The Austin Chronicle

male circle. Before the doors close in front of her, she sees her husband Michael, the new Don, graciously receive the best wishes of his confidantes and associates.

The film stands out for its clever dramatization of the balance of power enjoyed by Vito Corleone and his successor, Michael, as well as its scenes of gory violence, such as the severed horse's head in film producer Jack Woltz's bed, Sonny's bullet-riddled body, or the gunshot through the lens of casino owner Moe Green's glasses. The brilliant finale has an Old Testament-like intensity about it. But these drastic images are mere moments compared to the

"In scene after scene – the long wedding sequence, John Marley's bloody discovery in his bed, Pacino nervously smoothing down his hair before a restaurant massacre, the godfather's collapse in a garden – Coppola crafted an enduring, undisputed masterpiece."
San Francisco Chronicle

9 Big brother: when Carlo makes putty of wife Connie, Sonny puts a little love in his heart.

10 Gone with the wind: Sonny Corleone (James Caan) walks into a trap and goes up in smoke.

11 Paying the piper: Sonny's attempt to rescue sister Connie from a violent marriage had proved more dangerous than he imagined.

"Cast and designed to perfection, this epic pastiche of '40s and '50s crime movies is as rich in images of idyllic family life as it is in brutal effects." *Der Spiegel*

extensive family scenes. The business activities of the Corleones, which include murder and extortion, invariably take place outside the inner circle – they often follow car rides and trips, literally at a distance from the family core. This distance represents a lack of protection – the attempted hit on Vito Corleone occurs when he spontaneously stops to buy fruit from a street vendor, and hothead Sonny is killed when he leaves the family fortress with too great haste.

In a poignant reversal, Michael Corleone, the initially modern man, is unable to escape the chains of his family. Though he always considered himself an independent individual, he becomes a victim of the family tradition, a marionette whose strings are moved by the hands of fate, a metaphor the image on the book cover and film poster captures with perfection.

HK

THE DISCREET CHARM OF THE BOURGEOISIE ♟

LE CHARME DISCRET DE LA BOURGEOISIE

1972 - FRANCE - 102 MIN.

DIRECTOR

LUIS BUÑUEL (1900–1983)

SCREENPLAY

LUIS BUÑUEL, JEAN-CLAUDE CARRIÈRE

DIRECTOR OF PHOTOGRAPHY

EDMOND RICHARD

EDITING

HÉLÈNE PLEMIANNIKOV

MUSIC

GUY VILLETTE

PRODUCTION

SERGE SILBERMAN for GREENWICH FILM PRODUCTIONS

STARRING

FERNANDO REY (Rafaele Costa, Ambassador of Miranda), PAUL FRANKEUR (Monsieur Thévenot),
DELPHINE SEYRIG (Madame Thévenot), BULLE OGIER (Florence),
STÉPHANE AUDRAN (Madame Sénéchal), JEAN-PIERRE CASSEL (Monsieur Sénéchal),
MILENA VUKOTIC (Ines, the Maid), JULIEN BERTHEAU (Bishop Dufour),
CLAUDE PIÉPLU (Colonel), MICHEL PICCOLI (Minister)

ACADEMY AWARDS 1972

OSCAR for BEST FOREIGN FILM

SERGE SILBERMAN présente

le charme discret de la bourgeoisie

avec par ordre
d'entrée en scène
FERNANDO REY
PAUL FRANKEUR
DELPHINE SEYRIG
BULLE OGIER
STEPHANE AUDRAN
JEAN-PIERRE CASSEL
JULIEN BERTHEAU
MILENA VUKOTIC
MARIA GABRIELLA MAIONE
CLAUDE PIEPLU
MUNI
FRANÇOIS MAISTRE
PIERRE MAGUELON
MAXENCE MAILFORT

scénario de
LUIS BUNUEL
avec la collaboration de
JEAN-CLAUDE CARRIERE

décors de
PIERRE GUFFROY
Directeur de la Photographie
EDMOND RICHARD
Directeur de la Production
ULLY PICKARD
un film produit par
SERGE SILBERMAN
PANAVISION SPHERIQUE
EASTMANCOLOR
Distribué par 20th Century Fox

UNE PRODUCTION
GREENWICH FILM PRODUCTION
© COPYRIGHT MCMLXXII

UN FILM DE LUIS BUNUEL

"There's nothing like a martini, especially when it's dry!"

An anecdote from Oscars Night, 1972, encapsulates the spirit of this film. When Luis Buñuel's movie was officially nominated, the 72-year-old Surrealist and scourge of the bourgeoisie made a statement to Mexican journalists: he was quite sure, he announced, that he would indeed be awarded the Oscar; after all, he insisted, he'd forked out the 25,000 dollars demanded for the prize. The story hit the press, and all hell broke loose in Hollywood. Buñuel's producer, Serge Silbermann, had his work cut out pouring oil on the troubled waters. When *The Discreet Charm of the Bourgeoisie* actually went on to win the Academy Award for the Best Foreign Film, Buñuel smugly told anyone who'd listen: "The Americans may have their faults – but you can always count on them to keep their word."

FERNANDO REY He turned up in so many films that almost everyone must have seen him sometime – possibly without even noticing it, for his appearances were sometimes fleeting (though always worthwhile). In the '80s, he appeared in so many movies that one critic dared call him "a prop." His filmography comprises around 200 films.

Yet for all that, the Spaniard Fernando Rey (1917–1994) is best known and best loved for his performances in a handful of films by his friend Luis Buñuel, as well as for his major roles in *The French Connection I* and *II* (1971/1975). In the latter movies, he played a sophisticated French drug czar who's pursued obsessively by a tough, streetwise New York detective (Gene Hackman). The chase scene in the subway is unforgettable: when Rey, the man with the elegant walking stick and the perfectly manicured beard, waves nonchalantly as his train draws away from his frustrated nemesis on the platform, it's surely one of the great moments in movie history. Only Rey could have embodied this figure in all its rich ambiguity: gallant and decadent, cultivated and greedy – a memorably nuanced characterization.

His great career with the exiled Spaniard Buñuel began in Mexico with *Viridiana* (1961). There followed *Tristana* (1969/70), *The Discreet Charm of the Bourgeoisie (Le Charme discret de la bourgeoisie,* 1972), and *That Obscure Object of Desire (Cet obscur objet du désir,* 1977), Buñuel's last film. Though it may be hard to believe, Buñuel discovered Rey when he was playing the part of a corpse; the director was simply blown away by the actor's "expressive power." An encounter of crucial – indeed vital – importance to both …

1 The Mirandan ambassador (Fernando Rey) is a connoisseur of good food. Madame Thévenot (Delphine Seyrig) admires his excellent taste.

2 The more unattainable the goal, the more authoritative the moral law, the more unsuspecting the husband … the more desire grows.

3 Everybody's nightmare: suddenly on stage without a line in your head.

In his last film but three, the Old Master unleashed the beast of surrealism once more. This time, however, the result was less visually disturbing than the early masterpiece *An Andalusian Dog* (*Un chien andalou*, 1929), made in collaboration with Salvador Dalí. After years of struggle and exile, in his hard-boiled but still vital old age, Buñuel no longer had any need to prove his credentials as an anarchic, subversive, and unconventional artist. And though one might complain that the film has no plot, that its characters are as lifeless as marionettes, or that they're forced to caper through an all-too-theatrical set, this kind of criticism simply fails to recognize the film's truly revolutionary quality, as a grotesque cinematic carnival of bourgeois ideals, values, and clichés.

The story is easily summarized: six *grands bourgeois* are doing their damnedest to meet for an exquisitely cultivated evening meal – but something or other keeps stopping them from doing so. Either they mysteriously get the dates mixed up, or they're inconvenienced by a sudden death in the restaurant. So they try again; and this time, a

> **"The title's complacent *grandezza* not only characterizes the bourgeoisie itself, but the visual style of the film, and Buñuel's analytical approach. No other director treats his characters with such distance and apparent passivity (or indifference); and none grants them such unconditional freedom to act according to the milieu or the atmosphere they happen to inhabit – to be new and different in each scene."** *Die Zeit*

squad of paratroopers burst into the house in order to carry out a maneuver. The would-be diners persist undeterred; and just as they've all taken their places and lifted their cutlery, they realize they're on a theater stage; the chicken is made of rubber, the audience is booing, and the actors appear to have forgotten their lines …

This last scene is not the only one that turns out to have been dreamt by one of the protagonists. Various other nightmares disturb the diners, whose faultlessly polite but utterly trivial activity seems destined to peter out in one dead end after another. On one occasion, a dream within a dream leads to yet another dream. As the film proceeds, it becomes increasingly clear to the audience that they can rely on nothing they are shown. Reality and illusion dissolve and merge into a new actuality, a surreal cinematic universe. Yet however bizarre the events that invade their lives, these six ladies and gentlemen never lose their cool, persevering heroically with their cultivated poses and their gestures of hypocritical friendliness. Quite literally, they never lose face; for when all they have is a

succession of masks for every social eventuality, there's no face left to lose.

However elegantly the table is set, it's a uniquely hot, dry, and spicy meal that Buñuel serves up to his audience, and it's not for tender palates (though he does include an excellent recipe for an extra dry martini). In fact, the guests at this dinner table are so wonderfully adroit in their blasé bitchiness that it's hard not to end up liking them a little. The subtle pleasure of *schadenfreude* is something one could quite easily acquire a taste for.

SR

"You may note that I haven't really tried to say what the film is about, what it means. And the reason for that is that I don't know. But, I don't really care, either. A poem should not mean, but be, said someone, and if there was a film poem, this is it." *Guardian Weekly*

4 Opportunity strikes: while the party is hiding from terrorists, the ambassador grabs what he can.

5 Topsy-turvy: the dead hold a wake while the living sleep. Buñuel adopted and adapted the principles of carnival.

6 Absolution: a bishop with a shotgun (Julien Bertheau) executes his father's murderer during confession.

A WOMAN UNDER THE INFLUENCE

1974 - USA - 155 MIN.

DIRECTOR

JOHN CASSAVETES (1929–1989)

SCREENPLAY

JOHN CASSAVETES

DIRECTOR OF PHOTOGRAPHY

MITCH BREIT, CALEB DESCHANEL

EDITING

DAVID ARMSTRONG, TOM CORNWELL,
ROBERT HEFFERNAN

MUSIC

BO HARWOOD

PRODUCTION

SAM SHAW for FACES

STARRING

PETER FALK (Nick Longhetti), GENA ROWLANDS (Mabel Longhetti),
FRED DRAPER (George Mortensen), LADY ROWLANDS (Martha Mortensen),
KATHERINE CASSAVETES (Mama Longhetti), MATTHEW LABORTEAUX (Angelo Longhetti),
MATTHEW CASSEL (Tony Longhetti), CHRISTINA GRISANTI (Maria Longhetti),
O. G. DUNN (Garson Cross), MARIO GALLO (Harold Jensen), EDDIE SHAW (Doctor Zepp)

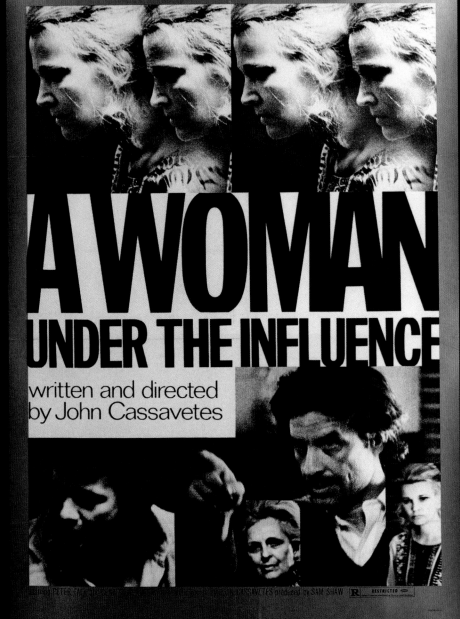

A WOMAN
UNDER THE INFLUENCE

written and directed
by John Cassavetes

"How you want me to be.
I can be that ... Just tell me, Nicky!"

Two adults try to play house and fail miserably. Two actors infuse their roles with every imaginable contour of human dignity and disgrace, taking their audience hostage for two and a half hours as they unleash the demons of Pandora's box on their rocky marriage.

This was the formula that led to one of the greatest cinematic triumphs for independent filmmaking icon John Cassavetes. In a riveting, powerhouse performance, Gena Rowlands plays a woman on the verge of a mental breakdown. For a long time now, there haven't been words to express what Mabel Longhetti has been feeling, and so she has substituted them with an arsenal of gesticulations and nervous ticks, mimicry, and pantomime. She combats the stress of her daily life, which confines her like an iron chastity belt, with deflective hand movements, eye rolls, and jerking jaws. These are the mouthed screams of a desperate woman; they pound the audience with an utter devastation that is at times hysterically funny. Peter Falk plays Mabel's husband Nick, a simple blue-collar worker, who has as little control over his words as he does over his own body. He is someone who hollers. His gestures die before completion, often ending in an admonishing pointer finger, or, as on one occasion in the film, in physical abuse. Three children stand in the crossfire as man and wife frantically grasp at straws in the hopes of pinpointing what originally made them fall in love. The couple are certain of their love for one another, yet they have no idea how to go about loving each other.

A Woman Under the Influence was originally conceived for the stage. The idea was scrapped because seasoned theater veteran Gena Rowlands didn't think she was capable of exerting such an extreme amount of emotional force night after night in front of a live audience. And so, with just a dialogue script and no true screenplay, an intimate film was shot almost exclusively within the four walls of a small family residence. No shots were predetermined. The camera was free to roam at will, thus partially accounting for the piece's almost documentary feel. Of course, this atmospheric touch is more the result of Cassavetes's unique directing style, chiseled in die-hard method-acted techniques. This is illuminated in the film by an act of associative thought processes reflected in Mabel's behavior such as when she improvises the "dying swan" from *Swan Lake*. Here, she not only takes on Cassavetes's dual role of actor-director, but also that of prima ballerina and choreographer. In another scene, the oblivious Nick surprises her at the door with ten work buddies and she instantly

JOHN CASSAVETES With his directorial debut, *Shadows* (1959), John Cassavetes (1929–1989) established himself as a permanent fixture in the world of indie filmmaking. Today's independent director has him to thank for making it possible to shoot a movie without stepping into financial quicksand. Cassavetes was born in New York in 1929 to Greek immigrant parents. He used his acting to raise funds for his directing projects, appearing in front of the camera in such films as *The Killers* (1964), *The Dirty Dozen* (1967), and *Rosemary's Baby* (1968). Friends and family often played a dual role in Cassavetes's works. Despite the little he could pay them, the actor-director received a high degree of commitment and dedication. Thespians like Seymour Cassel, Peter Falk, Ben Gazzara as well as producer Al Ruban were on board for some of his most ambitious undertakings like *Husbands* (1970), *Minnie and Moskowitz* (1971), *A Woman Under the Influence* (1974), and *The Killing of a Chinese Bookie* (1976). Gena Rowlands married Cassavetes in 1954 and portrayed the leading roles in many of his pictures such as in *Gloria* (1980). Although Cassavetes's pictures cover a wide range of genres, his constant themes remained individuality conveyed through unforgettable characters prone to double standards, the suffocating mechanisms of conventionality, and the full expression of a given personality. Cassavetes is the idol of a long list of cutting-edge filmmakers like Larry Clark of *Kids* fame (1995), and *Happiness* director Todd Solondz (1998).

transforms herself into a June Cleaver on amphetamines, whipping up a mess-hall portion of spaghetti and doing her best "hostess with the mostest" imitation. Mabel is emotionally electrified when one of the guys breaks into an aria and she implores yet another of the work crew to dance with her. She refuses to take no for an answer, prompting Nick to abruptly silence her. Her spirit and charm have, nonetheless, a miraculous impact on children. Yet upon seeing how the free-spirited Mabel allows the children to run naked through the house, one neighborhood father is convinced that she's off her rocker. Mabel, on the other hand, simply can't understand why he too doesn't just let loose and dance.

Observation of the pictures taken of Cassavetes on the set reveals the actor-director manifesting the same gestures as Mabel, from the ticking Cheshire Cat grin, to the chummy yet invasive hooking an arm around someone's shoulder while giving direction. The filmmaker readily encouraged his cast to search for authentic feelings and means of expression that often broke with Hollywood conventions. The product is a family drama and love story, whose tale itself also provides a map of the film's actual genesis.

Be that as it may, the real world is not run according to these rules; it adheres rather to the masculine leadership archetypes seen in Nick. Mabel, as well as all she represents, is too prone to the type of nervous breakdowns that Cassavetes often almost drove his team to. At one point, Nick just stands by and watches as his wife is institutionalized. Completely at a loss as a parent without

1 How much longer will Mabel Longhetti (Gena Rowlands) be able to ward off her nervous breakdown?

2 Loving you is easy 'cos you're beautiful ... Mabel's children are her only sanctuary.

3 Was that lonely woman really me? Mabel drinks away her sorrows at a local bar ... and falls into the arms of a total stranger.

4 Life of the party: construction worker Nick (Peter Falk) loves his wife, but is oblivious to her needs.

5 Big boys don't cry: but they have been known to beat their wives ...

3

her, he lets his children sip his beer on one of their family outings. When Mabel is released from the psychiatric hospital six months later, we see how all of his attempts to force his family into neat little roles have failed. Nick packs the house full of family and friends to welcome home his "healthy wife" in a gung-ho effort to "have a party!" Not to be overlooked in this film is that Nick is not one ounce less out of his mind than Mabel. His relentless need to prove his masculinity leads to disaster time after time, and he appears incapable of recognizing this.

Nonetheless, Cassavetes has no intention of pinning the blame on either of them. The film's leitmotif is much more wrapped up in Nick's schizophrenic and seemingly impossible plea to "just be yourself!" – a philosophy that is possibly to blame for the break-up of his marriage. Cassavetes's own take on the matter sheds a bit more light on the subject: "I don't believe that Mabel's collapse is a social problem. It is rooted in personal relationships. Someone can love you and still drive you insane."

PB

"Mabel's not crazy. She's unusual. She's not crazy, so don't say she's crazy!"

Film quote: Nick

CHINATOWN ⚲

1974 - USA - 131 MIN.

DIRECTOR
ROMAN POLANSKI (*1933)

SCREENPLAY
ROBERT TOWNE

DIRECTOR OF PHOTOGRAPHY
JOHN A. ALONZO

EDITING
SAM O'STEEN

MUSIC
JERRY GOLDSMITH

PRODUCTION
ROBERT EVANS for LONG ROAD, PENTHOUSE, PARAMOUNT PICTURES

STARRING

JACK NICHOLSON (J. J. "Jake" Gittes), FAYE DUNAWAY (Evelyn Cross Mulwray),
JOHN HUSTON (Noah Cross), PERRY LOPEZ (LAPD Lieutenant Lou Escobar),
JOHN HILLERMAN (Russ Yelburton), DARRELL ZWERLING (Hollis I. Mulwray),
DIANE LADD (Ida Sessions), ROY JENSON (Claude Mulvihill),
ROMAN POLANSKI (Man with the knife), RICHARD BAKALYAN (LAPD Detective Loach)

ACADEMY AWARDS 1974
OSCAR for BEST ORIGINAL SCREENPLAY (Robert Towne)

"Chinatown"

a Robert Evans production of a

Roman Polanski film

Jack Nicholson · Faye Dunaway

"Chinatown"

co-starring
JOHN HILLERMAN · PERRY LOPEZ · BURT YOUNG and JOHN HUSTON
production designer   associate producer   music scored by
RICHARD SYLBERT · C.O.ERICKSON · JERRY GOLDSMITH
written by   produced by   directed by
Robert Towne · Robert Evans · Roman Polanski

TECHNICOLOR® · PANAVISION®
A PARAMOUNT PRESENTATION

R RESTRICTED

"I'm just a snoop."

Los Angeles, 1937. When private detective J. J. Gittes (Jack Nicholson) is hired to keep tabs on an unfaithful husband, he assumes it's going to be just another routine job. But the investigation takes an unexpected turn. The guy he's been keeping an eye on, a high-ranking official for the city's water and power department, is bumped off. His attractive widow Evelyn (Faye Dunaway) retains Gittes's services to find out whodunit. Before he knows it, Gittes stumbles unexpectedly onto a foul-smelling real estate scheme, and soon finds himself entangled in one sordid affair after another. Gittes has several bloody run-ins with thugs determined to put an end to his work on the case, and uncovers clues pointing to the involvement of influential power-players in the sinister dealings. Even Gittes's alluring employer Evelyn seems to know more about the matter than she's letting on …

Chinatown is considered by many film critics to be not only one of the greatest films of the '70s, but of all time. How the movie came to be illustrates, like so many other similar moments in Hollywood history, that masterpieces can still be born within the framework of the imperious big studios. *Chinatown* was simply one of those rare instances when the perfect combination of people came together at just the right time. Jack Nicholson, who at the time was not a solid "A-list" star, brought prominent "script doctor" Robert Towne on board to write the screenplay. When he got wind of the project, Robert Evans, who was head of production at Paramount, wanted to try his hand at producing a

ROBERT EVANS Robert Evans (born 1930 in New York), is one of New Hollywood's most illustrious personalities and got his start performing in film at the age of 14. His big break into the business came when actress Norma Shearer, widow of legendary Hollywood tycoon Irving Thalberg, insisted that Evans play her husband in *Man of a Thousand Faces* (1957). Dissatisfied with the state of his acting career, he began to work as a freelance producer, without ever producing a single picture, and eventually signed a contract with Paramount in 1965. In the blink of an eye, Evans climbed the rungs of the corporate ladder and emerged as the studio's head of production. He was able to bring the old "mountain" back to its state of former glory as a major studio by taking on a number of blockbuster projects such as *Rosemary's Baby* (1968), *Love Story* (1970), *The Godfather* (1972), *The Godfather – Part II* (1974), and *Chinatown* (1974).
Chinatown marked the first time Evans was able to realize his long-harbored ambition of producing a film himself, which garnered him an Academy Award nomination for Best Picture. He left Paramount shortly thereafter to produce film independently, working on films like *Marathon Man* (1976) and *Black Sunday* (1977). These productions were, however, less popular at the box office. In 1984, Evans made headlines for his involvement in *The Cotton Club* (1984), which not only bombed, but also entangled him in disastrous private scandals. As a result, Evans disappeared from the scene completely for several years. He returned to the business in 1990 with *The Two Jakes*, a further installment of *Chinatown*, also starring Jack Nicholson. Evans published a book entitled *The Kid Stays in the Picture* (1994) about his personal life story, a constant target of media attention since his start in Hollywood. This gripping autobiography was made into a documentary film in 2002 under the same title.

"*Chinatown* was seen as a Neo-Noir when it was released – an update on an old genre. Now years have passed and film history blurs a little, and it seems to settle easily beside the original noirs. That is a compliment." *Chicago Sun-Times*

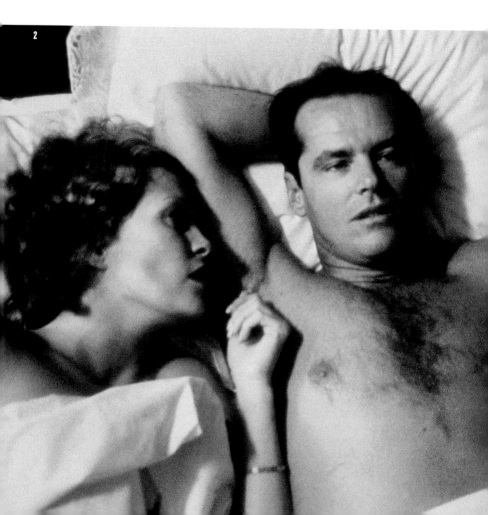

1 Portrait of a lady: *femme fatale* Evelyn (Faye Dunaway) awakens men's dreams and inspires them to action.

2 In her clutches: the private eye (Jack Nicholson) has lost all professional distance from his seductive client.

3 Mack the knife: Polanski in a striking cameo as the "nose-slitter."

film himself. He finalized an agreement with the writer and actor and secured Roman Polanski, with whom he had collaborated previously on *Rosemary's Baby* (1968), as the picture's director. (Polanski had been working in his native Europe following the brutal death of his wife Sharon Tate [1943–1969] in their Los Angeles home.) When Faye Dunaway was cast as the female lead, yet another famous personality was added to the mix. As one might expect, the shoot was not exactly plain sailing. Evans dubbed the verbal fireworks between Towne and Polanski "World War III." The problem probably had something to do with the fact that this was the first project Polanski had directed without writing it himself. The product was, nonetheless, an international smash. *Chinatown* reeled in a total of 11 Oscar nominations, although Robert Towne was the sole person who ended up taking a statuette home.

Yet what makes *Chinatown* truly fascinating, and the reason it attained its instant status as an uncontested mas-

terpiece, is by and large the film's grace in evoking the Golden Age of 1930s–1940s Hollywood, without losing itself in the nostalgia of the era or turning the production into just another stiffly stylized homage. Naturally, Polanski's film draws heavily on classic Bogart characters like detective Philip Marlowe from Howard Hawks's *The Big Sleep* (1946) or his more cynical counterpart Sam Spade from *The Maltese Falcon* (1941), directed by Hollywood legend John Huston. Huston himself plays a pivotal role in *Chinatown* as a ruthless and sickeningly sentimental patriarch, who seems to be the key to the entire mystery. Unlike Bogart, Nicholson's character is only capable of being a limited hero. Although J. J. "Jake" Gittes is a likeable small-time snoop, with a weakness for smutty jokes, the charming sheister fails miserably as a moralist and suffers terribly as a result. The scene featuring Polanski as a gangster who slits open Nicholson's nose is absolutely priceless. The Gittes character also lacks the romantic potential of a

4 Just the facts, ma'am: *Chinatown* evokes classic Hollywood cinema without ever romanticizing it.

5 Still nosing around: J. J. Gittes (Jack Nicholson), bloody but unbowed.

Bogart hero. Gittes doesn't embody desires; instead he stumbles on them. Yet his greatest weakness is Chinatown, the place where his career as a cop came to an end and a synonym for all the irresistible, exotic dangers of the urban jungle. This same sweet taboo seems to echo in Faye Dunaway's character. In the end, Chinatown presents Gittes with a double-edged defeat. Although Towne had originally written a happy ending, the film's final sequence, which just screams Polanski, sees Gittes inadvertently aiding the forces of evil and losing the love of his life at the same time.

Another great accomplishment of the piece is Polanski and cinematographer John A. Alonzo's triumph in achieving the impact of a black-and-white film noir piece with brilliant color photography. It is uncanny how little the city feels like a movie lot and how convincing the topography looks. Unlike in so many other so-called revisionist noir films, in *Chinatown* L.A. is not a black, smoldering hell's kitchen but rather a vast, often sunny countryside metropolis still in the early stages of development. The imagery lets the viewer sense that the city and its surrounding valleys exist in spite of the imposing desert. We are also made aware of the colossal pipeline, supplying the city with water, its artificial lifeblood. Water is, in fact, the major resource being manipulated in the story's diabolical real-estate venture, a scandal with genuine historical roots in the region. Robert Towne based his screenplay on non-fictional accounts dating back to early 20th-century Southern California. It was a time when the foundations for the future riches of the world's movie capital were in construction. The location was chosen primarily on account of the area's year-round sun, ideal for filming, and its affordable purchase price. The boom ushered in a wave of land speculators, corruption, and violence. It is a grim bit of earth that the City of Angels and Hollywood rests upon. A tale that unfolds in *Chinatown*. JH

JAWS ♟♟♟

1975 - USA - 124 MIN.

DIRECTOR
STEVEN SPIELBERG (*1946)

SCREENPLAY
CARL GOTTLIEB, PETER BENCHLEY,
based on his novel of the same name

DIRECTOR OF PHOTOGRAPHY
BILL BUTLER

EDITING
VERNA FIELDS

MUSIC
JOHN WILLIAMS

PRODUCTION
RICHARD D. ZANUCK, DAVID BROWN for
ZANUCK/BROWN PRODUCTIONS, UNIVERSAL PICTURES

STARRING
ROY SCHEIDER (Police Chief Martin Brody), ROBERT SHAW (Quint),
RICHARD DREYFUSS (Matt Hooper), MURRAY HAMILTON (Mayor Larry Vaughn),
LORRAINE GARY (Ellen Brody), CARL GOTTLIEB (Ben Meadows),
JEFFREY KRAMER (Lenny Hendricks), SUSAN BACKLINIE (Chrissie),
CHRIS REBELLO (Mike Brody), JAY MELLO (Sean Brody)

ACADEMY AWARDS 1975
OSCARS for BEST FILM EDITING (Verna Fields), BEST MUSIC (John Williams),
and BEST SOUND (Robert L. Hoyt, Roger Herman Jr., Earl Mabery, John R. Carter)

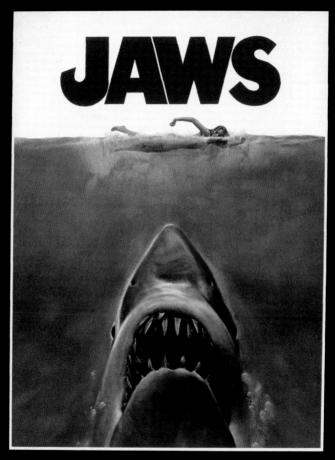

The terrifying motion picture from the terrifying No.1 best seller.

JAWS

ROY SCHEIDER · **ROBERT SHAW** · **RICHARD DREYFUSS**

JAWS

Co-starring LORRAINE GARY · MURRAY HAMILTON · A ZANUCK/BROWN PRODUCTION
Screenplay by PETER BENCHLEY and CARL GOTTLIEB · Based on the novel by PETER BENCHLEY · Music by JOHN WILLIAMS
Directed by STEVEN SPIELBERG · Produced by RICHARD D. ZANUCK and DAVID BROWN · A UNIVERSAL PICTURE ·
TECHNICOLOR® PANAVISION®   ORIGINAL SOUNDTRACK AVAILABLE ON MCA RECORDS & TAPES

"You're gonna need a bigger boat."

A hot summer night, a beach party, a little too much red wine, and some teenage sex is just the stuff Hollywood horror films are made of. While her drunken companion sleeps off his hangover on the beach, young Chrissie (Susan Backlinie) takes a midnight dip in the water and is torn to pieces by a shark. The fact that the monster with the dead eyes cynically emerges in innocent white from the depths of the water makes it all the more threatening. The shark – the fear and guilt in all of us – awakens our prehistoric terror of the incomprehensible, the truly wild. It is evil incarnate.

But in the small American beach town ironically named Amity, nobody wants to hear about the threat to a safe world and free-market economy, least of all from the mouth of visiting New York cop Martin Brody (Roy Scheider) who, to cap it all, is afraid of the water.

Accordingly, the authorities, in the form of the mayor Larry Vaughn (Murray Hamilton), and the profit- and pleasure-seeking public win out over Brody, who wants to close the beaches in light of the menacing danger. It comes as no surprise that the town has a new victim the very next day. A reward of $3,000 for the capture of the shark

THE END OF ARTIFICIAL CREATURES "Compressors, tanks, winches, pneumatic hoses, welding torches, blow lamps, rigging, generators, copper, iron, and steel wire, plastic material, electric motors, crammers, hydraulic presses" – just some of the trappings required to make "Bruce," as the film team christened the model of the white shark, come alive. In his book, "The Jaws Log," co-screenwriter Carl Gottlieb tells of the immense problems encountered trying to simulate real-life shark attacks with a life-sized model (because actually Bruce was made of three different models). Shooting was repeatedly interrupted by technical problems, most memorably when they first put Bruce in the water, only to see him sink like a stone. The hiring of long-retired Hollywood veteran Robert A. Mattey, creator of the special effects for Disney's *Mary Poppins* (1964) and countless other films, makes it clear that the mid-'70s marked the end of conventionally created film monsters. "Bruce" was one of the last of his kind and craftsmen like Bob Mattey were increasingly replaced by computer programmers. Spielberg proved his ability to incorporate their work into his projects in 1981 with *Raiders of the Lost Ark*, in which entire sequences were created with the help of computer animation.

"If *Jaws* was a kind of skeleton key to the angst of the '70s, from the puritanical fear of sex to the war in Vietnam, then its heroes were models of America's wounded masculinity, who meet and join to face a test of character." *Georg Seeßlen*

1 Baywatch: Police Chief Martin Brody (Roy Scheider) is fighting nature, the ignorance of those he's trying to protect, and his own fears.

2 Beach, blanket, bloodbath: beautiful Chrissie (Susan Backlinie) is the shark's first victim.

3 Smile for the camera: three separate models, each seven yards long and weighing over a ton, brought the monster to life. The film crew dubbed the shark "Bruce" – after Steven Spielberg's lawyer.

incites hunting fever in Amity, and the gawking mob on the pier is duly presented with a dead shark. But it is quickly determined that the captured shark can't possibly be the feared killer: upon cutting open its stomach they find a few small fish, a tin can, and a license plate from Louisiana.

It is a motley trio that sets out to capture the beast – a water-shy policeman, a "rich college boy" named Matt Hooper (Richard Dreyfuss), and shark-hunting Vietnam veteran Quint (Robert Shaw), a modern Captain Ahab who

unsuccessfully attempts to disguise a wounded psyche with a façade of disgust for everything around him. For each of the three men, the shark hunt also turns into a search for their true selves.

The unmistakably sexual aspect of the story of the unnamed monster – a terrifying mixture of phallus and vagina – which afflicts the home and the family has often been pointed out. But *Jaws* is also a film about human fears and character flaws, the overcoming of which gives

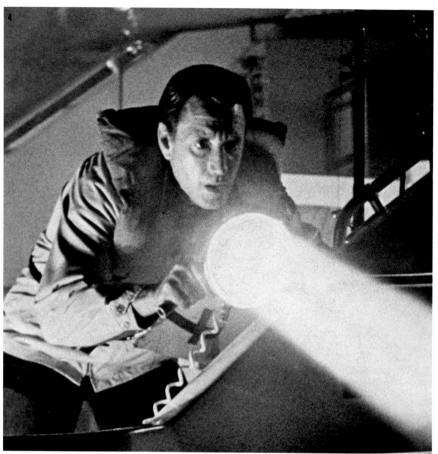

4 Brody's scared of water, but he's about to undergo some shock therapy…

5 Rub a dub dub, three men in a tub: *Jaws* is also a parable about social conflicts in the U.S.

6 Shark fin soup: evil feeds on ignorance and Americans.

birth to heroes. That the story also tells of the capitalistic, self-endangering society, of patriotic America, of mass hysteria, guilt, atonement, and the sacrifice of the individual for the good of the whole is proof of Spielberg's ability to give a simple story plausible readings on multiple levels.

But let's not forget that *Jaws* is one of the most nerve-wracking thrillers of all time. When Spielberg explains that during the filming he felt as if he could direct the audience with an electric cattle prod, it speaks volumes about the cold precision with which, supported by an exceptionally suggestive soundtrack, he was able to raise the tension and lower it again, all in preparation for the next dramatic highlight.

Just one example of Spielberg's virtuoso storytelling technique is the scene in which the men show one another their scars below deck. In the middle of the scene, the audience is told the story of the *USS Indianapolis*, the boat with which the Hiroshima bomb was transported to the Pacific. Under fire from Japanese submarines, the crew threw themselves into the ocean and the majority of them were eaten by sharks.

During this sequence, which is actually quite humorous, Spielberg and his writers succeed in setting a counterpoint even before the appearance of the shark illustrates the terror of the story. Quint's tale contains a political dimension. Ultimately, this scene also reveals something about storytelling itself – reality catches you up in a flash. Right when Quint and Hooper attempt to stem their apprehension with loud song, Mr. Spielberg is right there with his electric shocker.

SH

"If Spielberg's favorite location is the suburbs, *Jaws* shows suburbanites on vacation."

Chicago Sun-Times

ONE FLEW OVER THE CUCKOO'S NEST ♟♟♟♟♟

1975 - USA - 134 MIN.

DIRECTOR

MILOŠ FORMAN (*1932)

SCREENPLAY

LAWRENCE HAUBEN, BO GOLDMAN, based on the novel of the same name by
KEN KESEY, and a play by DALE WASSERMAN

DIRECTOR OF PHOTOGRAPHY

HASKELL WEXLER, WILLIAM A. FRAKER, BILL BUTLER

EDITING

LYNZEE KLINGMAN, SHELDON KAHN, RICHARD CHEW (Supervising editor)

MUSIC

JACK NITZSCHE

PRODUCTION

SAUL ZAENTZ, MICHAEL DOUGLAS for FANTASY FILMS, N. V. ZVALUW

STARRING

JACK NICHOLSON (Randle Patrick McMurphy), LOUISE FLETCHER (Nurse Mildred Ratched),
WILLIAM REDFIELD (Harding), BRAD DOURIF (Billy Bibbit),
WILL SAMPSON (Chief Bromden), DANNY DEVITO (Martini),
MICHAEL BERRYMAN (Ellis), PETER BROCCO (Colonel Matterson),
DEAN R. BROOKS (Doctor John Spivey), ALONZO BROWN (Miller)

ACADEMY AWARDS 1975

OSCARS for BEST PICTURE (Saul Zaentz, Michael Douglas), BEST DIRECTOR (Miloš Forman),
BEST ACTOR (Jack Nicholson), BEST ACTRESS (Louise Fletcher),
and BEST ADAPTED SCREENPLAY (Lawrence Hauben, Bo Goldman)

JACK NICHOLSON

ONE FLEW OVER THE CUCKOO'S NEST

Fantasy Films presents

A MILOS FORMAN FILM JACK NICHOLSON in "ONE FLEW OVER THE CUCKOO'S NEST"

Starring LOUISE FLETCHER and WILLIAM REDFIELD · Screenplay LAWRENCE HAUBEN and BO GOLDMAN

Based on the novel by KEN KESEY · Director of Photography HASKELL WEXLER · Music · JACK NITZSCHE

Produced by SAUL ZAENTZ and MICHAEL DOUGLAS · Directed by MILOS FORMAN

R RESTRICTED

United Artists

NOW AVAILABLE IN SIGNET PAPERBACK AND VIKING/COMPASS TRADE PAPERBACK

"But I tried didn't I?
Goddammit, at least I did that!"

The movie's opening shot evokes an image of paradise lost. Rolling hills are reflected in the glistening water by the rising sun, as a peaceful melody drifts through the air. The last shot is equally utopian. Chief Bromden (Will Sampson), a mountain of a man resident at the psychiatric rehabilitation facility tucked away in this picturesque countryside, wrenches a colossal marble bathroom fixture from its anchored position, hurls it through a window, and embarks on the road to freedom. What director Miloš Forman manages to pack into the action that takes place between these two points is a mesmerizing parable about both the urge to capitulate and an ideological system that seeks to crush the individual at any cost. The tale is ingeniously coated in a tragicomic drama about life, death, and the state of vegetative indifference exhibited by the residents of an insane asylum.

But all that is about the last thing assault and statutory rape convict Randle P. McMurphy (Jack Nicholson) has on his mind when he first arrives at the sterile building with barred windows for clinical observation. To McMurphy, the facility serves as a promising alternative to the hard labor he'd be subjected to at the state penitentiary. This is, of course, precisely why higher authorities suspect him of faking his mental ailments. It soon becomes evident that McMurphy is the sole person at the institution still possessing enough fantasy and initiative to combat the current reign of deadening boredom. His opposition comes in the form of the austere head nurse, Mildred Ratched (Louise Fletcher), who has made it her life mission to suck the marrow out of any bit of excitement within the ward in order to assure her patients' eternal sedation. McMurphy, however, slowly undermines her authority. He begins to question trivialities as well as the inalterable daily schedule by instigating "harmless" acts of defiance, even managing to get the patients to sneak out of the clinic and treating them to a fishing trip. Although McMurphy's actions infuse

JACK NICHOLSON Wily, devious, and lecherous at times, Jack Nicholson still possesses all the qualities required to portray characters driven by animal instincts rather than intellect. His caustic mimicry, gestures, and trademark sneer vitalize rebels (*One Flew Over the Cuckoo's Nest*, 1975), psychopaths (*The Shining*, 1980), career killers (*Prizzi's Honor*, 1985), and hardboiled PIs alike (*Chinatown*, 1974; *The Two Jakes*, 1990). Some might even regard the sinister, eternally grinning "Joker" in Tim Burton's *Batman* (1988) as the culminating fusion of his classic roles. Hard to believe that for many years it seemed that the movie star born in Neptune, New Jersey, in 1937 was not destined to make it big as an actor. In the late 1950s, he joined the team of legendary exploitation film director/producer Roger Corman, performing bit roles in his horror flicks and wannabe rockumentaries, as well as writing screenplays. His screenwriting credits include Monte Hellman's Western *Ride in the Whirlwind* (1965) and Corman's exploration into LSD entitled *The Trip* (1967). The turning point in his career came with his role as a perpetually inebriated lawyer in *Easy Rider* (1969). Dennis Hopper's drama about the disappearance of the American Dream quickly attained cult status and earned Nicholson his first of many Oscar nods. His rise to superstardom reached its inevitable height in the 1970s. Among his many credits and honors, Nicholson has been awarded three Oscars, not to mention the projects he has directed himself. Still very much alive in the business, his more recent movies often feature him as stubborn, eccentric types. He likewise proved his formidable skills as an actor in *About Schmidt* (2003) and *The Departed* (2006). *The Bucket List* (2010), a tragicomedy directed by Rob Reiner, however, was considered a flop by most critics.

1 It's your move: Randle P. McMurphy (Jack Nicholson) thinks he's in a game – and he thinks he can win.

2 Leading by example: Randle is the hero of the other patients in the psychiatric ward.

3 Shake, rattle and roll: Randle encourages his fellow patients to take control of their lives.

"*One Flew Over the Cuckoo's Nest* is a powerful, smashingly effective movie – not a great movie but one that will probably stir audiences' emotions and join the ranks of such pop-mythology films as *The Wild One*, *Rebel Without a Cause* and *Easy Rider*." *The New Yorker*

the sequestered men with newfound self-esteem, Nurse Ratched's festering anger reveals her personal disdain for anything other than the prescribed routine. She, of course, defends the prevailing order by enforcing a strict, borderline totalitarian regime rooted in pseudo-democratic doctrines.

To take the film as a critique of modern psychiatric medicine is to misinterpret it. Director Forman has clearly made an attempt at a more monumental allegory about the power structures at play in modern society. Among the poignant final scenes in *One Flew Over the Cuckoo's Nest* is the moment when we discover that the majority of patients at the clinic are there of their own volition. In other words, they have all willingly acquiesced to the tyranny and perpetual humiliation. The counterpoint to this mentality manifests itself in McMurphy's reticence to re-sign himself to such blind compliance. One of the few actually incarcerated hospital inhabitants, the unforgetta-ble words he utters, following his failed attempt at dis-lodging a marble bathroom fixture sum up the plea of For-man's picture: "But I tried didn't I? Goddammit, at least I did that!" Tragically, McMurphy never internalizes the ex-treme gravity of his own predicament and continues to gamble in a poker game where no one can afford to bluff. At one point he is presented with a *deus ex machina* in the form of an open window offering escape. The camera holds its focus on McMurphy's face for some time before a cunning grin finally unfolds across his lips. He will stay and continue on with the "game."

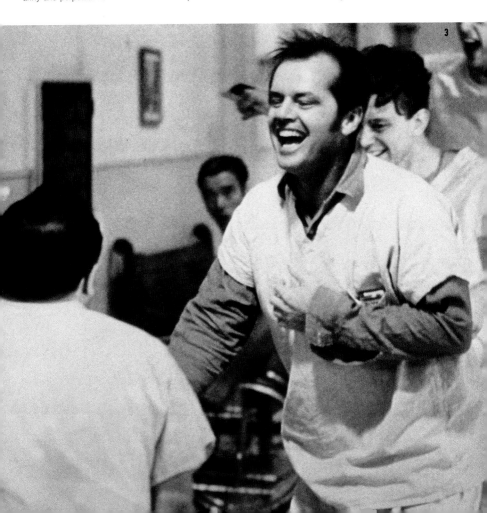

3

Be that as it may, his tournament is over before he even realizes it. The burgeoning self-confidence and associated mental resilience demonstrated in the wisecracks of the patients cause the hospital staff to implement more drastic physical and psychological measures. The film concludes with a "pacified" McMurphy, who was subjected to a lobotomy, being put out of his misery by his friend the chief. It is this character who continues what McMurphy has set into motion.

Miloš Forman earned his reputation in Hollywood as the most influential Czech "new wave" import in the 1960s

"The 'cuckoo's nest' described by Forman is our very own nest. It's the world we poor lunatics live in, subjected to the bureaucratic rule of one set of oppressors and the economic pressure of another; forever chasing the promise of happiness, which here appears in the guise of liberty – but always obliged to swallow Miss Ratched's bitter little pills." *Le Monde*

4 First Lady of a mock-democracy: Nurse Ratched (Louise Fletcher) brings the patients to their knees.

5 Born free: "Chief" Bromden carries on the torch when he flies the coop.

6 Sex, drugs, and fishing trips: there's nothing Dionysian Randle enjoys catching more than some female tail.

with his sarcastic reflections on everyday life. Although Ken Kesey's novel, on which the screen adaptation is based, is told from the perspective of the mute Native American, McMurphy served as the perfect vehicle for Forman to express his personal cinematic interests and set of reccurring themes. The director transforms the story into a lighter satire, whose socio-political potential takes a slight backseat to the entertainment value, allowing the piece to soar to stunningly beautiful heights. The actual directing in *One Flew Over the Cuckoo's Nest* is primarily evidenced in the world-class acting led by an energized Nicholson, his antithesis, the insidiously pleasant Louise Fletcher, and Will Sampson's gut-wrenching stoicism. Yet, it's not enough to speak of Sampson's Bromden character solely in these terms, for it is he who will undergo the most dramatic metamorphosis. From the ashes of his self-imposed silent retreat and symbolic emasculation arises a true warrior, who lets the eternal flame borne by McMurphy burn on inside him.

LP

TAXI DRIVER

1975 - USA - 113 MIN.

DIRECTOR

MARTIN SCORSESE (*1942)

SCREENPLAY

PAUL SCHRADER

DIRECTOR OF PHOTOGRAPHY

MICHAEL CHAPMAN

EDITING

TOM ROLF, MELVIN SHAPIRO, MARCIA LUCAS (Editing Supervisor)

MUSIC

BERNARD HERRMANN

PRODUCTION

JULIA PHILLIPS, MICHAEL PHILLIPS for BILL / PHILLIPS, COLUMBIA PICTURES CORPORATION

STARRING

ROBERT DE NIRO (Travis Bickle), CYBILL SHEPHERD (Betsy),
JODIE FOSTER (Iris), HARVEY KEITEL (Sport),
ALBERT BROOKS (Tom), PETER BOYLE (Wizard),
MARTIN SCORSESE (Passenger), STEVEN PRINCE (Andy the Gun Dealer),
DIAHNNE ABBOTT (Candy Saleswoman), VICTOR ARGO (Melio)

IFF CANNES 1976

GOLDEN PALM for BEST FILM (Martin Scorsese)

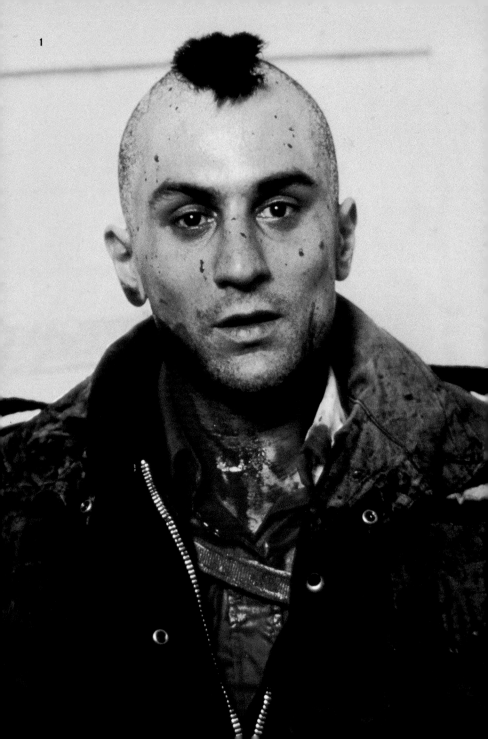

"You talkin' to me?"

The restless, metallic strokes of the musical theme in the opening sequence say it all: this film is a threat. A rising steam cloud hangs over the street and covers the screen in white. As if out of nowhere, a yellow cab penetrates the eerie wall of steam and smoke, gliding through in slow motion. The background music abruptly ends atonally; the ethereal taxi disappears, the cloud closing up behind it. Two dark eyes appear in close-up, accompanied by a gentle jazz theme. In the flickering light of the colorful street lamps they wander from side to side, as if observing the surroundings. They are the eyes of Travis Bickle (Robert De Niro), a New York taxi driver who will become an avenging angel.

Even at the premiere in 1976, *Taxi Driver* split the critics. Some saw the main character as a disturbed soul who revels in his role as savior of a young prostitute, for whom he kills three shady characters in an excessively bloody rampage, an act for which the press fetes him as a hero. Others looked more closely and detected a skillfully stylized film language in the melancholy images and a common urban

BERNARD HERRMANN He made a guest appearance in Hitchcock's *The Man Who Knew Too Much* (1956) as the conductor on the podium of the London Symphony, practically playing himself. He also wrote the music for the film. Born in New York on June 29, 1911, it was Bernard Herrmann who gave a number of film classics the final push towards immortality. He began working for radio, and then moved on to film, collaborating with Alfred Hitchcock, Orson Welles, François Truffaut, Brian De Palma, and Martin Scorsese, to name but a few. He gave films like *Vertigo* (1958), *Psycho* (1960), *North by Northwest* (1959), *Citizen Kane* (1941), *The Magnificent Ambersons* (1942), *Fahrenheit 451* (1966), and *Taxi Driver* (1975) an unmistakable musical face, an aura of tonality. No one used the orchestra as eclectically as Herrmann. He could make it sound conservative and classical, or send it into strange tonal regions in which the strings, accompanied by sonorous, dark horns, imitated the sounds of swinging metal wires.

Herrmann was fascinated by the sinister romantic literature of the Brontë sisters and by Melville's *Moby Dick*. The sea with its elemental force was an inspiration for the scores of his compositions. He could hear and compose the rising and falling of deep waters. Herrmann was not an affable man, perhaps because he was too much of an artist. He was known for his irascible and perverse behavior. He fell out of favor with Hitchcock during work on *Torn Curtain* (1966). He remained an artist through and through while working on his last soundtrack, which he finished on the day before his death on December 24, 1975. It was the music to *Taxi Driver*.

1 Robert De Niro in *The Last of the Mohicans?* Call central casting, quick!

2 Soldier of fortune at a buck a mile: ex-Marine Travis Bickle, at war with New York.

3 This screen ain't big enough for the two of us: both pimp (Harvey Keitel) and taxi driver are used to getting their own way.

4 Talk to the hand: Travis helps stamp out violent crime.

"Martin Scorsese's *Taxi Driver* is a homage to home from a homeless man; a New York Western, with a midnight cowboy cruising the canyons in a shabby yellow cab." *Der Spiegel*

sociopath behind the figure of the madman Travis Bickle: "On every street, in every city, there's a nobody who dreams of being somebody," reads one of the film posters.

Travis can't sleep at night. To earn a few cents he becomes a taxi driver. He'll drive anytime and anywhere, he says in his interview. He will even enter the neighborhoods his colleagues avoid at all costs – the districts with either too little or too much light, in which street gangs loiter around and teenage prostitutes wait for johns under bright neon lights. Travis is given the job. He and his taxi become one and the catastrophe takes its course.

Like Travis, the audience gazes out of the driving taxi into the night. Rarely was New York depicted as impressively. The camera style switches between half-documentary and subjective takes. Bernard Herrmann's suggestive music, which accompanies the film, lends it an acoustic structure, creating a unique combination of image and sound. The taxi driving becomes nothing less than a metaphor of film.

Travis's attempt to build a romantic relationship with campaign assistant Betsy (Cybill Shepherd) fails. He can neither express himself, nor his feelings, which is why in the end he turns to the gun. Isolated and aimless, he wanders through the city. Travis's story resembles the yellow taxi cab that slices through the cloud of smoke in the opening sequence. He too emerges out of nowhere, briefly appears in the night light of the city, and vanishes again into nothingness.

Travis is no hero, even if many applauded the brutal rampage at the premiere. Violence is naturally an important theme of the film, but the violence is not merely physical, but social. Travis embodies a person who has lost himself in the big city. Robert De Niro gave this type a face and an unmistakable body.

Scorsese is known for creating his films on paper. He draws them as sketches in a storyboard, and time and

"An utterly strange, disturbing, alarming and fascinating film. Syncretic and glamorous, it is a lurking reptile that changes color like a chameleon; a synthetic amalgam of conflicting influences, tendencies and metaphysical ambitions, raised to the power of a myth: comical, edgy, hysterical." *Frankfurter Rundschau*

5 Jodie Foster as the child prostitute, Iris. Foster's older sister who stood in as her body double for the more mature shots.

6 The facts of life: on tonight's episode, Mrs. Garrett tells Tootie what men really want.

7 Remember the Alamo: election campaigner Betsy (Cybill Shepherd) is the object of Travis's desire.

again he shows that images are his true language. The screenplay was the work of Paul Schrader, and marked the first close collaboration between two film-obsessed men. The scene in which Travis stands before the mirror shirtless, clutching his revolver and picks a fight with himself is unforgettable: "You talkin' to me? Well I'm the only one here. Who do you think you're talking to?" The scene has been cited over and over, but the original remains untouchable. It is a modern classic.

SR

STAR WARS ♊♊♊♊♊♊♊

1977 - USA - 121 MIN.

DIRECTOR
GEORGE LUCAS (*1944)

SCREENPLAY
GEORGE LUCAS

DIRECTOR OF PHOTOGRAPHY
GILBERT TAYLOR

EDITING
PAUL HIRSCH, MARCIA LUCAS, RICHARD CHEW

MUSIC
JOHN WILLIAMS

PRODUCTION
GARY KURTZ for LUCASFILM LTD.

STARRING
MARK HAMILL (Luke Skywalker), HARRISON FORD (Han Solo),
CARRIE FISHER (Princess Leia Organa), ALEC GUINNESS (Ben "Obi-Wan" Kenobi),
PETER CUSHING (Tarkin), DAVID PROWSE (Darth Vader),
JAMES EARL JONES (Darth Vader's voice), KENNY BAKER (R2-D2),
ANTHONY DANIELS (C-3PO), PETER MAYHEW (Chewbacca),
PHIL BROWN (Owen Lars), SHELAGH FRASER (Beru Lars)

ACADEMY AWARDS 1977
OSCARS for BEST MUSIC (John Williams), BEST FILM EDITING (Paul Hirsch, Marcia Lucas,
Richard Chew), BEST SET DESIGN (John Barry, Norman Reynolds, Leslie Dilley, Roger Christian),
BEST COSTUMES (John Mollo), BEST SOUND (Don MacDougall, Ray West, Bob Minkler, Derek Ball),
BEST SPECIAL EFFECTS (John Stears, John Dykstra, Richard Edlund, Grant McCune, Robert Blalack),
and SPECIAL PRIZE FOR SOUND EFFECTS (voices of the aliens and robots, Ben Burtt)

TWENTIETH CENTURY-FOX Presents A LUCASFILM LTD. PRODUCTION STAR WARS
Starring MARK HAMILL HARRISON FORD CARRIE FISHER
PETER CUSHING
and
ALEC GUINNESS

Written and Directed by   Produced by   Music by
GEORGE LUCAS   GARY KURTZ   JOHN WILLIAMS

PANAVISION®   PRINTS BY DE LUXE®   TECHNICOLOR®

Making Films Sound Better
DOLBY SYSTEM®
Noise Reduction · High Fidelity

Original Motion Picture Soundtrack on 20th Century Records and Tapes

ONE SHEET STYLE "C"

1

off off

STAR WARS

"May the Force be with you!"

There's something rotten in the state of the galaxy. With the blessings of the emperor, Grand Moff Tarkin (Peter Cushing) and the sinister Lord Vader (David Prowse / James Earl Jones) have been conquering and subjugating one planet system after the other in the old Republic. Tarkin commands a massive spaceship, whose firepower has the ability to annihilate entire planets. This "Death Star" is the most dangerous weapon in the universe – perhaps with the exception of "the Force," a mysterious, all-pervading energy. Anyone who learns to master this force through years of ascetic training is possessed with superhuman powers. In the past, the Jedi Knights secured justice and kept the peace with the help of the Force. But now Darth Vader, a renegade Jedi, is one of the last people with control of its powers, forming with Tarkin an almost invincible alliance of evil in the once peaceful expanses of the universe.

Only a small group of rebels resist the might of the Empire and fight to restore the old order. To achieve their aspirations, the construction plans of the Death Star, which the rebels have acquired, could be of great assistance. But the spaceship of Princess Leia (Carrie Fisher) is captured just as she is returning to her home planet with the plans in hand. At the last moment she is able to save the blueprint of the Death Star inside the droid R2-D2 (Kenny Baker). If this tiny robot can get the plans to the old Jedi Knight Obi-Wan Kenobi (Alec Guinness) in time, there could still be a remote hope for the rebels' cause.

SERIAL SPACE OPERAS The overture to *Star Wars* (1977) begins with a long block of text rolling up the screen which sets the stage and recounts the background story. What follows is no singular adventure; it is an entire universe. From the very beginning *Star Wars* was created as a multi-episode project. After the first episode came *Star Wars: Episode V – The Empire Strikes Back* (1980) and then *Star Wars: Episode VI – The Return of the Jedi* (1983). With *Star Wars: Episode I – The Phantom Menace* from 1999, three prequels tell the history of the space saga. Even during the first screenplay drafts, Lucas's star world was getting bigger and bigger. This is no exception in the fantasy and science-fiction genre. Where new, exotic worlds are created, there will always be questions about how it all began. With the interest in both past and future, the plot possibilities are endless.

Serial science-fiction stories were already prevalent and popular in the 1930s. The space heroes of *Flash Gordon* (1936) and *Buck Rogers* (1939) helped their comic forefathers to big-screen success. Each 13-part series told of despotic rulers, beautiful women, and heroic men saving the universe; after 20 minutes the plot stopped at the most exciting moment – to be continued next week in this theater!

The *Star Trek* universe has been massively popular and has experienced considerable expansion. Since the first episode of the television series about the Starship Enterprise was broadcast in 1966, five spin-off series and 12 films have been created, each piece of this long chain of individual stories adding to the colossal inventory of characters, events, time periods, and places that make up this fantastic world.

1 May the Force be with you: with a monk's habit and lightsaber, Ben "Obi-Wan" Kenobi (Alec Guinness) links medieval mythology to a hi-tech future.

2 Iron lung of evil: Darth Vader (David Prowse) will stop at nothing to conquer the galaxy.

3 Man's best friend according to Lucas: Princess Leia (Carrie Fisher) confides in R2-D2 (Kenny Baker).

The journey of R2-D2 and his companion, the dithering and etiquette-conscious communication robot C-3PO (Anthony Daniels), takes them to the planet Tatooine, where they are purchased by farmer Owen Lars (Phil Brown). His nephew, Luke Skywalker (Mark Hamill) longs for a life more exciting than that of an agricultural worker. He would much rather fight with the rebels against the Empire – just as his father, a legendary Jedi whom he has never met, once did ...

Skywalker's dreams of adventure begin to become reality when the two droids meet Obi-Wan. Soon the imperial Stormtroopers are at their heels, and the old Jedi Knight is left with no other alternative but to travel with Luke and the droids to Alderaan, Leia's home planet, bringing the plans of the Death Star to help plan a counter-attack.

They receive assistance from Han Solo (Harrison Ford), an old pro who, with his ship the *Millennium Falcon*, manages to speed away from the fast-approaching imperial cruisers in the nick of time. Even so, they do not reach their destination: Tarkin and Darth Vader have already destroyed the planet Alderaan.

After our heroes free Princess Leia from the Death Star, nothing stands in the way of the final battle between the Empire and the rebels in the Javin System. The Achilles heel of the gigantic space station is a small ventilation shaft, and in the end, after several intense battles, it is Luke who is able to hit the weak spot and destroy the Death Star in a powerful explosion. Only Darth Vader escapes the blazing inferno. And while one battle may have been won in this war in the stars, it won't be long before the Empire strikes back ...

"I wanted to make a film for kids, something that would present them with a kind of elementary morality. Because nowadays nobody bothers to tell those kids, 'Hey, this is right and this is wrong.'"

George Lucas, interview with David Sheff

4

"A combination of past and future, Western and space odyssey, myth and dream world, *Star Wars* may be the most enduring piece of escapism ever put on film." *Sacramento Bee*

George Lucas began working on his star saga just as his teenage drama, *American Graffiti*, was poised to become the surprise hit of 1973 – a success from which the director profited much less than the studios that produced the film. For Lucas, this experience was the driving motivation never to give control of one of his projects to anyone else again. *Star Wars* was produced entirely by his own company and the special effects were created by Industrial Light & Magic, also a Lucas company. Rounding out the deal was a clause giving rights to merchandising (toys, clothing, etc.) and the use of film music to Lucas, initiating a new era in cinema in which the biggest proceeds of a film were no longer made at the box office. The blockbuster movie was born.

Real success always did depend on reaching the largest possible audience. Lucas stressed over and over that he wrote the screenplay with eight and nine-year-olds in mind. But in the end, the film was able to connect with

4 Rebels without a shave: individualists Chewbacca (Peter Mayhew) and Han Solo (Harrison Ford) battle against the evil empire.

5 About face: the imperial stormtroopers are trained and ruthless killers.

virtually every age group, primarily because with his "space opera," Lucas was neither attempting to depart from old genres, nor to enthusiastically deconstruct them. In fact, his goal was just the opposite. Like his colleague Steven Spielberg, Lucas pursued a higher path, which led him back to the classical narrative form, meeting the expectations of the public and employing the highest levels of technical mastery.

The subject matter of *Star Wars* is akin to a trip through the annals of cultural and film history. Lucas fused elements from the tales of knights and the myths of heroes with the hi-tech world of spaceships, was inspired by German and Soviet military uniforms, based the Jedi religion on the shaman cults of Central America, and cre-

ated the Empire in the image of an Orwellian dictatorship. The android C-3PO is unmistakably based on the machine woman from Fritz Lang's *Metropolis* (1926), and the concluding hero-honoring ceremony is an obvious reference to Leni Riefenstahl's Nazi party film, *The Triumph of the Will* (*Triumph des Willens*, 1935). In short, with *Star Wars*, an intercultural super-cosmos was created, containing something for every audience member to recognize.

The real highlight, however, was that Lucas's film, despite its complex plot, tells a story easily reduced to the battle of good versus evil. *Star Wars* is not a story of broken heroes. Lucas sends clearly defined characters into battle, and the audience is never left in doubt as to who will triumph in the end.

6 Budget getaway: protocol droid C-3PO (Anthony Daniels) speaks millions of languages; but unlike brave little R2-D2, he's an exasperating penny-pincher.

7 Putting their lives on the line for a pleasant tomorrow: Princess Leia and Luke Skywalker (Mark Hamill).

8 Everyday life in the not-too-distant future: the accoutrements of the *Star Wars* universe is sometimes credibly and recognizably shabby.

"It's a terrifically entertaining war story, it has memorable characters and it is visually compelling. What more do we want in movies?" *San Francisco Chronicle*

The result is that the science-fiction opus became an effortlessly digestible mixture of vignettes, whose charm lay not in complicated conceptual worlds, but rather in its fantastic moments and visual spectacles. It was these moments that made the film an ideal springboard for the budding entertainment industry of video and computer games. The space battles were replicated and prolonged on consoles and monitors all over the world, helping to reduce the time between episodes …

EP

ANNIE HALL ♟♟♟♟

1977 - USA - 93 MIN.

DIRECTOR
WOODY ALLEN (*1935)

SCREENPLAY
WOODY ALLEN, MARSHALL BRICKMAN

DIRECTOR OF PHOTOGRAPHY
GORDON WILLIS

EDITING
RALPH ROSENBLUM, WENDY GREENE BRICMONT

MUSIC
CARMEN LOMBARDO, ISHAM JONES

PRODUCTION
CHARLES H. JOFFE, JACK ROLLINS
for UNITED ARTISTS

STARRING
WOODY ALLEN (Alvy Singer), DIANE KEATON (Annie Hall),
TONY ROBERTS (Rob), CAROL KANE (Allison), PAUL SIMON (Tony Lacey),
COLLEEN DEWHURST (Mother Hall), JANET MARGOLIN (Robin),
SHELLEY DUVALL (Pam), CHRISTOPHER WALKEN (Duane Hall),
SIGOURNEY WEAVER (Alvy's Date), BEVERLY D'ANGELO (TV Actress)

ACADEMY AWARDS 1977
OSCARS for BEST PICTURE (Charles H. Joffe), BEST DIRECTOR (Woody Allen),
BEST ACTRESS (Diane Keaton), and BEST ORIGINAL SCREENPLAY
(Woody Allen, Marshall Brickman)

WOODY
ALLEN

DIANE
KEATON

TONY
ROBERTS

CAROL
KANE

PAUL
SIMON

JANET
MARGOLIN

SHELLEY
DUVALL

CHRISTOPHER
WALKEN

COLLEEN
DEWHURST

"ANNIE HALL"

A nervous romance.

A JACK ROLLINS - CHARLES H. JOFFE PRODUCTION

Written by WOODY ALLEN and MARSHALL BRICKMAN • Directed by WOODY ALLEN

"You know, it's one thing about intellectuals, they prove that you can be absolutely brilliant and have no idea what's going on."

"There's an old joke. Two elderly women are at a Catskills mountain resort, and one of them says: 'Boy, the food at this place is really terrible.' The other one says, 'Yeah, I know, and such … small portions.' Well, that's essentially how I feel about life," says *Annie Hall*'s actual protagonist, Alvy Singer (Woody Allen) at the top of the film. "[It's] full of loneliness and misery and suffering and unhappiness, and it's all over much too quickly."

Singer is a stand-up comedian, professional cynic, and full-time misanthrope. When a big tall blond crew-cutted guy in a record store tells him that Wagner is on sale this week, Jewish Alvy knows exactly how to take it. He also despises Los Angeles for being a city whose only cultural advantage is that you can make a right turn on a red light. What ties this seemingly unrelated hodge-podge of scenes and sketches pieced together by editor Ralph Rosenblum from a heap of over 50,000 feet of film is Alvy's relationship to the movie's title character, Annie Hall.

We meet the couple after the two of them have called it quits for the very last time, and then take an endearing yet heartbreaking trip with them down memory lane to discover what led to the demise of their year-long romance. Annie (Diane Keaton) is the quintessential pseudo-intellectual, a caricature of the urban woman. Alvy brands her as eternally flawed for being born with original sin – she grew up in rural America. On the other hand Alvy's condemning remarks about everyone and everything (including himself) are just his way of concealing his own unique, neurotic blend of self-loathing, self-pity, and self-worship, which not even 15 years of therapy could cure him of. As he explains in a TV interview he was deemed "4-P" by a personality assessment test: a hostage in the event of war.

Allen biographer Marion Meade rightly stated that *Annie Hall* could have just as easily been entitled *Alvy Singer* or even better, *Allan Konigsberg*, Woody Allen's given name. The Alvy character is an unmistakable self-portrait of the director, who himself started out as a gag writer for stand-up comics. Up until three weeks before the premiere, Allen insisted that the film be called *Anhedonia* (the debilitating absence of pleasure or the ability to

DIANE KEATON In a quirkily perfect performance that won her the Best Actress Oscar, Woody Allen's then flame Diane Keaton reveals Annie Hall's and her own zany yet huggable nature through the character's stumbling, flailing gestures. These are reinforced by self-conscious, shyly banal statements, particularly her self-effacing "La-dee-dah." The similarities between these two women include their over the top and "not quite with it" manner as well as their taste in clothing, which according to Allen, includes an affinity for football jerseys matched to skirts, combat boots, and mittens. Given all this, it should come as no surprise that Keaton's original surname was used for the character.

The actress born on January 5, 1946, in Los Angeles, met Allen in 1969 while acting with him in his Broadway play *Play it Again, Sam*. A few years later, she appeared for the first time in an often-overlooked performance at the side of Al Pacino in the role of Michael Corleone's wife in Francis Ford Coppola's *Godfather* trilogy (1972, 1974, 1990).

She worked on numerous Woody Allen films, both before and after their relationship came to an end. In 1981, she collaborated with Warren Beatty, with whom she was also romantically involved for some time, on the film *Reds*. Before long, Keaton proved she had what it took to join the male-dominated world of directing and has been making pictures and TV shows, including an episode of the legendary TV show *Twin Peaks*, since the 1980s. Her 1995 work *Unstrung Heroes* is a little-known masterpiece in filmmaking. Her 1996 acting and comedic bravado in *The First Wives Club* (1996) and dramatic eloquence in *Marvin's Room* (1996) reconfirmed her star appeal. Today, it is hard to imagine that this star in her own right was once inextricably tied up with Allen.

experience it). Arthur Krim, head of United Artists and Allen's paternal role model, allegedly threatened to throw himself out the window if he went through with it.

The almost non-existent cinematic structure of the piece allowed Allen to pack the movie full of amusing quips and snide remarks; more concisely, it supplied him with a vehicle for unabated hilarity. Nonetheless, *Annie Hall* remains a particularly significant work for two main reasons. The first being that the director makes a point of tweaking classic modes of cinematic depictions of reality and storytelling. Whereas he filmed his 1969 piece *Take*

"**Personal as the story he is telling may be, what separates this film from Allen's own past work and most other recent comedy is its general believability. His central figures and all who cross their paths are recognizable contemporary types. Most of us have even shared a lot of their fantasies.**" *Time Magazine*

DINO DE LAURENTIIS PRESENTS
INGMAR BERGMAN
"FACE TO FACE"
Starring
LIV ULLMANN
Directed and Produced by INGMAR BERGMAN · Film
A Paramount Release

1 He'd never join a club that would have him as a member: Alvy Singer is Woody Allen's filmic alter ego.

2 A walk on the mild side: neurotic New Yorkers Annie (Diane Keaton), Alvy, and Dick (Dick Cavett) analyze life, art, and above all themselves.

3 New York is full of interesting, undiscovered places to hang out …

4 Uppers and downers: Alvy reveres European cinema – and especially Ingmar Bergman.

the Money and Run (1969) in the style of a news exposé, Annie Hall is a veritable cornucopia of narrative conventions and even manages to weave in an animated sequence. Time and again, Alvy directly addresses his audience sitting in the theater. Such is the case in a movie ticket line, when he wishes to one-up and embarrass the wannabe film buff who loudly pontificates, claims to teach a course on TV, Media and Culture at Columbia University, and quotes extensively from influential Canadian media theorist Marshall McLuhan. Alvy quickly wins their debate by surreally calling upon McLuhan to personally step in and set matters straight. In another memorable sequence, Allen uses a split screen to illustrate two incompatible worlds, as Alvy's New York Jewish family is compared in similar, juxtaposed dinner scenes to Annie's family. On the left third of the screen is the brightly lit, affluent, politely gracious, aloof, and sober Hall family discussing subjects such as the Christmas play and the 4-H Club. On the right two-thirds

of the screen is a darkly lit, sloppy and informal, noisily argumentative, competitively babbling Singer family talking about illness (diabetes, heart disease) and unemployment (illustrating that Alvy's argumentative nature and fear of marriage were inherited from his family). The genius of the episode is born out of the actual conversation of the two families that takes place *across* this divided split screen. This brand of narrative anarchy was both a liberating artistic breakthrough and a triumph for Allen.

The second significant achievement for Allen that came out of *Annie Hall* was the creation of his alter ego, which finally succeeded in distancing him from his purely comic self. Since this picture, Allen's cosmopolitan neurotic has been a free-floating entity who can be readily integrated into the context of more serious pieces like *Hannah and Her Sisters* (1985) and *Husbands and Wives* (1992), or just observe the action from the sidelines as in his 1978 drama, *Interiors* (1978).   SH

THE DEER HUNTER ♟♟♟♟♟

1978 - USA - 183 MIN.

DIRECTOR
MICHAEL CIMINO (*1943)

SCREENPLAY
DERIC WASHBURN, MICHAEL CIMINO,
LOUIS GARFINKLE, QUINN K. REDEKER

DIRECTOR OF PHOTOGRAPHY
VILMOS ZSIGMOND

EDITING
PETER ZINNER

MUSIC
STANLEY MYERS

PRODUCTION
BARRY SPIKINGS, MICHAEL DEELEY, MICHAEL CIMINO,
JOHN PEVERALL for EMI FILMS LTD., UNIVERSAL PICTURES

STARRING
ROBERT DE NIRO (Michael), JOHN CAZALE (Stan),
JOHN SAVAGE (Steven), CHRISTOPHER WALKEN (Nick),
MERYL STREEP (Linda), GEORGE DZUNDZA (John),
CHUCK ASPEGREN (Axel), SHIRLEY STOLER (Steven's Mother),
RUTANYA ALDA (Angela), PIERRE SEGUI (Julien)

ACADEMY AWARDS 1978
OSCARS for BEST FILM (Barry Spikings, Michael Deeley, Michael Cimino, John Peverall),
BEST DIRECTOR (Michael Cimino), BEST SUPPORTING ACTOR (Christopher Walken),
BEST FILM EDITING (Peter Zinner), and BEST SOUND
(C. Darin Knight, Richard Portman, Aaron Rochin, William L. McCaughey)

THE DEER HUNTER

EMI Films present

ROBERT DE NIRO IN A **MICHAEL CIMINO** Film **THE DEER HUNTER**

co-starring

JOHN CAZALE · JOHN SAVAGE · MERYL STREEP · CHRISTOPHER WALKEN

Music composed by STANLEY MYERS · Director of Photography VILMOS ZSIGMOND, A.S.C.

Associate Producers MARION ROSENBERG · JOANN CARELLI · Production Consultant JOANN CARELLI

Story by MICHAEL CIMINO, DERIC WASHBURN and LOUIS GARFINKLE, QUINN K. REDEKER

Screenplay by DERIC WASHBURN · Produced by BARRY SPIKINGS · MICHAEL DEELEY · MICHAEL CIMINO and JOHN PEVERALL

Directed by **MICHAEL CIMINO**

Technicolor® · Panavision® ☐☐ DOLBY SYSTEM® Stereo Distributed by EMI Films Limited ©1978 by EMI Films, Inc.

"One shot is what it's all about. A deer has to be taken with one shot."

There are films that lose all their magic as soon as you know how they end; and there are others that keep their thrill even after several viewings. One of the cinema's undying magic moments is the scene at the end of *The Deer Hunter*, in which Nick (Christopher Walken) walks out of the back room of a Saigon gambling den with a red scarf around his head. His old friend Michael (Robert De Niro) steps towards him – he wants him to come home. But Nick can no longer recognize him; he's spent too long with his temple pressed to the barrel of a revolver with just one bullet in the chamber. He's gambled with his life so often,

he can't believe it's still his. He moves towards the crowded gaming table with a bunch of banknotes in his hand. Michael tries in vain to persuade him to leave. And suddenly there's a flicker of recognition in Nick's eyes. He laughs, takes the gun, holds it to his head and pulls the trigger.

It's the end of the '60s. Michael, Nick, and Steven (John Savage), three friends from a steel town in Pennsylvania, are sent to Vietnam. By coincidence, they meet again in the midst of war. And by misfortune, they end up in the hands of the Vietcong. The prisoners are forced to

---

MICHAEL CIMINO His films are always controversial: *The Deer Hunter* (1978) was showered with Oscars in Hollywood and condemned as a falsification of the Vietnam War in Europe. The epic late Western *Heaven's Gate* (1980) was hailed as a masterpiece in Europe, and decried as a "catastrophe" in the USA. *Year of the Dragon* (1985), in which a sole cop takes on the Chinese mafia in New York, brought accusations of racism. *The Sicilian* (1987), an opulent biography of the Sicilian popular hero Salvatore Giuliano, was dismissed as historical kitsch.

Michael Cimino (*1943) came to filmmaking after studying architecture and painting. By the end of the '60s, he was making commercials. In 1973, he joined with John Milius to write the screenplay to *Magnum Force*, starring Clint Eastwood. Cimino's first feature film was *Thunderbolt and Lightfoot* (1974), a tragicomic thriller about a gangster in search of his money, with Eastwood and Jeff Bridges in the leading roles. The debut signaled some of the motifs that would be found throughout Cimino's work: male friendship, detailed milieu studies, and gorgeous landscape panoramas. His expensive obsession with authenticity drove United Artists to bankruptcy, and to this day, *Heaven's Gate* is a synonym for megaflops. Although his last film *The Sunchaser* (1996) was a fairly conventional effort, Michael Cimino is still regarded as one of the most visually brilliant directors in America.

1 War on the home front: Linda (Meryl Streep) and Michael (Robert De Niro) tackle daily life and its many ghosts.

2 Birds of prey: Michael and Nick (Christopher Walken) on a hunting trip in the mountains.

3 Fun and games in Clairton, Pennsylvania. Cimino shot the Clairton scenes in eight separate locations to breathe life into the fictitious town.

"There can be no quarrel about the acting. De Niro, Walken, John Savage, as another Clairton pal who goes to war, and Meryl Streep, as a woman left behind, are all top actors in extraordinary form." *Time Magazine*

play Russian roulette while their captors lay bets on the outcome. Finally, only Michael and Nick are left, face-to-face across the table. Michael demands three bullets instead of one, in order to raise the stakes. His ruse is successful: the two friends overcome the Vietcong guerillas, free Steven from the "tiger cage" (a half-submerged bamboo basket) and flee for their lives. But Michael is the only

one who makes it home intact. Steven loses his legs, and Nick gets stuck in Saigon, making money with the game of death.

Only around one-third of this great epic takes place in Vietnam – the middle part. These are among the most impressive images of war ever filmed. The contempt for human life so typical of any war – the hatred, the power-

4 Caught in the crossfire: Robert De Niro called this role "his toughest yet" after shooting was completed.

5 "One of the most frightening, unbearably tense sequences ever filmed – and the most violent excoriation of violence in screen history," wrote *Newsweek*.

6 Secret admirer: back from the war, decorated soldier Michael visits the true love of his life – Nick's girl, Linda.

lessness, the fear, and the pride – Michael Cimino brings all these together in a single symbolic action: Russian roulette. Yet Cimino shows the Americans purely as victims of the Vietnam War, and this provoked a lot of protest, especially in Europe. The Americans, it was claimed, were much more guilty than their opponents of torturing POWs. The film was accused of being racist, and the controversy came to a head at the Berlin Film Festival in 1979, as the Soviet Union, followed by the rest of the Eastern Bloc, withdrew all

its films in protest. But Cimino is not even attempting to provide a political commentary to the Vietnam War. Instead, his film tells the story of people uprooted from everything they used to call home, and it shows the destruction of everything that once made friendship possible. The first hour of the film is devoted to the rituals of the two friends, Michael and Nick. We see their last day in the steel mill; we see them drinking with their buddies from the little community of Belorussian immigrants; we see their wild

Equally at ease in the lyrical and the realistic modes, a virtuoso of the shocking image who never loses sight of the whole, a consummate master of his technique, Michael Cimino is a supremely accomplished filmmaker."

Le Monde

celebrations at Steven's wedding reception, after the Russian Orthodox ceremony. One last time before Vietnam, the friends go hunting in the mountains of Pennsylvania, a pristine contrast to the dirty steel town. Michael's hunting ambition, to kill a deer with a single shot, will not survive his experiences in Vietnam. Indeed, when he returns in the third part of the film, he'll have difficulties even finding his home – because someone's missing, and he's made a promise. That's why he leaves once more, to search for Nick in Saigon.

At the end, the little group of mourners in the bar will strike up "God Bless America," but their rendition of the hymn is anything but triumphant. These people are the walking wounded, and each of them has lost something: a friend, physical wholeness, trust in life, or hope for the future. The fault lies with America; and yet America is their home, a part of their very selves. In *The Deer Hunter*, Cimino shows us this painful contradiction, and gives us a subtle, exact, and outstandingly photographed portrait of American society after Vietnam.   NM

THE TIN DRUM 🏆

DIE BLECHTROMMEL/LE TAMBOUR

1979 - FRG / FRANCE / POLAND / YUGOSLAVIA - 145 MIN.

DIRECTOR

VOLKER SCHLÖNDORFF (*1939)

SCREENPLAY

JEAN-CLAUDE CARRIÈRE, VOLKER SCHLÖNDORFF, FRANZ SEITZ,
based on the novel of the same name by GÜNTER GRASS

DIRECTOR OF PHOTOGRAPHY

IGOR LUTHER

EDITING

SUZANNE BARON

MUSIC

MAURICE JARRE, FRIEDRICH MEYER

PRODUCTION

FRANZ SEITZ, ANATOLE DAUMAN for BIOSKOP FILM, ARTÉMIS PRODUCTIONS,
ARGOS FILMS, HALLELUJAH FILMS

STARRING

DAVID BENNENT (Oskar Matzerath), ANGELA WINKLER (Agnes Matzerath),
MARIO ADORF (Alfred Matzerath), DANIEL OLBRYCHSKI (Jan Bronski),
KATHARINA THALBACH (Maria), HEINZ BENNENT (Greff),
ANDRÉA FERRÉOL (Lina Greff), CHARLES AZNAVOUR (Sigismund Markus),
MARIELLA OLIVERI (Roswitha), ILSE PAGÉ (Gretchen Scheffler),
OTTO SANDER (The Musician Meyn)

ACADEMY AWARDS 1979

OSCAR for BEST FOREIGN FILM

IFF CANNES 1979

GOLDEN PALM (Volker Schlöndorff)

Der Film
nach dem Roman
von Günther Grass
Die Blechtrommel
Ein Film von
Volker Schlöndorff
Im Verleih UIP

"I first saw the light of the world in the form of a 60-watt bulb."

The film starts and ends in a field of potatoes. "I begin long before me," says the narrator, and describes the events that led to the conception of his mother. We see policemen pursuing a man, before a country girl grants him refuge under her voluminous skirts, where matters take their course. The begetting of Oskar, our narrator, is no less strange: his kindly mother Agnes (Angela Winkler) is married to the loudmouthed grocer Alfred Matzerath (Mario Adorf) and in love with the sensitive Pole, Jan Bronski (Daniel Olbrychski). Oskar is conceived "within this trinity." When he's born, his mother promises him a tin drum; on his third birthday he gets it. And on the same day, already disgusted by the drunken, gluttonous, cacophonous world of the adults around him, he makes an important decision: he's going to stay small. He throws himself down the cellar stairs and immediately stops growing. For the next 18 years, he'll go through life in the body of a three-year-old, with a tin drum hanging around his neck. And anyone who tries to take this drum away from him will be subjected to little Oskar's unearthly, glass-shattering scream.

Oskar is no normal child. From the day he's born, he can think and make decisions for himself; and his strangeness sets him apart. *The Tin Drum* is an opulent panorama of German-Polish history, seen through the eyes of an outsider. We are witness to the years between 1899 and 1945, from the peaceful coexistence of Germans and Poles in Danzig, to the German attack on the city, to Oskar's flight westwards as the war draws to a close. In the film's final image, the camera watches from the potato field as he fades into the distance. Tectonic shifts in politics are

VOLKER SCHLÖNDORFF The German weekly *Die Zeit* once had the following to say about Volker Schlöndorff: "Together with Fassbinder, he's undoubtedly the most skilled craftsman in German cinema; but he's not a director whose films can be said to add up to an inimitable style." Yet most of his films can be brought under a single heading: literary adaptations. So Volker Schlöndorff was perhaps an ideal director for *The Tin Drum (Die Blechtrommel / Le Tambour*, 1979).

He learned his trade in the Paris of the Existentialists and the Nouvelle Vague. He assisted Jean-Pierre Melville and Louis Malle before making *Young Toerless (Der junge Törless / Les Désarrois de l'élève Törless)* in 1966 – based on a story by Robert Musil. The works of other great writers would follow: Heinrich von Kleist *(Michael Kohlhaas – der Rebell*, 1969), Marcel Proust (*Swann in Love / Eine Liebe von Swann / Un amour de Swann*, 1983), and Arthur Miller (*Death of a Salesman*, 1985). In the '70s, he turned his attention to the contemporary political scene. Together with his then wife Margarethe von Trotta, he made *The Lost Honor of Katharina Blum (Die verlorene Ehre der Katharina Blum*, 1975), based on a short novel by Heinrich Böll. He then took part in a collective project involving directors such as Alexander Kluge, Rainer Werner Fassbinder and others: *Germany in Autumn (Deutschland im Herbst*, 1977/78) described the atmosphere in the country after the abduction of Hanns Martin Schleyer by the Red Army Faction, otherwise known as the Baader-Meinhof Group. In 1999, Schlöndorff returned to this theme in the drama *Legends of Rita (Die Stille nach dem Schuss)*, which tells the story of former terrorists gone to ground in East Germany.

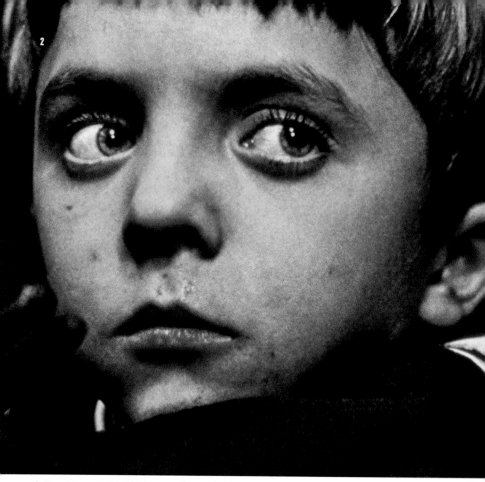

1 Toy soldier: on his third birthday, Oskar Matzerath (David Bennent) is given a tin drum…

2 … and, disgusted at the adult world, he resolves to stop growing immediately.

3 Sins of the fatherland: Oskar's father, grocer Matzerath (Mario Adorf), is a fervent fan of Adolf Hitler.

> ## "Schlöndorff deliberately looked for a simpler narrative style. Whole fragments of the book were simply left out. Yet I still feel that he's succeeded in casting a new light on the whole story." *Günter Grass in: Sequenz*

made visible in tiny details, as when Beethoven's portrait makes way for Hitler's. Oskar takes no sides in all this; he remains an outsider. Once, however, his drumming causes chaos at a Nazi meeting. Oskar carries on drumming till everyone present is swaying happily to the strains of "The Blue Danube." It's reminiscent of the scene in *Casablanca* (1942), where the "Marseillaise" does battle with "Die Wacht am Rhein." On another occasion, Oskar lets the Nazis draw him in: he meets some kindred spirits at a circus, dwarves employed as clowns and later as "a tonic for the troops." Oskar joins them, and soon he too is wearing a Nazi uniform.

If the story is episodic and discontinuous, the cinematic style is a riot. Adapted from the novel by Nobel Prize–winner Günter Grass, the film is a kind of comical yarn, a burlesque bubbling over with ideas, by turns naturalistic (as in the unforgettable scene in which a horse's head is used to catch eels), grotesque (Oskar's view from the womb), or even slapstick (when Oskar's grandfather is chased across the field in a jumpy, flickering silent-film sequence). These disparate elements are held together by Oskar's precocious and knowing off-screen commentary. The actor who plays Oskar is perhaps the film's most fortunate find. While planning the filming of what the German weekly *Die Zeit* called "the most unfilmable novel ever written," Volker Schlöndorff's attention was drawn to the 12-year-old David Bennent. The son of the well-known German actor Heinz Bennent, he suffers from a growth

"A very German fresco: world history seen and experienced from below. Huge, spectacular images, held together by tiny Oskar." *Volker Schlöndorff*

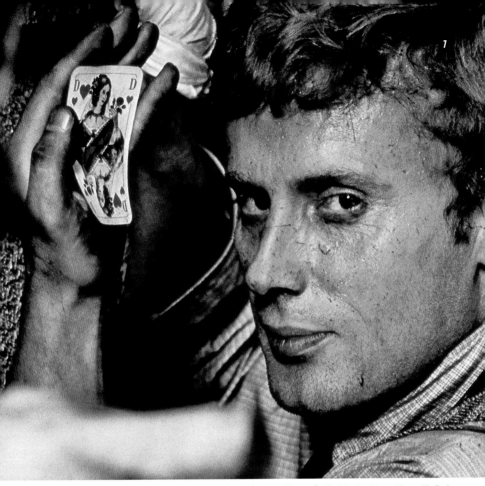

4 Maid to order: a belly button full of sherbet marks Oskar's first sexual experience with servant Maria (Katharina Thalbach).

5 Marching band: Oskar's musical interludes disrupt his mother's

regular Thursday rendezvous with Jan.

6 An officer and a gentleman: Oskar falls in love with the midget Roswitha (Mariella Oliveri).

7 The joker's wild: gambler and ladies' man, Jan Bronski (Daniel Olbrychski), is also an antifascist.

disorder. He brings a wonderful seriousness, depth, and presence to the role of Oskar. Schlöndorff was so delighted by David Bennent that he decided not to film the part of the book that takes place after 1945, when Oskar grows up – for he couldn't face replacing Bennent with another actor. In the '80s, Schlöndorff wrote the screenplay for a follow-up, but the film was never made.

In Cannes, *The Tin Drum* shared the Golden Palm with *Apocalypse Now* (1979), and in 1980 it won the Oscar for Best Foreign Film. And in 1997 came a suitably absurd epilogue: a judge in Oklahoma City had videos of *The Tin Drum* confiscated, saying the film was obscene because it showed a person under the age of 18 indulging in sexual intercourse. HJK

MAD MAX

1979 - AUSTRALIA - 93 MIN.

DIRECTOR
GEORGE MILLER (*1945)

SCREENPLAY
JAMES MCCAUSLAND, GEORGE MILLER

DIRECTOR OF PHOTOGRAPHY
DAVID EGGBY

MUSIC
BRIAN MAY

EDITING
TONY PATERSON, CLIFF HAYES

PRODUCTION
BYRON KENNEDY for MAD MAX FILMS,
KENNEDY MILLER PRODUCTIONS, CROSSROADS

STARRING
MEL GIBSON (Max Rockatansky), JOANNE SAMUEL (Jessie Rockatansky),
HUGH KEAYS-BYRNE (Toecutter), STEVE BISLEY (Jim Goose),
ROGER WARD (Fifi Macaffee), TIM BURNS (Johnny),
VINCENT GIL (Nightrider), GEOFF PARRY (Bubba Zanetti),
DAVID BRACKS (Mudguts), PAUL JOHNSTONE (Cundalini)

"You've seen it! ... You've heard it! ... and you're still asking questions?"

He's simply trying to make sense of it all, policeman Max Rockatansky (Mel Gibson) explains to his wife Jessie (Joanne Samuel), after one of his colleagues is burned alive by a marauding gang of rockers. But he is unable to unearth any explanation.

Max is not alone in his helplessness. Indeed, Australian director George Miller's low-budget production also gives the audience no explanation for the openly waged "war" between cops and rockers. A blend-in at the beginning of the film succinctly identifies the time and location of the plot: "Somewhere in the near future." A street sign on a dusty highway specifies that "Anarchy Road" stretches from this point on, and another sign displays the number of people who have recently died in the area. Without further ado comes the spectacular car chase between the

Nightrider (Vincent Gil), who has declared himself a gas-propelled suicide machine, and the custodians of the law, for whom the murderous race on the desolate country highways is apparently just as much fun as it is for the psychopathic rocker. After several spectacular stunts and a half dozen crashes, he stalls – ultimately there is one obstacle too many on the highway.

Logic plays virtually no role in the story of the worn-down "Interceptor," Max, who turns into a merciless avenger after a band of bikers under the leadership of Toecutter (Hugh Keays-Byrne) murders his wife and child: although the adversaries never seek each other out, they continually meet.

Though the plot of *Mad Max* could have sprung directly from a vengeance Western of the 1950s, the

STUNTS A film like *Mad Max* (1979) certainly doesn't belong to those cinematic masterpieces noted for their sleek character portraits or philosophical depths. But even virulent opponents of the film are forced to recognize director George Miller's sovereign command of cinematic forms of expression and the technical brilliance of the stunts coordinated by Grant Page. Presented as a visual attraction, the circus-like perfection of the stunts points to the inception of the cinema – the markets and vaudeville shows where nickelodeons and cinematographs served as entertainment for a wide public. In the early days of the industry (in American films at least), stuntmen were simply extras who realized their chances of employment would increase if they mastered skills not everyone could master. In the labor-divided world of film, a profession quickly developed out of this realization that soon included not only the use of body doubles in dangerous situations, but also the coordination (and dramatization) of action sequences. A special sort of daring was not required, but the opposite: technical perfection and risk minimization are paramount for the stunt coordinator because ultimately a botched take can cost the production not only money, but more importantly, the lives of the stuntmen.

3

1 Officer down: when the highway's a battlefield, there are bound to be some casualties.

2 A light breather: Max (Mel Gibson) will stop at nothing to avenge his murdered family.

3 Remodeling: a rocker practices for the demolition derby.

4 The bad boys of Melbourne: the future's tax collectors.

5 Car on the barbie: *Mad Max* has some grilling action scenes.

scenery and the characters have a comic-like stylization; the protagonists speak in memorable bubbles, and they are motivated by the basic joy of movement.

In a way, *Mad Max* seems like the final stopover in a string of films like Dennis Hopper's *Easy Rider* (1969) and Richard C. Safarian's *Vanishing Point* (1970), which at the beginning of the decade raised the car and/or motorcycle into the consummate expression of individual freedom. But in *Two-Lane Blacktop* (1971) director Monte Hellman had already signified the motor-madness of his heroes as an element of their communication disorders. In *Mad Max*, all that is left for the protagonists is pointless violence.

But we should not label this as social criticism – the film is based on the commercial appeal of action and violence, and accentuates them as cleverly constructed highlights within the plot. Ultimately, it is an exploitative product.

Nonetheless, George Miller only seldom dramatizes the violence against people as the focal point of the images, with plot-related aspects remaining in the foreground (at one point a biker's arm is ripped off). Often the enormously violent and powerful impression of the film is a result of the dynamic montage. The most horrifying details are thus left to the viewer's imagination. In the scene in which the bikers kill Max's family, Jessie and the child run into the middle of the street while the rockers steadily approach on their bikes from the distance. After the edit, the bikers have already sped past the camera and Jessie's fate is simply suggested by a stray shoe that tumbles to the side of the road. And when Max belatedly arrives on the scene, the camera retains a wide shot – one can see him sinking over the corpses on the highway in the distance.

Mel Gibson was a completely unknown actor when he made his debut in the role of Max, as a star could not and would not have taken the risk of participating in the production. But the film offers its hero an exceptionally interesting entrance: Miller combines takes of Max's boots, gloves, leather gear, and sunglasses to create the mythical image of the cool policeman. And when we finally get to see the cop's face, we're almost surprised to look into Gibson's still boyish features.   LP

"*Mad Max* is a Western. It has the same story, but instead of riding horses they are riding motorcycles and cars. People say the Western's dead, but it's not; it's become the car-action film." *Cinema Papers*

APOCALYPSE NOW ♟♟

1979 - USA - 153 MIN.

DIRECTOR
FRANCIS FORD COPPOLA (*1939)

SCREENPLAY
JOHN MILIUS, FRANCIS FORD COPPOLA, MICHAEL HERR (off-screen commentary),
based on motifs from the novella *Heart of Darkness* by JOSEPH CONRAD

DIRECTOR OF PHOTOGRAPHY
VITTORIO STORARO

EDITING
LISA FRUCHTMAN, GERALD B. GREENBERG, RICHARD MARKS, WALTER MURCH

MUSIC
CARMINE COPPOLA, FRANCIS FORD
COPPOLA, THE DOORS (Song: "The End")

PRODUCTION
FRANCIS FORD COPPOLA for ZOETROPE CORPORATION, OMNI ZOETROPE

STARRING
MARLON BRANDO (Colonel Walter E. Kurtz),
ROBERT DUVALL (Lieutenant Colonel William Kilgore),
MARTIN SHEEN (Captain Benjamin L. Willard), FREDERIC FORREST ("Chef" Jay Hicks),
ALBERT HALL (Chief Quartermaster Phillips), SAM BOTTOMS (Lance B. Johnson),
LAURENCE FISHBURNE (Tyrone "Clean" Miller), DENNIS HOPPER (Photo-journalist),
G. D. SPRADLIN (General R. Corman), HARRISON FORD (Colonel G. Lucas)

ACADEMY AWARDS 1979
OSCARS for BEST CINEMATOGRAPHY (Vittorio Storaro), and BEST SOUND
(Walter Murch, Mark Berger, Richard Beggs, Nathan Boxer)

IFF CANNES 1979
GOLDEN PALM (Francis Ford Coppola)

FRANCIS FORD COPPOLA
PRESENTS
Apocalypse Now
MARLON BRANDO ROBERT DUVALL MARTIN SHEEN APOCALYPSE NOW
FREDERIC FORREST ALBERT HALL SAM BOTTOMS LARRY FISHBURNE DENNIS HOPPER
FRANCIS COPPOLA
JOHN MILIUS FRANCIS COPPOLA MICHAEL HERR
FRED ROOS GRAY FREDERICKSON TOM STERNBERG
VITTORIO STORARO DEAN TAVOULARIS RICHARD MARKS
WALTER MURCH CARMINE COPPOLA FRANCIS COPPOLA
United Artists AN OMNI ZOETROPE PRODUCTION

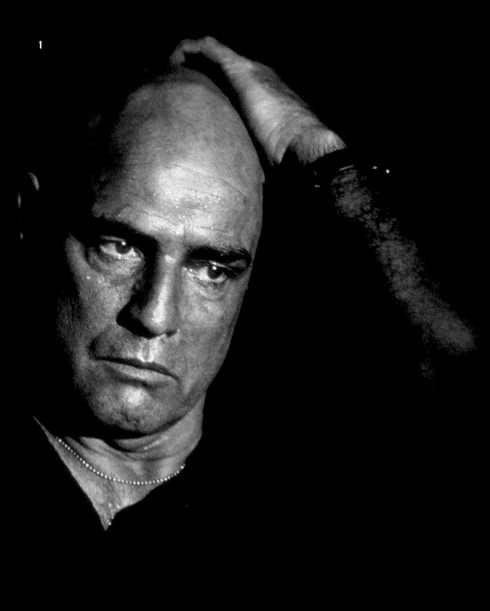

APOCALYPSE NOW

"I love the smell of napalm in the morning."

Vietnam, 1969. Captain Willard (Martin Sheen) is on a top-secret mission to find Colonel Kurtz (Marlon Brando), a highly decorated U.S. Army officer. And when he's located the man, his next task will be to kill him; for Kurtz has clearly gone mad, is defying the control of his superior officers, and now commands a private army in the jungle beyond the Cambodian border. His soldiers are a mixed bag of indigenous people, South Vietnamese, and rogue GIs, whom he uses to his own unauthorized and murderous ends. Willard boards a patrol boat and heads upriver through the rainforest in search of Kurtz; and the further he penetrates into the jungle, the more intensely he and his four comrades experience the horror of war.

No other movie of the '70s received so much attention before it was even released. Francis Ford Coppola was the first director to risk making a big-budget film about the Vietnam War, and he did so with almost demonstrative independence. As his own production company American Zoetrope financed the film, *Apocalypse Now*

could be made without the usual assistance – and interference – from the Pentagon. (Even today, such help is practically obligatory when a war film is made in the United States.) Coppola said later that he had originally aimed to make a lucrative action movie. Instead, the film became an unparalleled nightmare for the celebrated director of *The Godfather* (1972) – and not just in financial terms.

Coppola was looking for a country with a climate similar to Vietnam's, so he chose to film in the Philippines. As the necessary infrastructure was lacking, conditions were quite hair-raising from the word go. The military equipment, for instance, was the result of a deal with the dictatorial President Marcos, who was fighting a civil war against communist rebels while the film was being made. As a consequence, helicopters were sometimes requisitioned from the set at short notice and sent off by the military to take part in real battles. Conditions as tough as these made it hard to find stars willing to take part. Initially, the role of Willard was taken by Harvey Keitel, but he was

FRANCIS FORD COPPOLA Francis Ford Coppola (*1939 in Detroit) enjoyed a sheltered middle-class childhood in a suburb of New York. His father Carmine was a composer and musician who would later write the music to some of his son's films. Coppola studied theater at Hofstra University, then film at UCLA. While still a student, he worked as an assistant director to Roger Corman, who also produced his first feature film, *Dementia 13* (1963). Coppola made his breakthrough at the early age of 31, when his screenplay to *Patton* (1969) was awarded an Oscar.

A short time later, he became world famous as a director – and as the Boy Wonder of the New Hollywood: the Mafia saga *The Godfather* (1972) became one of the biggest hits in movie history and won three Oscars, including Best Film. Two years later, he topped even this: *The Godfather – Part II* (1974) scooped six Academy Awards, including Best Director. In the meantime, Coppola had also made an outstanding movie about an alienated surveillance expert: *The Conversation* (1974), which carried off the Palme d'Or at the Cannes Festival.

In 1976, Coppola began work on the Vietnam film *Apocalypse Now* (1979), which he produced himself, and which came very close to ruining him. But after four years in production, that film also won the Golden Palm and two Oscars, and even recouped the huge sum that had been spent making it. Only two years later, however, the failure of the love story *One from the Heart* (1981) drove him and his production company, American Zoetrope, into horrendous debt. Though he has since directed other films, such as *The Cotton Club* (1984) and *The Godfather – Part III* (1990), none have been as successful as his huge hits of the '70s.

1 Tribal titan: Marlon Brando rocked the screen in his role as Colonel Kurtz although he only appeared at the end of the movie.

2 Battle of the bulge: Captain Willard (Martin Sheen) and the photographer (Dennis Hopper) flesh out the fate of Colonel Kurtz.

3 Duty calls: filmed on location in the Philippines, where helicopters were taken off the set and flown into the front lines of battle.

"My film is not a movie. My film is not about Vietnam. It is Vietnam. That's what it was really like. It was crazy." *Francis Ford Coppola, IFF Cannes*

replaced by the little-known Martin Sheen after only three weeks' filming, as his expressive acting was not to Coppola's taste, and he wanted a more passive protagonist. This was an expensive mistake, but harmless in comparison to the problems the director would later face. There was the deadly typhoon that destroyed the expensive sets; the almost fatal heart attack suffered by Martin Sheen; the difficulty of working with the grossly overweight Brando; and above all, the trouble caused by the director's own constant

departures from the script. As a result, work had to stop on several occasions, and the filming period expanded from four to 15 months. Soon, the 16-million-dollar budget was exhausted, and Coppola – close to physical and mental collapse – was forced to mortgage his own property in order to raise the same sum all over again. The press could smell a disaster of previously unheard of proportions. But though two more years were taken up by post-production, the film ultimately became a box-office hit – despite mixed

reviews, and the fact that other "Vietnam movies" had by then already reached the screen.

The legendary status of *Apocalypse Now* is inseparable from the spectacular circumstances of its making. Many people, including Coppola himself, have drawn an analogy between the Vietnam conflict itself and the agonized struggle to complete the film. It's all the more remarkable, then, that Coppola succeeded in freeing himself, gradually but radically, from the superficial realism that tends to typify the war-film genre. The Vietnam War has often been described as a psychedelic experience, but Coppola and his cameraman Vittorio Storaro created images that actually do justice to the description. Willard's trip upriver, inspired by Joseph Conrad's novella *Heart of*

Darkness, is a journey into the darkness of his own heart, and so the various stages on his journey acquire an increasingly fantastic, dreamlike quality. At the beginning of his odyssey, Willard encounters the surfing fanatic Lieutenant Colonel Kilgore (Robert Duvall), who sends his squad of choppers in to obliterate a peasant village so that he can enjoy the perfect waves on the neighboring beach. Kilgore's insane euphoria is heightened by the musical accompaniment: Wagner's "Ride of the Valkyrie." At this point, Willard is no more than a passive observer of a monstrous spectacle, which is ironically depicted by Coppola as a kind of hi-tech U.S. Cavalry. It's a grimly satirical scene, in which the director makes masterly use of aesthetic conventions for his own purposes.

4 The river wild: civilization on a voyage downstream.

5 The buck stops here: having made it to the end of his journey, Willard is prepared to kill Colonel Kurtz.

"It is not so much an epic account of a grueling war as an incongruous, extravagant monument to artistic self-defeat." *Time Magazine*

Willard's journey terminates in a realm of the dead: Kurtz's bizarre and bloody jungle kingdom, a garishly exotic and obscenely theatrical hell-on-earth. As embodied by Marlon Brando, Kurtz has the quality of a perverted Buddha. When he first receives Willard in his murky temple residence, both men are sunk in the surrounding shadows. At the end of the line, in the heart of darkness, good and evil have grown indistinguishable, and Willard has lost what distance he ever had: Kurtz has become part of his very self. When Willard finally kills him, the act – like an archaic ritual – is at once an exorcism and a manifestation of the darkness at the heart of mankind, a black

stain no civilization will ever erase. Ultimately, it's the cause and the irreducible essence of war – whatever the epoch, and whatever the weapons deployed.

In 2001, Coppola brought out *Apocalypse Now Redux*, a director's cut that was 49 minutes longer. It contains some sequences that had fallen victim to the cutter's shears, and the director says it's the closest possible approximation to his original intentions. Yet although the *Redux* version is undoubtedly somewhat more complex than the original, it constitutes neither a radical alteration to, nor a significant improvement on the original.

JH

RAGING BULL ♟♟

1980 - USA - 129 MIN.

DIRECTOR

MARTIN SCORSESE (*1942)

SCREENPLAY

PAUL SCHRADER, MARDIK MARTIN from the autobiography
of JAKE LA MOTTA together with JOSEPH CARTER and PETER SAVAGE

DIRECTOR OF PHOTOGRAPHY

MICHAEL CHAPMAN

EDITING

THELMA SCHOONMAKER

MUSIC

PIETRO MASCAGNI ("Cavalleria Rusticana"),
diverse songs arranged by ROBBIE ROBERTSON

PRODUCTION

ROBERT CHARTOFF, IRWIN WINKLER
for CHARTOFF-WINKLER PRODUCTIONS, UNITED ARTISTS

STARRING

ROBERT DE NIRO (Jake La Motta), CATHY MORIARTY (Vickie La Motta),
JOE PESCI (Joey La Motta), FRANK VINCENT (Salvy),
NICHOLAS COLASANTO (Tommy Como), THERESA SALDANA (Lenore La Motta),
MARIO GALLO (Mario), FRANK ADONIS (Patsy),
JOSEPH BONO (Guido), FRANK TOPHAM (Toppy)

ACADEMY AWARDS 1980

OSCARS for BEST ACTOR (Robert De Niro),
and BEST EDITING (Thelma Schoonmaker)

ROBERT DE NIRO

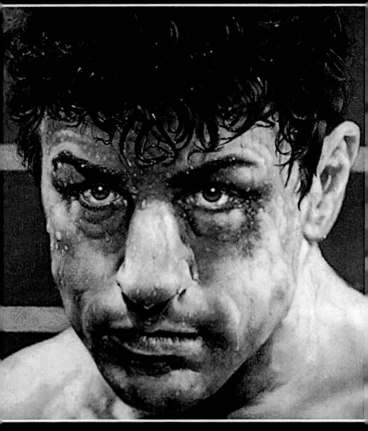

"RAGING BULL"

A ROBERT CHARTOFF·IRWIN WINKLER PRODUCTION
ROBERT DE NIRO
in A MARTIN SCORSESE PICTURE
"RAGING BULL"
Produced in association with PETER SAVAGE   Screenplay by PAUL SCHRADER and MARDIK MARTIN
Based on the book by JAKE LA MOTTA with JOSEPH CARTER and PETER SAVAGE
Director of photography MICHAEL CHAPMAN
Produced by IRWIN WINKLER and ROBERT CHARTOFF   Directed by MARTIN SCORSESE
Read the Bantam Book

R RESTRICTED
UNDER 17 REQUIRES ACCOMPANYING
PARENT OR ADULT GUARDIAN

United Artists

"You didn't get me down, Ray!"

It is the beginning of the 1940s and Jake La Motta (Robert De Niro) is one of the top middleweight boxers in the world. He's the "Raging Bull," famous for an almost inhuman ability to take a beating and notorious for his unpredictable attacks. He's not a stylist, he's a brutal puncher whose strength comes from a deep-seated aggression he is unable to control – inside or outside of the ring. The brunt of Jake's aggression is leveled at his wife, but his brother and manager Joey (Joe Pesci) are also forced to weather his temper. Even in his interaction with the Mafiosi from Little Italy, Jake is anything but diplomatic. This erratic behavior contributes to his continually being denied a title fight. He soon meets Vickie (Cathy Moriarty),

a blonde beauty who is already hanging out with the gangsters of Hell's Kitchen, despite being only 15 years old. Jake gets a divorce and marries her. But he is not calmed down. In fact, his jealous outbursts intensify and he terrorizes everyone around him. When he finally gets the chance to fight for the title in 1949, his predictable demise has been years in the making.

Robert De Niro had long dreamed of acting in a cinematic adaptation of Jake La Motta's autobiography. In the midst of shooting of *Alice Doesn't Live Here Anymore* (1974), he tried to convince Martin Scorsese to direct the project. Though initially unsuccessful, De Niro did not relent. He took another shot at it while Scorsese lay in a hospital

---

MICHAEL CHAPMAN Michael Chapman (*1935 in New York) became one of the most sought-after American cameramen toward the middle of the '70s. He began by working as a camera operator for Gordon Willis, whose "classicism" became a major influence. The films he worked on during this period include Alan J. Pakula's thriller *Klute* (1971) and Coppola's *The Godfather* (1972). In 1973, Chapman became director of photography for the first time in Hal Ashby's tragicomedy *The Last Detail*, followed by the Arctic film *The White Dawn* (1974), the first of four collaborations with Philip Kaufman. Chapman worked as operator once again for Spielberg's *Jaws* (1975) before experiencing his real breakthrough with the legendary Scorsese film *Taxi Driver* (1975), in which he beautifully transmitted the threatening atmosphere of a film noir into color images. Chapman proved his mastery of black-and-white photography with another Scorsese film, *Raging Bull* (1980), for which he received his first Oscar nomination, and later with Carl Reiner's lovely film noir homage, *Dead Men Don't Wear Plaid* (1981). Chapman built on his reputation in the years that followed, but only really hit the limelight again in 1993 when he received his second Oscar nomination for *The Fugitive*. Chapman repeatedly appears in small roles as an actor, and has been directing films himself since 1983, though without the impact he has had as a cameraman.

"I put everything I knew and felt into this film, and I thought it would finish my career. I call it 'kamikaze,' this way of making films: put all of yourself into it, then forget it and start a new life."

Martin Scorsese, in: Martin Scorsese, David Thompson, Ian Christie (Ed.), Scorsese on Scorsese

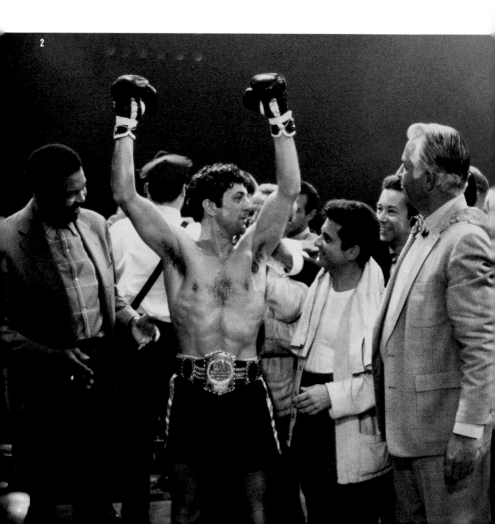

1 Blood, sweat and tears: *Raging Bull* captures the sheer physicality of the fights in merciless close-up.

2 Method acting and a few black eyes: in order to give a convincing depiction of "The Bronx Bull," Robert De Niro spent months training as a boxer, and even fought some fights as an amateur. He was rewarded for his efforts with an Oscar.

3 Professional scene-stealer: Joe Pesci (left) also worked alongside Robert De Niro in the Scorsese master-pieces *Goodfellas* (1989) and *Casino* (1995).

bed, psychologically and physically lacerated by the disaster of *New York, New York* (1977). This time around the director was fascinated by the subject matter, seizing on La Motta's self-destructive life story as a chance to exorcise his own demons. The film therefore focuses less on the boxer's career – the fight scenes are relatively brief – than the story of a man tortured by his own existence, a man who has only himself to blame for his downfall. The fact that La Motta grew up in the same milieu of Italian immigrants that Scorsese knew well from his own childhood intensified his identification with the subject matter.

Raging Bull was the challenge of a lifetime for De Niro. In the role of Jake La Motta, he radically explored the limits of his craft. The convincing physical presence De Niro lends to the violence La Motta turned on himself and

others is as fascinating as it is terrifying. In order to make the fight scenes as believable as possible, he trained – partially under the guidance of La Motta – for months and on several occasions even fought a real bout. Legend has it that De Niro gained over fifty pounds to personify the aging La Motta, who traveled from nightclub to nightclub as a fat has-been entertainer.

The film's technical quality – its skillful sound design and editing – is just as extraordinary as De Niro's Oscar-winning performance, and the rest of the acting. Michael Chapman deserves a special mention for his excellent black-and-white photography, which captures the private life of the boxer with a merciless sobriety that recalls Italian neorealism and the "semi-documentaries" of the '40s. The camera often stands still and focuses on La

4 Sick with jealousy: mindless violence soon characterizes Jake's relationship with wife Vicky (Cathy Moriarty).

5 & 6 A beached whale: De Niro put on 50 pounds to depict Jake La Motta in his decline.

7 That's *amore*: Martin Scorsese, the son of Sicilian immigrants, depicts the Italian milieu in '40s and '50s New York with a documentary filmmaker's attention to detail.

Motta's violent outbursts. Squeezed into the frame, he resembles an animal caught in a cage, unable to come to terms with the lack of space, and powerless to free himself from its constraints. Jake's torturous frustrations are so painfully depicted in these images that the boxing matches begin to seem like a necessary consequence of his life. The extent of his spiritual barrenness becomes clear during the fights. The camera zooms in on the action in the ring, approaching La Motta's subjective perception. Fists pummel body and face from close range, spraying blood and sweat, the images acoustically underscored by dull blows that sound as if they come from the inside out. The violence exploding in these rapidly edited images have an edge of soothing intimacy. It appears that La Motta is only able to truly express himself within the confines of the ring. He is a lonely man for whom punches are not only a reward, but a means of communication.

JH

"An American masterwork, a fusion of Hollywood genre with personal vision couched in images and sounds that are kinetic and visceral, and closer to poetry than pulp." *The Village Voice*

FITZCARRALDO

1981 - FRG - 158 MIN.

DIRECTOR

WERNER HERZOG (*1942)

SCREENPLAY

WERNER HERZOG

DIRECTOR OF PHOTOGRAPHY

THOMAS MAUCH

EDITING

BEATE MAINKA-JELLINGHAUS

MUSIC

POPOL VUH

PRODUCTION

WERNER HERZOG, LUCKI STIPETIC for WERNER HERZOG
FILMPRODUKTION, PRO-JECT FILMPRODUKTION, FILMVERLAG DER AUTOREN, ZDF

STARRING

KLAUS KINSKI (Brian Sweeney Fitzgerald, aka "Fitzcarraldo"),
CLAUDIA CARDINALE (Molly), JOSÉ LEWGOY (Don Aquilino),
MIGUEL ÁNGEL FUENTES (Cholo), PAUL HITTSCHER (Orinoco-Paul),
HUEREQUEQUE ENRIQUE BOHORQUEZ (Cook), GRANDE OTHELO (Stationmaster),
PETER BERLING (Opera Director)

IFF CANNES 1982

SILVER PALM for BEST DIRECTOR (Werner Herzog)

Klaus Kinski in
Fitzcarraldo
Der Film von Werner Herzog
KLAUS KINSKI
CLAUDIA CARDINALE
in »Fitzcarraldo«
mit JOSÉ LEWGOY · MIGUEL ANGEL FUENTES
PAUL HITTSCHER · HUEREQUEQUE ENRIQUE BOHÓRQUEZ
GRANDE OTHELO · PETER BERLING Kamera THOMAS MAUCH Musik POPOL VUH
Produziert von WERNER HERZOG und LUCKI STIPETIC
Eine Werner Herzog Filmproduktion mit der Pro-ject Filmproduktion
im Filmverlag der Autoren, München
FILMVERLAG DER AUTOREN

"I will move a mountain!"

It's the beginning of the 20th century, and it feels like there's a gold rush on the banks of the Amazon. Actually it's a rubber rush, for the market in rubber is booming. And while the businessmen of Iquito rake in the money, Fitzcarraldo (Klaus Kinski) dreams of building an opera house in the middle of the jungle. For the city's rich entrepreneurs, this is no more than another of the eccentric Irishman's mad plans; but after consulting an old map, Fitzcarraldo has a brilliant idea how to finance his dream. On an Amazon tributary, here are countless rubber trees that cannot be exploited because the way is blocked by impassable rapids. Fitzcarraldo's plan is to bypass the rapids by cruising down a neighboring river until he reaches a point where the two watercourses almost meet; there, he will transport his steamship over land. The

adventure begins – but seems doomed to end very quickly, when almost the entire crew abandons ship for fear of the warlike natives. Fitzcarraldo, however, succeeds in winning the Indios over to his side with the help of Enrico Caruso, by winding up the gramophone and broadcasting the tenor's voice into the rainforest. Even when the anticipated narrow strip of land turns out to be a steep hill in the jungle, Fitzcarraldo is undeterred. With the help of the natives, he simply attempts the impossible: dragging the heavy steamship over the mountain.

Fitzcarraldo tells the story of an obsession, and it also seems to be the film of an obsessed man. Werner Herzog had already made a movie with Klaus Kinski in the Peruvian jungle: *Aguirre, Wrath of God* (*Aguirre, der Zorn Gottes*, 1972). But the hair-raising conditions under which

WERNER HERZOG Alongside Rainer Werner Fassbinder, Wim Wenders, and Volker Schlöndorff, Werner Herzog is one of the best-known directors of the New German Cinema. He was born in Munich on September 5, 1942, and grew up in a remote, rural area. An autodidact, he formed his own film production company in 1963. Since then, he has written, directed, and produced more than 60 documentaries and feature films; they focus mainly on social outsiders, with whom Herzog clearly sympathizes. He attracted great attention with five films starring Klaus Kinski in the leading role: *Aguirre, Wrath of God* (*Aguirre, der Zorn Gottes*, 1972); *Nosferatu* (*Nosferatu – Phantom der Nacht*, 1978); *Woyzeck* (1979); *Fitzcarraldo* (1981); and *Cobra Verde* (1987). In 1999, Herzog looked back on his unusual relationship with the eccentric Kinski in the documentary film *My Best Fiend* (*Mein liebster Feind*). In recent years Herzog, more widely known and popular abroad than in his native country, has filmed primarily in the United States.

2

"The whole project was total lunacy – the same stark staring madness the film itself is about. It is the sweat-drenched story of a man besotted with the idea of building an opera in the rotting city of Iquitos, for the sole reason that his heart belongs to Caruso." *Die Zeit*

this second jungle project took place have been matched, if at all, only by those prevailing when Francis Ford Coppola made *Apocalypse Now* (1979). A documentary by Les Blank, *Burden of Dreams* (1982), provides a gripping account of the making of *Fitzcarraldo*. Shooting was dogged by a series of catastrophes: the loss of the original leading actors, Jason Robards and Mick Jagger; involvement in a border war between Peru and Ecuador; droughts, floods, snakebites, and severe accidents. A further shadow was cast by Kinski's notorious outbursts of rage, which (as Herzog reported) were so extreme that an Indio chief even

offered to kill him for the director. Herzog, who knew only too well how unpredictable his star could be, had anticipated such problems, and had not originally planned to cast Kinski; only when Mick Jagger dropped out of the project did Herzog bring Kinski on board as a replacement. But Kinski was, without question, ideal for the role; no one else had his particular charisma, the aura of a lonely and quite possibly insane visionary. It made him the perfect embodiment of a hero who, in the depths of the primeval rainforest, declares the supremacy of art. The leading character is thus a mirror image of the director, to an

3

4

1 No actor embodies geniality and madness as convincingly as Klaus Kinski.

2 The star and the extras: the Brazilian Indians often felt that Kinski was an intruding presence.

3 No trick photography: the ship was really towed by hand across the mountain of the virgin forest.

4 A most difficult star: on account of his unpredictability, Kinski was not originally considered for the part.

But when Mick Jagger and Jason Robards jumped ship, Werner Herzog brought the notorious eccentric on board.

" 'I'm a dream-weaver,' says Herzog. Though it's questionable whether we can dream about Fitzcarraldo, we can see enough of Herzog's own vision to let him do the dreaming for us."

Jeune Cinéma

extent unparalleled in any other Herzog film. In the end, *Fitzcarraldo* is a further fruit of the collaboration between Herzog and his "favorite enemy."

It's possible to argue whether Herzog was justified in his savage determination to see the project through at all costs – a ruthlessness that bears obvious comparisons to Fitzcarraldo himself. What's undeniable is that *Fitzcarraldo*, as a special-effects film, would have been unthinkable without the film team's remarkable readiness to get involved in such a risky, unpredictable project. The film's visionary power is rooted in the fact that one cannot doubt the genuineness of the images it presents; these are pictures we can trust. That ship was really pulled over that mountain by those Indians; we know it for sure, even though we've never seen anything like it in our lives. Herzog's declared intention as a filmmaker is to show things that may have been dreamt but have never yet been seen; in *Fitzcarraldo*, he succeeds in doing so. These are utterly original images, filled with the pathos of veracity. Today, in the age of digital technology and an ironic self-referential cinema of quotations, the effect of these images on the audience may well be even more overwhelming than it was when the film first came out. *Fitzcarraldo* is first-hand film.

JH

5

5 *Fitzcarraldo* was the fourth of five Werner Herzog films in which Kinski played the leading role. Their legendary partnership dates back to 1972 when the two teamed up for *Aguirre, Wrath of God (Aguirre, der Zorn Gottes)*. This project, also shot in a virgin forest, starred Kinski as a power-hungry conquistador.

6 Molly is the only one who believes in Fitzcarraldo's visionary ideas: Claudia Cardinale endows the country madam with an unbridled temper and an equally kind heart characteristic of the lovely Italian actress.

"... The lensing is top-flight, and Kinski is delightfully mad from start to finish. In fact, Herzog's handling of the thesps, non-professionals in particular, is unique. All said and done, this is a fun film. *Fitzcarraldo* is an adult daydream. A magnificent one at that." *Variety*

FANNY AND ALEXANDER ♟♟♟♟

FANNY OCH ALEXANDER

1982 - SWEDEN / FRANCE / FRG - 187 MIN.

DIRECTOR

INGMAR BERGMAN (1918–2007)

SCREENPLAY

INGMAR BERGMAN

DIRECTOR OF PHOTOGRAPHY

SVEN NYKVIST

EDITING

SYLVIA INGEMARSSON

MUSIC

DANIEL BELL

PRODUCTION

JÖRN DONNER for SWEDISH FILMINSTITUTE, SVT DRAMA,
GAUMONT, PERSONAFILM, TOBIS

STARRING

BÖRJE AHLSTEDT (Carl Ekdahl), PERNILLA ALLWIN (Fanny),
BERTIL GUVE (Alexander), ALLAN EDWALL (Oscar), EWA FRÖLING (Emilie),
JARL KULLE (Gustav Adolf Ekdahl), GUNN WÅLLGREN (Helena Ekdahl),
JAN MALMSJÖ (Bishop Edvard Vergerus), HARRIET ANDERSSON (Justina),
ANNA BERGMAN (Hanna Schwartz), LENA OLIN (Rosa)

ACADEMY AWARDS 1983

OSCARS for BEST FOREIGN LANGUAGE FILM (Jörn Donner),
BEST CINEMATOGRAPHY (Sven Nykvist), BEST ART DIRECTION (Anna Asp, Susanne Linghelm),
and BEST COSTUMES (Marik Vos-Lundh)

Fanny och Alexander
En film av Ingmar Bergman

SANDREWS

"Anything can happen, anything is possible and likely. Time and space do not exist. Against a faint background of reality, imagination spins out and weaves new patterns."

In the very first scenes of *Fanny and Alexander*, Ingmar Bergman defines his position and signals his intentions. We see a boy looking at a puppet theater. Layer by layer, he lifts up the painted elements of the decoration. In a similar fashion, he will penetrate and see through the fronts and façades of the adult world. The film's perspective is primarily that of a child, and the drama unfolds before the eyes of Bergman's ten-year-old alter ego.

Alexander (Bertil Guve) and his eight-year-old sister Fanny (Pernilla Allwin) are the youngest members of the Ekdahl clan, which runs the theater in a sleepy Swedish town at the beginning of the 20th century. The grandmother rules the roost with wisdom and forbearance. The Ekdahls' family life is turbulent and colorful, constantly inspiring Alexander to invent new and imaginative games. His ambition is to have a brilliant career on the stage, just like his mother and grandmother, but the death of his father changes everything. At the end of the year of mourning, Emilie (Ewa Fröling), the young widow, marries the bishop, Edvard Vergerus (Jan Malmsjö). For the sake of love and

respectability, she abandons acting and moves into the bishop's residence together with her children. In the strict (and hypocritical) atmosphere of their new home, the children are bullied and harassed. But Alexander is a rebel. Instead of saying grace before meals, he mutters unchristian indecencies, and infuriates his stepfather with childish slyness and cruelty. The bishop retaliates mercilessly, and instead of the love of God, the boy makes the acquaintance of the cane and the humiliating methods of the Inquisition. Home is a puritanical hell and it seems like a miracle when Emilie, Alexander, and Fanny finally manage to escape.

Fanny and Alexander is a baroque and highly dramatic tissue of images in which Ingmar Bergman reworks the raw material of his own childhood. It is no coincidence that the name Ekdahl reminds us of the photographer's family in Ibsen's play *The Wild Duck*, for this is a story about the need for theater – for imagination – in human life. Ingmar Bergman was the son of a pastor, and the film leaves us in no doubt about his attitude towards sanctimonious clergymen for whom love and the fear of God are no

MAGIC LANTERN Alexander possesses not only a puppet theater but a Magic Lantern – Bergman's homage to the medium of moving pictures. This first step towards contemporary cinema was made in the 17th century by Athanasius Kircher, an Austrian Jesuit. The device used a candle and a lens to project an image onto the wall. Inside a casing resembling the normal lanterns of the day, it had a turntable holding little pictures painted on glass. Lens covers were also sometimes used. This entirely mechanical construction made it possible to produce visible movement – sled rides or windmills with turning blades, for example. Around 1820, the invention of limelight introduced a new phase in cinema history. This novel method of lighting did a lot to further the dissemination of the Magic Lantern and the "Phantasmagorias" that followed. Dissolves and surprising effects with movement now became possible. For the first time, rain, snowfall, fire, and the waves of the sea could all be imitated with deceptive accuracy.

1 Peeking into the grown-up world: Alexander (Bertil Guve) and his sister Fanny (Pernilla Allwin).

2 All smiles: a picture-perfect Ekdahl family poses with friends and servants for the annual Christmas photo. Fanny and Alexander are seated in the first row.

3 Nothing but the truth: much like appearing before a court tribunal, Fanny and Alexander often have to account for their actions at Bishop Vergerus's (Jan Malmsjö, right) "humble abode."

4 Saying their goodnight prayers under the bishop's watchful eye was always a trial for Fanny and Alexander.

5 A visit from the great beyond: Oscar (Allan Edwall), Fanny and Alexander's dearly departed father, appears to his son in the form of a ghost and shares some words of comfort.

6 Bacchanal at the Ekdahl manor: the boisterous Christmas celebration that opens the film instantly puts the audience in festive spirits.

more than instruments of power over their fellow human beings.

Oscar Ekdahl, the father of Alexander and Fanny, dies of a heart attack during a rehearsal of *Hamlet*. His role was the Ghost. Later, he will indeed appear to his son from beyond the grave, offering help and support. In this way, Bergman unhesitatingly extends his naturalist novel of family life to include the supernatural. He goes beyond contrasting the Ekdahl household's Dionysian love of life with the oppressive discipline of the Episcopal residence, and explores the fundamental conflict between imagination and reason.

The version made for cinema is far from short, with a running time of three and a half hours. However, the four-part TV version, 312 minutes long, is regarded as the director's cut. For Bergman, *Fanny and Alexander* was a resumé of his entire life and art, and his last work for the cinema. Although he was not idle later, directing a large number of works for the theater and television in the last 25 years of his life. *Fanny and Alexander* was, incidentally, the first foreign-language film in history to receive four Oscars.

RF

"Fanny and Alexander emerges as a sumptuously produced period piece that is also a rich tapestry of childhood memoirs and moods, fear and fancy, employing all the manners and means of the best of cinematic theatrical from high and low comedy to darkest tragedy with detours into the gothic, the ghostly and the gruesome." Variety

SCARFACE

1982/83 - USA - 170 MIN.

DIRECTOR
BRIAN DE PALMA (*1940)

SCREENPLAY
OLIVER STONE

DIRECTOR OF PHOTOGRAPHY
JOHN A. ALONZO

EDITING
JERRY GREENBERG, DAVID RAY

MUSIC
GIORGIO MORODER

PRODUCTION
PETER SAPHIER, MARTIN BREGMAN for UNIVERSAL PICTURES

STARRING
AL PACINO (Tony Montana), STEVEN BAUER (Manny Ray),
MICHELLE PFEIFFER (Elvira), MARY ELIZABETH MASTRANTONIO (Gina),
ROBERT LOGGIA (Frank Lopez), MIRIAM COLON (Mama Montana),
F. MURRAY ABRAHAM (Omar Swarez), PAUL SHENAR (Alejandro Sosa),
HARRIS YULIN (Bernstein), ÁNGEL SALAZAR (Chi Chi)

AL PACINO SCARFACE

In the spring of 1980,
the port at Mariel Harbor
was opened, and thousands
set sail for the United States.
They came in search
of the American Dream.

One of them found it on the
sun-washed avenues of
Miami...wealth, power and
passion beyond
his wildest dreams.

He was Tony Montana.
The world will remember
him by another name
...SCARFACE.

A **MARTIN BREGMAN**
PRODUCTION

A **BRIAN De PALMA**
FILM

AL PACINO
"SCARFACE"

SCREENPLAY BY
OLIVER STONE

MUSIC BY
GIORGIO MORODER

DIRECTOR OF PHOTOGRAPHY
JOHN A. ALONZO
A.S.C.

EXECUTIVE PRODUCER
LOUIS A. STROLLER

PRODUCED BY
MARTIN BREGMAN

DIRECTED BY
BRIAN De PALMA

He loved the American Dream.
With a vengeance.

SCARFACE

"You know what capitalism is? Getting fucked!"

The final scene of this film is the one everybody remembers: Cuban refugee drug lord Tony Montana (Al Pacino) is caught in the gigantic stairwell of his villa, his body riddled with bullets, but he keeps on firing his machine gun unremittingly at his enemies, who stream in through the doorway. Ultimately his body slumps forward, arms spread out in a crucified pose, and he falls headfirst into the fountain in the cavernous foyer. It is a death as violent and merciless as his own life. Perhaps it is a bit too heroic, considering the atrocious trail of murder and mayhem that he left in his wake on the way to the top.

This unsettling epic has often been misunderstood as a brutal action film, but it's a film with many sides. Montana's inability to assert himself without using brute force and his tendency to express affection by humiliating the people he loves lend the film a powerful dramatic effect.

Brian De Palma's remake of Howard Hawks's 1932 classic, *Scarface: Shame of a Nation*, was greeted with harsh reviews, mainly on account of its occasionally graphic depictions of violence. Hawks's *Scarface*, based upon the life of Al Capone, also faced biting criticism because its "negative version of an American entrepreneurial career" (*Filmdienst*), went against etiquette.

De Palma's remake shifts the plot to 1980s Miami, when Fidel Castro briefly opened the Cuban border to allow emigrants out, and used the opportunity to rid Cuba of many of its criminals. Tony Montana and his friend Manny Ray (Steven Bauer) belong to this group and quickly rise from dishwashers to drug millionaires in the greed-driven America of the Reagan era.

Before long, the dark side of this uncompromising and unscrupulous craving for wealth and power comes to

"In this country, you gotta make the money first. Then when you get the money, you get the power. Then when you get the power, then you get the women."

Quotation from film: Tony Montana

1 The slaphappy couple: Tony (Al Pacino) and Elvira's (Michelle Pfeiffer) marriage is soon knocked out by drugs, alcohol, and egomania.

2 A great white among sharks: Tony Montana knows no mercy – not even for those who used to watch his back.

3 Lead poisoning: the closing sequence is among the most controversial in film history.

4 Tony sweeps Elvira off her feet with intoxicating glitz.

5 Knowing how the caged bird sings: Elvira wards off boredom with cocaine and cynicism.

6 Paranoia rides wealth's coattails: Montana senses enemies in every corner.

the fore. Along with excess comes the beginning of the end. "We're getting sloppy," says Montana to his friend and accomplice, now head of his bodyguards, and drifts further and further into a drug-induced stupor and paranoia. Suspicion and hate increasingly exert their influence in Montana's stronghold, where he has secluded himself with his drug-addicted wife, Elvira (Michelle Pfeiffer), and his entourage.

Similar to the Tony "Scarface" Camonte (Paul Muni) character in Hawks's version, Tony Montana is also a lost soul, who as his mother (Miriam Colon) predicts, ultimately destroys everyone he loves. And like its predecessor and model, De Palma's film possesses both a psychological and a political dimension. This is hardly surprising considering that the screenplay was written by Oliver Stone.

At one point, Montana explains that society needs men like him, so that people can point a finger at him and still feel righteously innocent. Politicians would rather fight the legalization of drugs than take on organized crime, for black sheep like Montana justify election campaign promises, excuse police brutality, and help cover up their own machinations. The powerful don't even need to be corrupt to profit from organized crime. At the end Montana is not gunned down by the police, but by the Mafia. This divergence from Howard Hawks's original could scarcely make its point more effectively – in a decade of Reaganite neo-liberal economic practices, it's a statement as meaningful as it is provocative.

SH

BLADE RUNNER

1982 - USA - 117 MIN.

DIRECTOR

RIDLEY SCOTT (*1937)

SCREENPLAY

HAMPTON FANCHER, DAVID PEPLOES,
based on the novel *Do Androids Dream of
Electric Sheep?* by PHILIP K. DICK

DIRECTOR OF PHOTOGRAPHY

JORDAN CRONENWETH

EDITING

MARSHA NAKASHIMA, TERRY RAWLINGS

MUSIC

VANGELIS

PRODUCTION

MICHAEL DEELEY for THE LADD COMPANY, BLADE RUNNER PARTNERSHIP

STARRING

HARRISON FORD (Rick Deckard), RUTGER HAUER (Roy Batty),
SEAN YOUNG (Rachael), EDWARD JAMES OLMOS (Gaff),
M. EMMET WALSH (Bryant), DARYL HANNAH (Pris),
WILLIAM SANDERSON (Sebastian), BRION JAMES (Leon),
JOE TURKEL (Eldon Tyrell), JOANNA CASSIDY (Zhora),
MORGAN PAULL (Holden)

MAN HAS MADE HIS MATCH
...NOW IT'S HIS PROBLEM

HARRISON FORD is
BLADE RUNNER™

JERRY PERENCHIO and BUD YORKIN PRESENT
A MICHAEL DEELEY-RIDLEY SCOTT PRODUCTION
STARRING HARRISON FORD
IN BLADE RUNNER™ WITH RUTGER HAUER · SEAN YOUNG
EDWARD JAMES OLMOS SCREENPLAY BY HAMPTON FANCHER AND DAVID PEOPLES
EXECUTIVE PRODUCERS BRIAN KELLY AND HAMPTON FANCHER VISUAL EFFECTS BY DOUGLAS TRUMBULL
ORIGINAL MUSIC COMPOSED BY VANGELIS ASSOCIATE PRODUCER IVOR POWELL PRODUCED BY MICHAEL DEELEY DIRECTED BY RIDLEY SCOTT
ORIGINAL SOUNDTRACK ALBUM AVAILABLE ON POLYDOR RECORDS · PANAVISION® · TECHNICOLOR® · · IN SELECTED THEATRES

"You're so different. You're so perfect."

Los Angeles, 2019. Earth-toned high-rise temples soar up into smog-covered skies. Factory towers spit fire, and acid rain collects between the neon-illuminated fissures that separate the mammoth buildings. The city has become a mutant hybrid, a futuristic yet archaic urban leviathan. The L.A. streets are home to an exotic blend of races, while whites are housed in forbidding, monolithic skyscrapers. Everyone who can afford it has relocated to one of the "off world colonies." To make this prospect even more enticing, the Tyrell Corporation has designed humanoids called replicants to be used as slave labor on the foreign planets. These synthetic beings are virtually indistinguishable from real humans, but the law forbids them from setting foot on Earth. Yet some of these androids manage to slip through the net, and it is the job of the "blade runners" to hunt them down and "decommission" them. Is this an allusion to the Day of Judgment, where only the innocent can escape the confines of hell? Perhaps. Nothing in this film rich with philosophical and theological admonishments would seem to indicate the contrary.

Rick Deckard (Harrison Ford) used to work as a blade runner. Now a disillusioned ex-cop, he roams the damp streets with a chip on his shoulder like a film noir crusader. He was the best in the business, which is why the bureau want to reactivate him when a band of four rogue androids, two men and two women, makes their way into L.A. Their "life expectancy" has been programmed to four years. Now, they want to know how much time they have left to live, and they'll do anything to prolong it.

Roy Batty (Rutger Hauer), the leader of these humanoid bandits, is blond, buff, and demonic. Meeting his maker Eldon Tyrell (Joe Turkel), a futuristic Dr. Frankenstein, proves an existential disappointment for Roy. Tyrell lives in a pyramid-shaped structure reminiscent of that of the ancient Mayans and sleeps in a bed like the pope's. Unfortunately, the great creator is in no position to grant the android a new lease of life, and the fallen angel kills his maker in a dual father-God assassination.

Blade Runner is based on the novel *Do Androids Dream of Electric Sheep?* (1968) by Philip K. Dick, who

RIDLEY SCOTT Alan Parker dubbed him "the greatest visual stylist working today." With a deep-rooted love for Hollywood, the films of English director Ridley Scott have played an enormous role in determining Tinseltown's film aesthetics for more than 20 years. Whether the sci-fi thrillers like *Alien* (1979) and *Blade Runner* (from 1982 – a film which would enjoy cult status ten years later with the release of its director's cut), or a feminist road movie like *Thelma & Louise* (1991), Scott's films are a triumph with critics and audiences alike. A graduate of the London Royal College of Art, the *auteur* got his start working for the BBC and then went on to shoot advertising spots with his own production company.

Born in 1937, his first feature film, *The Duellists* (1977), won the prize for best directorial debut at Cannes. Ridley Scott has also enjoyed tremendous success as a producer. Together with his brother Tony Scott (*Top Gun*, 1985), he purchased Shepperton Studios in 1995. Neither genre nor quality links the resulting films. Fantasy flick *Legend* (1985), featuring a young Tom Cruise, met with a more modest reception; thriller *Someone to Watch Over Me* (1987) was a veritable grand slam; and *Black Rain* (1989) with Michael Douglas, a film on the Japanese Yakuza, is certainly worth seeing. Clearly, in addition to the numerous hits, Scott has also had his share of misses. The Columbus-glorifying *1492: Conquest of Paradise* (1992) and *G.I. Jane* (1997) starring Demi Moore bombed at the box office and were panned by critics. In 2000, Ridley Scott landed himself another smash hit with *Gladiator*, the first big budget Hollywood production about Ancient Rome in more than 30 years. He was also successful with the epic *American Gangster* (2007), the spy thriller *Body of Lies* (2008), and *Alien* prequel *Prometheus* (2012).

also wrote the story that inspired *Total Recall* (1990). The film bombed at the box office, but is nonetheless seen as a milestone in sci-fi. It is a dismal, philosophical fairy tale with mind-boggling sets, sophisticated lighting design, and a grandiose score by Vangelis. Alongside *Liquid Sky* (1982) and *The Hunger* (1983), *Blade Runner* is among the most significant '80s New Wave films. One could label it "postmodern" or attribute its power to the director's eclecticism. Scott's mesmerizing layering technique showcases his knack for integrating architectural elements, the intricacies of clothing articles, and symbols originating from a wide array of cultures and eras.

The film makes productive use of astoundingly diverse codes, synthesizing their Babylonian confusion into a compact means of communication on the L.A. city streets. In a mélange of Fritz Lang's *Metropolis* (1926), film noir, the imagery of Edward Hopper, and the comic-book sketches of Moebius, Ridley Scott creates a wildly driven piece that demands its audience to consider the essence of human identity. The film's subtext gradually unfolds throughout its story, raising issues of the conscious and subconscious. The homonymic link between protagonist Deckard and mathematician Descartes is only part of the rich body of motifs that hint at the film's underlying philosophy. Also not to be overlooked are the variations on the "eye" motif throughout the picture. Here, too, the film synthesizes a word's homonymic potential, alluding to the "I" inherent in the word "eye." The eye is a universal symbol of recognition

1 The other, that's who I am: Rachael (Sean Young), attractive and unapproachable like a film noir vamp. She doesn't know that she's a replicant. Even her memories are just implants.

2 More human than human: Roy Batty (Rutger Hauer) is the *Übermensch* in the Nietzschean sense of the word. The blond beast and yet a slave who suffers and shows compassion.

3 Harrison Ford plays blade runner Deckard. In hot pursuit of renegade replicants, although perhaps he's one himself.

"*Blade Runner* was the science fiction of the '80s. The gritty gray counterpart to Kubrick's *2001*."

epd Film

and a sense of self-awareness "unique" to humans. Yet in *Blade Runner*, the androids are also equipped with this level of consciousness. "We're not computers, Sebastian, we're physical," Batty declares at one point, laying claim to his humanity as well as his body and physicality, one of the most important topics of the '80s.

For their bodies are precisely what make the androids indistinguishable from their human counterparts. Upon first meeting, Rachael (Sean Young), Eldon Tyrell's secretary, reminds Deckard of the dangers of his occupation when she asks him whether he has ever killed a

human by mistake. Her question sensitizes the viewer to the predicament at hand; sometimes the fine line between humans and their replicas is intangible. Rachael herself has sat on both sides of the fence. Although she has always believed herself to be human, at one point in the film she is forced to confront the reality that she too is an android. There is, however, something "unique" about her. Rachael is the product of an experiment and has been programmed with the memories of Tyrell's niece, which she latches on to as her own. Her memories are rooted in photos. Likewise, it is photos that help Deckard zero in on the

4 What does it mean to be human? A question the film puts forth in an aesthetically brilliant framework. The film set the standard for 1980s style.

5 Artificial humans are a recurrent phenomenon in both literature and film – from the Greek myth of Pygmalion, E. T. A. Hoffmann's doll Olympia in *The Sandman*, to Fritz Lang's *Metropolis* and Spielberg's *A.I.*, to name but a few. Here, the mannerisms of replicant Pris (Daryl Hannah) almost make her seem like a china doll.

"At first the villain of the piece, he suddenly becomes its mythic, emphatic center. Batty turns Frankenstein's monster to Biblical Adam; Deckard veers from hunter to homomorph." *Film Comment*

whereabouts of the renegade androids. He uses a picture of an empty hotel room as only a 21st-century detective would, or at least, as we might have imagined him to from an '80s perspective. Aided by a contraption known as an Esper machine, he enlarges segments of the photo onto a monitor. This provides him with a sort of X-ray vision that allows him to travel into the depths of the image's two-dimensional space. He soon discovers a woman's reflection from within a mirror. The detective embarks on an investigation, which takes the audience on a course through the history of Western art. Ridley Scott cites various paintings in this scene, including Jan van Eyck's *The Arnolfini Wedding*

6 The sun doesn't rise here anymore: bathed in neon light, the streets of L.A. are ruled by a gangland mix of Chinese, Mexicans, and punks.

7 Harrison Ford's laconic and somewhat cynical portrayal of Deckard brings many a film noir protagonist to mind. Not only the visual aesthetics and characters evoke elements of film noir, but also the voice-over narrative technique, later eliminated in the director's cut, is typical of the genre.

"We used a lot of real punks for the street scenes in *Blade Runner*. Because I had so much 'crowd,' it was better to save time and money by recruiting a huge number of extras: 200 punks, 100 Chinese, another 100 Mexicans."

Ridley Scott in: Film Comment

7

(1434), a piece which, though focused on its two main sub-jects, also allowed the spectator to see the artist and his assistant peering out from a mirror. Scott's knack for turning cultural paradigms on their heads undoubtedly contributes to the intriguing fabric of the film, many of whose images have become ingrained in our collective visual memories. One such example shows Deckard chasing exotic snake dancer Zhora through the chaotic, mazelike L.A. streets, inundated with people. He finally shoots her dead, causing her to fall in slow motion through a store window. One could argue that these shards of glass signify the shattered real-ity brought about by the role reversals at the film's conclu-sion. The blade runner becomes the bounty, and the android Batty is revealed as a compassionate, "selfless" individual.

It is indeed Batty who saves the blade runner's life in the nick of time and who dies in the end. The moral disparity between android and human no longer exists. This holds even truer if one accepts the hypothesis that Deckard is himself an android. There is some proof in the original version to favor this ongoing debate. The director's cut, released in 1992, has no voice over and no happy ending, differences that make this theory even more prob-able. In July 2000, Scott went on record as saying that Deckard definitively was a replicant. An outraged Harrison Ford countered that while making the film, Scott had sworn the opposite. And so the debate goes on …

KK

THE FOURTH MAN

DE VIERDE MAN

1983 - THE NETHERLANDS - 105 MIN.

DIRECTOR

PAUL VERHOEVEN (*1938)

SCREENPLAY

GERARD SOETEMAN, based on the
novel of the same name by GERARD REVE

DIRECTOR OF PHOTOGRAPHY

JAN DE BONT

EDITING

INE SCHENKKAN

MUSIC

LOEK DIKKER

PRODUCTION

ROB HOUWER for DE VERENIGDE NEDERLANDSCHE FILMCOMPAGNIE

STARRING

JEROEN KRABBÉ (Gerard Reve), RENÉE SOUTENDIJK (Christine Halsslag),
THOM HOFFMAN (Herman), DOLF DE VRIES (Dr. de Vries),
GEERT DE JONG (Ria), PAMELA TEVES (Nurse),
HANS VEERMAN (Undertaker), HERO MULLER (Josefs),
CAROLINE DE BEUS (Adrienne), PAUL NYGAARD (Violinist)

DE FILM VIERDE MAN

THOM HOFFMAN/DOLF DE VRIES/GEERT DE JONG/HANS VEERMAN E.V.A.

JEROEN KRABBÉ/RENEE SOUTENDIJK

PAUL VERHOEVEN/ROB HOUWER

REGIE PRODUCENT

SCENARIO: GERARD SOETEMAN NAAR DE GELIJKNAMIGE ROMAN VAN GERARD REVE
KAMERA: JAN DE BONT/MUZIEK: LOEK DIKKER/MONTAGE: INE SCHENKKAN

MÉÉR DAN EEN THRILLER....NÚ IN DE BIOSCOPEN!

"I lie the truth, until I no longer know whether something really happened or not."

Amsterdam. Writer Gerard Reve (Jeroen Krabbé) no longer knows what to believe: is he hallucinating, or is he the witness to a deadly conspiracy? His lively imagination, fed by the twin sources of strict Catholicism and homoeroticism, supplies him with plenty of welcome inspiration for his novels, but it begins to take on a deeply disturbing quality when he meets a seductive young woman during a stay at the seaside town of Vlissingen. Her aura is mysterious and her intentions may well be murderous.

When the Vlissingen Literary Society asks him to give a reading, Gerard accepts gratefully, for he is chronically short of money. After a night haunted by terrible dreams, he sets off on his journey. At the station in Amsterdam, a young man awakens his interest, but he fails in his attempt to strike up an acquaintance. On the train to Vlissingen, his eye is caught by a photograph of a hotel. Soon, however, he falls asleep – and is once again beleaguered by ghastly nightmares. On arrival at his destination, he meets Christine Halslag (Renée Soutendijk), who takes care of financial matters for the Literary Society, and who will make a Super 8 film of Gerard's reading. After the event, she brings the writer to his hotel. Gerard recoils in horror: this is the building he had seen in the photo in his train compartment. Christine is sympathetic, and invites him back to her place, where they spend the night in a close embrace; but Christine's warm attentions can't save Gerard from his nightmares. In his dream, he sees himself enter a tomb in which three bloody corpses are hanging, and it's clear that a fourth victim is about to be slaughtered: Gerard himself. Christine castrates him with a pair of scissors – then he awakes, screaming, and finds comfort in her arms. The following day, he is pottering about in her apartment when he discovers a photo of the young man he had found so fascinating at the station in Amsterdam; it's Herman (Thom Hoffman), Christine's fiancé. In the hope of meeting this young Adonis, Gerard decides to stay in Vlissingen a little longer. As he gets to know Christine better, he discovers that she has already been married

JAN DE BONT Paul Verhoeven, born in Amsterdam in 1938, gained international recognition with a series of provocative and visually outstanding films, before making it in Hollywood. His career is closely bound up with that of the cameraman Jan de Bont, responsible for the cinematography on Verhoeven's first major success, *Turkish Delight* (*Turks fruit*, 1973). Even prior to Verhoeven, de Bont had also worked in Hollywood, but *Private Lessons* (1981) was his first film as Director of Photography. He shot several photographically impressive films, including *Die Hard* (1987), *Black Rain* (1989), and, with Verhoeven as director again, *Basic Instinct* (1992). In 1994, de Bont made his debut as a director with the visceral action thriller *Speed*, a film that set new standards for the genre and became a global box-office hit.

three times, and that each of her husbands suffered a premature death. He suspects that Herman is destined to be her fourth victim, but Herman scornfully dismisses his warning.

Gerard is finding it increasingly difficult to distinguish between reality and illusion. Further disturbing experiences leave him with raw nerves, and he resolves to return to Amsterdam. Herman drives him to the station, but on the way there, they are involved in accident that is as bizarre as it is tragic. Herman dies and Gerard is taken

"I don't consider sex the main thing in life, of course, but it's a real possibility for expressing yourself. And I'm always amazed that people fucking each other in films is so completely boring." *Paul Verhoeven, in: Cinema Papers*

1 Reve (Jeroen Krabbé) wakes up from a ghastly vision: his inner goblins will soon follow him into the outside world.

2 Tactile literature lover or deadly siren: Christine Halsslag (Renée Soutendijk).

3 Homoerotic imagery and Christine Halsslag's mysterious aura pervade Gerard Reve's feverish, waking dreams.

4 If Reve's grueling premonitions are correct, Christine's interlocking embrace will be accompanied by death.

to hospital, suffering from extreme shock. Meanwhile, Christine is outside, flirting with a hunky surfer, before climbing into his car. Is this her fifth victim?

"Every film I've made forms a contrast to the previous one," said Paul Verhoeven, when *The Fourth Man* reached cinemas. "I have a preference for things that are visually spectacular, and feel more drawn to images than sound, although sound, of course, also has an important function." The most spectacular element in this film was Verhoeven's provocative treatment of religious symbols, which many critics regarded as a breaking of taboos. The avowed Catholic Gerard sees Herman, the object of his intense desire, as a crucified Christ – and he approaches him with sexual in-

tentions. Seen in the context of the film's carefully developed supernatural atmosphere, these scenes are thoroughly fitting. Just like Gerard, the viewer is unnerved by a maelstrom of disturbing images and tableaux, whereby it never quite becomes clear whether the notorious drinker, Gerard, is in a delirium or actually living through a series of dreadful events.

This film is a bold and sardonic mixture of Christian motifs, open homosexual eroticism and pure "scary movie." It caused a worldwide furor, and brought Verhoeven a series of awards, including in 1984 the International Critics' Award at the Toronto International Film Festival, and the prize for Best Foreign Film from the Los Angeles Film Critics Association.   HK

BLUE VELVET

1985 - USA - 120 MIN.

DIRECTOR
DAVID LYNCH (*1946)

SCREENPLAY
DAVID LYNCH

DIRECTOR OF PHOTOGRAPHY
FREDERICK ELMES

EDITING
DUWAYNE DUNHAM

MUSIC
ANGELO BADALAMENTI

PRODUCTION
FRED CARUSO for DE LAURENTIIS ENTERTAINMENT

STARRING
KYLE MACLACHLAN (Jeffrey Beaumont), ISABELLA ROSSELLINI (Dorothy Vallens),
DENNIS HOPPER (Frank Booth), LAURA DERN (Sandy Williams),
HOPE LANGE (Mrs. Williams), DEAN STOCKWELL (Ben),
GEORGE DICKERSON (Detective Williams), BRAD DOURIF (Raymond),
FRANCES BAY (Aunt Barbara), JACK HARVEY (Mr. Beaumont)

"BLUE VELVET is a mystery…a masterpiece…
a visionary story of sexual awakening,
of good and evil, a trip to the underworld."
—David Thompson, CALIFORNIA MAGAZINE

"A nightmarish, intensely disturbing exploration
of the hidden side of the soul. It is sure to cause a sensation."
—Ken Turan, GQ

"Brilliant and unsettling…this is the work of
an all-American visionary—and a master film stylist."
—Stephen Schiff, VANITY FAIR

Blue Velvet

DE LAURENTIIS ENTERTAINMENT GROUP
PRESENTS
A DAVID LYNCH FILM
"BLUE VELVET" KYLE MACLACHLAN ISABELLA ROSSELLINI DENNIS HOPPER
and LAURA DERN with HOPE LANGE GEORGE DICKERSON and DEAN STOCKWELL
Director of Photography FREDERICK ELMES Sound Design ALAN SPLET Production Designer PATRICIA NORRIS Edited by DUWAYNE DUNHAM
Music Composed and Conducted by ANGELO BADALAMENTI Executive Producer RICHARD ROTH Written and Directed by DAVID LYNCH

RESTRICTED
UNDER 17 REQUIRES ACCOMPANYING
PARENT OR ADULT GUARDIAN

DOLBY STEREO

DEG
DE LAURENTIIS ENTERTAINMENT GROUP INC. ALL RIGHTS RESERVED

"I'll bet a person could learn a lot by getting into that woman's apartment. You know, sneak in and hide and observe."

The camera sweeps over Lumberton, USA, a charming American small town with white picket fences, tulip-filled gardens, and amiable people. Jeffrey Beaumont (Kyle MacLachlan) is on the way to hospital to visit his father, who suffered a heart attack while watering his lawn. While walking home across a field, he pauses to throw rocks at some bottles. He is soon stopped in his tracks – partially hidden by the grass at his feet lies a milky-looking, rotting human ear, covered with crawling ants. The ear is a completely foreign object in this American small-town idyll, and becomes a mesmerically compelling object. Little does he realize that it is to become his entry ticket into another world. For the moment, he brings the ear to the police.

In Sandy (Laura Dern), the blonde daughter of the investigating detective, Jeffrey finds a hesitant, but eventually more and more curious accomplice and partner. She informs him of a clue in the case that leads to the nightclub singer Dorothy Vallens (Isabella Rossellini). He decides to sneak into her apartment. The thought of forcing his way into this woman's private sphere arouses him more than he will admit to himself, let alone to Sandy.

Blue Velvet is a film about seeing and about the camera as an eye. Jeffrey observes more than he would like to in Dorothy Vallens's apartment. When Dorothy unexpectedly returns, rips the closet door open and orders him out, the boundless terror in his eyes exposes him as a peeping

ANGELO BADALAMENTI From *Blue Velvet* (1985) to *Mulholland Drive* (2001) Angelo Badalamenti has played a key role in every David Lynch project; the celestial sounds of his music have become an integral part of Lynch's universe. A classically trained composer, he was born in 1937 in New Jersey. Towards the beginning of the '70s he wrote scores for two films under the pseudonym Andy Badale, but only with *Blue Velvet* did his career as a film composer truly begin. In addition to his scores for films – including *Wild at Heart* (1990), *Twin Peaks* (1990), *Lost Highway* (1997), and *The Straight Story* (1999) – there are two albums on which Julee Cruise sings the songs of Badalamenti (music) and Lynch (lyrics): *Floating Into the Night* (1989) and *The Voice of Love* (1993). Ranking among his many compositions are the scores to *The City of Lost Children* (*La cité des enfants perdus*, 1995) and *The Beach* (2000).

"As wicked and contradictory as it may seem to be, *Blue Velvet* is quite clearly one of the few great films of the Eighties, perhaps even the most sensational film since *Last Tango in Paris*. No film has blown me away like this for years." *L.A. Weekly*

3

1 Mysterious nightclub singer Dorothy Vallens (Isabella Rossellini) is suspicious of an unannounced visitor.

2 Jeffrey Beaumont (Kyle MacLachlan) is about to drive into the unknown depths of his soul.

3 Under duress: Dorothy forces Jeffrey to take his clothes off and make love to her. Suddenly, there is a knock at the door.

Tom caught red-handed. When Dorothy threatens him and even calls him by name, the object has suddenly become the subject, the subject the object.

The voyeur experiences arousal, pleasure, and power. Director David Lynch plays with these phenomena and makes the viewer an accomplice, but then turns the tables. In Lynch's film, the voyeur is degraded and ultimately becomes the helpless witness of a brutal act. The scene in which Dorothy is brutally raped by the perverted Frank Booth (Dennis Hopper) is just as shocking and disturbing

as the shower murder scene in Hitchcock's *Psycho* (1960). And *Blue Velvet* is as important for 1980s cinema as *Psycho* was for film of the early '60s. The following day, his experience in Dorothy's apartment truly seems like a bad dream to Jeffrey. For just as it would be in a dream, he was alternately observer and participant, and Frank was the representation of the dark side of his soul.

Towards the end of *Blue Velvet*, when the worst is over, the camera shows a close-up of an ear, but this time, it is Jeffrey's own ear. The fissures in the perfect world are

4 Shutter speed: Jeffrey bears witness to a bizarre scene from inside Dorothy's closet.

5 Dorothy sings "Blue Velvet" at the Slow Club: Lynch composer Angelo Badalamenti at the piano.

6 Sandy (Laura Dern) is appalled by Dorothy Vallens's morbid power over Jeffrey. Yet Sandy's romantic feelings compel her to help him.

7 "Mommy… Baby wants to fuck!" With her family in his clutches, Frank Booth (Dennis Hopper) strokes Dorothy Vallens with blue velvet.

"*Blue Velvet* is a big film about the innocence and perversion that characterizes childhood." David Lynch

apparently sealed, and Jeffrey's journey into the dark depths of the soul is over. But is it entirely over for good, or is this just a temporary respite? …

While *Blue Velvet* was initially met with much controversy at the time of its release, its status as one of the best American films of the '80s is indisputable. The film established David Lynch as a visionary of modern cinema, marked the well-deserved comeback of the incomparable Dennis Hopper, and shattered the constricting perception of Isabella Rossellini as merely the flawless daughter of the great Ingrid Bergman. RF

DEAD RINGERS

1988 - USA / CANADA - 115 MIN.

DIRECTOR

DAVID CRONENBERG (*1943)

SCREENPLAY

BARI WOOD, JACK GEASLAND

DIRECTOR OF PHOTOGRAPHY

PETER SUSCHITZKY

MUSIC

HOWARD SHORE

PRODUCTION

MARC BOYMAN, DAVID CRONENBERG for MANTLE CLINIC II,
MORGAN CREEK PRODUCTIONS, TÉLÉFILM CANADA

STARRING

JEREMY IRONS (Beverly Mantle / Elliot Mantle), GENEVIÈVE BUJOLD (Claire Niveau),
HEIDI VON PALLESKE (Cary), BARBARA GORDON (Danuta),
SHIRLEY DOUGLAS (Laura), STEPHEN LACK (Anders Wolleck),
NICK NICHOLS (Leo), LYNNE CORMACK (Arlene),
DAMIR ANDREI (Birchall), MIRIAM NEWHOUSE (Mrs. Bookman)

FROM THE DIRECTOR OF "THE FLY" COMES A NEW KIND OF THRILLER

TWO BODIES. TWO MINDS. ONE SOUL.

DAVID CRONENBERG'S

DEAD RINGERS

JAMES G. ROBINSON AND JOE ROTH PRESENT JEREMY IRONS · GENEVIEVE BUJOLD IN DAVID CRONENBERG'S DEAD RINGERS EDITED BY RONALD SANDERS
PRODUCTION DESIGNER CAROL SPIER MUSIC BY HOWARD SHORE DIRECTOR OF PHOTOGRAPHY PETER SUSCHITZKY COSTUME DESIGNER DENISE CRONENBERG ASSOCIATE PRODUCER JOHN BOARD EXECUTIVE PRODUCER CAROL BAUM
AND SYLVIO TABET WRITTEN BY DAVID CRONENBERG AND NORMAN SNIDER BASED ON THE BOOK "TWINS" BY BARI WOOD AND JACK GEASLAND
PRODUCED BY DAVID CRONENBERG AND MARC BOYMAN DIRECTED BY DAVID CRONENBERG

"Pain creates character distortion, it's simply not necessary."

Identical twins Elliot and Beverly Mantle (Jeremy Irons in a dual role) are both renowned physicians. After completing their studies at Cambridge, Massachusetts, the brothers moved out to Toronto where they open up a clinic for gynecology. Aided by state of the art technology, the Mantles specialize in fertilizing the eggs of seemingly barren women. However, there are naturally some patients whom even they cannot help. Such is the case when they discover a physical abnormality in actress Claire Niveau (Geneviève Bujold) that prevents her from ever getting pregnant. Following the diagnosis, Elliot and Claire enter into an affair and it soon becomes clear that the actress has a taste for exotic pleasures. Fascinated by her masochistic tendencies, Elliot decides to contribute to them. Unbeknownst to Claire, Elliot lets brother Beverly slip into his intimate role, once he has had his fill of her. After all, sharing is what these twins do best. But when Beverly falls in love with the fragile actress, the siblings' equilibrium begins to falter.

Until now, the lives of the two brothers have thrived on the perfect balance between their personal and private lives. Elliot's charismatic personality allowed him to play the part of the go-getting daredevil. The rather shy and reserved Beverly, on the other hand, was the brilliant researching strength. Elliot, in turn, would then deftly package his brother's results for the open market. Now and again, they take advantage of their uncanny physical resemblance and trade places. This goes undetected by those around them, as the two are "perceived as a single person," as Elliot puts it. Their complementary yin and yang even succeeds in pulling the wool over Claire's eyes. Much time passes before she starts to distinguish the ambivalent behavior of her two lovers, and she is livid upon discovering that her monogamous relationship has grown new feet.

Guilt drives Beverly to drink and drugs. He is torn between wanting to start a new life with Claire independently of his brother, and fearing the prospect of life without him.

DAVID CRONENBERG Few directors have polarized the masses like David Cronenberg, revered among horror film fans and highbrows alike. Many people first became aware of the Toronto-born Canadian filmmaker through his first Hollywood film *Videodrome* (1982). Prior to that, the 1943-born baby boomer made a slew of pictures that won him acclaim in sci-fi and horror film circles, including *Fast Company* (1979), *The Brood* (1979), and *Scanners* (1980). Cronenberg's thematic cornerstone is the human body and physical anomalies. He has dazzled audiences time and again with a seemingly limitless arsenal of masterfully executed special effects. As a director he is less interested in the shock value of gore than in the potential of science and technology to alter our relationship to our bodies. *Naked Lunch* (1991), *Crash* (1996), and *eXistenZ* (1998) plunge into the dark side of the engulfing worlds of drugs, cars, and video games. He argues that depletion of identity is a typical symptom of addiction whose negative effects are on a par with those of physical atrophy. Identity was also a dominant theme in Cronenberg's recent films like *A History of Violence* (2005) and *A Dangerous Method* (2011), where the focus shifted away from the corporeal towards the psychological.

"*Dead Ringers* is Narcissus' worst nightmare. He wakes up one morning and finds his reflection lying beside him." *epd Film*

In a narcotic state, his sleep is tormented by mad visions of Claire vainly trying to sever the twins' shared umbilical cord with her teeth. Elliot, meanwhile, makes a concerted effort to rehabilitate his drug-addicted brother, but is sucked into the same quagmire. He too has started to take "medication" to be "in sync" with Beverly, as he refers to it. This downward spiral soon takes a deadly turn for the two doctors who can live neither with nor without each other.

David Cronenberg's exploration of the phenomenon of twins in *Dead Ringers* (a term from dog racing meaning an identical substitute used to defraud bookmakers) has its roots in biological studies. Himself a former medical student, the director was fascinated by the findings of twin research. Some published reports indicate that identical twins raised apart from each another often develop remarkably similar predispositions, affinities, and characteristics. It is Cronenberg's assertion that "the behavior demonstrated by twins turns our entire concept of individuality on its head. We understand that we are dealing with two distinct individuals but are simultaneously thrown for a loop by their homogeneity. We want to "see" them as individuals, despite the apparent physical replication we are

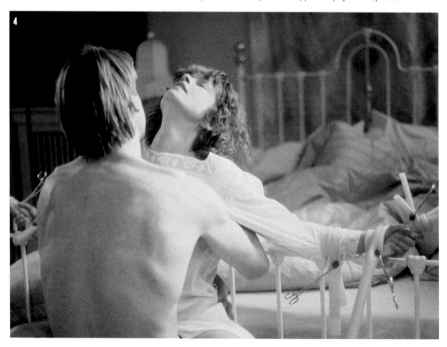

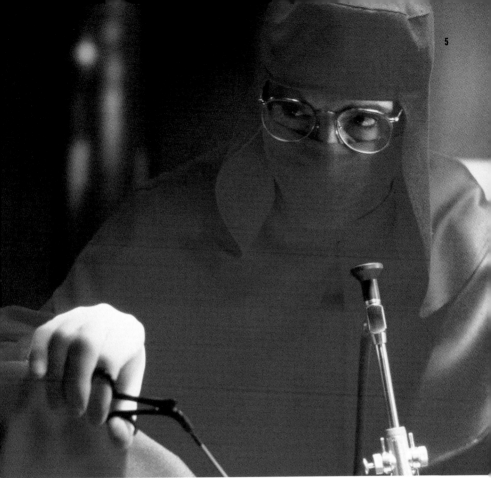

1 Just can't be himself: Beverly Mantle (Jeremy Irons) mourns the loss of his twin brother.

2 One last reunion: Mantle twins Elliot and Beverly.

3 Female intuition: actress Claire Niveau (Geneviève Bujold) knows she's been had in the worst of ways.

4 Claire falls victim to a little death in Elliot's arms.

5 Quarantine: good doctor Elliot dissects the ailments of childless mothers at his fertility clinic.

presented with. It is therefore clear that we can no longer legitimately view the body as the source of individuality." Cronenberg believes body and soul, as manifested by Elliot and Beverly, to be inseparable.

If we limit ourselves to valuing only one of these aspects, as is often the case in the medical field, the other will directly suffer as a result. Fittingly, *Dead Ringers* treats self-renunciation and loss of identity as two slow-moving, malignant processes that accompany physical decay. In later films like *eXistenZ* (1998), Cronenberg takes this reasoning to new heights. The human body becomes virtually disbanded in the simulative realms of video games and no longer constitutes a hold on reality.

HM

THE SILENCE OF THE LAMBS 🏆🏆🏆🏆🏆

1991 - USA - 118 MIN.

DIRECTOR
JONATHAN DEMME (*1944)

SCREENPLAY
TED TALLY, based on the novel of the same name by THOMAS HARRIS

DIRECTOR OF PHOTOGRAPHY
TAK FUJIMOTO

EDITING
CRAIG MCKAY

MUSIC
HOWARD SHORE

PRODUCTION
GARY GOETZMAN, EDWARD SAXON, KENNETH UTT,
RON BOZMAN for STRONG HEART PRODUCTIONS (for ORION)

STARRING
JODIE FOSTER (Clarice Starling), ANTHONY HOPKINS (Dr. Hannibal Lecter),
SCOTT GLENN (Jack Crawford), TED LEVINE (Jame Gumb),
ANTHONY HEALD (Dr. Frederick Chilton), BROOKE SMITH (Catherine Martin),
DIANE BAKER (Senator Ruth Martin), KASI LEMMONS (Ardelia Mapp),
ROGER CORMAN (FBI Director Hayden Burke), GEORGE A. ROMERO (FBI Agent in Memphis)

ACADEMY AWARDS 1991
OSCARS for BEST PICTURE, BEST DIRECTOR (Jonathan Demme),
BEST ACTRESS (Jodie Foster), BEST ACTOR (Anthony Hopkins), and BEST SCREENPLAY
based on material previously produced or published (Ted Tally)

jodie foster / anthony hopkins / scott glenn

the silence of the lambs

from the terrifying best seller

a jonathan demme picture / jodie foster / anthony hopkins / scott glenn / "the silence of the lambs" / ted levine / music by howard shore / production designer kristi zea / director of photography tak fujimoto / edited by craig mckay, a.c.e. / executive producer gary goetzman / based upon the novel by thomas harris / screenplay by ted tally / produced by kenneth utt edward saxon and ron bozman / directed by jonathan demme

"I'm having a friend for dinner."

Clarice Starling (Jodie Foster), daughter of a policeman shot in the line of duty, wants to join the FBI. At the FBI Academy in Woods, Virginia, she races over training courses, pushing herself to the limit. Wooden signs bear the legend "HURT-AGONY-PAIN: LOVE IT" – they're not just there to exhort the rookies to excel, they also reveal the masochism involved. The movie goes through the whole range of this theme, from heroic selflessness to destructive self-hate. Jack Crawford (Scott Glenn), who is Starling's boss and the head of the FBI's psychiatric department, sends her to Baltimore to carry out a routine interview with an imprisoned murderer who is resisting questioning. As well as being a psychiatrist, the prisoner is also an extreme pathological case who attacked people and ate their organs.

For eight years Dr. Hannibal "The Cannibal" Lecter (Anthony Hopkins) has lived in the windowless cellar of a high security mental hospital. Crawford hopes the interview will provide clues to the behavior of a second monster, a killer known as "Buffalo Bill" who skins his female victims and has so far skillfully evaded the FBI. Crawford's plan works, and the professorial cannibal agrees to discuss the pathology of mass murderers with his visitor Clarice – on one condition. Lecter will give her expert advice on Buffalo Bill in exchange for the tale of her childhood trauma. "Quid pro quo" – she lays bare her psyche, he gives her a psychological profile of her suspect. The gripping dialogue that develops between the ill-matched couple can be understood on many levels. On one hand, we see a psychoanalyst talking to his patient, on the other, a young detective interrogating an unpredictable serial killer, and that ambiguity is the determining quality in Lecter and Starling's relationship.

Both follow their own aims unerringly, refusing to give way, and the struggle that results is one of the most brilliant and sophisticated duels in cinema history. The daughter of a U.S. senator falls into the hands of Buffalo Bill, and suddenly the FBI is under increasing pressure to find the murderer. Lecter's chance has come. In return for his help in capturing Jame Gumb alias Buffalo Bill (Ted Levine), he asks for better conditions and is transferred to a temporary prison in Memphis. He kills the warders and escapes in the uniform of a policeman, whose face he has also removed and placed over his own.

His last exchange with Starling takes place over the telephone, when he rings from a Caribbean island to congratulate her on her promotion to FBI agent and bids her farewell with the words: "I'm having a friend for dinner". After hanging up, Lecter follows a group of tourists in which the audience recognize the hated Dr. Chilton (Anthony Heald), director of the secure mental hospital in Baltimore, who clearly will be Lecter's unsuspecting dinner "guest."

The Silence of the Lambs marked a cinematic high point at the beginning of the '90s. It is impossible to categorize in any one genre as it combines several. There are elements from police movies (where crime does not pay),

---

PARALLEL MONTAGE A process developed early in the history of cinema. Editing enables two or more events happening in different places to be told and experienced at the same time. The best-known kind of parallel montage in movies is the "last-minute rescue," where images of an endangered or besieged character are juxtaposed in rapid succession with those of the rescuers who are on their way. Action movies use such sequences over and over as a means of increasing the tension, and the device has remained basically the same from David Griffith's 1916 film *Intolerance* to today's thrillers. Parallel montage allows us to be a step ahead of the figures in a film. We are allowed to know things that the characters do not themselves realize, and we are also in several places at the same time, an experience which is only possible in fiction.

1 The naked man and the dead: "Buffalo Bill" (Ted Levine) uses a sewing machine to make himself a new identity from the skin of his victims; above him are butterflies, a symbol of that metamorphosis.

2 The staring matches between Starling (Jodie Foster) and Lecter (Anthony Hopkins) are a battle for knowledge: Lecter is to help the FBI build a profile of the killer; Starling is to surrender the secret of her childhood.

3 The eyes have it: in the serial killer genre, eyes become a tool for appropriation, destruction, and penetration.

"*The Silence of the Lambs* is just plain scary – from its doomed and woozy camera angles to its creepy Freudian context." *The Washington Post*

but it's also a thriller that borrows much from real historical figures: the model for both Gumb and Lecter is Edward Gein (1906–1984), who was wearing suspenders made from his victims' skin when arrested in 1957.

But *The Silence of the Lambs* is also a movie about psychiatry. Both murderers are presented as psychopaths whose "relation" to one another forms the basis for criminological research, even though their cases are not strictly

4 The cannibal clasps his hands. Cage and pose are reminiscent of Francis Bacon's portraits of the pope.

5 A policeman is disemboweled and crucified on the cage. With his outstretched arms, he looks like a butterfly.

6 The pair meet in the lowest part of the prison system, a basement dungeon from the underworld.

7 The monster is restrained with strait-jacket and muzzle; the powers of the state have the monopoly on violence for the time being.

8 Lecter overpowers the guards with their own weapons: one policeman is given a taste of his own pepper spray.

"It has been a good long while since I have felt the presence of Evil so manifestly demonstrated ..." *Chicago Sun-Times*

comparable. The movie was so successful that it became one of the most influential models for the decade that followed, enriching cinema history to the point of plot plagiarism and quotation.

Hannibal Lecter had already appeared on the silver screen before *The Silence of the Lambs*. In 1986, Michael Mann filmed Thomas Harris's 1981 novel *Red Dragon* under the title *Manhunter*. Five years later, Jonathan Demme refined the material, and the changing perspectives of his

camera work give what is fundamentally a cinematic re-telling of *Beauty and the Beast* a new twist. Demme films his characters from both within and without.

The director plays with the fluid border between external and internal reality, between memory and the present, as when we see Clarice's childhood in two flash-backs for which we are completely unprepared. Jodie Foster's eyes remain fixed on the here and now while the camera zooms beyond her into the past, probing her psy-

chological wounds. During the final confrontation between Clarice and Jame Gumb, the perspective changes repeatedly. We see the murderer through Clarice's eyes but we also see the young FBI agent through the eyes of Jame, who seeks out his victims in the dark using infrared glasses.

This changing perspective in the movie's final scenes emphasizes the extreme danger that Clarice is in. Other sequences are straightforward trickery, like the changing perspectives in the sequence which builds up to the finale. A police contingent has surrounded the house where they expect to find Jame Gumb, and a black police

officer disguised as a deliveryman rings the bell. On the other side of the door, we hear the bell ring. Jame dresses and answers the door.

The police break into the house, while we see the murderer open the door to find Clarice standing before him – alone. In the next take, the police storm an empty house. This parallel montage combines two places that are far apart, two actions with the same aim, two houses, of which one is only seen from outside, the other from inside. We are made to think that both actions are happening in the same place. The parallel montage is revealed as a trick and

9 In Buffalo Bill's basement lair, Starling is just about to be plunged into
total darkness ...

10 ... where she has to feel her way
blindly, straining to hear, while
Buffalo Bill watches her through
infrared goggles.

"I go to the cinema because I feel like being shocked."
Jonathan Demme

increases the tension: we suddenly realize that Clarice must face the murderer alone.

More than one film critic assumed that this ploy meant that even Hollywood films had moved into an era of self-reflexivity. Instead of consciously revealing a cinematic device, however, the parallel montage serves primarily to heighten the movie's atmosphere of danger and uncertainty. Nevertheless, *The Silence of the Lambs* works on two levels, both as exciting entertainment and as a virtuoso game with key cultural figures and situations. Some critics went so far as to interpret the perverted killer Buffalo Bill as Hades, god of the underworld, and although analyses like

that may be interesting, they are not essential to an understanding of the film or its success.

At the 1992 Oscar awards, *The Silence of the Lambs* carried off the so-called Big Five in the five main categories, something which only two films (*It Happened One Night* [1934] and *One Flew Over the Cuckoo's Nest* [1975] had managed previously. Ten years after his escape, Hannibal Lecter appeared again on the silver screen (*Hannibal*, 2001). Jodie Foster refused to play the role of Clarice for a second time and was replaced by Julianne Moore *(Magnolia)* and Ridley Scott took over from Jonathan Demme as director.   RV

FORREST GUMP ♟♟♟♟♟♟

1994 - USA - 142 MIN.

DIRECTOR
ROBERT ZEMECKIS (*1952)

SCREENPLAY
ERIC ROTH, based on the novel
of the same name by WINSTON GROOM

DIRECTOR OF PHOTOGRAPHY
DON BURGESS

EDITING
ARTHUR SCHMIDT

MUSIC
ALAN SILVESTRI

PRODUCTION
WENDY FINERMAN, STEVE TISCH,
STEVE STARKEY, CHARLES NEWIRTH FOR PARAMOUNT

STARRING
TOM HANKS (Forrest Gump), ROBIN WRIGHT (Jenny Curran),
GARY SINISE (Lt. Dan Taylor), SALLY FIELD (Mrs Gump),
MYKELTI WILLIAMSON (Benjamin Buford "Bubba" Blue),
MICHAEL CONNER HUMPHREYS (Forrest as a boy), HANNA HALL (Jenny as a girl),
TIFFANY SALERNO (Carla), MARLA SUCHARETZA (Lenore),
HALEY JOEL OSMENT (Forrest Junior)

ACADEMY AWARDS 1994
OSCARS for BEST PICTURE, BEST DIRECTOR (Robert Zemeckis), BEST ACTOR (Tom Hanks),
BEST VISUAL EFFECTS (Allen Hall, George Murphy, Ken Ralston, Stephen Rosenbaum),
BEST FILM EDITING (Arthur Schmidt), and BEST ADAPTED SCREENPLAY (Eric Roth)

The world
will never be the same
once you've
seen it through the eyes of
Forrest Gump.

Tom Hanks is Forrest Gump

Paramount Pictures presents a Steve Tisch/Wendy Finerman production a Robert Zemeckis film Tom Hanks Forrest Gump Robin Wright Gary Sinise
Mykelti Williamson and Sally Field producer Charles Newirth music by Alan Silvestri music producer Joel Sill editor Arthur Schmidt production designer Rick Carter director of photography Don Burgess based on the novel by Winston Groom screenplay by Eric Roth
READ THE PAPERBACK   SPECIAL VISUAL EFFECTS BY   produced by Wendy Finerman Steve Tisch Steve Starkey   directed by Robert Zemeckis   A Paramount Communications Company
FROM POCKET BOOKS   INDUSTRIAL LIGHT & MAGIC   SOUNDTRACK AVAILABLE ON EPIC SOUNDTRAX   TM & Copyright © 1994 by Paramount Pictures. All Rights Reserved.

FORREST GUMP

"Shit happens!"

A bus stop in Savannah, Georgia. A man with the facial expression of a child sits on the bench, a small suitcase next to him and a box of chocolates in his hand. While he is waiting for the bus, he tells the story of his life to the others sitting around him.

The story begins sometime in the 1950s in a place called Greenbow in Alabama. Here Forrest Gump (Michael Conner Humphreys), a young boy named after a hero from the Civil War, is growing up without a father. He is different from the other children: his IQ of 75 is way below average, and as his mother (Sally Field) says, his spine is as bent as a politician's morals. But his mother is a strong-willed woman, and she manages to balance out these defects. She makes her boy wear leg braces and although she's prepared to use her body to convince the headmaster that Forrest doesn't need to go to a special school, she teaches her son morals: "Dumb folks are folks who act dumb," being one of the many pearls of wisdom from her rich repertoire.

Forrest, who is friendly and unsuspecting, doesn't have an easy life. No one wants to sit next to him on the school bus, apart from Jenny (Hanna Hall), who soon becomes his only friend. When Forrest is being teased by his schoolmates for the thousandth time, she tells him to run away. Forrest always does what people tell him, and suddenly he discovers hidden gifts like speed and endurance. The leg braces shatter, and with them the limitations of his simple mind fall away. Swifter than the wind, Forrest runs and runs and runs through his youth.

Years later, when he's almost an adult, Forrest is running away from his schoolmates again and by mistake ends up on a football field. Simple-minded Forrest is offered a college scholarship and a place on an All-American football team.

"Life is like a box of chocolates. You never know what you're gonna get" – another gem from Mrs. Gump's treasury. There's a lot in this for Forrest. Thanks to his knack for being in the right place at the right time, his football career is followed by military service and the Vietnam War, where he becomes not only a war hero but also a first-class table tennis player. After the war he fulfills a promise he made to Bubba (Mykelti Williamson), his friend and comrade in arms, and he makes his fortune as the captain of a shrimping boat. He becomes even richer when he invests his millions in what he believes to be a fruit firm by the name of "Apple."

BLUE/GREEN SCREEN Blue/green screen is a process by which moving silhouettes can be combined with a picture background. The actors, figures, or objects are first filmed in front of a blue screen. Then two versions of the movie are made: in the first all the colors are filtered out of the background, in the second only the silhouettes of the actors remain on a white background. The layers can be amalgamated either in an optical printer or digitally. The computer process, known as compositing, was used in films including *Jurassic Park* (1993), *Godzilla* (1997), and *Gladiator* (2000).

2

1 As simple as they come: Forrest Gump (Tom Hanks) fulfills the American dream in his own way.

2 A safe seat: one of his mother's sayings was "Dumb folks are folks who act dumb" and this stays with him all his life.

3 Jenny (Hanna Hall) is Forrest's (Michael Conner Humphreys) only friend. She sticks by him, even though everybody teases him because he is so slow physically and mentally.

4 A woman's wiles: Forrest's single mother (Sally Field) uses everything in her power, even her own body, to ensure that her son leads a normal life.

Forrest Gump's life is a 40-year long-distance run through American postwar history. He shakes hands with Presidents Kennedy and Nixon, shows Elvis Presley the hip thrust and inspires John Lennon's song "Imagine." He invents the Smiley as well as the "Shit happens" sticker. By pure chance his finger is always on the pulse of the times. He gets mixed up in a protest action for racial inte-

gration, in a demonstration against the Vietnam War, and accidentally witnesses the Watergate Affair.

Just as Forrest's career and his experiences of American history are unintentional, his meetings with the love of his life, Jenny (Robin Wright), are also unplanned. Instead of fulfilling her dream and becoming a folk singer she has ended up a junkie hanging around the hippie scene,

"Hanks is a kid again in director Robert Zemeckis' *Forrest Gump*. Slow-witted and likeable, Forrest races through the rubble of the '50s, '60s and '70s."

Time Magazine

singing in a third-rate nightclub. When his mother dies, Forrest moves back to Greenbow, where he has a short but unsuccessful affair with Jenny. Once more, Forrest tries to run away from his destiny and he runs through America for three years without a concrete destination, accompanied by a growing band of followers.

Director Robert Zemeckis is known for being a specialist in technically demanding entertainment movies. He literally turned Meryl Streep's head in *Death Becomes Her* (1992) and his *Back to the Future* trilogy suggests that he has a weakness for time travel (*Back to the Future I–III*,

1985, 1989, 1990). *Forrest Gump*, adapted by Eric Roth from the novel of the same name by Winston Groom, is also a strange journey into the past.

With the help of George Lucas's special effects firm Industrial Light & Magic (ILM), Zemeckis uses sophisticated visual tricks and original film footage to create the illusion that Forrest was actually present at various historical occasions. For the scene where Forrest shakes hands with President Kennedy in the Oval Office, the digital technicians of ILM used archive material with the real people cut out and a superimposed image of Forrest

"Throughout, Forrest carries a flame for Jenny, a childhood sweetheart who was raised by a sexually abusive father and is doomed to a troubled life. The character's a bit obvious: Jenny is clearly Forrest's shadow — darkness and self destruction played against his lightness and simplicity." *San Francisco Chronicle*

Gump put in. Tom Hanks was filmed in front of a blue screen and this was combined with the archive film by computer. Computer technology is present throughout *Forrest Gump*, though audiences are unlikely to notice it. With its help, a thousand real extras were transformed into a hundred thousand simulated demonstrators.

The naïve boy-next-door image which Tom Hanks had developed elsewhere made him the ideal actor for this part, which one critic described as "Charlie Chaplin meets Lawrence of Arabia." His Forrest Gump is the counterpart of Josh Baskin, the 12-year-old who grows into the body of a man overnight in Penny Marshall's hit comedy *Big* (1988).

    Forrest Gump is not a direct reflection of contemporary history, but it does reflect a distinctly American mentality. History is personalized and shown as a series of coincidences. The moral of the movie is as simple as the sayings of Forrest's mother. Everything is possible – you just have to want something to happen, or be at the right place at the right time, even if you hardly realize what is going on and don't take an active part in events. International moviegoers loved the unique and entertaining worldview of this simple soul from Alabama, underscored by a soundtrack which is a musical cross section of the whole century. The movie made 330 million dollars in the U.S., and almost doubled that sum worldwide. It was awarded six Oscars in 1995, and suddenly Smileys were in fashion again and everyone went around saying "Shit happens!" Winston Groom's novel and Bubba's shrimp cookbook stood on many bookshelves. *Forrest Gump* is somewhat reminiscent of Hal Ashby's comedy *Being There* (1979), where Peter Sellers plays a simple gardener who only knows the world from his television. Ashby's movie is an intelligent and sometimes highly comic satire, but *Forrest Gump* didn't take that opportunity, or didn't want it: it's pure entertainment which only pretends to reflect on modern history. That combination of historical reproduction and conventional Hollywood plot links *Forrest Gump* to Steven Spielberg's *Schindler's List* (1993): the audience flick through the movie like a photo album, reassure themselves about their own past and leave the movie theater two hours later, satisfied and by no means unpleasantly moved. APO

---

5 Love, peace and happiness? Jenny (Robin Wright) resorts to drugs while running away from herself.

6 An inspired move: *Forrest Gump* owes a large part of its authentic feel to the special effects of Industrial Light & Magic. These lead the viewer to think that Forrest really did meet President Nixon.

7 A promise with consequences: Forrest promises his dying friend Bubba (Mykelti Williamson) that he will fulfill their shared dream of going shrimp fishing.

CHUNGKING EXPRESS

CHONGQING SENLIN

1994 - HONG KONG - 97 MIN.

DIRECTOR

WONG KAR-WAI [WANG JIAWEI] (*1958)

SCREENPLAY

WONG KAR-WAI

DIRECTOR OF PHOTOGRAPHY

CHRISTOPHER DOYLE, ANDREW LAU [LIU WEIQIANG]

EDITING

WILLIAM CHANG, KAI KIT-WAI, KWONG CHI-LEUNG

MUSIC

ROEL A. GARCIA, FRANKIE CHAN [CHEN SHUNQI]

PRODUCTION

CHAN YI-KAN [CHEN YIJIN] for JET TONE PRODUCTIONS

STARRING

BRIGITTE LIN [Lin Qingxia] (woman with the blond wig), TAKESHI KANESHIRO [He Qiwu] (# 223),
TONY LEUNG [Liang Chaowei] (# 663), FAYE WONG [Wang Jinwen] (Faye),
VALERIE CHOW [Shou Jialing] (Stewardess), "PIGGY" CHAN [Chen Jinquan],
GUAN LINA, HUANG ZHIMING, ZHEN LIANG, ZUO SONGSHEN

"California Dreamin'."

To begin with, *Chungking Express* was just occupational therapy for Wong Kar-wai: he had a couple of months' break in the middle of a big production called *Ashes of Time* (*Dung che sai duk*, 1992–94) and he wanted to fill it in by knocking out a short movie. He started with little more than a couple of clearly defined characters and locations to go with them. The internal links and the plot, were all to be found in the process of filming.

April 30, 1994. A woman (Brigitte Lin) in a garish blond wig and enormous sunglasses has to pass on a packet of drugs, but she loses it and has to go and look for it. At the same time policeman He Qiwu – officer no. 223 – sits in a snack bar drowning his sorrows, as his girlfriend left him exactly a month ago. Since then he has survived on cans of pineapple whose sell-by date is today, symbolizing the end of his love. Gloomily he gets more and more drunk and empties his last can of pineapple. To cap it all, today is his 25th birthday. He decides to fall in love with the first woman who comes into the snack bar. Enter the blonde with the sunglasses, worn out from a chaotic day and looking for comfort.

Another policeman – officer no. 663 – has also split up with his girlfriend, a stewardess. She has left her key to his apartment in his regular bar with Faye the waitress, who constantly listens to the promises of "California Dreamin'." Faye has secretly been in love with the policeman for a long time, and has absolutely no intention of passing on the keys. She starts creeping into his apartment every day. Sometimes she simply cleans up, often she plays some kind of trick, swaps labels on tin cans, dissolves sleeping pills in drinks, or puts new fish in his aquarium. One day she finds a message from the policeman: he wants to meet her and arranges a date in the Restaurant California.

The particular conditions of the movie's production, meant that Wong had to fight not only with his inspiration but also with the plans of his film team, who were booked up for months ahead. Apparently the set was the scene of the most extraordinary comings and goings as both the actors and the technicians were constantly disappearing off to other film sets. Wong improvised a lot and filmed lots of individual scenes that had to be self-contained, as it

CHRISTOPHER DOYLE Christopher Doyle was born in Sydney in 1952. His work with director Wong Kar-wai, whose movies he filmed from *Days of Being Wild* (*A Fei zhengzhuan*, 1990) onwards, made him into one of the most-imitated cameramen of the '90s. His sensitive approach to color combined with precise handheld camera work came to express the melancholy of the period's *fin-de-siècle* school of international art films. Doyle, who speaks fluent Mandarin and Cantonese, moved to Hong Kong and then adopted a Chinese name: Duk Ke-feng (lord, master, like the wind). From 1998 onward, Doyle has worked as director of photography on English language productions like *Liberty Heights* (1999), *The Quiet American* (2002), and *Ondine* (2009).

1 "[I'm the] DJ of my own films."
Wong Kar-wai

2 Self-reflection, Hong Kong style: Cantonese pop superstar Faye Wong [Wang Jinwen] as Faye in a typical Wong game with the identities of his actors.

3 Another icon of 1990s cinema: Asian hit woman Brigitte Lin [Lin Qingxia] in a blonde wig.

4 "There is so little space in Hong Kong that you would have no chance with a fixed camera. You have to work with a handheld camera."
Cameraman Christopher Doyle

5 "The scenes in *Chungking Express* […] are set in places that he [Wong Kar-wai] himself frequents, such as the 'Midnight-Express' fastfood stand in the Lan Kwai Fong district."
Production Manager & Chief Editor William Chang

"It's beautiful, simple, funny and smart. I wish more films were like it." *Le Monde*

was unclear how the scenes would fit together at the end. Despite the movie's transitory character, this gives every moment a high degree of concentration. Wong withdrew to the editing room with the piecemeal material and two months later, *Chungking Express* was finished.

The movie became Wong Kar-wai's greatest international success, the blonde with the sunglasses the icon of a whole generation and Chris Doyle one of the most important cameramen of the '90s. Wong Kar-wai became a style. Wong Kar-wai came to mean loose plots structured like poems, eccentric voice-overs, bright colors, spectacular handheld camera work and outlandish picture composition: an urbane cinema of memories, where romance is only possible in retrospect, set in a city which is constantly changing, which denies its past and which will soon cease to exist.   OM

PULP FICTION ♦

1994 - USA - 154 MIN.

DIRECTOR
QUENTIN TARANTINO (*1963)

SCREENPLAY
QUENTIN TARANTINO, ROGER AVARY

DIRECTOR OF PHOTOGRAPHY
ANDRZEJ SEKULA

MUSIC
VARIOUS SONGS

PRODUCTION
LAWRENCE BENDER for JERSEY FILMS, A BAND APART (for MIRAMAX)

STARRING
JOHN TRAVOLTA (Vincent Vega), SAMUEL L. JACKSON (Jules Winnfield),
UMA THURMAN (Mia Wallace), HARVEY KEITEL (Winston Wolf),
VING RHAMES (Marsellus Wallace), ROSANNA ARQUETTE (Jody),
ERIC STOLTZ (Lance), QUENTIN TARANTINO (Jimmie),
BRUCE WILLIS (Butch Coolidge), MARIA DE MEDEIROS (Fabienne),
CHRISTOPHER WALKEN (Koons), TIM ROTH (Ringo /Pumpkin),
AMANDA PLUMMER (Yolanda / Honey Bunny)

ACADEMY AWARDS 1995
OSCAR for BEST ORIGINAL SCREENPLAY (Quentin Tarantino, Roger Avary)

IFF CANNES 1994
PALME D'OR

WINNER·BEST PICTURE·1994 CANNES FILM FESTIVAL

PULP FICTION

a Quentin Tarantino film

10¢

produced by
Lawrence Bender

JOHN TRAVOLTA
SAMUEL L. JACKSON
UMA THURMAN
HARVEY KEITEL
TIM ROTH
AMANDA PLUMMER
MARIA de MEDEIROS
VING RHAMES
ERIC STOLTZ
ROSANNA ARQUETTE
CHRISTOPHER WALKEN
and
BRUCE WILLIS

MIRAMAX FILMS PRESENTS A BAND APART AND JERSEY FILMS PRODUCTION A FILM BY QUENTIN TARANTINO PULP FICTION MUSIC SUPERVISOR KARYN RACHTMAN
COSTUME DESIGNER BETSY HEIMANN PRODUCTION DESIGNER DAVID WASCO EDITOR SALLY MENKE DIRECTOR OF PHOTOGRAPHY ANDRZEJ SEKULA
CO-EXECUTIVE PRODUCERS BOB WEINSTEIN HARVEY WEINSTEIN RICHARD N. GLADSTEIN EXECUTIVE PRODUCERS DANNY DEVITO MICHAEL SHAMBERG
STACEY SHER STORIES BY QUENTIN TARANTINO & ROGER AVARY PRODUCED BY LAWRENCE BENDER WRITTEN AND DIRECTED BY QUENTIN TARANTINO

R RESTRICTED

SOUNDTRACK AVAILABLE ON MCA LP'S CASSETTES & CD'S

DOLBY STEREO
DIGITAL

MIRAMAX

PULP FICTION

"Zed's dead, baby. Zed's dead."

After his amazing directorial debut, *Reservoir Dogs* (1991), Quentin Tarantino had a lot to live up to. The bloody studio piece was essentially a purely cinematic challenge, and such an unusual movie seemed difficult to beat. But Tarantino surpassed himself with *Pulp Fiction*, a deeply black gangster comedy. Tarantino had previously written the screenplay for Tony Scott's uninspired gangster movie *True Romance* (1993) and the original script to Oliver Stone's *Natural Born Killers* (1994). At the beginning of his own movie, he presents us with another potential killer couple. Ringo and Yolanda (Tim Roth and Amanda Plummer), who lovingly call each other Pumpkin and Honey Bunny, are sitting having breakfast in a diner and making plans for their future together. They are fed up of robbing liquor stores whose multicultural owners don't even understand simple orders like "Hand over the cash!" The next step in their career plan is to expand into diners – why not start straight away with this one? This sequence, which opens and concludes *Pulp Fiction* serves a framework for the movie's other three interwoven stories, which overlap and move in and out of chronological sequence. One of the protagonists is killed in the middle of the movie, only to appear alive and well in the final scene, and we only understand how the stories hang together at the very end.

The first story is "Vincent Vega and Marsellus Wallace's Wife." Vincent and Jules (John Travolta and Samuel L. Jackson), are professional assassins on their way to carry out an order. Their boss Marsellus Wallace (Ving Rhames) wants them to bring him back a mysterious briefcase. A routine job, as we can tell from their nonchalant chitchat. Their black suits make them look as if they have stepped out of a '40s *film noir*. Vincent is not entirely happy, as he has been given the job of looking after Marsellus's wife Mia (Uma Thurman) when the boss is away. In gangster circles, rumor has it that Vincent's predecessor was thrown out of a window on the fourth floor – apparently for doing nothing more than massaging Mia's feet.

"The Golden Watch," the second story in the film, is the story of has-been boxer Butch Coolidge (Bruce Willis). He too is one of Marsellus's "niggers" as the gangster boss calls all those who depend on him. Butch has accepted a bribe and agreed to take a dive after the fifth round in his next fight. At the last minute, he decides to win instead and to run away with the money and his French girlfriend Fabienne (Maria de Medeiros).

In the third story, "The Bonnie Situation," a couple of loose narrative strands are tied together. Jules and

PULP Cheap novels in magazine format, especially popular in the '30s and '40s, owing their name to the cheap, soft paper they were printed on. The themes and genres of these mostly illustrated serial novels and short stories ranged from comics to science fiction to detective stories. The first pulp stories appeared in the 1880s in the magazine *The Argosy*. In the 1930s there were several hundred pulp titles available, but by 1954 they had all disappeared – pulp was replaced by the cinema, the radio and above all, the new paperback book.

2

"Hoodlums Travolta and Jackson – like modern-day Beckett characters – discuss foot massages, cunnilingus and cheeseburgers on their way to a routine killing job. The recently traveled Travolta informs Jackson that at the McDonald's in Paris, the Quarter Pounder is known as 'Le Royal.' However a Big Mac's a Big Mac, but they call it 'Le Big Mac.' "

The Washington Post

1 Do Mia's (Uma Thurman) foot massages turn into an erotic experience?

2 The Lord moves in mysterious ways: Jules (Samuel L. Jackson) is a killer who knows his Bible by heart.

3 Completely covered in blood: Vincent (John Travolta) after his little accident.

Vincent have done their job. However, on the way back, Vincent accidentally shoots his informer who is sitting in the back of the car. The bloody car and its occupants have to get off the street as soon as possible. The two killers hide at Jim's (Quentin Tarantino), although his wife Bonnie is about to get back from work at any moment, so they have to get rid of the evidence as quickly as they can. Luckily they can call upon the services of Mr. Wolf (Harvey Keitel), the quickest and most efficient cleaner there is.

To like *Pulp Fiction*, you have to have a weakness for pop culture, which this film constantly uses and parodies, although it never simply ridicules the source of its inspiration. Quentin Tarantino must have seen enormous quantities of movies before he became a director. The inside of his head must be like the restaurant where Vincent takes Mia; the tables are like '50s Cabrios, the waiters and waitresses are pop icon doubles: Marilyn Monroe, James Dean, Mamie van Doren and Buddy Holly (Steve Buscemi in a cameo appearance). Vincent and Mia take part in a Twist competition. The way the saggy-cheeked, aging John Travolta dances is a brilliant homage to his early career and *Saturday Night Fever* (1977).

With his tongue-in-cheek allusions to pop and film culture, Tarantino often verges on bad taste: in one scene from "The Golden Watch," a former prisoner of war and Vietnam veteran (Christopher Walken) arrives at a children's home to give the little Butch his father's golden watch. The scene begins like a kitsch scene from any Vietnam movie, but quickly deteriorates into the scatological and absurd when Walken tells the boy in great detail about the dark place where his father hid the watch in the prison camp for so many years.

Tarantino has an excellent feel for dialogue. His protagonists' conversations are as banal as in real life, they talk about everything and nothing, about potbellies, embarrassing silences, or piercings. He also lays great value on those little details which really make the stories, for example the toaster, which together with Vincent's habit of long sessions

in the bathroom will cost him his life – as he prefers to take a detective story rather than a pistol into the lavatory.

Tarantino's treatment of violence is a theme unto itself. It is constantly present in the movie, but is seldomly explicitly shown. The weapon is more important than the victim. In a conventional action movie, the scene where Jules and Vincent go down a long corridor to the apartment where they will kill several people would have been used to build up the suspense, but in Tarantino's film Vincent and Jules talk about trivial things instead, like two office colleagues on the way to the canteen.

One of the movie's most brutal scenes comes after Vincent and Mia's restaurant visit. The pair of them are in Mia's apartment, Vincent as ever in the bathroom, where he is meditating on loyalty and his desire to massage Mia's feet. In the meantime Mia discovers his supply of

4 Everything's under control: as the "Cleaner" Mister Wolf (Harvey Keitel) takes care of any dirty work that comes up.

5 In his role as Major Koons Christopher Walken plays an ex-Vietnam prisoner of war, as he did in *The Deer Hunter*.

6 Echoes of *Saturday Night Fever*: Mia and Vincent risk a little dance.

4

> **"Tarantino's guilty secret is that his films are cultural hybrids. The blood and gore, the cheeky patter, the taunting mise-en-scène are all very American – the old studios at their snazziest."**
> *Time Magazine*

heroin, thinks it is cocaine and snorts an overdose. Vincent is then forced to get physical with her, but not in the way he imagined. To bring her back to life, he has to plant an enormous adrenaline jab in her heart.

Pulp Fiction also shows Tarantino to be a master of casting. All the roles are carried by their actors' larger-than-life presence. They are all "cool": Samuel L. Jackson as an Old-Testament-quoting killer, and Uma Thurman in a black wig as an enchanting, dippy gangster's moll. Bruce Willis drops his habitual grin and is totally convincing as an aging boxer who refuses to give up. Craggy, jowly John

"Split into three distinct sections, the tale zips back and forth in time and space, meaning that the final shot is of a character we've seen being killed 50 minutes ago." *Empire*

Travolta plays the most harmless and good-natured assassin imaginable. If *Pulp Fiction* has a central theme running through it, then it's the "moral" which is present in each of the three stories. Butch doesn't run away when he has the opportunity but stays and saves his boss's life. Vincent and Jules live according to strict rules and principles and are very moral in their immoral actions. Vincent is so loyal that it finally costs him his life. Jules's moment of revelation comes when the bullets aimed at him miraculously miss. Coincidence or fate? Jules, who misquotes a Bible passage from Ezekiel before each of the murders he commits, decides that henceforth he will walk the path of righteousness. In the last scene when Ringo and Honey Bunny rob the diner, Ringo tries to take the mysterious shiny briefcase. He fails to spot Jules draw his gun and under normal circumstances he would be a dead man. But Jules, who has decided to turn over a new leaf, has mercy on both of them – and that's not normal circumstances. APO

7 You gotta change your life! Jules and Vincent talk about chance and predestiny.

8 Hand over the cash! Yolanda (Amanda Plummer) carries out …

9 … the plan that she and Ringo (Tim Roth) hatched a few moments before.

L.A. CONFIDENTIAL ♛♛

1997 - USA - 138 MIN.

DIRECTOR
CURTIS HANSON (*1945)

SCREENPLAY
CURTIS HANSON, BRIAN HELGELAND,
based on the novel *L.A. Confidential* by JAMES ELLROY

DIRECTOR OF PHOTOGRAPHY
DANTE SPINOTTI

MUSIC
JERRY GOLDSMITH

PRODUCTION
CURTIS HANSON, ARNON MILCHAN, MICHAEL G. NATHANSON
for REGENCY ENTERPRISES

STARRING
RUSSELL CROWE (Bud White), KEVIN SPACEY (Jack Vincennes),
GUY PEARCE (Ed Exley), KIM BASINGER (Lynn Bracken),
DANNY DEVITO (Sid Hudgeons), JAMES CROMWELL (Dudley Smith),
DAVID STRATHAIRN (Pierce Patchett), RON RIFKIN (D. A. Ellis Loew),
MATT MCCOY (Brett Chase), PAUL GUILFOYLE (Mickey Cohen)

ACADEMY AWARDS 1997
OSCARS for BEST SUPPORTING ACTRESS (Kim Basinger),
and BEST ADAPTED SCREENPLAY (Curtis Hanson, Brian Helgeland)

"Why did you become a cop?"
"I don't remember."

Sun, swimming pools, beautiful people: "Life is good in L.A., it's a paradise …" That Los Angeles only exists in commercials. In *L.A. Confidential* – set in the early '50 s – the city looks quite different, and is a morass of crime and corruption. Three policemen try to combat this with varying dedication and varying motives. Ambitious young police academy graduate Ed Exley (Guy Pearce) is a champion of law and order, and his testimony against his colleagues in an internal police trial catapults him straight to the top of the station house hierarchy. Bud White (Russell Crowe) is a hardened cynic who is prepared to extract confessions with force, but cannot stand violence against women and Jack Vincennes (Kevin Spacey) is nothing more than a corrupt phony who uses his police job to get in with the entertainment in-dustry. He is advisor to the television series *Badge Of Honor* and sets up stories for Sid Hudgeons (Danny DeVito), slimy reporter on the gossip magazine *Hush-Hush.*

Exley's first case is a spectacular bloodbath in the Nite Owl bar. Five lie dead in the bathroom, killed with a shotgun. Three black youths seen near the scene of the crime are swiftly arrested, and with his brilliant interrogation technique, Exley gets them to admit to having kidnapped and raped a Mexican girl. While White frees the victim and shoots her captor, the three suspects escape from police custody. Exley hunts them down and shoots them dead. He is hailed as a hero and awarded a medal, and it would seem that that is the end of the case. But it doesn't seem to quite add up, and Exley, White and Vincennes continue their investigations until they discover a conspiracy which reaches up into the highest echelons of police and city administration, involving drugs, blackmail, and a ring of porn traders.

L.A. Confidential is a reference to the first and perhaps most brazen American gossip magazine *Confidential* (1952–1957), and Hudgeons, the reporter played by Danny DeVito (who is also the off-screen narrator) is an alter ego of Robert Harrison, its infamous editor. Hudgeons gets his kicks from filth and sensationalism, and typifies the moral decadence that seems to have infected the

JAMES ELLROY: L.A.'S INDEFATIGABLE CHRONICLER His own life sounds like a crime story. James Ellroy was born in Los Angeles in 1948. When he was ten, his mother fell victim to a sex killer, a crime he works through in his 1996 novel *My Dark Places.* The shock threw Ellroy completely off the rails: drugs, petty crime, and 50 arrests followed and he came to writing relatively late. His first novel *Brown's Requiem* was published in 1981 and made into a movie with the same name in 1998. He then wrote a novel trilogy on the figure of the policeman Lloyd Hopkins. The first of this series *Blood on the Moon* (1984) was filmed in 1988 as *Cop* starring James Woods in the title role. Ellroy's masterpiece is the L.A. tetralogy, novels on historical crimes from the period 1947 to 1960. Brian De Palma made the first volume in the series, *The Black Dahlia,* into a film with the same title in 2006. *L.A. Confidential* (1997) was based on the third volume in the series; it took director Curtis Hanson and coauthor Brian Helgeland a whole year and seven different versions to adapt this complex novel into a screenplay.

3

4

entire city. The police make deals with criminals, the cops who uncover the conspiracy are far from blameless and even the naïve greenhorn Exley looses his innocence in the course of the film.

Director Curtis Hanson conjures up the brooding atmosphere of the film noir crime movies of the '40s and '50s, but *L.A. Confidential* is far more than a throwback of a simple nostalgia trip. Cameraman Dante Spinotti shoots clear images free from any patina of age and avoids typical genre references like long shadows. The crime and the corruption seem even more devastating when told in pictures of a sunny, crisp Los Angeles winter. The plot is complex and difficult to follow on first viewing, but Hanson does not emphasize this so much as individual scenes which condense the city's amorality into striking images, like Vincennes saying he can no longer remember why he became a cop. Above all, the director focuses on his brilliant ensemble. Australians Russell Crowe and Guy Pearce, who were virtually unknown before the movie was made, make a great team with the amazing Kevin Spacey. Kim Basinger is a worthy Oscar winner as prostitute and Veronica Lake look-alike Lynn.   HJK

1 He may have deserved it much more for this film, but Russell Crowe didn't win an Oscar until 2001 for *Gladiator*.

2 Bud White (Russell Crowe) doesn't waste any time with the kidnapper of the Mexican girl.

3 A few moments of melancholy apart, Bud White doesn't let the corruptness of the world get to him.

4 Brief moments of happiness: is there a future for Bud and Lynn's love?

5 Kim Basinger's Oscar for the part of Lynn Bracken brought her long-overdue universal acclaim.

6 A Christmas angel: Lynn out on business until late in the evening with her employer.

7 Lynn the prostitute's little trick: she does herself up to look like 1940s glamour star Veronica Lake.

"It's striking to see how the elegance and lightness of touch in the atmosphere of *L.A. Confidential* seem both to derive from and influence the actors." *Cahiers du cinéma*

"When I gave Kevin Spacey the script, I said I think of two words: Dean Martin."

Curtis Hanson in: Sight and Sound

8 Tabloid reporter Sid Hudgeons (Danny DeVito) loves digging up other people's dirt.

9 Officer Vincennes (right) likes to take Hudgeons and a photographer along to his arrests.

10 Vincennes (Kevin Spacey) makes sure that first and foremost he's looking after number one.

11 Officer Ed Exley (Guy Pearce) earns praise from the press and from his boss Dudley Smith (James Cromwell, right).

FACE/OFF

1997 - USA - 138 MIN.

DIRECTOR

JOHN WOO (*1946)

SCREENPLAY

MIKE WERB, MICHAEL COLLEARY

DIRECTOR OF PHOTOGRAPHY

OLIVER WOOD

MUSIC

JOHN POWELL

PRODUCTION

DAVID PERMUT, BARRIE M. OSBORNE, TERENCE CHANG, CHRISTOPHER GODSICK
for DOUGLAS-REUTHER PRODUCTION, WCG ENTERTAINMENT

STARRING

JOHN TRAVOLTA (Sean Archer), NICOLAS CAGE (Castor Troy),
JOAN ALLEN (Eve Archer), ALESSANDRO NIVOLA (Pollux Troy),
GINA GERSHON (Sasha Hassler), DOMINIQUE SWAIN (Jamie Archer),
NICK CASSAVETES (Dietrich Hassler), HARVE PRESNELL (Victor Lazarro),
COLM FEORE (Dr. Malcolm Walsh), CCH POUNDER (Dr. Hollis Miller)

JOHN   NICOLAS
TRAVOLTA/CAGE

IN
ORDER
TO
TRAP
HIM,
HE
MUST
BECOME
HIM.

FACE/OFF

PARAMOUNT PICTURES PRESENTS A DOUGLAS/REUTHER PRODUCTION A WCG ENTERTAINMENT PRODUCTION A DAVID PERMUT PRODUCTION A JOHN WOO FILM JOHN TRAVOLTA NICOLAS CAGE "FACE/OFF" JOAN ALLEN
GINA GERSHON ALESSANDRO NIVOLA MUSIC JOHN POWELL EDITOR CHRISTIAN ADAM WAGNER CO-PRODUCER JEFF LEVINE WRITTEN MIKE WERB and MICHAEL COLLEARY EXECUTIVE PRODUCERS MICHAEL DOUGLAS, STEVEN REUTHER and JONATHAN D. KRANE
PRODUCED DAVID PERMUT, BARRIE OSBORNE, TERENCE CHANG and CHRISTOPHER GODSICK WRITTEN MIKE WERB & MICHAEL COLLEARY DIRECTED JOHN WOO

www.face-off.com

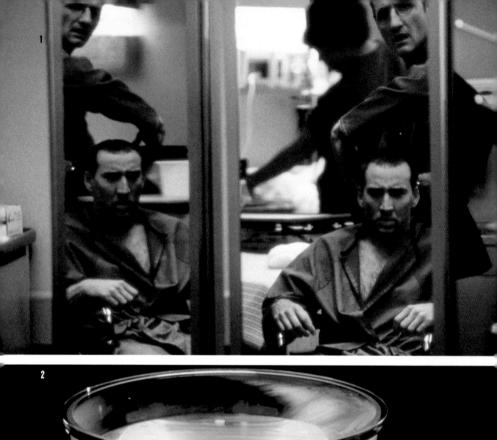

"In order to catch him, he must become him."

Sepia pictures, images in someone's memory. A father rides with his son on a carousel horse. A shot rings out. The father is wounded and the son is killed. Six years later L.A. cop Sean Archer (John Travolta) still hasn't caught up with Castor Troy (Nicolas Cage), the psychopathic sharpshooter who killed his son. He gets another chance at a private airfield. Castor and his brother Pollux (Alessandro Nivolla) are about to take off, and Archer tries to stop them.

A shoot-out ensues where Pollux is arrested and Castor is injured and falls into a coma. But Archer still hasn't shaken off Castor Troy's evil legacy. His brother is carrying a disc that contains information on a gigantic bomb attack in Los Angeles, but the whereabouts of the bomb is a mystery. Pollux insists that he will only speak to his brother. To find out the truth about the bomb, a team of scientists from a secret project make Archer an unbelievable offer.

JOHN TRAVOLTA John Travolta's career began in 1975 with the role of Vinnie Barbarino in the popular television series *Welcome Back, Kotter*. After his enormous success in the dance movies *Saturday Night Fever* (1977) and *Grease* (1978), based on the clichéd role of hunky ladies' man, Travolta practically disappeared from the screen in the 1980s. He wasn't able to return to Hollywood's premiere league until Quentin Tarantino cast him as the off-beat killer Vincent Vega in *Pulp Fiction* (1994). Since then, Travolta has established himself as a versatile character actor who is just as at home in comedy roles as in action films (for example, *Operation: Broken Arrow*, 1995) or in existential dramas such as *Mad City* (1996). At the same time, he has moved up to become one of Hollywood's biggest earners: *Pulp Fiction* earned him $140 000, but subsequent films like *Swordfish* (2001) and *Ladder 49* (2004) saw his fee rise to $20 million. A series of flops, including the self-produced space disaster movie *Battlefield Earth* (2000), form the flipside of his amazing comeback.

"Woo is such an action wizard that he can make planes or speedboats kick‑box, but his surprising strength this time is more on a human level."

New York Times

The parallel between hunter and hunted is a well-worn theme: the cop has to empathise with the criminal in order to predict his next move. Many movies have used this device, perhaps none so systematically as *Heat* (1995), where cop Al Pacino and gangster Robert De Niro meet for a tête-à-tête. *Face/Off*'s director John Woo takes the motif to new heights when he turns the cop into the gangster. With the help of the latest medical technology, Archer is given the face, stature, and voice of the gangster Troy. He already knows more than enough about Troy's story, deeds, and accomplices as he has been chasing him for years. To get the information out of him, Archer is admitted to the high-security prison where Pollux is being kept. The mission remains a secret, and not even Archer's boss or his wife know anything about it. At any time, with the help of the same techniques, he can be given back his own body. But that escape route is suddenly blocked. Troy wakes from his coma and appears in the prison – as Archer. He has had

1 A shock: police officer Archer (John Travolta) wearing the face of the villain he has been pursuing like a man possessed for the last six years.

2 "Ridiculous chin," says Castor (Nicolas Cage) when Archer's face is fixed onto his.

3 The parallel between the hunter and the hunted is a well-known film motif, but nobody has ever taken it as far as John Woo.

4 It's not easy for Archer: locked up in the body of Castor in a hi-tech jail.

5 The moment of truth: Archer (as Castor) runs his archenemy to the ground.

the cop's face put on and shot the scientists and the people who witnessed the "swap." Archer manages to escape from the prison and has to make his way as an outlaw while Troy lives in his comfortable home with his wife and daughter.

Two movies gave new life to the Hollywood action film genre in the '90s: *Speed* (1994) and *Face/Off*. *Speed* is a fast-paced, light-footed celebration of pure movement, whereas *Face/Off* – despite its virtuoso action scenes – has dark, elegiac undertones and a much more complex plot. Archer is a tragic figure from the outset, first losing his son and then his life. The idea of changing bodies might seem far-fetched, but it offers the director plenty of opportunities to play with the hunter/hunted motif. John

Woo goes through all of them one by one. Troy in Archer's body becomes a more subtle kind of gangster: he defuses his own bomb, becomes a hero and decides he wants to run the whole police department. Archer in Troy's body holds Troy's son in his arms as he used to hold his own. And Archer's wife Eve is delighted with the reawakened passion of her husband, who seems like a new man.

The doppelgänger motif reaches a visual highpoint in the scene where Archer and Troy stand on two sides of a mirror and aim their pistols at their own reflections, each of them wearing the face of their archenemy. The visual stylization typical of Woo is everywhere in the movie – like the white doves in a church, or the slow-motion billowing overcoat. HJK

THE CELEBRATION
FESTEN (DOGME 1)
1998 – DENMARK – 106 MIN.

DIRECTOR

THOMAS VINTERBERG (*1969)

SCREENPLAY

THOMAS VINTERBERG, MOGENS RUKOV

DIRECTOR OF PHOTOGRAPHY

ANTHONY DOD MANTLE

EDITING

VALDÍS ÓSKARSDÓTTIR

MUSIC

MORTEN HOLM

PRODUCTION

BRIGITTE HALD, MORTEN KAUFMANN for NIMBUS FILM

STARRING

ULRICH THOMSEN (Christian), THOMAS BO LARSEN (Michael),
PAPRIKA STEEN (Helene), HENNING MORITZEN (Helge),
BIRTHE NEUMANN (the mother), TRINE DYRHOLM (Pia),
HELLE DOLLERIS (Mette), BJARNE HENRIKSEN (Chef),
GBATOKAI DAKINAH (Gbatokai), KLAUS BONDAM (Master of Ceremonies),
THOMAS VINTERBERG (Taxi Driver), JOHN BOAS (Grandfather)

IFF CANNES 1998

SPECIAL JURY PRIZE

DOGME #1

THOMAS VINTERBERG

FESTEN

ALLE FAMILIER HAR EN HEMMELIGHED

1

"Here's to the man who killed my sister, a toast to a murderer."

A dogma is a religious teaching or a doctrine of belief. When four Danes got together to draw up ten commandments in 1995, baptized them "Dogme 95," and described them as a cinematic vow of chastity, it seemed a bizarre act of self-chastisement in a post-ideological age. Perhaps, critics suggested, the whole thing was a bid for freedom at a time of computer animation and postmodern indifference. They wanted to do away with all the trappings of technology and to get back to the basics: strict classical form following crazy, ornate Baroque. Perhaps, the skeptics replied, it was nothing more than a publicity stunt: Tarantino meets *It's a Wonderful Life*.

Nobody could have guessed at that point that the same four Danes would go on to open an agency that watched over the keeping of the commandments and distributed certificates. By the beginning of 2001 a dozen films had been adjudged worthy to promote themselves as "produced in accordance with the rules of the Dogme Manifesto." Both the manifesto and the certification process are inspired by deadly seriousness tempered with a certain dose of ironic humor, and certificates cost anything from nothing at all to 2000 dollars, according to the budget of the

film in question. One of the signatories, Thomas Vinterberg, director of the first brilliant Dogme film *The Celebration*, admitted in an interview that the whole thing oscillated between being "a game and in deadly earnest."

That is also a good description of *The Celebration*'s relationship to its subject matter: whenever viewers attempt to look at it purely as a comedy or solely as drama, it is guaranteed to topple over into the opposite. Drama and comedy are most likely to meet at their extremes. *The Celebration* is not exactly a black comedy, more a bitter reckoning with the deceptive façade of the institution of family life. The best ideas often come from a new look at traditional models and the movie's departure point is very simple: patriarch Helge (Henning Moritzen) is celebrating his 60th birthday with his family at a country mansion. The party turns into a night of grim revelations and innumerable skeletons are dragged out of the family closet.

Basically, the film is about the accusations of the oldest son Christian (Ulrich Thomsen). He claims that he and his twin sister were abused by their father, and that this was the reason for his sister's recent suicide. After a shocked pause, the guests return to the festivities as if nothing had

DOGME 95 1. Shooting must be done on location. Props and sets must not be brought in. 2. The sound must never be produced apart from the images or vice versa. 3. The camera must be handheld. 4. The film must be in color. Special lighting is not acceptable. (If there is too little light for exposure the scene must be cut or a single lamp be attached to the camera.) 5. Optical work and filters are forbidden. 6. The film must not contain superficial action. (Murders, weapons, etc. must not occur.) 7. Temporal and geographical alienation are forbidden. (That is to say that the film takes place here and now.) 8. Genre movies are not acceptable. 9. The film format must be Academy 35 mm. 10. The director must not be credited. For a time, the Dogme 95 movement – an avant-garde film collective initiated in Denmark by Lars von Trier – influenced independent cinema in Europe, and to an extent the US. Between 50 and 100 films are attributed to the genre; one of the last Dogme films, which was explicitly guided by the manifesto from 1995, is *Open Hearts (Elsker dig for evigt*, 2002, Denmark) by Susanne Bier.

happened. At first, Christian's repeated accusations are received with the same equanimity as the table speeches of the grandfather (John Boas) who always tells the same anecdote. Later his mother (Birthe Neumann) attempts to smooth over the situation and finally his hot-tempered youngest brother Michael (Thomas Bo Larsen) explodes. It takes a message from the next world to convince those present of Christian's story.

Some critics consider the Dogme commandments to be a self-important waste of time, but the rules for the use of natural sound and handheld cameras result in films that look like home movies, giving a picture and sound quality which contributes greatly to the believability of their story lines. At first sight, high-resolution video shot without artificial light and transferred onto 35 mm looks like an amateur recording of a private birthday party. The unusual, often underexposed or unfocused pictures force the audience to concentrate. Like a source of purity and liberation, they contrast with the family's repression of the party's shocking revelations. The Dogme films' rejection of skillfully produced, artificial images gives them a feeling of undiluted directness and a whole new pallet of expressive means. This is the attack of the documentary handheld camera on the bastion of the feature film – direct cinema as a presentation of the truth in fiction.

Once spectators get used to the grainy, wobbly pictures, which have quite a different beauty from polished Hollywood pictures, the movie itself is highly coherent both visually and dramatically. The camera angles have been chosen with extreme care: there is a bird's-eye view from the corner of the room, a jump shot over a fence and a camera hidden behind the banisters. Furniture or objects often obstruct the camera's viewfinder. There are two possible interpretations of this: firstly, a blocked viewpoint implies that the place of filming is treated spontaneously and that potential obstacles are dealt with as they arise. Secondly, obscured viewpoints give the movie a documentary feel, as if the camera were a hidden witness or a passerby. The plot follows the classic division in three acts with Christian as the hero and focal point overcoming opposition and obstacles. At the beginning he only has the support of the hotel staff who have known him since he was little, like the chef Kim, who spirits away the guests' keys so that they are isolated in

1 Two brothers still fighting for their father's favor: Christian (Ulrich Thomsen) is thrown out of the house at the instigation of his younger brother Michael (Thomas Bo Larsen).

2 "When my sister died a couple of months ago, it became clear to me that with all the baths he took, Helge was a very clean man." Christian accuses his father.

3 The patriarch Helge shortly before his fall from power: Henning Moritzen, Birthe Neumann.

the country house like the guests in Buñuel's *The Exterminating Angel* (*El ángel exterminador*, 1962). But Mexico or Denmark, 1962 or 1998, bourgeois charm is revealed to be nothing but a veneer of civilization that peels away all too easily.

With great intensity and directness, Vinterberg and his actors show how the respectable bourgeois atmosphere is rapidly transformed into hate-filled racism, how finally the aggressive brother Michael changes sides and erupts against his father instead of shouting at his wife and children, his sister's black boyfriend, and his brother. The abyss in *The Celebration* lurks just below the surface: the official face of the family only just manages to conceal the grimace behind it. Vinterberg is so committed and uncompromising, he almost seems like a descendent of the iconoclasts of the '68 generation.

Vinterberg grew up in a hippie commune. In interviews, he often points out that the Catholic terminology of the Dogme Manifesto came from co-signatory Lars von Trier and has nothing to do with him. He prefers the communist component implicit in the word "Manifesto." To him, this artistic manifesto is also a compelling call to revolt, a return to the basics of collective filmmaking and an appeal for the rejection of production hierarchies, so as a protest against the cult of the auteur, the director's name is not allowed to appear on the film.

The aim above all is to reclaim film from the spirit of post-modernism. Dogma means nothing less than forgetting everything you've already seen and done, beginning again from the beginning, and reinventing cinema. Vinterberg is still filled with awe and wonder in the face of "living pictures" and he shares this with his audience.   MH

ALL ABOUT MY MOTHER ♟

TODO SOBRE MI MADRE

1999 - SPAIN / FRANCE - 101 MIN.

DIRECTOR
PEDRO ALMODÓVAR (*1951)

SCREENPLAY
PEDRO ALMODÓVAR

DIRECTOR OF PHOTOGRAPHY
AFFONSO BEATO

MUSIC
ALBERTO IGLESIAS

PRODUCTION
AGUSTIN ALMODÓVAR, CLAUDE BERRI for EL DESEO,
RENN PRODUCTIONS, FRANCE 2 CINÉMA

STARRING
CECILIA ROTH (Manuela), ELOY AZORÍN (Estéban),
MARISA PAREDES (Huma Rojo), PENÉLOPE CRUZ (Sister Rosa),
ANTONIA SAN JUAN (Agrado), CANDELA PEÑA (Nina),
ROSA MARÍA SARDÀ (Rosa's mother), FERNANDO FERNÁN GÓMEZ (Rosa's father),
TONI CANTÓ (Lola), CARLOS LOZANO (Mario)

ACADEMY AWARDS 2000
OSCAR for BEST FOREIGN LANGUAGE FILM

IFF CANNES 1999
SILVER PALM for BEST DIRECTOR (Pedro Almodóvar)

EL DESEO S.A. presenta:

TODO SOBRE MI MADRE

la producción EL DESEO S.A. / RENN PRODUCTIONS / FRANCE 2 CINEMA

ECILIA ROTH   MARISA PAREDES   PENÉLOPE CRUZ

ANDELA PEÑA   ANTONIA SAN JUAN   ROSA MARÍA SARDÁ

con la colaboración especial de FERNANDO FERNÁN-GÓMEZ   FERNANDO GUILLÉN   TONI CANTÓ   ELOY AZORÍN   y CARLOS LOZANO
nido MIGUEL REJAS   Director Artístico ANTXÓN GÓMEZ   Montaje JOSÉ SALCEDO   Música ALBERTO IGLESIAS   Directora de Producción ESTHER GARCÍA
ductor AGUSTÍN ALMODÓVAR   Director de fotografía AFFONSO BEATO
ión y dirección PEDRO ALMODÓVAR

nda Sonora UNIVERSAL

Con la colaboración de MA   Distribuida por WARNER SOGEFILMS

Un film de ALMODÓVAR

"The only genuine thing about me is my feelings."

The loss of a child is the worst thing that can happen to a mother. Manuela (Cecilia Roth) never mentioned the child's father, even when asked, but now that she is completely on her own she continues her son's search for his other parent. Bowed by suffering and yet filled with strength she is driven back deep into her own past, and she travels from Madrid to Barcelona, from her present existence back to an earlier one. The people she meets on this journey to the end of the night generally only appear on our screens as the bad crowd in television crime series, as pathetic informers or more likely as corpses. Here, transsexuals and junkie prostitutes, pregnant nuns and touchy divas are not only the main characters, but with all their failings and weaknesses, they also win our sympathy.

In her search for comfort, Manuela eventually finds the father of her dead son Estéban (Eloy Azorín), and he has now become a dark angel of death, a terminally ill transsexual who earns his living as a prostitute. Eighteen years ago when they were a couple he was also called Estéban, but now (s)he calls herself Lola (Toni Cantó). Although (s)he was once attractive, those days are long gone: Estéban the First no longer exists and Lola is not long for this world either. Nevertheless, at the end of the movie a third Estéban is born, giving us a utopian hope against all the odds.

The audience shares Manuela's perspective and the Spanish director guides us skillfully through the glittering microcosm of Barcelona's transsexual scene. Almodóvar however has no intention of giving us a documentary; he does not claim to portray objective reality in an authentic manner, and neither is it his intention to teach us a lesson in pity. Instead he takes all the expressive means at the disposal of a melodrama to their extreme: tears, blood, blows, violence, fucking, birth, love, hate, life, and death. The plot may sound unlikely, but nothing seems artificial or false and that is the true miracle of this movie, an effect due in no small part to its fantastic actresses.

They all play actresses in the movie as well: Manuela does role plays with hospital employees to teach them how to deal with the families of deceased patients, and when Nina (Candela Peña), partner of the theater diva Huma (Marisa Paredes), can't go on stage because she's too doped up, Manuela takes her place. The faithful companion Agrado (Antonia San Juan) is perhaps the greatest actress in the true sense of the word; her body has been operated on innumerable times until it is nothing but artificial illusion. One of the best scenes is where she has to announce the cancellation of a play but manages to whip up the disappointed audience into storms of enthusiasm with an autobiographical monologue. This movie about mothers is also dedicated to all actresses who have ever played actresses.

At their best the men in Almodóvar's films are senile like the father (Fernando Fernán Gómez) of AIDS sufferer Rosa (Penélope Cruz), but for the most part men are

PEDRO ALMODÓVAR In the 1980s Almodóvar was hailed as an icon of Spain's gay subculture and was a welcome guest at international festivals. His biting satire ensured that midnight showings of his films were invariably sold out and eventually he became a great figure of European art cinema. In the '90s he was awarded all of cinema's most important prizes and came to be considered one of the most important contemporary filmmakers. He started off being provocative for the sake of it, but gradually he has given his figures depth and complexity while still taking a critical look at conventional bourgeois family life and sexual morals. Nowadays Almodóvar is seen as part of the great tragicomic tradition alongside directors such as Fassbinder or Buñuel.

1 Women in the mirror: Marisa Paredes (with lip-pencil) and Cecilia Roth.

2 Three women, three different stories: Manuela (Cecilia Roth, left), whose son died, and Rosa (Penélope Cruz, right), whose son provides a glimmer of hope at the end of the film, on either side of Rosa's mother (Rosa María Sardà).

3 The actress Huma Rojo (Marisa Paredes), larger than life, looks through the railings at her fan Estéban (Eloy Azorín), who is soon to die.

4 Penélope Cruz, shooting star of Spanish cinema, finds herself on the road to Hollywood.

5 It's the "end of the line for desire" not only for the dreams of Almodóvar's heroines, but also as a play in the film.

"*All About My Mother* is all about art, women, people, life, and death, and must be one of the most intense films I've ever made." *Pedro Almodóvar in: Cahiers du cinéma*

conspicuous by their absence. However, even in his short appearances the double father Estéban/Lola – who is in theory the villain of the piece – is given a dignity which no other character acquires in the course of the whole movie. Almodóvar respects every single human emotion, however bizarre his characters might appear. "The only genu-

ine thing about me is my feelings," says Agrado, the faithful transsexual girlfriend in *All About My Mother*. This also applies to Almodóvar's movie, where feelings always remain genuine despite the visual artistry. And that's more than can be said of most films.

MH

AMERICAN BEAUTY ⚊⚊⚊⚊⚊

1999 - USA - 121 MIN.

DIRECTOR
SAM MENDES (*1965)

SCREENPLAY
ALAN BALL

DIRECTOR OF PHOTOGRAPHY
CONRAD L. HALL

MUSIC
THOMAS NEWMAN

PRODUCTION
BRUCE COHEN, DAN JINKS for DREAMWORKS SKG,
JINKS/COHEN COMPANY

STARRING
KEVIN SPACEY (Lester Burnham), ANNETTE BENING (Carolyn Burnham),
THORA BIRCH (Jane Burnham), WES BENTLEY (Ricky Fitts),
MENA SUVARI (Angela Hayes), PETER GALLAGHER (Buddy Kane),
CHRIS COOPER (Colonel Frank Fitts), ALLISON JANNEY (Barbara Fitts),
SCOTT BAKULA (Jim Olmeyer), SAM ROBARDS (Jim "JB" Berkley)

ACADEMY AWARDS 1999
OSCARS for BEST PICTURE, BEST ACTOR (Kevin Spacey),
BEST CINEMATOGRAPHY (Conrad L. Hall), BEST DIRECTOR (Sam Mendes),
and BEST ORIGINAL SCREENPLAY (Alan Ball)

"You have no idea what I'm talking about, I'm sure. But don't worry, you will someday."

In one year's time Lester Burnham (Kevin Spacey) will be dead: that much we learn right at the beginning of the movie. And he already knows this himself, for he's the one who tells his own story. A dead man speaks to us from off screen, and the strangest thing about it is his amused detachment. With a sweeping movement making the narration seem like a message of salvation, the camera moves down on the world from above and closes in on the dismal suburban street where Lester lives. We are introduced to the situation in which he finds himself: his marriage to Carolyn (Annette Bening) is over, and she considers him a failure, while his daughter Jane (Thora Birch) hates him for not being a role model. The only highpoint of Lester's sad daily routine is masturbating under the shower in the morning while his wife gathers roses in the garden to decorate the dinner table where they conduct their daily fights.

Family happiness, or whatever passed for it, only ever existed in the photos that Lester often looks at to remind himself of his past, and of the interest in life which he once had but which is now buried under the pressure of conformity. It is only when he falls in love with Angela (Mena Suvari), his daughter's Lolita-like friend, that he rediscovers his zest for life. This second spring changes Lester, but his wife Carolyn meanwhile is doing worse and worse as a property dealer. He reassesses his position and discovers old and forgotten strengths. She by contrast becomes inextricably entwined in the fatal cycle of routine and self-sacrifice. As Lester puts it, trying to live as though their life were a commercial nearly destroys them both. Outward conformity and prosperity result in inner impoverishment. The business mantras that Carolyn repeats over and over to herself to bolster her self-confidence sound increasingly ridiculous under the circumstances.

At this point, it becomes abundantly clear what we are intended to understand by "American Beauty." The title is not a reference to the seductive child-woman who helps Lester break out of the family prison – that would be too superficial. The subject of *American Beauty* is the question of the beauty of life itself. Mendes's movie is about whether or not it is possible to live a fulfilling life in a society where superficiality has become the norm. In more philosophical terms, *American Beauty* uses the expressive means of drama and satire to go through all the possibilities for

KEVIN SPACEY What would the cinema of the '90s have been without Kevin Spacey? Born in 1959, this friendly-looking actor with his ordinary face portrayed some of the most complex and disturbing characters of the decade with impressive depth. Nobody demonstrated so clearly the difference between being and appearance, between a deceptive façade and the brutal reality behind it as drastically as Kevin Spacey playing John Doe, "The Man Without Qualities" in *Se7en* (1995), or the sinister Keyser Soze who pulls the strings in *The Usual Suspects* (1995). Spacey is an enigmatic minimalist who needs only a few striking gestures, and with cool irony can play great emotional cinema as he shows in the role of Lester Burnham in *American Beauty*. When he dies at the turning point of a story – as he does in *L.A. Confidential* – it's a great loss, both for us and for the movie.

1 A seductively beautiful image.

2 Hollywood's new bright young things: saucy Angela (Mena Suvari) …

3 … and sensitive Jane (Thora Birch).

4 Carolyn Burnham (Annette Bening) on the brink of madness.

5 Liberation from the familial cage brings happiness to Lester Burnham (Kevin Spacey).

> **"When I made *American Beauty*, I wanted the film's vision to offer every spectator a very intimate experience. I hope it's a universal work, which helps one understand life that little bit better."** *Sam Mendes in: Le Figaro*

leading an honest life in a dishonest environment. Sadly this turns out to be impossible, or at least Lester's attempt ends in death.

It's a gem of a movie, thanks to Sam Mendes's careful use of film techniques. He never exposes his characters to ridicule and he protects them from cheap laughs by giving them time to develop. He also gives depth to their relationships and arranges them in dramatic constellations. Mendes' experience as a theater director shows in a number of carefully staged scenes whose strict form is well suited to the Burnhams' oppressive and limited family life. Many scenes put us in mind of plays by Samuel Beckett, like the backyard sequence where Rick teaches

Lester not to give in to circumstance. The symmetrical arrangements of characters around the table or the television are further reminders of family dramas on the stage.

In an important subplot, Lester's daughter Jane falls in love with Rick, the boy next door, who is never seen without his video camera and films constantly, to "remind himself," as he says. He documents the world and discovers its beauty in grainy video pictures of dead animals and people. It is his father, the fascist ex-marine Colonel Frank Fitts – brilliantly acted by Chris Cooper – who in a moment of emotional turmoil shoots Lester Burnham and thereby fulfills the prophecy made at the beginning of the film. The hopeless struggle between internal and external beauty

comes to a bloody end, but the issue remains open. The movie points to a vague possibility for reconciling these two opposites, but at the end this seems to have been an illusion. Despite our right to the "pursuit of happiness," material and spiritual wealth seem to be mutually exclusive, and the good life remains a promise of happiness which is yet to be fulfilled. With irony and humor, *American Beauty* shows that modern American society's mental state is by no means as rosy as the initiators of the Declaration of Independence would have hoped.

BR

"At first the film judges its characters harshly; then it goes to every effort to make them win back their rights."
Frankfurter Allgemeine Zeitung

6 Grotesque victim of his own ideology: sinister neighbor Colonel Fitts (Chris Cooper) shortly before his surprise coming out.

7 Scenes from a marriage in ruins.

8 Wes Bentley is very convincing as Ricky Fitts, the introverted young man from next door.

9 Life's true beauty can only be appreciated in a video image.

MAGNOLIA

1999 - USA - 188 MIN.

DIRECTOR

PAUL THOMAS ANDERSON (*1970)

SCREENPLAY

PAUL THOMAS ANDERSON

DIRECTOR OF PHOTOGRAPHY

ROBERT ELSWIT

MUSIC

JON BRION, AIMEE MANN

PRODUCTION

PAUL THOMAS ANDERSON, JOANNE SELLAR for GHOULARDI FILM COMPANY,
NEW LINE CINEMA, THE MAGNOLIA PROJECT

STARRING

JOHN C. REILLY (Jim Kurring), TOM CRUISE (Frank T. J. Mackey),
JULIANNE MOORE (Linda Partridge), PHILIP BAKER HALL (Jimmy Gator),
JEREMY BLACKMAN (Stanley Spector), PHILIP SEYMOUR HOFFMAN (Phil Parma),
WILLIAM H. MACY (Quiz Kid Donnie Smith), MELORA WALTERS (Claudia Wilson Gator),
JASON ROBARDS (Earl Partridge)

IFF BERLIN 2000

GOLDEN BEAR

mag·no´li·a

THE NEW FILM FROM P.T. ANDERSON,
WRITER AND DIRECTOR OF BOOGIE NIGHTS

www.magnoliamovie.com

NEW LINE CINEMA
A Time Warner Company
© MCMXCIX NEW LINE PRODUCTIONS, INC. ALL RIGHTS RESERVED.

"It would seem that we're through with the past, but it's not through with us."

According to Quentin Tarantino, the plot of *Pulp Fiction* (1994) is three stories about a story. Shortly before that, the film virtuoso Robert Altman gave the episodic movie new elegance with *Shorts Cuts* (1993), where many short stories revolve around a center, overlap, move away from each other again and form new combinations. Although director Paul Thomas Anderson originally tried to play down the link, *Magnolia* can definitely be seen in relation to these earlier movies. The denial was probably just the reaction of a promising young filmmaker who wanted audiences to take a second look at his *Boogie Nights* (1997).

At the center of the tragicomedy *Magnolia* is Big Earl Partridge (Jason Robards), a TV tycoon of the worst kind. He lies dying, a wilting magnolia. Earl is the key figure, the man behind the scenes and the origin of all evils. His name alone is a program for the movie … Earl is the only figure who always stays in the same place, unable to move from his deathbed. When the camera looks down on him from above and the mighty fanfare from Richard Strauss's *Also sprach Zarathustra* sounds, it's not just an ironic reference to his once all-powerful influence, but also to the end of Stanley Kubrick's *2001 – A Space Odyssey* (1968). There we see the astronaut David Bowman as an old man alone on a big bed, shortly before the next evolutionary leap transforms him into the famous fetus from the final shot of *2001* and the cycle of human development moves onto a higher plane. Earl's end also signifies new beginnings, but before that can come about all the suffering that he has brought into the world must be dealt with. And that is no easy task.

With great humor and sympathy, *Magnolia* tells the stories of all the people on whose lives he has had such a lasting influence. First of all comes Earl's son Frank (Tom Cruise) who trains frustrated men to become supermacho in his "Seduce and Destroy" seminars. He got this motto from his father, who destroyed his wife with his complete lack of consideration. Now, shortly before his death, the shallow patriarch searches for his lost son, who he had abandoned as a teenager when his mother fell ill with cancer. When the two come together at the end, their broken relationship is shown in all its misery. Earl's young wife Linda (Julianne Moore) only married him for his money. She realizes the shallowness of her own character and starts to go through a crisis of identity. Quiz master Jimmy Gator (Philip Baker Hall) presents the bizarre show *What Do Kids Know?* for Big Earl Partridge TV Productions,

PAUL THOMAS ANDERSON Anderson first worked as a production assistant on television films, video productions, and game shows in Los Angeles and New York, before leaving film school at New York University after only two days to get back to the practical side of things again. He developed his short film *Cigarettes & Coffee* (1993) into his first feature film *Hard Eight*, which was presented at the 1996 Cannes Film Festival. *Boogie Nights* (1997) was nominated for three Oscars. His innovative directing style doesn't balk at confusing plots or complex characters. With recent films like the oil driller drama *There Will Be Blood* (2007), which won two Oscars, and the cult parable *The Master* (2012), Paul Thomas Anderson ranks as one of the most important directors around today.

"Almost exactly in the middle is *Magnolia* – which lasts for three hours and isn't a second too long – so close to its characters that we can almost feel their breath."

Frankfurter Allgemeine Zeitung

1 Prodigal son (Tom Cruise) and hated father (Jason Robards).

2 Relationship at an end: scenes from a marriage on its deathbed. Julianne Moore in the role of Linda Partridge.

3 The incarnation of law and order: good-natured police officer Jim Kurring (John C. Reilly).

4 Claudia (Melora Walters), abused by her own father and addicted to drugs, provides an optimistic ending to the film.

5 Phil (Philip Seymour Hoffman), the carer of ailing patriarch Earl, demonstrates patience and sensitivity.

6 Confessions under duress: homosexual Donnie (William H. Macy) becomes the victim of his inferiority complex.

where three children compete against three adults answering general knowledge questions. Jimmy has absorbed his boss's way of thinking to such a degree that his extramarital affairs even include his daughter Claudia, who is now a cocaine addict and funds her habit with occasional prostitution. When the neighbors complain about her loud music, she gets a visit from a policeman who promptly falls in love with her, and even greater confusion ensues. Finally, there are the two child prodigies who have become famous through the quiz show. Former child star Donny now tries vainly to chat up a good-looking barman and Stanley wets his pants at the show's decisive moment, as the production team's strict rules don't allow him to go to the lavatory before the broadcast.

The movie's interpersonal conflicts run along the fault lines between parents and children and men and women. All these relationships have been ruined by an inability to build up and maintain friendships, and by the impossibility of any real communication. *Magnolia* is an affectionate but cynical critique of the medium of television, and all the people in the movie seem to be trying to emulate its clichés. Behind everything is the television magnate Earl. The characters' lives are nothing more than television made flesh, absurd TV drama on the wrong side of the screen.

The movie begins with a macabre, satirical undertone and it becomes increasingly sarcastic and even cynical. An amused, concise voice-over at the beginning talks about the absurdity of life and denies the existence of coincidence, and the film goes on to prove that thesis. Although at first the episodes appear to be a transitory collection of unconnected events, a dense network of links gradually appears. The movie draws the audience into a whirl of failed relationships and unfulfilled yearnings for

7 The strain of the TV quiz is written all over the face of young genius Stanley (Jeremy Blackman).

8 Learning from children: a hard task even for MC Jimmy Gator (Philip Baker Hall).

"*Magnolia* takes a long run-up, then jumps and lands in the middle of our present. It is the first film of the new millennium." *Frankfurter Allgemeine Zeitung*

freedom, love, and mutual respect. This descent influences the movie's images, and their rhythm becomes slower and their colors darker, and spectators start to feel that the downward spiral could go on forever. But *Magnolia* is anything but a pessimistic movie: shortly before the final catastrophe, all the figures suddenly begin to sing the same song wherever they happen to be. After the initial surprise, this absurd directorial idea turns out to be a wonderful trick, which counteracts the seemingly inevitable end with off-beat humor in a manner not dissimilar to the song at the end of *Monty Python's Life of Brian* (1979).

When it rains frogs at the very end, spectators heave a sigh of relief along with the characters in the movie. This surreal event makes it clear that anything is possible in this movie. We may not be able to believe our eyes, but "it did happen" as the text under the pictures tells us. The event shakes the characters out of their lethargy and reminds them of the incredible opportunities that life can offer. And a small smile into the camera in the final shot holds the key to the way out of this crisis whose name is life.

BR

9 Tom Cruise in the unusual role of a repulsive advocate of machismo.

10 Victim of self-delusion: Julianne Moore is a convincing Beauty and the Beast.

"The film pauses for a moment: suicides forget to press the trigger, addicts forget their fix, and those in pain their pain. Then the play is over, the world appears fresh once more, the dead are buried and the living are given a second chance." *Süddeutsche Zeitung*

CROUCHING TIGER, HIDDEN DRAGON ♟♟♟♟

WO HU ZANG LONG

2000 - CHINA / HONG KONG / TAIWAN / USA - 120 MIN.

DIRECTOR

ANG LEE (*1954)

SCREENPLAY

JAMES SCHAMUS, WANG HUI LING,
TSAI KUO JUNG, based on a novel by WANG DU LU

DIRECTOR OF PHOTOGRAPHY

PETER PAU

MUSIC

TAN DUN

PRODUCTION

BILL KONG, HSU LI KONG, ANG LEE for UNITED CHINA VISION, SONY,
COLUMBIA, GOOD MACHINE, EDKO FILMS

STARRING

CHOW YUN-FAT (Li Mu Bai), MICHELLE YEOH (Yu Shu Lien),
ZHANG ZIYI (Jiao Long Yu/Jen), CHANG CHEN (Xiao Hu Luo/Lo),
LUNG SIHUNG (Sir Te), CHENG PEI-PEI (Jade Fox),
LI FAZENG (Yu), GAO XIAN (Bo),
HAI YAN (Madam Yu), WANG DEMING (Tsai)

ACADEMY AWARDS 2001

OSCARS for BEST FOREIGN LANGUAGE FILM, BEST CINEMATOGRAPHY (Peter Pau),
BEST MUSIC (Tan Dun), BEST ART DIRECTION (Tim Yip)

IMPRINT

CREDITS

The publishers would like to thank the distributors, without whom many of these films would never have reached the big screen.

Columbia Tri Star, Filmverlag der Autoren, MGM, Paramount, RKO, Tobis, 20th Century Fox, United Artists, Universal, Warner Bros.

Academy Award® and Oscar® are the registered trademark and service mark of the Academy of Motion Picture Arts and Sciences.

If, despite our concerted efforts, a distributor has been unintentionally omitted, we apologize and will amend any such errors brought to the attention of the publishers in the next edition.

PHOTOGRAPHS

defd and CINEMA, Hamburg
Deutsche Kinemathek, Berlin
(pages 24–27, 82–89, 639)
Deutsches Filminstitut – DIF e.V./
Deutsches Filmmuseum, Frankfurt
(page 669)
British Film Institute (BFI), London
Bibliothèque du Film (BiFi), Paris
Herbert Klemens Filmbild Fundus
Robert Fischer, Munich
Ciné-Images, Paris (page 73)
Photofest, New York (pages 9, 15, 65)

TEXTS

Ulrike Bergfeld (UB), Philipp Bühler (PB), Malte Hagener (MH), Jörn Hetebrügge (JH), Heinz-Jürgen Köhler (HJK), Petra Lange-Berndt (PLB), Nils Meyer (NM), Lars Penning (LP), Stephan Reisner (SR), Burkhard Röwekamp (BR), David Gaertner (DG), Eckhard Pabst (EP), Steffen Haubner (SH), Jörg Schweinitz (JS), Oliver Küch (OK), Eric Stahl (ES), Rainer Vowe (RV), Katja Kirste (KK), Harald Keller (HK), Anne Pohl (APO), Robert Fischer (RF), Helmut Merschmann (HM), Steffen Lückehe (SL), Olaf Möller (OM), Anka Ziefer (AZ)

EDITING

20s: Gill Paul, Grapevine Publishing Services Ltd., London
30s and 40s: Daniela Klein for English Express, Berlin
50s, 60s, 70s, and 80s: Daniela Klein for English Express, Berlin, and Jonathan Murphy, Brussels
90s: Jonathan Murphy, Brussels

TECHNICAL EDITING

David Gaertner, Bertram Kaschek and Malte Hagener, Berlin, and Steffen Haubner, Hamburg

ENGLISH TRANSLATIONS

20s: Isabel Varea, Caroline Durant, Karen Waloschek and Monika Bloxam, for Grapevine Publishing Services Ltd., London
30s, 40s, 50s and 60s: Patrick Lanagan, Shaun Samson for English Express, Berlin
70s and 80s: Daniel A. Huyssen, Patrick Lanagan and Shaun Samson for English Express, Berlin
90s: Deborah Caroline Holmes, Vienna, Harriet Horsfield in association with First Edition Translations Ltd., Cambridge, Katharine Hughues, Oxford

DESIGN

Sense/Net Art Direction, Andy Disl and Birgit Eichwede, Cologne, www.sense-net.net

EACH AND EVERY TASCHEN BOOK PLANTS A SEED!

TASCHEN is a carbon neutral publisher. Each year, we offset our annual carbon emissions with carbon credits at the Instituto Terra, a reforestation program in Minas Gerais, Brazil, founded by Lélia and Sebastião Salgado. To find out more about this ecological partnership, please check: www.taschen.com/zerocarbon

INSPIRATION: UNLIMITED. CARBON FOOTPRINT: ZERO.

To stay informed about TASCHEN and our upcoming titles, please subscribe to our free magazine at www.taschen.com/magazine, follow us on Twitter, Instagram, and Facebook, or e-mail your questions to contact@taschen.com.

© 2018 TASCHEN GmbH
Hohenzollernring 53, D-50672 Köln
www.taschen.com

ORIGINAL EDITION

© 2011 TASCHEN GmbH

© for the work of Marcel Jeanne:
VG Bild-Kunst, Bonn 2018

Printed in China
ISBN 978-3-8365-5618-7

CHOW YUN-FAT MICHELLE YEOH CHANG CHEN ZHANG ZI YI

A TIMELESS STORY OF STRENGTH, SECRETS
AND TWO WARRIORS
WHO WOULD NEVER SURRENDER.

A FILM BY ANG LEE

CROUCHING TIGER
HIDDEN DRAGON

www.crouchingtiger.com

"Sharpness is a state of mind"

Crouching Tiger, Hidden Dragon is in every sense a fairy tale, while still remaining a classic martial arts film. This is no contradiction; the martial arts film genre is a perfect medium for telling fairy tales and has never been afraid of the extreme exaggeration that is necessary to film the fantastic. In *Crouching Tiger, Hidden Dragon*, the world of the fairy tale is already evoked by the setting: the synthesized studio shots, the fantastic landscapes shot on location in the People's Republic of China, and the original costumes and architecture. The historic reconstruction of an idyllic past goes hand in hand with its stylization. Into this opulent scenario steps Wudang master Li Mu Bai (Chow Yun-fat). Wudang is a style of swordsmanship that teaches self-negation and internal strength. Sharp wits become the practitioner's greatest weapon. Li Mu Bai wishes to turn his back on his earlier life as a swordsman, in search of greater enlightenment, and therefore entrusts his fabled sword "Green Destiny" to the keeping of the state administrator in Peking. The sword is delivered by his female colleague Yu Shu Lien (Michelle Yeoh), who is bound to him in a sort of platonic imprisonment through a secret bond of unspoken love. Jen (Zhang Ziyi), the daughter of an aristocratic family, also lives in the city but is trapped in the gilded cage of her social circumstances. She is being forced into an arranged marriage. Jen has a servant and companion who is interested in far more than her socially appropriate upbringing. She is in fact the witch Jade Fox, wanted by the police for the murder of Li Mu Bai's teacher. Not only does she assist the beautiful Jen in maintaining her flawless looks and behavior, she also secretly trains her

MARTIAL ARTS FILMS Generally, martial arts films are films featuring oriental combat sports and their accompanying philosophical traditions. The plots normally revolve around a hero figure whose sense of loyalty and justice free him from moral scruples in meting out vengeance to evildoers. The martial arts film developed into a mass product in Hong Kong and gradually shifted its focus away from psychological complexity towards the representation of spiritual states through choreographed motion, and dynamic movement therefore takes on a metaphorical perspective. In the '70s martial arts found their way into American action movies via Hong Kong cinema. Martial arts movies had an increasing influence in the '80s on the related genres of gangster movies, historical epics, and even comedy. Alongside Bruce Lee and the no less popular Jackie Chan, directors like John Woo or Tsui Hark have made martial arts acceptable within the action movie genre, giving it a whole new dimension.

1 Fairylike grace and unbridled energy are not mutually exclusive: beautiful and willful Jen (Zhang Ziyi) casts her spell over the film.

2 The sword of power is reason, and nobody knows this better than the monk Li Mu Bai (Chow Yun-fat).

3 Love beyond death: earthly barriers are no obstacle. Michelle Yeoh in the role of Hu Shu Lien.

in various martial arts. Jen much prefers adventure to the dreariness of her sheltered life in the city. A lengthy flashback relates how she fell in love with the desert bandit Lo following his assault on her caravan. In spite of his wild appearance, Lo is a warm-hearted person. As a pair, they counterbalance Li Mu Bai and Yu Shu Lien. Although their youth makes it easier for them to ignore social constraints, their love is also destined for an unhappy end.

But before the film leads us into this web of relationships, a crime occurs: the priceless sword is stolen. A furi-

ous chase ensues, but the masked thief just manages to escape. The film's repeated chase scenes, where the participants follow each other over rooftops, through alleyways, and even over treetops may at first appear absurd, but are in fact an integral part of Chinese folk mythology. By collaborating with the same team that choreographed the fight scenes in *The Matrix* (1999), Ang Lee reaches new heights of intercultural film style in *Crouching Tiger, Hidden Dragon*. The stolen sword acts as a kind of "McGuffin," carrying the story forward without playing an important

"Sword and saber shiver and redound like lovers in this portrait of contrasted temperaments locked in battle. This is a whirligig of literal revenges, slings and arrows ... Ang Lee enters the ranks of his past masters." *Libération*

role in its outcome. Even before all the relationships in the film are clearly established, transformations begin. During the chase and fight scenes they are literally set in motion. At times, the camera work reduces the action into dancing graphic patterns. Where the human eye can only discern lines of motion – in the rapid oscillation between long and short-range shots – the fight scenes nonetheless remain carefully controlled. They are a reflection of the same ethic of discipline and self-control that governs social behavior in the film. The art of fighting is also a social art.

Ang Lee's *Crouching Tiger, Hidden Dragon* is a remarkable martial arts film. While respecting the conven- tions of the genre, it is also a fascinating vehicle for the portrayal of tragic-romantic love stories in a poetic setting. The movie owes its persuasiveness to the manner in which Ang Lee extends the boundaries of the genre without betraying its innate virtues. As in his other films – especially *Eat, Drink, Man, Woman* (1994), *The Wedding Banquet* (1993), *Sense and Sensibility* (1995), *The Ice Storm* (1997), and *Ride with the Devil* (1999), the film whose production practically coincided with *Crouching Tiger, Hidden Dragon,* Lee's strength lies in the careful balance between the powerful visual images and the mastery of epic storytelling. This reflects Lee's equal experience of

3

Western and Eastern culture. *Crouching Tiger, Hidden Dragon* has reflective moments where it devotes itself to its protagonists' personal concerns, but then it erupts into phases of extreme action, before settling effortlessly back into contemplative situations. The film never loses its rhythm, and great attention is paid to every detail.

Crouching Tiger, Hidden Dragon combines images of the director's youth in Taiwan with a story from the fourth book of a pentology by Du Lu Wang. The novel is a product of East Asian popular literature comparable with the penny romance, featuring stereotyped heroes and predictable love stories. Ang Lee adapts this cultural tradition with great skill. In his version, virtues like bravery, friendship, and honor turn out to be impossible ideals. He does not reject them, but takes leave of them with melancholy regret and not before he has pointed a way out of the resulting emptiness.

In contrast to the value system of a male-dominated society, the film emphasizes womanly virtues. In an irony typical of Ang Lee's films, the fate of the male protagonist lies in the hands of three women who are all struggling for independence from the patriarchal norm. Finally, *Crouching Tiger, Hidden Dragon* is an ideal film realization of the principle of yin and yang: contemplative stillness and furious action, peaceful dialogue and sword battles, the cramped city and the wide-open Chinese landscapes. The balanced harmony of its composition makes *Crouching Tiger, Hidden Dragon* a fairy tale constructed on an epic scale.   BR

4 Jen's desire for a life full of adventure and love is being fulfilled, but not quite as she imagines.

5 At the moment of maximum concentration, body and soul fuse together.

6 In the fantasy world of *Crouching Tiger, Hidden Dragon* the normal laws of physics don't apply.

7 During the fight, the rival women's bodies hover and fly through space with no apparent effort.

"The choreography was new to me. It had its roots in the Peking Opera, and they are completely different from the Western method of producing action scenes." *Ang Lee in: epd Film*

1920s OSCARS

1927/28

BEST PICTURE *Sunrise – A Song of Two Humans*
(in "Unique and Artistic Picture" category)
BEST PICTURE *Wings* (in "Best Production" category)
BEST DIRECTOR Lewis Milestone for *Two Arabian Knights*
(Comedy)
BEST DIRECTOR Frank Borzage for *Seventh Heaven* (Drama)
BEST ACTRESS Janet Gaynor in *Seventh Heaven,*
Sunrise – A Song of Two Humans and *Street Angel*
BEST ACTOR Emil Jannings in *The Last Command* and *The Way of All Flesh*
BEST ORIGINAL Screenplay Ben Hecht for *Underworld*
BEST ADAPTED SCREENPLAY Benjamin Glazer for *Seventh Heaven*
BEST TITLE WRITING Joseph Farnham, George Marion Jr.
BEST CINEMATOGRAPHY Charles Rosher, Karl Strauss for
Sunrise – A Song of Two Humans
BEST ART DIRECTION William Cameron Menzies for
The Dove and *Tempest*
BEST ENGINEERING EFFECTS Roy Pomeroy for *Wings*

1928/29

BEST PICTURE *The Broadway Melody*
BEST DIRECTOR Frank Lloyd for *The Divine Lady*
BEST ACTRESS Mary Pickford in *Coquette*
BEST ACTOR Warner Baxter in *In Old Arizona*
BEST SCREENPLAY Hanns Kräly for *The Patriot*
BEST CINEMATOGRAPHY Clyde De Vinna for *White Shadows in the South Seas*
BEST ART DIRECTION Cedric Gibbons for *The Bridge of San Luis Rey*

1929/30

BEST PICTURE *All Quiet on the Western Front*
BEST DIRECTOR Lewis Milestone for *All Quiet on the Western Front*
BEST ACTRESS Norma Shearer in *The Divorcee*
BEST ACTOR George Arliss in *Disraeli*
BEST SCREENPLAY Frances Marion for *The Big House*
BEST CINEMATOGRAPHY Joseph T. Rucker, Willard Van der Veer for *With Byrd at the South Pole*
BEST ART DIRECTION Herman Rosse for *King of Jazz*
BEST SOUND RECORDING Douglas Shearer for *The Big House*

1930s OSCARS

1931

BEST PICTURE *Cimarron*
BEST DIRECTOR Norman Taurog for *Skippy*
BEST LEADING ACTRESS Marie Dressler in *Min and Bill*
BEST LEADING ACTOR Lionel Barrymore in *A Free Soul*
BEST SUPPORTING ACTRESS Not awarded
BEST SUPPORTING ACTOR Not awarded

1932

BEST PICTURE *Grand Hotel*
BEST DIRECTOR Frank Borzage for *Bad Girl*
BEST LEADING ACTRESS Helen Hayes in *The Sin of Madelon Claudet*
BEST LEADING ACTOR Wallace Beery in *The Champ* and Fredric March in *Dr. Jekyll and Mr. Hyde*
BEST SUPPORTING ACTRESS Not awarded
BEST SUPPORTING ACTOR Not awarded

1933

BEST PICTURE *Cavalcade*
BEST DIRECTOR Frank Lloyd for *Cavalcade*
BEST LEADING ACTRESS Katharine Hepburn in *Morning Glory*
BEST LEADING ACTOR Charles Laughton in *The Private Life of Henry VIII*
BEST SUPPORTING ACTRESS Not awarded
BEST SUPPORTING ACTOR Not awarded

1934

BEST PICTURE *It Happened One Night*
BEST DIRECTOR Frank Capra for *It Happened One Night*
BEST LEADING ACTRESS Claudette Colbert in *It Happened One Night*
BEST LEADING ACTOR Clark Gable in *It Happened One Night*
BEST SUPPORTING ACTRESS Not awarded
BEST SUPPORTING ACTOR Not awarded

1935

BEST PICTURE *Mutiny on the Bounty*
BEST DIRECTOR John Ford for *The Informer*
BEST LEADING ACTRESS Bette Davis in *Dangerous*
BEST LEADING ACTOR Victor McLaglen in *The Informer*
BEST SUPPORTING ACTRESS Not awarded
BEST SUPPORTING ACTOR Not awarded

1936

BEST PICTURE *The Great Ziegfeld*
BEST DIRECTOR Frank Capra for *Mr. Deeds Goes to Town*
BEST LEADING ACTRESS Luise Rainer in *The Great Ziegfeld*
BEST LEADING ACTOR Paul Muni in *The Story of Louis Pasteur*
BEST SUPPORTING ACTRESS Gale Sondergaard in *Anthony Adverse*
BEST SUPPORTING ACTOR Walter Brennan in *Come and Get It*

1937

BEST PICTURE *The Life of Emile Zola*
BEST DIRECTOR Leo McCarey for *The Awful Truth*
BEST LEADING ACTRESS Luise Rainer in *The Good Earth*
BEST LEADING ACTOR Spencer Tracy in *Captains Courageous*
BEST SUPPORTING ACTRESS Alice Brady in *In Old Chicago*
BEST SUPPORTING ACTOR Joseph Schildkraut in *The Life of Emile Zola*

1938

BEST PICTURE *You Can't Take It With You*
BEST DIRECTOR Frank Capra for *You Can't Take It With You*
BEST LEADING ACTRESS Bette Davis in *Jezebel*
BEST LEADING ACTOR Spencer Tracy in *Boys Town*
BEST SUPPORTING ACTRESS Fay Bainter in *Jezebel*
BEST SUPPORTING ACTOR Walter Brennan in *Kentucky*

1939

BEST PICTURE *Gone with the Wind*
BEST DIRECTOR Victor Fleming for *Gone with the Wind*
BEST LEADING ACTRESS Vivien Leigh in *Gone with the Wind*
BEST LEADING ACTOR Robert Donat in *Goodbye, Mr. Chips*
BEST SUPPORTING ACTRESS Hattie McDaniel in *Gone with the Wind*
BEST SUPPORTING ACTOR Thomas Mitchell in *Stagecoach*

1940s OSCARS

1940
BEST PICTURE *Rebecca*
BEST DIRECTOR John Ford for *The Grapes of Wrath*
BEST LEADING ACTRESS Ginger Rogers in *Kitty Foyle*
BEST LEADING ACTOR James Stewart in *The Philadelphia Story*
BEST SUPPORTING ACTRESS Jane Darwell in *The Grapes of Wrath*
BEST SUPPORTING ACTOR Walter Brennan in *The Westerner*

1941
BEST PICTURE *How Green Was My Valley*
BEST DIRECTOR John Ford for *How Green Was My Valley*
BEST LEADING ACTRESS Joan Fontaine in *Suspicion*
BEST LEADING ACTOR Gary Cooper in *Sergeant York*
BEST SUPPORTING ACTRESS Mary Astor in *The Great Lie*
BEST SUPPORTING ACTOR Donald Crisp in *How Green Was My Valley*

1942
BEST PICTURE *Mrs. Miniver*
BEST DIRECTOR William Wyler for *Mrs. Miniver*
BEST LEADING ACTRESS Greer Garson in *Mrs. Miniver*
BEST LEADING ACTOR James Cagney in *Yankee Doodle Dandy*
BEST SUPPORTING ACTRESS Teresa Wright in *Mrs. Miniver*
BEST SUPPORTING ACTOR Van Heflin in *Johnny Eager*

1943
BEST PICTURE *Casablanca*
BEST DIRECTOR Michael Curtiz in *Casablanca*
BEST LEADING ACTRESS Jennifer Jones in *The Song Of Bernadette*
BEST LEADING ACTOR Paul Lukas in *Watch on the Rhine*
BEST SUPPORTING ACTRESS Katina Paxinou in *For Whom the Bell Tolls*
BEST SUPPORTING ACTOR Charles Coburn in *The More The Merrier*

1944
BEST PICTURE *Going My Way*
BEST DIRECTOR Leo McCarey for *Going My Way*
BEST LEADING ACTRESS Ingrid Bergman in *Gaslight*
BEST LEADING ACTOR Bing Crosby in *Going My Way*
BEST SUPPORTING ACTRESS Ethel Barrymore in *None But the Lonely Heart*
BEST SUPPORTING ACTOR Barry Fitzgerald in *Going My Way*

1945
BEST PICTURE *The Lost Weekend*
BEST DIRECTOR Billy Wilder for *The Lost Weekend*
BEST LEADING ACTRESS Joan Crawford in *Mildred Pierce*
BEST LEADING ACTOR Ray Milland in *The Lost Weekend*
BEST SUPPORTING ACTRESS Anne Revere in *National Velvet*
BEST SUPPORTING ACTOR James Dunn in *A Tree Grows in Brooklyn*

1946
BEST PICTURE *The Best Years of Our Lives*
BEST DIRECTOR William Wyler for *The Best Years of Our Lives*
BEST LEADING ACTRESS Olivia de Havilland in *To Each His Own*
BEST LEADING ACTOR Fredric March in *The Best Years of Our Lives*
BEST SUPPORTING ACTRESS Anne Baxter in *The Razor's Edge*
BEST SUPPORTING ACTOR Harold Russell in *The Best Years of Our Lives*

1947
BEST PICTURE *Gentleman's Agreement*
BEST DIRECTOR Elia Kazan for *Gentleman's Agreement*
BEST LEADING ACTRESS Loretta Young in *The Farmer's Daughter*
BEST LEADING ACTOR Ronald Colman in *A Double Life*
BEST SUPPORTING ACTRESS Celeste Holm in *Gentleman's Agreement*
BEST SUPPORTING ACTOR Edmund Gwenn in *Miracle on 34th Street*

1948
BEST PICTURE *Hamlet*
BEST DIRECTOR John Huston for *The Treasure of the Sierra Madre*
BEST LEADING ACTRESS Jane Wyman in *Johnny Belinda*
BEST LEADING ACTOR Laurence Olivier in *Hamlet*
BEST SUPPORTING ACTRESS Claire Trevor in *Key Largo*
BEST SUPPORTING ACTOR Walter Huston in *The Treasure of the Sierra Madre*

1949
BEST PICTURE *All the King's Men*
BEST DIRECTOR Joseph L. Mankiewicz for *A Letter to Three Wives*
BEST LEADING ACTRESS Olivia de Havilland in *The Heiress*
BEST LEADING ACTOR Broderick Crawford in *All the King's Men*
BEST SUPPORTING ACTRESS Mercedes McCambridge in *All the King's Men*
BEST SUPPORTING ACTOR Dean Jagger in *Twelve o'Clock High*

1950s OSCARS

1950

BEST PICTURE *All About Eve*
BEST DIRECTOR Joseph L. Mankiewicz for *All About Eve*
BEST LEADING ACTRESS Judy Holliday in *Born Yesterday*
BEST LEADING ACTOR José Ferrer in *Cyrano de Bergerac*
BEST SUPPORTING ACTRESS Josephine Hull in *Harvey*
BEST SUPPORTING ACTOR George Sanders in *All About Eve*

1951

BEST PICTURE *An American in Paris*
BEST DIRECTOR George Stevens for *A Place in the Sun*
BEST LEADING ACTRESS Vivien Leigh in *A Streetcar Named Desire*
BEST LEADING ACTOR Humphrey Bogart in *The African Queen*
BEST SUPPORTING ACTRESS Kim Hunter in *A Streetcar Named Desire*
BEST SUPPORTING ACTOR Karl Malden in *A Streetcar Named Desire*

1952

BEST PICTURE *The Greatest Show on Earth*
BEST DIRECTOR John Ford for *The Quiet Man*
BEST LEADING ACTRESS Shirley Booth in *Come Back, Little Sheba*
BEST LEADING ACTOR Gary Cooper in *High Noon*
BEST SUPPORTING ACTRESS Gloria Grahame in *The Bad and the Beautiful*
BEST SUPPORTING ACTOR Anthony Quinn in *Viva Zapata!*

1953

BEST PICTURE *From Here to Eternity*
BEST DIRECTOR Fred Zinnemann for *From Here to Eternity*
BEST LEADING ACTRESS Audrey Hepburn in *Roman Holiday*
BEST LEADING ACTOR William Holden in *Stalag 17*
BEST SUPPORTING ACTRESS Donna Reed in *From Here to Eternity*
BEST SUPPORTING ACTOR Frank Sinatra in *From Here to Eternity*

1954

BEST PICTURE *On the Waterfront*
BEST DIRECTOR Elia Kazan for *On the Waterfront*
BEST LEADING ACTRESS Grace Kelly in *The Country Girl*
BEST LEADING ACTOR Marlon Brando in *On the Waterfront*
BEST SUPPORTING ACTRESS Eva Marie Saint in *On the Waterfront*
BEST SUPPORTING ACTOR Edmond O'Brien in *The Barefoot Contessa*

1955

BEST PICTURE *Marty*
BEST DIRECTOR Delbert Mann for *Marty*
BEST LEADING ACTRESS Anna Magnani in *The Rose Tattoo*
BEST LEADING ACTOR Ernest Borgnine in *Marty*
BEST SUPPORTING ACTRESS Jo Van Fleet in *East of Eden*
BEST SUPPORTING ACTOR Jack Lemmon in *Mister Roberts*

1956

BEST PICTURE *Around the World in Eighty Days*
BEST DIRECTOR George Stevens for *Giant*
BEST LEADING ACTRESS Ingrid Bergman in *Anastasia*
BEST LEADING ACTOR Yul Brynner in *The King and I*
BEST SUPPORTING ACTRESS Dorothy Malone in *Written on the Wind*
BEST SUPPORTING ACTOR Anthony Quinn in *Lust for Life*

1957

BEST PICTURE *The Bridge on the River Kwai*
BEST DIRECTOR David Lean for *The Bridge on the River Kwai*
BEST LEADING ACTRESS Joanne Woodward in *The Three Faces of Eve*
BEST LEADING ACTOR Alec Guinness in *The Bridge on the River Kwai*
BEST SUPPORTING ACTRESS Miyoshi Umeki in *Sayonara*
BEST SUPPORTING ACTOR Red Buttons in *Sayonara*

1958

BEST PICTURE *Gigi*
BEST DIRECTOR Vincente Minnelli for *Gigi*
BEST LEADING ACTRESS Susan Hayward in *I Want to Live!*
BEST LEADING ACTOR David Niven in *Separate Tables*
BEST SUPPORTING ACTRESS Wendy Hiller in *Separate Tables*
BEST SUPPORTING ACTOR Burl Ives in *The Big Country*

1959

BEST PICTURE *Ben-Hur*
BEST DIRECTOR William Wyler for *Ben-Hur*
BEST LEADING ACTRESS Simone Signoret in *Room at the Top*
BEST LEADING ACTOR Charlton Heston in *Ben-Hur*
BEST SUPPORTING ACTRESS Shelley Winters in *The Diary of Anne Frank*
BEST SUPPORTING ACTOR Hugh Griffith in *Ben-Hur*

1960s OSCARS

1960
BEST PICTURE *The Apartment*
BEST DIRECTOR Billy Wilder for *The Apartment*
BEST LEADING ACTRESS Elizabeth Taylor in *Butterfield 8*
BEST LEADING ACTOR Burt Lancaster in *Elmer Gantry*
BEST SUPPORTING ACTRESS Shirley Jones in *Elmer Gantry*
BEST SUPPORTING ACTOR Peter Ustinov in *Spartacus*

1961
BEST PICTURE *West Side Story*
BEST DIRECTOR Robert Wise, Jerome Robbins for *West Side Story*
BEST LEADING ACTRESS Sophia Loren in *Two Women*
BEST LEADING ACTOR Maximilian Schell in *Judgment at Nuremberg*
BEST SUPPORTING ACTRESS Rita Moreno in *West Side Story*
BEST SUPPORTING ACTOR George Chakiris in *West Side Story*

1962
BEST PICTURE *Lawrence of Arabia*
BEST DIRECTOR David Lean for *Lawrence of Arabia*
BEST LEADING ACTRESS Anne Bancroft in *The Miracle Worker*
BEST LEADING ACTOR Gregory Peck in *To Kill a Mockingbird*
BEST SUPPORTING ACTRESS Patty Duke in *The Miracle Worker*
BEST SUPPORTING ACTOR Ed Begley in *Sweet Bird of Youth*

1963
BEST PICTURE *Tom Jones*
BEST DIRECTOR Tony Richardson for *Tom Jones*
BEST LEADING ACTRESS Patricia Neal in *Hud*
BEST LEADING ACTOR Sidney Poitier in *Lilies on the Field*
BEST SUPPORTING ACTRESS Margaret Rutherford in *Hotel International*
BEST SUPPORTING ACTOR Melvyn Douglas in *Hud*

1964
BEST PICTURE *My Fair Lady*
BEST DIRECTOR George Cukor for *My Fair Lady*
BEST LEADING ACTRESS Julie Andrews in *Mary Poppins*
BEST LEADING ACTOR Rex Harrison in *My Fair Lady*
BEST SUPPORTING ACTRESS Lila Kedrova in *Zorba the Greek*
BEST SUPPORTING ACTOR Peter Ustinov in *Topkapi*

1965
BEST PICTURE *The Sound of Music*
BEST DIRECTOR Robert Wise for *The Sound of Music*
BEST LEADING ACTRESS Julie Christie in *Darling*
BEST LEADING ACTOR Lee Marvin in *Cat Ballou*
BEST SUPPORTING ACTRESS Shelley Winters in *A Patch of Blue*
BEST SUPPORTING ACTOR Martin Balsam in *A Thousand Clowns*

1966
BEST PICTURE *A Man for all Season*
BEST DIRECTOR Fred Zinnemann for *A Man for All Seasons*
BEST LEADING ACTRESS Elizabeth Taylor in *Who's Afraid of Virginia Woolf?*
BEST LEADING ACTOR Paul Scofield in *A Man for All Seasons*
BEST SUPPORTING ACTRESS Sandy Dennis in *Who's Afraid of Virginia Woolf?*
BEST SUPPORTING ACTOR Walter Matthau in *The Fortune Cookie*

1967
BEST PICTURE *In the Heat of the Night*
BEST DIRECTOR Mike Nichols for *The Graduate*
BEST LEADING ACTRESS Katharine Hepburn in *Guess Who's Coming to Dinner*
BEST LEADING ACTOR Rod Steiger in *In the Heat of the Night*
BEST SUPPORTING ACTRESS Estelle Parsons in *Bonnie and Clyde*
BEST SUPPORTING ACTOR George Kennedy in *Cool Hand Luke*

1968
BEST PICTURE *Oliver!*
BEST DIRECTOR Carol Reed for *Oliver!*
BEST LEADING ACTRESS Barbra Streisand in *Funny Girl* / Katharine Hepburn in *The Lion In Winter*
BEST LEADING ACTOR Cliff Robertson in *Charly*
BEST SUPPORTING ACTRESS Ruth Gordon in *Rosemary's Baby*
BEST SUPPORTING ACTOR Jack Albertson in *The Subject Was Roses*

1969
BEST PICTURE *Midnight Cowboy*
BEST DIRECTOR John Schlesinger for *Midnight Cowboy*
BEST LEADING ACTRESS Maggie Smith in *The Prime of Miss Jean Brodie*
BEST LEADING ACTOR John Wayne in *True Grit*
BEST SUPPORTING ACTRESS Goldie Hawn in *Cactus Flower*
BEST SUPPORTING ACTOR Gig Young in *They Shoot Horses, Don't They?*

1970s OSCARS

1970
BEST PICTURE *Patton*
BEST DIRECTOR Franklin J. Schaffner for *Patton*
BEST LEADING ACTRESS Glenda Jackson in *Women in Love*
BEST LEADING ACTOR George C. Scott in *Patton*
BEST SUPPORTING ACTRESS Helen Hayes in *Airport*
BEST SUPPORTING ACTOR John Mills in *Ryan's Daughter*

1971
BEST PICTURE *The French Connection*
BEST DIRECTOR William Friedkin for *The French Connection*
BEST LEADING ACTRESS Jane Fonda in *Klute*
BEST LEADING ACTOR Gene Hackman in *The French Connection*
BEST SUPPORTING ACTRESS Cloris Leachman in *The Last Picture Show*
BEST SUPPORTING ACTOR Ben Johnson in *The Last Picture Show*

1972
BEST PICTURE *The Godfather*
BEST DIRECTOR Bob Fosse for *Cabaret*
BEST LEADING ACTRESS Liza Minnelli in *Cabaret*
BEST LEADING ACTOR Marlon Brando in *The Godfather* (the award was declined)
BEST SUPPORTING ACTRESS Eileen Heckart in *Butterflies Are Free*
BEST SUPPORTING ACTOR Joel Grey in *Cabaret*

1973
BEST PICTURE *The Sting*
BEST DIRECTOR George Roy Hill for *The Sting*
BEST LEADING ACTRESS Glenda Jackson in *A Touch of Class*
BEST LEADING ACTOR Jack Lemmon in *Save the Tiger*
BEST SUPPORTING ACTRESS Tatum O'Neal in *Paper Moon*
BEST SUPPORTING ACTOR John Houseman in *The Paper Chase*

1974
BEST PICTURE *The Godfather – Part II*
BEST DIRECTOR Francis Ford Coppola for *The Godfather – Part II*
BEST LEADING ACTRESS Ellen Burstyn in *Alice Doesn't Live Here Anymore*
BEST LEADING ACTOR Art Carney in *Harry and Tonto*
BEST SUPPORTING ACTRESS Ingrid Bergman in *Murder on the Orient Express*
BEST SUPPORTING ACTOR Robert De Niro in *The Godfather – Part II*

1975
BEST PICTURE *One Flew Over the Cuckoo's Nest*
BEST DIRECTOR Miloš Forman for *One Flew Over the Cuckoo's Nest*
BEST LEADING ACTRESS Louise Fletcher in *One Flew Over the Cuckoo's Nest*
BEST LEADING ACTOR Jack Nicholson in *One Flew Over the Cuckoo's Nest*
BEST SUPPORTING ACTRESS Lee Grant in *Shampoo*
BEST SUPPORTING ACTOR George Burns in *The Sunshine Boys*

1976
BEST PICTURE *Rocky*
BEST DIRECTOR John G. Avildsen for *Rocky*
BEST LEADING ACTRESS Faye Dunaway in *Network*
BEST LEADING ACTOR Peter Finch in *Network*
BEST SUPPORTING ACTRESS Beatrice Straight in *Network*
BEST SUPPORTING ACTOR Jason Robards in *All the President's Men*

1977
BEST PICTURE *Annie Hall*
BEST DIRECTOR Woody Allen for *Annie Hall*
BEST LEADING ACTRESS Diane Keaton in *Annie Hall*
BEST LEADING ACTOR Richard Dreyfuss in *The Goodbye Girl*
BEST SUPPORTING ACTRESS Vanessa Redgrave in *Julia*
BEST SUPPORTING ACTOR Jason Robards in *Julia*

1978
BEST PICTURE *The Deer Hunter*
BEST DIRECTOR Michael Cimino for *The Deer Hunter*
BEST LEADING ACTRESS Jane Fonda in *Coming Home*
BEST LEADING ACTOR Jon Voight in *Coming Home*
BEST SUPPORTING ACTRESS Maggie Smith in *California Suite*
BEST SUPPORTING ACTOR Christopher Walken in *The Deer Hunter*

1979
BEST PICTURE *Kramer vs. Kramer*
BEST DIRECTOR Robert Benton for *Kramer vs. Kramer*
BEST LEADING ACTRESS Sally Field in *Norma Rae*
BEST LEADING ACTOR Dustin Hoffman in *Kramer vs. Kramer*
BEST SUPPORTING ACTRESS Meryl Streep in *Kramer vs. Kramer*
BEST SUPPORTING ACTOR Melvyn Douglas in *Being There*

1980s OSCARS

1980

BEST PICTURE *Ordinary People*
BEST DIRECTOR Robert Redford for *Ordinary People*
BEST LEADING ACTRESS Sissy Spacek in *Coal Miner's Daughter*
BEST LEADING ACTOR Robert De Niro in *Raging Bull*
BEST SUPPORTING ACTRESS Mary Steenburgen in *Melvin and Howard*
BEST SUPPORTING ACTOR Timothy Hutton in *Ordinary People*

1981

BEST PICTURE *Chariots of Fire*
BEST DIRECTOR Warren Beatty for *Reds*
BEST LEADING ACTRESS Katharine Hepburn in *On Golden Pond*
BEST LEADING ACTOR Henry Fonda in *On Golden Pond*
BEST SUPPORTING ACTRESS Maureen Stapleton in *Reds*
BEST SUPPORTING ACTOR Sir John Gielgud in *Arthur*

1982

BEST PICTURE *Gandhi*
BEST DIRECTOR Richard Attenborough for *Gandhi*
BEST LEADING ACTRESS Meryl Streep in *Sophie's Choice*
BEST LEADING ACTOR Ben Kingsley in *Gandhi*
BEST SUPPORTING ACTRESS Jessica Lange in *Tootsie*
BEST SUPPORTING ACTOR Louis Gossett Jr. in *An Officer and a Gentleman*

1983

BEST PICTURE *Terms of Endearment*
BEST DIRECTOR James L. Brooks for *Terms of Endearment*
BEST LEADING ACTRESS Shirley MacLaine in *Terms of Endearment*
BEST LEADING ACTOR Robert Duvall in *Tender Mercies*
BEST SUPPORTING ACTRESS Linda Hunt in *The Year of Living Dangerously*
BEST SUPPORTING ACTOR Jack Nicholson in *Terms of Endearment*

1984

BEST PICTURE *Amadeus*
BEST DIRECTOR Miloš Forman for *Amadeus*
BEST LEADING ACTRESS Sally Field in *Places in the Heart*
BEST LEADING ACTOR F. Murray Abraham in *Amadeus*
BEST SUPPORTING ACTRESS Peggy Ashcroft in *A Passage to India*
BEST SUPPORTING ACTOR Haing S. Ngor in *The Killing Fields*

1985

BEST PICTURE *Out of Africa*
BEST DIRECTOR Sydney Pollack for *Out of Africa*
BEST LEADING ACTRESS Geraldine Page in *The Trip to Bountiful*
BEST LEADING ACTOR William Hurt in *Kiss of the Spider Woman*
BEST SUPPORTING ACTRESS Anjelica Huston in *Prizzi's Honor*
BEST SUPPORTING ACTOR Don Ameche in *Cocoon*

1986

BEST PICTURE *Platoon*
BEST DIRECTOR Oliver Stone for *Platoon*
BEST LEADING ACTRESS Marlee Matlin in *Children of a Lesser God*
BEST LEADING ACTOR Paul Newman in *The Color of Money*
BEST SUPPORTING ACTRESS Dianne Wiest in *Hannah and Her Sisters*
BEST SUPPORTING ACTOR Michael Caine in *Hannah and Her Sisters*

1987

BEST PICTURE *The Last Emperor*
BEST DIRECTOR Bernardo Bertolucci for *The Last Emperor*
BEST LEADING ACTRESS Cher in *Moonstruck*
BEST LEADING ACTOR Michael Douglas in *Wall Street*
BEST SUPPORTING ACTRESS Olympia Dukakis in *Moonstruck*
BEST SUPPORTING ACTOR Sean Connery in *The Untouchables*

1988

BEST PICTURE *Rain Man*
BEST DIRECTOR Barry Levinson for *Rain Man*
BEST LEADING ACTRESS Jodie Foster in *The Accused*
BEST LEADING ACTOR Dustin Hoffman in *Rain Man*
BEST SUPPORTING ACTRESS Geena Davis in *The Accidental Tourist*
BEST SUPPORTING ACTOR Kevin Kline in *A Fish Called Wanda*

1989

BEST PICTURE *Driving Miss Daisy*
BEST DIRECTOR Oliver Stone for *Born on the Fourth of July*
BEST LEADING ACTRESS Jessica Tandy in *Driving Miss Daisy*
BEST LEADING ACTOR Daniel Day-Lewis in *My Left Foot*
BEST SUPPORTING ACTRESS Brenda Fricker in *My Left Foot*
BEST SUPPORTING ACTOR Denzel Washington in *Glory*

1990s OSCARS

1990

BEST PICTURE *Dances with Wolves*
BEST DIRECTOR Kevin Costner for *Dances with Wolves*
BEST LEADING ACTRESS Kathy Bates in *Misery*
BEST LEADING ACTOR Jeremy Irons in *Reversal of Fortune*
BEST SUPPORTING ACTRESS Whoopi Goldberg in *Ghost*
BEST SUPPORTING ACTOR Joe Pesci in *GoodFellas*

1991

BEST PICTURE *The Silence of the Lambs*
BEST DIRECTOR Jonathan Demme for *The Silence of the Lambs*
BEST LEADING ACTRESS Jodie Foster in *The Silence of the Lambs*
BEST LEADING ACTOR Anthony Hopkins in *The Silence of the Lambs*
BEST SUPPORTING ACTRESS Mercedes Ruehl in *The Fisher King*
BEST SUPPORTING ACTOR Jack Palance in *City Slickers*

1992

BEST PICTURE *Unforgiven*
BEST DIRECTOR Clint Eastwood for *Unforgiven*
BEST LEADING ACTRESS Emma Thompson in *Howards End*
BEST LEADING ACTOR Al Pacino in *Scent of a Woman*
BEST SUPPORTING ACTRESS Marisa Tomei in *My Cousin Vinny*
BEST SUPPORTING ACTOR Gene Hackman in *Unforgiven*

1993

BEST PICTURE *Schindler's List*
BEST DIRECTOR Steven Spielberg for *Schindler's List*
BEST LEADING ACTRESS Holly Hunter in *The Piano*
BEST LEADING ACTOR Tom Hanks in *Philadelphia*
BEST SUPPORTING ACTRESS Anna Paquin in *The Piano*
BEST SUPPORTING ACTOR Tommy Lee Jones in *The Fugitive*

1994

BEST PICTURE *Forrest Gump*
BEST DIRECTOR Robert Zemeckis for *Forrest Gump*
BEST LEADING ACTRESS Jessica Lange in *Blue Sky*
BEST LEADING ACTOR Tom Hanks in *Forrest Gump*
BEST SUPPORTING ACTRESS Dianne Wiest in *Bullets Over Broadway*
BEST SUPPORTING ACTOR Martin Landau in *Ed Wood*

1995

BEST PICTURE *Braveheart*
BEST DIRECTOR Mel Gibson for *Braveheart*
BEST LEADING ACTRESS Susan Sarandon in *Dead Man Walking*
BEST LEADING ACTOR Nicolas Cage in *Leaving Las Vegas*
BEST SUPPORTING ACTRESS Mira Sorvino in *Mighty Aphrodite*
BEST SUPPORTING ACTOR Kevin Spacey in *The Usual Suspects*

1996

BEST PICTURE *The English Patient*
BEST DIRECTOR Anthony Minghella for *The English Patient*
BEST LEADING ACTRESS Frances McDormand in *Fargo*
BEST LEADING ACTOR Geoffrey Rush in *Shine*
BEST SUPPORTING ACTRESS Juliette Binoche in *The English Patient*
BEST SUPPORTING ACTOR Cuba Gooding Jr. in *Jerry Maguire*

1997

BEST PICTURE *Titanic*
BEST DIRECTOR James Cameron for *Titanic*
BEST LEADING ACTRESS Helen Hunt in *As Good As It Gets*
BEST LEADING ACTOR Jack Nicholson in *As Good As It Gets*
BEST SUPPORTING ACTRESS Kim Basinger in *L.A. Confidential*
BEST SUPPORTING ACTOR Robin Williams in *Good Will Hunting*

1998

BEST PICTURE *Shakespeare in Love*
BEST DIRECTOR Steven Spielberg for *Saving Private Ryan*
BEST LEADING ACTRESS Gwyneth Paltrow in *Shakespeare in Love*
BEST LEADING ACTOR Roberto Benigni in *Life Is Beautiful*
BEST SUPPORTING ACTRESS Judi Dench in *Shakespeare in Love*
BEST SUPPORTING ACTOR James Coburn in *Affliction*

1999

BEST PICTURE *American Beauty*
BEST DIRECTOR Sam Mendes for *American Beauty*
BEST LEADING ACTRESS Hilary Swank in *Boys Don't Cry*
BEST LEADING ACTOR Kevin Spacey in *American Beauty*
BEST SUPPORTING ACTRESS Angelina Jolie in *Girl Interrupted*
BEST SUPPORTING ACTOR Michael Caine in *The Cider House Rules*

GENERAL INDEX

ABOUT THE AUTHORS

ULRIKE BERGFELD (UB), *1969, studied Art. Numerous publications on art-related subjects. Lives in Berlin.

PHILIPP BÜHLER (PB), *1971, studied Political Science, History, and British Studies. Film journalist. Writes for various regional German publications. Lives in Berlin.

ROBERT FISCHER (RF), *1954, filmmaker and film historian, published numerous film books, essays, and articles as author, editor, and translator. Lives in Vaterstetten near Munich.

DAVID GAERTNER (DG), *1978, studied Film and Art History. Researcher and teacher at the Free University of Berlin. Author and editor of publications on film. Lives in Berlin.

MALTE HAGENER (MH), *1971, Professor of Media Studies, specializing in film history, theory, and aesthetics, at the Philipps University of Marburg. Main research areas: film theory and history; media education. Author of an introduction to film theory (with Thomas Elsaesser) and *Moving Forward, Looking Back: The European Avant-garde and the Invention of Film Culture, 1919–1939*, Amsterdam, 2007. Lives in Marburg.

STEFFEN HAUBNER (SH), *1965, studied Art History and Sociology. Author of many academic and press articles. Runs a press office in Hamburg, the city he lives in.

JÖRN HETEBRÜGGE (JH), *1971, studied German Literature. Author and journalist; many articles on film. Lives in Berlin.

HARALD KELLER (HK), *1958, media journalist, works for national newspapers, has written essays and books on the history of film and television. Lives in Osnabrück.

KATJA KIRSTE (KK), *1969, studied Literature and Film in Kiel; works for the The Independent State Board for Broadcasting (ULR) in Schleswig-Holstein and the broadcaster Premiere; project leader of a film research project; director of press and PR with Discovery Channel; lectures at the University of Kiel and Passau, and the Media College in Stuttgart; currently freelance journalist and communications consultant. Lives in Munich.

HEINZ-JÜRGEN KÖHLER (HJK), *1963, Film & TV journalist; author of many academic and press articles. Lives in Hamburg.

OLIVER KÜCH (OK), *1972, studied English Literature and British History; works for Fraunhofer SIT (Sichere Informationstechnologie) in Darmstadt, head of PR and Marketing. Author of various articles on film, television, and IT themes. Lives in Darmstadt.

PETRA LANGE-BERNDT (PLB), *1973, Lecturer / Assistant Professor in History of Art department, University College London. Publications on art and science, animal studies, history, and the history and theory of materiality and mediality. Writings include a book on animal art, and she has co-edited a book on the artist Sigmar Polke. Lives in London and Dresden.

STEFFEN LÜCKEHE (SL), *1962, film gallerist, manages "Mr. & Mrs. Smith," a film archive and video library. Author of many articles in various magazines. Lives in Mannheim.

HELMUT MERSCHMANN (HM), *1963, media journalist, works for several national newspapers, numerous radio programs; articles and books on the history of film and television. Lives in Berlin.

NILS MEYER (NM), *1971, studied German Literature and Politics, trainee at the Evangelische Journalistenschule in Berlin, research assistant in Dresden, editor in Bremen. Articles for print, radio, and television. Works as a public relations officer. Lives in Hanover.

OLAF MÖLLER (OM), author, translator, program curator. Film journalist, writes for the national press. Lives in Cologne.

ECKHARD PABST (EP), *1965, PhD, lectures at Institute for Contemporary German Literature and Media in Kiel. Publications on film and television include a book on images of the city in two German TV series. Lives in Rendsburg, near Kiel.

LARS PENNING (LP), *1962, studied Journalism, Theatre Studies, and General and Comparative Literature. Freelance film journalist. Writes for, among others, *tip* and *taz*. Author of books on Cameron Diaz and Julia Roberts, as well as many critical articles on film history for various publications. Lives in Berlin.

ANNE POHL (APO), *1961, active as a journalist since 1987. Author of numerous academic articles. Lives near Hamburg.

STEPHAN REISNER (SR), *1969, Literature and Philosophy. Many articles on film, photography, art, and literature. Lives and works as a freelance writer in Berlin.

BURKHARD RÖWEKAMP (BR), *1965, PhD, media scholar and lecturer at the Institute for Media Studies at the Philipps University in Marburg. Author of books on film aesthetics, history and theory. Specialist areas: the militarization of perception in AV media; the aesthetics, theory and history of film; media pragmatics. His most recent work is on the antiwar film. Lives in Marburg.

JÖRG SCHWEINITZ (JS), *1953, Professor of Film Studies at the University of Zürich, Switzerland. Visiting Professorships at the Free University of Berlin, the Universities of Marburg and Klagenfurt, the University of Chicago, and the Ruhr University in Bochum. Numerous publications on the history and theory of film. Author of *Film and Stereotype: A Challenge for Cinema and Theory*, Berlin, 2011. Lives in Zurich.

ERIC STAHL (ES), 1965–2009, German Studies graduate, specializing in communication science. Film journalist and cultural editor, wrote many articles in various journals.

RAINER VOWE (RV), *1954, PhD, historian, teaches at the Institute for Film and Television Studies at the Ruhr University in Bochum. Numerous articles on the history of cinema and television. Lives in Bochum.

ANKA ZIEFER (AZ), *1980, studied History of Art, Economics and History in Dresden, Milan, Pisa. Currently PR / editorial office / press communication at Bibliotheca Hertziana, Max Planck Institute for Art History in Rome. Lives in Rome.

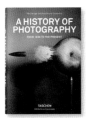

A History of
Photography

Photographers A–Z

20th Century
Photography

Karl Blossfeldt

Stieglitz.
Camera Work

Eugène Atget.
Paris

Curtis. The North
American Indian

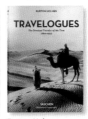

Burton Holmes.
Travelogues

New Deal
Photography

André de Dienes.
Marilyn Monroe

Lewis W. Hine

Bookworm's delight:
never bore, always excite!

TASCHEN
Bibliotheca Universalis

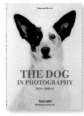

The Dog in
Photography

Julius Shulman

Eadweard Muybridge

Norman Mailer.
MoonFire

Frédéric Chaubin.
CCCP

Film Posters of the
Russian Avant-Garde

100 All-Time
Favorite Movies

Movies of the 50s

Movies of the 70s

Movies of the 80s

Movies of the 2000s

Horror Cinema

Film Noir

The Stanley Kubrick
Archives

David Bowie. The Man
Who Fell to Earth

Steinweiss

Extraordinary
Records

1000 Record Covers

Jazz Covers

Funk & Soul Covers

100 Contemporary
Fashion Designers

Industrial Design

Design of the
20th Century

Scandinavian Design

1000 Chairs

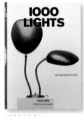

1000 Lights

100 Interiors around
the World

100 Contemporary
Houses

Small Architecture

The Grand Tour

Tree Houses

Modern Art

Interiors Now!

Living in Japan

Living in Bali

Living in Tuscany